Privileged Horses

The Italian Renaissance Court Stable

Sarah G Duncan

STEPHEN MORRIS

First published in 2020 by Stephen Morris, London
www.stephen-morris.co.uk
smc@freeuk.com

ISBN 978-1-9160953-6-6

© Sarah Duncan
British Library Cataloguing-in-Publication Data
A catalogue record for this book is available from the British Library
All rights reserved. Except for the purpose of review, no part of this book
may be reproduced, stored in a retrieval system, or transmitted, in
any form or by any means, electronic, mechanical, photocopying,
recording or otherwise, without the prior permission of the publishers.

design and typesetting © Stephen Morris 2020
set in Minion Pro 11/14
Printed and bound via Akcent Media

Front cover: Massimiliano Sforza on Horseback, Giovan Ambrogio de' Predis or his workshop.
Massimiliano Sforza's schoolbook, Milan, 1493-99.
Milan, Archivio Storico Civico e Biblioteca Trivulziana, Triv. 2167, 10v
akg-images/De Agostini Picture Library

Contents

The Stables 7

Introduction 9

PART ONE: PERCEPTIONS OF THE RENAISSANCE HORSE

Introduction 21

Ch 1 *The Perfect Horse*: A Valued Commodity 23

Ch 2 The Horse and Magnificence at the Renaissance Court 41

Ch 3 *Second only to Man*: The God-given Virtues of the Renaissance Horse 63

PART TWO: THE COURT STABLE

Introduction 89

Ch 4 *Facing the Heavens:* Choosing a Location 93

Ch 5 The Stable as Spectacle 117

Ch 6 *As Beauty demands:* Inside the Stable 153

PART THREE: CARING FOR THE COURT HORSE

Introduction 189

Ch 7 *Faithful and loving*: Stable Staff and their Duties 191

Ch 8 *Il Maniscalco*: Spells, Potions and Prayer 221

A Summary of the Stables: location, architect, capacity etc 237

Appendices 253

Currency, weights and measures 258

Notes to the Reader 260

A Glossary of equestrian terms and terminology 262

Bibliography 273

Index 280

The Author 288

Acknowledgements

The gestation of *Privileged Horses* has taken much longer than it should have done, having developed from my 2013 thesis on Italian Renaissance court stables. Unsurprisingly, over the intervening years, many people have contributed to the evolution of the book and if I have failed to mention their names, I ask for their forgiveness. However, I particularly thank the Isobel Thornley Fund for their financial contribution; Kate Lowe and Amanda Lillie for their continued encouragement and support, Stephen Morris for his limitless patience in the book's production and publication and Pauline Hubner for her indexing.

In many instances a chain of people has led to those who could show me round stables: Fabio Soldatini, Marco Giardano and Carlo Proveddi at Cafaggiolo; Giulia Bozzi in the Museo Soffici and Luigi Corsetti, Maria Pia Atzori and Gian Franco at Poggio a Caiano; Fiorella Belpoggi and Federica Scagliarini at the Ramazzini Institute in Bentivoglio; Fabrizio Nevola, Laura Martini and Dr Pogni of La Pia Dispozione for Pienza and Mario Ciolfi for guiding me through the cavernous ruins of Pius II's stables; Clare Robertson and Tommasso Casini, who put me in touch with Luciano Passini at Caprarola and Arcangelo who showed me round Lo Stallone.

Others include the staff in Italian state archives in Modena, Naples, Rome and Mantua; Signora Laura, secretary at the Palazzo d'Arco in Mantua, for showing me a facsimile of Ottolengo's treatise; the staff at the Warburg Institute, London and the British School in Rome; Alberto Pavan who, with Angelo Maria Monaco, helped me with Latin translations and informed me of the Vigevano stables; Paola Tinagli for help with unusual fifteenth-century Italian texts; Jane Bridgeman for Catalan texts and Cristina Bellorini for information on medical herbs and spices as well as finding a copy of Giancarlo Malacarne's book; Philippa Jackson for extracts from Sienese archives regarding saddlery; Pia Cuneo and Esther Münzberg with advice on bit books and coloured horses; the late Henry Dietrich Fernández for information on the Chigi stables, Bramante's stable designs and Philip II's stables; Elizabeth Tobey for access to her articles; Catherine Fletcher for help on Bologna; Peter Fane Saunders for sources on architecture and depictions of horses; and to Simon Adams, Susan Simpson and Charlotte Boland for information on Claudio Corte's time in England. Also The Royal Collection Trust, Christie's Images Ltd, The Biblioteca Estense in Modena, The Archivio Storico Diocesano, Fondazione Ambrosianeum and Biblioteca Trivulziana in Milan; Ugo Bazzotti, Jan Pieper, William Curtis Rolf and Alberto Muciaccia for allowing me to use their images and photographs.

I am also grateful to my family and friends: Mary Longden, Priscilla Mayall and Christopher and Fran Marriott for their help with horse matters and my daughter Julia for technical help. Finally, I would like to thank my husband Hedley not only for his encouragement but also for his patience during these last few years. Thank you.

Sarah Duncan, London 2020

In memory of my parents

Tommy and Frankie Inglis

The approximate locations of stables in *Privileged Horses*

The Stables

ALBEROBELLO	see VENETIAN REPUBLIC
BENTIVOGLIO (Ponte Poledrano)	Castello Bentivoglio
BOLOGNA	Castello Bentivoglio and Bentivoglio garrison stables
CAFAGGIOLO	Medici stables
CAPRAROLA	Alessandro Farnese's stables, Lo Stallone
FERRARA	Este stables: Belfiore, Belriguardo, Reggio and Palazzo San Francesco
FLORENCE	Medici San Marco stables Medici Uffizi stables
MANTUA	Gonzaga stables: Island of Te, Gonzaga, Pietole, Margonara, Marmirolo, Roversella
MILAN	Carlo Borromeo, La Rotonda Galeazzo Sanseverino Mariolo de' Guiscardi
NAPLES	The Caserta *cavallerizza* at Falciano, Maddalena stables, Royal Marcianise *cavallerizza*, S. Giovanni a Carbonara
PAVIA	Castello Visconteo
PIENZA	Pius II, Palazzo Piccolomini
POGGIO A CAIANO	Villa Medici stables
ROME	Agostino Chigi's stables, Trastevere Vatican stables (plans for Pope Julius II) La Magliana
TREBBIO	Pierfrancesco de'Medici's stables
URBINO	Federico da Montefeltro's stables, Ducal Palace and La Data
VENETIAN REP.	Masseria *cavallerizza* in Alberobello, Puglia
VIGEVANO	Sforza stables
VITERBO	Stallone del Papa for Julius II

M de la Guerinière,
L' École de Cavalerie, Paris, 1733.
The movements of *maneggio*

Introduction

> The usefulness provided by the horse to man is almost infinite...
> and the multitude of examples could alone make a book.
> Claudio Corte, 1562.[1]

> No subject is too trivial to help historians understand another culture.
> The history of men and horses helps us to explore a particular vision
> of the world through its social practices, conflicts and representations,
> and also through interweaving the understanding of material things
> with the materialization of ideas.
> Daniel Roche, 2008.[2]

Over many centuries the horse would become a necessary part of man's cultural history, serving as his trusted companion in times of both war and peace; vital for agriculture and logistical support as well as for the more elite pastimes of hunting and racing. And so it is important that equestrian culture should be considered relevant to the history of the general populace. Indeed, the attention to detail for the care and stabling of highly valued Italian horses in the period between the mid-fifteenth century and the end of the sixteenth century shows that the horse was particularly important for the Renaissance court, with both the animal and the culture surrounding it becoming essential elements of court life. This was especially evident with regard to aspects of entertainment, display and magnificence. Because, in addition to being a companion and servant, the court horse became an important Renaissance commodity, valued for the quality of its breeding and provenance and for the many ways in which it contributed to its master's public and private persona. Contemporary treatises and archival documents show that the horse offered princes ways to display their wealth through extravagant caparisons and saddlery; that it was a means for entertaining courtiers and visiting dignitaries, as well as an introduction for opening up diplomatic channels and royal friendships. As such, horses required secure housing and specific and often expensive maintenance in order to fulfil their potential. Throughout Italy, sites of equestrian culture included pastures, farms, markets and inns but, at Renaissance courts, horses were housed in elegant stabling, allowing ruling princes a further means of showing their magnificence through architectural design. A comparison of many of these Italian stables – ranging across the peninsula from Naples, Rome, Florence and Milan to Urbino and Mantua – shows that wealthy men did indeed use stabling as a means of displaying their status. Furthermore, in addition to elegant stabling, horses required a considerable number of staff to look after them; some directly concerned with grooming and training, others skilled in trades such as saddlery, bit making, shoeing and equine health. And it was the standard of care and stabling in addition to the quality and quantity of these horses (whether owned by *condottiere*, royal prince or prelate), which reflected his wealth as well as his knowledge of horseflesh. Not only did cavalry horses help the prince keep his state secure, they also contributed to a *condottiere*'s success and wealth whilst other lighter breeds, often of exotic origin, contributed to the prestige and magnificence of the prince by entertaining his courtiers and people. The importance attached to the horse and the new status attached to the courtly art of horsemanship led to two specific developments in the Renaissance. First, from the mid-sixteenth century there was a flourishing of treatises on the horse's care and training, with equitation given a similar status to other classical arts and sciences. Second, the court stable developed a status of its own, making it worthy as a category of court architecture. Indeed, while the various Renaissance treatises and court ordinances illustrate the status that Renaissance society held for the horse and horsemanship, they also reflect the attention to detail considered necessary for the care of this domesticated animal, while allowing an insight into the living conditions of the stable staff. These texts show that as with many other aspects of Renaissance culture, classical and early Italian precedents are evident in theories of both stable design and equine care, with authors such as Pliny, Columella and Varro being quoted alongside late-medieval writers such as the Calabrian, Giordano Ruffo and the imperial Roman farrier, Lorenzo Rusio.[3]

During the Renaissance, the stable would develop from the safety of the subterranean area of a castle, alongside prisons and kitchens, to an autonomous and often eye-catching building near to the prince's castle or villa. Court architects such as Francesco di Giorgio Martini, Leonardo da Vinci, Raphael and Bramante designed stables often with detailed specifications that included elaborate drainage and watering systems as well as the exact placement of hayrack and manger.[4] These magnificent buildings and the large stable staff, which may at times have cared for as many as three hundred horses, meant that a significant amount of the ruler's money went towards stable running costs which often included stabling and fodder for courtiers' or visitors' horses. Built of brick or stone and often two or three storeys high, the stables might house up to one hundred horses in a single unit or contain guest accommodation on the first floor. High-vaulted stone ceilings, preferred as protection against fire, were usually supported by rows of classically inspired columns which defined the interior aisles and created a ground plan reminiscent of a basilica. Sometimes, as in the Medici, Sforza, Gonzaga and Bentivoglio stables at Florence, Vigevano, Mantua and Ponte Poledrano (now known as Bentivolgio), frescoes decorated the exterior and interior walls, varying in design from geometric patterns and Mantegnesque arabesques to depictions of neighing horses or dressage movements. Such stables had developed a status of their own, providing the Renaissance prince with an additional way to display his magnificence with at least one building, Agostino Chigi's Roman stables, resembling a Renaissance palace.

Nevertheless, despite the importance attached to the Renaissance horse, its stabling and the stable staff, there still seems to have been a distinct void in things equestrian amongst Renaissance historians. In the case of hunting – an important courtly pursuit – this may well be because, as Anthony Pollard has pointed out, many late twentieth-century historians 'disapproved of hunting' and subsequently 'tended to underrate its significance in the medieval centuries'. As a result, they would 'note [the hunt's] popularity, especially amongst the aristocracy and pass on, regretting the frivolity (or the cruelty), to more weighty matters'.[5] This negative trend was broken in 1993, when Jeremy Kruse described how hunting and magnificence were central to Leo X's pontificate[6] and, ten years later, Richard Almond's book on *Medieval Hunting* would place different forms of hunting at the centre of English life for both rich and poor during the Medieval period.[7] More recently in Italy, a two-day conference at La Venaria Reale rightfully linked the words 'culture' and 'hunting' in 2009.[8] But Renaissance equestrian culture needs to extend far beyond hunting, with its ceremonies and organised pageantry. There is no doubt that any study of the Italian Renaissance court is incomplete without considering not only the court horse but the equestrian culture that surrounded it, not least for the fact that some aspects of the world surrounding the horse had their roots in classical precedent. Certainly, many aspects of stable architecture were based on classical theory and high school dressage, known as *maneggio* or *haute école*– with its demanding displays of the *levada*,[9] *corbetta*[10] and *capriola*[11] – was inspired by the wide readership of Xenophon's rediscovered *On the Art of Horsemanship*, which showed that a scientific study of horsemanship had been practised in classical Greece.[12] As Giles Worsley has pointed out, the occupation of Naples by the Spanish in 1504, together with the establishment of a Viceroy's court not only 'provided the necessary courtly-based culture on which *haute école* thrived' it also brought the classic performance horse to Italy: the Spanish *gineta*.[13] Consequently, this rediscovered interest in horsemanship resulted in Federico Grisone founding the first riding academy in Naples in 1532 and the printing of his book, *Gli ordini di cavalcare* in 1550, both of which helped establish Neapolitan supremacy in *haute école* for much of the sixteenth century. Furthermore, the Italian fashion for high school dressage would spread across Europe and remain popular in the eighteenth century.

Regarding stabling, Worsley's comprehensive book on the English stable also mentions the lack of interest in equestrian matters amongst academics, adding that 'nobody has found stables because nobody has tried looking for them.'[14] In Italy, the case is different. Here stables have been 'found' and studied often prior to extensive alterations for present-day use but, as yet, no comparison has been made of these court buildings. Regarding France, Daniel Roche writes that the void both in architectural and equestrian study may well be because 'the status of the horse stimulated strong feelings [as] it endorsed the identity of socially dominating groups and symbolised wealth and power' but, he adds, nor has there been any 'passing trend relating the horse to other, more fashionable topics of interest requiring less erudite specialization'.[15] However, a few years before Roche's 2008 article, there was an increasing interest amongst British and American academics regarding the horse and horsemanship, which began to fill this void. Both Peter Edwards and Ann Hyland have written comprehensive studies concerning the horse, especially with regard to its service to man; Anne McCabe has written on the *Hippiatrica* and veterinary medicine and others have dwelt on the representation of the horse and on the horse trade between East and West.[16] More recently Pita Kelekna has discussed the horse in the context of human history,[17] a collection of essays entitled *The Culture of the Horse* has included papers on status, discipline and identity in the modern world,[18] and papers given in 2009 at Roehampton University, London have been published under the title *The Horse as Cultural Icon*.[19] But whilst these studies have the horse as their central subject it was not until 2018, when The Society for Court Studies held a conference entitled *Horses and Courts: The Reins of Power*, that the horse was put centre stage in the context of the court.[20] It is still nevertheless rare to find the word 'horse' or 'stable' in the index of a work concerning the Italian Renaissance court. And, despite the architectural studies and archaeological surveys mentioned above, these have been considered within the confines of a specific court or ruler, not as a comparative architectural study. Neither are there studies of the prescribed or actual hierarchy, living conditions and responsibilities of the men involved in the various aspects of the horse's care, despite the importance of their roles within court life.

It is not within the scope of this book to consider every Italian court stable, as it is certain that many have yet to be located across the peninsula. Nor can every aspect of horsemanship and equine care specified in Renaissance hippological texts be analysed. There is no single source for equine culture. It is a vast and cross-disciplinary subject, involving art and architectural history, archaeology, social history, literature, veterinary medicine, European diplomacy and to some extent agriculture, astrology and even witchcraft. *Privileged Horses: the Italian Renaissance Court Stable* lifts these various subjects out of the confining limits of their disciplinary channels and reconsiders them in a broader historical context. It shows that the culture surrounding the court horse deserves to be considered as an important aspect of Renaissance social history because horses played a significant and valuable part in court life and entertainment. But it was not only the carefully bred and magnificently turned out horse that was considered a significant attribute of the Renaissance prince; so was its stabling.

Of necessity, therefore, the sources have been widespread and varied, with archives, diaries and letters being used in addition to contemporary architectural treatises and some extant stables. It should be noted that many Renaissance authors refer to classical and earlier Italian or Sicilian texts to substantiate their theories, whether on stable design or on stable management. Certainly, many early works were in circulation in manuscript, but printing many of them during the Renaissance created a much wider readership.[21] For both design and management a variety of treatises have been studied but four texts stand out as particularly significant: Leon Battista Alberti's *De equo animante* (c.1445); a late fifteenth-century treatise attributed to the Gonzaga *maniscalco*, Zanino de Ottolengo;[22] Claudio Corte's *Il cavallarizzo* (1562)[23] and Pasqual Caracciolo's *La gloria del cavallo* (1566).[24] All four men were qualified to write about the horse, each basing his treatise on personal experience and three of them often referring to early works. Alberti's Latin text and Ottolengo's Italian treatise were concise works written for individuals and remained in manuscript.[25] In contrast, both Corte's and Caracciolo's works were published in Italian and were known to have had a wide readership, but whilst *Il cavallarizzo* consists of three books with a total of 114 short chapters, Caracciolo's encyclopaedic work extends to over one thousand pages.

Ottolengo, the leading *maniscalco* (farrier-surgeon) for the Mantuan ruler Ludovico Gonzaga, wrote to Ludovico's son Federico I in January 1480, requesting to serve him in the same post.[26] In 1991, a manuscript of 141 pages dealing with medical and behavioural problems of horses, was ascribed to him with certainty by Carra and Golinelli,[27] allowing an insight into the ways Ottolengo diagnosed horse ailments and the various treatments he used, often with the assistance of prayer, magic and astrological charts. It would seem that there were at least two versions of the treatise. The copy used here was given by the Duke of Mantua to the riding master Ruberto Fera, before being passed to Ruberto's brother on his death. The second copy, now in the Mantuan Biblioteca Comunale,[28] contains a note, attributed to Ludovico Gonzaga, Duke of Nevers and dated 1571, which criticises as 'diabolical' Ottolengo's use of 'spells, heresy and superstition'.[29] Certainly, the *maniscalco*'s treatise differs significantly from the three other Renaissance works in that he does not deem it necessary to refer to earlier authors but relies on his reputation and experience.

One of the principle influences on Renaissance equestrian writers was Xenophon, the Greek general who had written two treatises concerning horses in the fourth century BC: *The Cavalry Commander* and *On the Art of Horsemanship* – the latter being the oldest complete equestrian text that survives.[30] It is almost certain that Xenophon had, himself, served in the Athenian cavalry, in which every recruit had to appear with his horse before a committee in order to pass a test.[31] It is no doubt for this reason that his treatise was so influential, not only for care of the horse but also for its training – in which Xenophon is notably sympathetic to the animal's welfare. And, although not all Renaissance writers had the same empathy for the horse, many did. At the beginning of his treatise, Xenophon mentions the earliest known text on horsemanship, written by Simon of Athens in the fifth century BC.[32] No complete manuscript survives of Simon's work although Emmanuel College, Cambridge owns a twelfth-century manuscript containing a chapter entitled, 'Simon of Athens on the choice of horses'.[33] Xenophon mentions that Simon's 'feats were recorded in relief on the pedestal' of a bronze equestrian statue, dedicated by the Athenian and placed in the temple of the Eleusinian Order at Athens.[34] One of the three laws of this secret society was to treat animals kindly[35] and, presumably, Simon himself had advocated a sympathetic treatment of horses, a concept that Xenophon continued. Both these Athenians described the horse's ideal conformation by starting with the feet and continuing up the body to the head, a practice that was reversed by Renaissance authors, all of whom started with the horse's head – reflecting the Renaissance interest in the psychology of the horse. Although Xenophon's *On Horsemanship* had been circulated in manuscript, as shown by Alberti's knowledge of it in *De equo animante*, it was first published in Greek in 1516 (Florence, F. Giunta), in Latin in 1525 (Venice, Aldo Manuzio and Andrea Torresani), and in Italian in 1580 (Venice, Francesco Ziletti). Three other early treatises also had a significant impact on Renaissance works: Vegetius' fifth-century treatise *Of the distempers of horses*,[36] which was printed in Latin (Basil, 1528) and in Italian (Venice, 1544); the Calabrian Giordano Ruffo's 'Liber mareschalchie' written *c.*1250, which was first printed in Italian as *Libro della mascalcia* in 1490 (Rome) and in 1493 (Venice)[37] and the Roman Lorenzo Rusio's[38] treatise the *Hippiatria sive marescalia* written in the early fourteenth century and heavily influenced by Ruffo, and which had been printed no later than 1489 (Johan and Conrad Hist, Spire).[39]

There is no doubt that the invention of the printing press in the mid-fifteenth century lead to a significant spread of literacy throughout Europe, which not only increased readership but, in turn, improved knowledge on horsemanship. And although early printed editions would have numbered between 200 and 1,000 copies, this does not necessarily indicate the size of the readership. Neither does a lengthy title listing the proposed readers indicate that these were the actual readers of the work. In fact, many vernacular manuals were written about already well-known practices and it is quite possible that writers wished to show off their knowledge on specific subjects. No doubt those writing equestrian texts were no different in this respect, as many writers were horsemen. The equestrian subjects covered by treatises were wide ranging both in topic and in length, some covering aspects of breeding, breaking in and training horses, others covering the more detailed aspects of remedial shoeing or producing extravagantly illustrated books on horse bits and horse caparisons. But whilst those works printed in Greek or Latin were for an educated elite, many other books printed in Italian, such as Caracciolo's *La gloria del cavallo*, had the possibility of a much wider readership.

Inevitably, the many Renaissance hippological texts varied in length and format depending on the number of equestrian subjects they contained and the detail in which they were covered. Writers such as Cesare Fiaschi[40] wrote at length on remedial shoeing, while Corte omitted this aspect of care for fear of being criticised by those who knew more than he. Although breaking in and schooling the horse are not covered in this book, it should be noted that for these aspects of horsemanship both Corte's and Caracciolo's treatises were influential abroad, alongside Federico Grisone's *Gli ordini di cavalcare* of 1550 which was the first western book on horsemanship. Widely read within Italy, in 1560 *Gli ordini* was translated into English by Queen Elizabeth I's Master of Horse Thomas Blundeville, with some alterations and criticisms,[41] as well as into French, Portuguese, German and Spanish.[42] However, unlike Alberti, Corte and Caracciolo, Grisone does not go into detail on the stabling and care of the horse. Consequently, *Gli ordini* will not be a primary source for this book.

Although primarily known as a diplomat, writer and architect, Leon Battista Alberti has also been described as an excellent horseman[43] and it has been suggested that his knowledge of horses led to his first 'professional' involvement with the visual arts – judging a competition for an equestrian statue of Niccolò III of Ferrara in the mid-fifteenth century.[44] Certainly, during this period, the Este were by far the most important horse breeders in Italy and it is significant that Niccolò's son, Leonello d'Este, should ask for Alberti's judgement.[45] The competition would result in the choice of two sculptors, the Florentine Niccolò Baroncelli for the horse and Antonio di Cristoforo for the rider.[46] It also spurred Alberti into writing his short Latin treatise, *De equo animante*, the thirteen folios of which include advice on breeding, stabling and training. In his dedication to Leonello, Alberti explains that he has 'looked into all the uses of horses, both public and private: in the violence of war as well for aspects of peacetime'. He then summarises the horse's contribution to society,

> In essence, they bring materials from the countryside, destined for the construction of houses or, at any rate, what is necessary for a family's upkeep; in camps or on the battlefield they contribute to the quest for glory and honour or liberty. Surely to accomplish these tasks, it is to the strength and labour of these animals that man must turn most often – to such an extent that, without the assistance of the horse, it seems to me impossible for man to be assured of respect and dignity.[47]

Alberti explains that his treatise was 'not written for the men who look after horses but for a prince, who is a great savant' and that he has, therefore, been more careful than if he had written 'for the ignorant masses'. In doing so, he would 'attempt to unite all the authors possible, known and obscure, who have written on the horse', first listing the Greeks: Xenophon, Apsyrtus, Chiro, Hippocrates and Pelagonius and then the Latin writers: Cato, Varro, Virgil, Pliny, Columella, Vegetius, Palladius, 'the Calabrian' (probably Giordano Ruffo), Crescentius, Alberto, Abbas 'and many others, native of Gaules or Etruria' as well as leading physicians.[48] Throughout his treatise Alberti, like Xenophon, advocates sympathetic and considerate training and care, writing extensively on the separation of a colt from its dam and the subsequent training of the young horse. Unlike the widespread dispersal and survival of some treatises, there are only two known manuscript copies of Alberti's work, neither of which are autograph, and three copies of a rare 1556 edition, printed in Basle by Michele Martino Stella.[49]

In contrast to the sparse information on Alberti's horsemanship, a considerable amount is known about Claudio Corte's professional life as a riding master. From the 1562 and 1573 editions of *Il cavallarizzo* (The Riding Master) and some letters, it is possible to construct parts of his life and his importance to European courts. From the 1562 dedication to his patron Cardinal Alessandro Farnese, it is known that Corte was born *c.*1514[50] and that his father, Messer Giovan Maria della Girola di Corte da Pavia,[51] who died before his birth, was a noble at the Sforza court in Pavia, where he had been riding master in 'that happy era when the horses were really excellent and good riding instructors were highly valued and well remunerated'. Subsequently, Claudio had been left in the care of his great-grandfather, the 'renowned' Evangelista Corte, who had taught his father horsemanship.[52] Corte became one of 35 pages at the Neapolitan court of Isabella of Aragon, wife of Gian Galeazzo Maria Sforza and Duchess of Milan.[53] He must have gone to France around 1543 as in the later 1573 edition, *Il cavalerizzo*, dedicated to Charles IX,[54] he explains that he has been living in France for thirty years – the last seven of which were in Paris[55] – during which time he had never seen a *palio* nor heard anyone show any desire for horseracing in France.[56] At some stage during his time in France he was working for Jacques, Duke of Nemours[57] and from the 1573 text and the accounts of Robert Dudley, Earl of Leicester, Queen Elizabeth I's Master of Horse, it is known that from November 1564 to about April 1565 Corte was in England as court riding master – although he is quick to point out that his tenure in Protestant England was with the permission of Pope Pius IV.[58] Despite his short time at the English court, Corte must have created a significant impression as Lord Leicester presented Sir William Pickering with a copy of *Il cavallarizzo* in 1565[59] and fifteen years after Corte returned to the Continent, Robert Dudley's nephew, Sir Philip Sidney, advised his younger brother Robert,

> At Horsemanshipp when you exercise it, reade *Crimson Claudio*,[60] and a book that is called *La Gloria de l'Cavallo*,[61] withal, that yow may ioyne the through Contemplation of it with the Exercise; and so shall yow profite more in a moneth, than in others in a Yeare, and marke the Bitting, Sadling, and Curing of Horses.[62]

In 1584 the second book of *Il cavallarizzo*, concerning the breaking in and training of horses, was translated into English as *The Art of Riding* by Thomas Bedingfield.[63] Like Grisone's *Gli ordini*, many copies of Corte's book still exist, with at least one known seventeenth-century German manuscript,[64] and several copies of Bedingfield's English translation, indicating the wide popularity of this text. Corte, who styled himself as 'Pavian', was the first to make the riding master central to his book's title, rather than the horse or horsemanship. His 1562 dedication explains that the treatise

> will be divided into three principal headings, in the first we discuss the nature of the horse, the way to manage a stud, raising foals, choosing them and managing them and many other useful and necessary things for this; in the second we will discuss the style of riding, of breaking in, and apart from this, things relevant to horsemanship; in the third and last, we will speak of what makes a good riding master; leaving aside medicating, shoeing (according to my judgement) the work of the *marescalco*[65] and the farrier.[66]

Corte's treatise is sometimes erroneously referred to as a treatise on riding but this term should only be applied to the second book which was translated into English. It is the first book of *Il cavallarizzo* which is most relevant for understanding how a stable should function, explaining the stable master's responsibilities as well as the grooms' expected daily routine and care of the horse, which sixteenth-century stable records show were indeed put into practice.

As yet little is known about the life of the Neapolitan nobleman Pasqual Caracciolo, although the Caraccioli were one of the most important and powerful aristocratic clans (*casate*) in the Kingdom of Naples, forming part of the city's ruling elite.[67] Dedicating *La gloria del cavallo* to his two sons, Giovambattista and Francesco, Caracciolo later explains he has written the book in Italian so that it can be read throughout the whole of Italy.[68] First published in 1566, it seems that *La gloria* may have been known in England by 1580, when Sir Philip Sidney recommended it to his brother with Corte's treatise. Caracciolo's dedication explains that 'from birth [he has] carried an incredible affection for this noble animal' and he describes the horse as 'a generous animal, worthy of glory, such that amongst all the other [animals], it should be considered as being [in] the first category after man'.[69] Divided into ten books *La gloria* includes many aspects of the horse's care both in the stable and in training and it is for this reason that it has been chosen as a principal text. Whilst *La gloria* is dedicated to his two sons, Caracciolo also mentions several other members of his family in his list of excellent gentleman riders, amongst whom are his brothers, Virgilio, Fabio and Giulio.[70] Indeed, given the wide variety of sources used and subjects covered, Caracciolo's work has been described as a culmination of a genus that covers a wide development of such treatises, putting *La gloria* at the centre of a stream of theoretical Neapolitan works.[71]

These works, together with other equestrian and architectural texts, remaining court stables, archival material and modern surveys, create a picture of both the horses' housing and care during the Renaissance. Fortunately, some of these magnificent buildings have been saved as a new use has been found for them such as part of a luxury resort (Cafaggiolo); library, art gallery and museum (Poggio a Caiano); hospitality and catering school (Caprarola); hospital (La Magliana); and museums (Vigevano and Viterbo). Others are now ruined, although contemporary paintings and drawings give an idea of their original appearance (La Data stable, Urbino and Chigi stables, Rome). These buildings provide evidence that patrons considered their horses valuable Renaissance commodities which required impressive housing and meticulous care, both of which gave them further opportunities to display their magnificence.

The book is divided into three parts. The first shows how the court horse was perceived, looking at its importance as a commodity, the different ways in which it and its stabling contributed to a court's magnificence and its status in the Renaissance psyche, through its comparison to man in both its character and in the ways in which it was perceived medically. The second part shows how classical precedent was combined with Renaissance theories of cleanliness in the actual design of the stable exterior and interior. The third part describes the hierarchy and responsibilities of the stable staff as well as considering their living conditions. The final chapter considers the important role of the *maniscalco* (farrier-surgeon) and how his position within the court has sometimes been misunderstood. It also considers the different methods for maintaining the horses' health and their treatment when sick or injured. Evidence shows that, as for men or women in privileged positions, no expense was spared or method excluded for the court horse, with imported ingredients used in potions and ointments, astrological charts consulted and both prayer and spells recommended for healing purposes.

1 Corte, 1562, I, 11r.
2 D. Roche, 'Equestrian culture in France from the sixteenth to the nineteenth Century', *Past and Present* 199:1 (2008), pp. 113-45, p. 113.
3 Although Lorenzo Rusio lived 50 or 60 years after Giordano Ruffo, these two men were often confused when referred to in Renaissance texts, their surnames being misspelt. According to Smith, there were 9 or 10 different ways of spelling Ruffus (Ruffo) and more than 25 different methods for Rusius (Rusio), with the result that the two names often resembled one another. Added to this confusion is the fact that Rusio's treatise takes much from Ruffo (including whole chapters), although he also added his own text. See F. Smith, *The Early History of Veterinary Literature and its British Development*, 4 vols (London, 1976), I, pp. 75-6 and 93.
4 Francesco di Giorgio Martini for Federico da Montefeltro at Urbino, Leonardo da Vinci's ideal stable, Raphael for Agostino Chigi in Rome and Bramante for Julius II at the Vatican.
5 A. Pollard, 'Foreword', R. Almond, *Medieval Hunting* (Stroud, 2003), p. vii.
6 J. Kruse, 'Hunting and magnificence at the court of Leo X', *Renaissance Studies* 7:3 (1993), pp. 243-57.
7 R. Almond, *Medieval Hunting* (Stroud, 2003).
8 Conference 'Caccia e cultura nello stato Sabaudo, XVI-XVIII secolo' (La Venaria Reale), Convegni della Reggia di Venaria, 11-12 September 2009.
9 In the *levada* the horse lifts its front legs off the ground, with its haunches lowered and stands at 30°, holding the position as long as possible.
10 In the *corbetta* the horse rears up and, standing on its hind legs, performs several leaps into the air without touching the ground with its forelegs. The movement was used in battle, the horse shielding the rider with its body. See Corte, 1562, II, ch. 15, 70v and Caracciolo, 1589, p. 427.
11 The *capriola* is the most difficult *maneggio* movement. The horse jumps off the ground and, with its body parallel to the ground, simultaneously kicks out its back legs. This battle movement was used in defence to create space, when surrounded by the enemy. See Corte, 1562, II, ch. 18, 73v.
12 Xenophon, *On the Art of Horsemanship,* trans. E.C. Marchant, *Scripta minora* (London & Cambridge MA, 1962), pp. 295-363.
13 G. Worsley, 'The design and development of the stable and riding house in Great Britain from the thirteenth century to 1914', Ph. D. thesis, Courtauld Institute of Art, 1989, p. 247.
14 G. Worsley, *The British Stable* (New Haven and London, 2004), p. 2.
15 Roche, 'Equestrian culture' (2008), pp. 114 and 126.
16 See in particular: P. Edwards, *Horse and Man in early Modern England* (London and New York, 2007), *The Horse Trade of Tudor and Stuart England* (Cambridge, 1988); A. Hyland, *The Medieval Warhorse: from Byzantium to the Crusades* (Stroud, 1994), *The Warhorse, 1250-1600* (Stroud, 1998), *The Horse in the Middle Ages* (Stroud, 1999); A. McCabe, *A Byzantine Encyclopaedia of Horse Medicine: The Sources, Compilation, and Transmission of the "Hippiatrica"* (Oxford, 2007); L. Jardine and J. Brotton, *Global Interests: Renaissance Art between East and West* (London, 2000), pp. 132-85; E.M. Tobey, 'The *Palio* in Renaissance art, thought and culture', Diss., University of Maryland, 2005.
17 P. Kelekna, *The Horse in Human History* (Cambridge, 2009).
18 K. Raber, T.J. Tucker, eds, *The Culture of the Horse: Status, Discipline and Identity in the Early Modern World* (New York & Basingstoke, 2005).
19 P. Edwards *et al.* eds, The *Horse as Cultural Icon: The Real and the Symbolic Horse in the Early Modern World* (Leiden and Boston, 2012).
20 *Horses and Courts: The Reins of Power,* The Wallace Collection, London, 21-23 March 2018. Some papers have been published in *The Court Historian: The International Journal of Court Studies*, 24:3 (Dec. 2019).
21 Early printed editions: Cato and Varro, *On Agriculture*, printed as a single edition (Venice, 1472); Lorenzo Rusio, *Hippiatria sive marescalia* (Spire, before 1489); Giordano Ruffo, *Libro della mascalcia* (Rome, 1490); Columella, *On Agriculture* (Venice, 1514); Xenophon, *On the Art of Horsemanship* (Venice, 1516); Vegetius, *On the Distempers of Horses* (Basle, 1528 in Latin and Venice, 1544 in Italian); the *Hipppiatrica* (Venice, 1543).
22 Mantua, Museo di Palazzo d'Arco, Inv. 547, Zanino de Ottolengo, 'Trattato'. The late-fifteenth-century treatise has been transcribed and edited by G. Carra and C. Golinelli as *Sulle infermità dei cavalli: dal codice di Zanino de Ottolengo (sec. XV)* (Mantua, 1991).
23 Corte's *Il cavallarizzo* (Venice, 1562), dedicated to Cardinal Alessandro Farnese, consists of three books and totals 114 chapters and three dialogues. Corte's later edition has a different spelling, *Il cavalerizzo* (Lyons, 1573). This edition was dedicated to Charles IX of France; it follows a similar format as *Il cavallarizzo* but has 134 chapters.
24 Pasqual Caracciolo, *La gloria del cavallo.* The first edition of *La gloria* was published in Venice, 1566. In the 1589 edition used here, the *proemio* has folio numbers 2r-4v. The poems, indices and summaries of the 10 books are unpaginated, as are the 24 pages at the end of the book. The main text has 969 pages.
25 Alberti's *De equo animante*, written *c.*1445, survives in only two fifteenth-century manuscript copies and three printed editions from 1556. See n.49 below for a further discussion on these five copies. There are only two known manuscripts of Ottolengo's treatise.

26 Mantua, ASMa, AG, b. 2424 (F. II. 8). Letter from Zanino de Ottolengo to Marquis Federico I Gonzaga.

27 Ottolengo, 'Prefazione', pp. 7-8.

28 Mantua, Biblioteca Comunale, MS A III 17 81. See D. Chambers & J. Martineau eds, *The Splendours of the Gonzaga* (Milan, 1981), p. 146.

29 Ludovico Gonzaga di Nevers (1539-95), *e quelli che vedrano scangellati alcune ricette, sappiano che erano incanti et erelie (ersie) et superstitioni, le quale sonon cose diaboliche et pertanto non conveniente a ver cristiano*. See R. Signorini *La dimora dei conti d'Arco in Mantova* (Mantua, 2000).

30 Both works are included in Xenophon, *Scripta minora*, trans. E.C. Marchant (London and Cambridge, MA, 1962).

31 Marchant, *Scripta Minora* (1962), pp. xxviii-xxxi.

32 *On Horsemanship*, 1962, p. 297.

33 Cambridge, Emmanuel College Library, MS 251 (III. 3.19). An English translation by H.T. Francis is in Smith, *The Early History* (1976), I, pp. 7-8.

34 *On Horsemanship*, 1962, p. 297.

35 The information on Simon of Athens and on the Eleusinian Order is taken from Smith, *The Early History* (1976), I, p. 7.

36 Vegetius' treatise was published in French (Paris, 1527); Latin (Basil, 1528); Italian (Venice, 1544) and (Rome, 1624). For this book an eighteenth-century English translation will be used: Publius Vegetius Renatus, trans. Anon., *Vegetius Renatus of the distempers of horses, and of the art of curing them* (London, 1748).

37 Giordano Ruffo, *Libro della mascalcia* ed. P. Crupi (Soveria Mannelli, 2002).

38 Lorenzo Rusio, *La mascalcia di Lorenzo Rusio volgarizzamento del secolo XIV. Messo per la prima volta in luce da Pietro Delprato aggiuntovi il testo Latino*, ed. L. Barbieri (Bologna, 1867).

39 Dates for the printed editions of Xenophon, Ruffo and Rusio are taken from P. Arquint & M. Gennero, *Escuirie de M. de Pavari venitien* (La Venaria Reale, 2008), pp. 5-6, 'Introduction'.

40 Cesare Fiaschi (1523-1592?), *Trattato dell'imbrigliare, maneggiare, et ferrare cavalli, diviso in tre parti, con alcuni discorsi sopra la natura di cavalli* (Bologna, 1556), which was dedicated to Henri II of France. A later edition entitled *Trattato dell'imbrigliare atteggiare e ferrare cavalli* etc. (Venice, 1603) is sometimes used here.

41 F. Grisone, *Gli ordini di cavalcare, et modi di conoscere le natura de' cavalli* (Naples, 1550). Thomas Blundeville, *The Arte of Rydinge and Breakinge Greate Horses* (London, 1560) and a revised version forming part of Blundeville's *The Fower Chiefyst Offices belonging to Horsemanshippe* (London, 1565). In 2014 an English translation by Elizabeth Tobey and Federica Deigan was published: *Federico Grisone's 'The Rules of Riding': an Edited Translation of the First Renaissance Treatise on Classical Horsemanship* (ACMRS, Tempe, Arizona, 2014).

42 Translations *Gli ordini di cavalcare*: French (1559), English (1560), Spanish (1568), German (1570). There were eight Italian editions by 1600.

43 Franco Borsi, *Leon Battista Alberti: the Complete Works* (Oxford, 1977), p. 20.

44 J. Rykwert, *Leon Battista Alberti, 'On the Art of Building in Ten Books'* (Cambridge, MA and London, 1988), p. xiv.

45 By the end of the fifteenth century, the Gonzaga of Mantua would replace the Este as the leading Italian horse owners and breeders.

46 This separate sculpting of man and horse was not unique. In 1479, Andrea del Verrocchio won a competition to make a statue of the Venetian Captain General, Bartolomeo Colleoni but it was decided that Verrocchio should only make the horse and Vellano da Padova should make the figure. See Giorgio Vasari, *Vite de' più eccellenti pittori scultore e architettori nelle redazione del 1550 e 1568* ed. R. Bettarini, P. Barocchi, 11 vols (Florence, 1966), III, p. 541.

47 Alberti, CV, pp. 5, 7. Videtta, p. 86.

48 Alberti, CV, p. 13. Videtta, pp. 92, 94, 96.

49 One manuscript copy is dated 30 July 1487, Oxford, Bodleian Library, MS Canoniciano, Misc. 172, 21v- 28v. The second manuscript, dated 7 March 1468 is in Vatican City, Biblioteca Vaticana, MS Ottoboniano. The three printed Basle copies are in: Paris, Bibliothèque Nationale; in Montecassino and Basle, Biblioteca Universitaria. See *Il cavallo vivo*, A. Videtta (Naples, 1991), p. 12.

50 Corte, 1562, Proemio, *2i v, 'à chi ne ha fatto isperienza per quaranta & otto anni ch'io son al mondo, & travagliato com'ho fatt'io'.

51 Corte 1562, II, 102r. See also Corte, 1573, *Proemio*, ***2r in which Corte writes of 'that happy and golden age'.

52 Corte, 1573, *Proemio*, ***2r.

53 Corte, 1562, III, Dialogue 2, 124v, 'quando noi eravamo paggi in Napoli della felice memoria della Signora Duchessa di Milano'.

54 It should be noted that this later 1573 edition, published in Lyons, has a different spelling – *Cavalerizzo* - to the 1562 edition - *Cavallarizzo*. Although the work was dedicated to Charles IX, the treatise is written in Italian, the language of the King's mother, Catherine de' Medici, Corte's dedication explains that he had hoped to have the work translated into French and printed in Paris, see *4r of his dedication.

55 Corte, 1573, *4r, . . . *che fu nel suo senza par Parigi, dov'io son dimorato gia sett'anni.*

56 Ibid. II, ch. 52, 115r.
57 Ibid. *Proemio*, **4r, *E vi direi, se pur non havesse detto, che mirassevo il mio gran Duca di Nemorse* . . . See N. Borsellino and B. Germano eds, *L'Italia letteraria e l'Europa*, 3 vols (Rome, 2001- *c.*2007), II, p. 310. See also Simon Adams correspondence with the author (December, 2009) concerning the various payments to Corte in the Dudley papers at Longleat House, Wiltshire. Adams believes that Corte may have been in Rouen.
58 Ibid. *Proemio* **2r-v, . . . *havendo servito la Gran Regina d'Inghilterra Elizabetta con consenso però del sommo pontefice, e gran Vicario di Christo Pio Quarto*. As late as 1571, Corte was requesting payment from Dudley for his work in England. See Longleat, Dudley Papers DU/vol. 1, 1559-72, no. 72 'Claudio Corte asking Leicester for payment due to him when he left Leicester's service. Paris, 4 Feb. 1571, 214r'. Information acc. on-line, 5 October 2011, under 'Dudley Papers, Longleat'.
59 William Pickering's copy of *Il cavallarizzo* was sold at Sotheby's in 1909.
60 The adjective 'crimson' may refer to Corte's clothing. During the Tudor period sumptuary laws allowed crimson to be worn only by royalty, nobility and members of the council. And under Henry VIII crimson velvet had been prohibited to anyone under the level of Knight of the Garter. By describing Corte as 'crimson' this reflected his status as a crown employee. See W. Hooper, 'The Tudor sumptuary laws', *The English Historical Review* (1915), XXX, pp. 433-49, p. 433.
61 'La Gloria' is most probably Caracciolo's *La gloria del cavallo* (Venice, 1566).
62 A. Collins, *Letters and Memorials of State in the Reigns of Queen Mary, Queen Elizabeth, King James, King Charles the First, Part of the Reign of King Charles the second, and Oliver's Usurpation,* 2 vols (London, 1746), 1, 'Letters and memorials of State: Collections made by Sir Henry Sydney', pp. 1-396, p. 285, 18 October 1580.
63 Thomas Bedingfield, *The Art of Riding, conteining diverse necessarie instructions, demonstrations, helps, & corrections apperteining to horssemanship, not heretofore expressed by anie other Author: Written at large in the Italian toong, by Maister Claudio Corte, a man most excellent in this Art. Here brieflie reduced into certeine English discourses to the benefit of Gentlemen & others of such knowledge* (Henry Denman, London, 1584).
64 Seventeenth-century MS in German, *Bereitkunst. Claudij Corte von Pavia. Warinnen gehandelt wirdt von Natur unndt Eigenschaft der Pfert von der RoSzucht unndt wie man die RoS aufmancherleij* (sold at Christie's, 2010).
65 *Marescalco* is the equivalent of today's veterinary surgeon. See discussion of the words *marescalco* and *maniscalco* in Chapter 8.
66 Corte, 1562, *Proemio*, *2v.
67 See T. Astarita, *The Continuity of Feudal Power: the Caracciolo di Brienza in Spanish Naples* (Cambridge, 1992), pp. 22-4.
68 Caracciolo, 1589, 4r.
69 Carracciolo, 1589, 4v, 5r.
70 Ibid. II, p. 142.
71 C.J. Hernando Sánchez, '"La Gloria del cavallo": saber ecuestre y cultura caballeresca en el reino de Nápoles durante el siglo XVI', in ed. J. Martines Milan, *Filipe II (1527-1598) Europa dividida y la monarquía católica de Felipe II, Universidad Autónoma de Madrid, 20-23 April, 1998*, lectures ed. J. Martines Milan, 4 vols (Madrid, 1998), III, pp. 277-310, p. 288.

Part One

Perceptions of the Renaissance Horse

Introduction

The splendours of the Renaissance are nothing but a gorgeous and solemn masquerade in the accoutrements of an idealised past . . . There are two play idealisations par excellence, 'Golden Ages of Play' as we might call them: the pastoral life and the chivalrous life.
Johan Huizinga, 1955.[1]

Renaissance society considered the horse not only as a valuable commodity but having particular qualities that gave some horses more value than others. The following three chapters consider these admirable qualities and look at how such a commodity was used or seen to its best advantage. They also consider how men sought to understand the horse's mentality, attributing to it human characteristics such that it could not only be trained but also properly looked after. Using Arjun Appadurai's concept of the 'politics of value',[2] Chapter 1, '*The Perfect Horse*: A Valued Commodity', suggests that many aspects of the horse's cultural biography are comparable to those of other commodities of the period and that, similarly, they contributed to the animal's value: its origins, training and performance, its perceived beauty and equally important, perhaps, its association with a particular owner or breeder. Chapter 2, 'The Horse and Magnificence at the Renaissance Court', considers the different ways in which the horse might add to the magnificence and honour of both princes and republican rulers, not only through chivalric pageants and parades but also through the more private displays of skilled horsemanship or visits to stud farms and court stables. Chapter 3, '*Second only to Man*. The God-given virtues of the Renaissance Horse', analyses why the horse was held in such high esteem and considers similarities believed to exist between man and the animal that he wished to dominate. It will also discuss the ways in which some Renaissance owners followed classical precedent by commemorating their horses.

---

1 J. Huizinga, *Homo Ludens: a Study of the Play-Element in Culture* (1938), trans. to English (Boston, 1955), pp. 180-1.
2 Arjun Appadurai, *The Social Life of Things: Commodities in cultural Perspective* (Cambridge, 1992), 'Introduction: commodities and the politics of things', pp. 3-63.

On the left cheek. Brand for the breed of the Illustrious Signore Don Francesco d'Este, they are good quality, beautiful horses and the stud farm is in Basilicata in the Kingdom of Naples

Chapter 1

The Perfect Horse:

A Valued Commodity

Commodity: a raw material or primary agricultural product that can
be bought and sold: a useful or valuable thing.
Oxford Dictionary of English, 2010

In his introduction to *The Social Life of Things: Commodities in cultural Perspective*, Arjun Appadurai extends the Oxford Dictionary's definition of a commodity by placing it 'in a space between pure desire and immediate enjoyment,' which gave it 'a particular type of social potential'.[1] If the definition of 'social potential' is taken as 'a quality giving an object social or political advantage', it is not difficult to include the Renaissance horse amongst other more obvious inanimate objects which were considered as commodities. But what was it that gave the horse economic value and how did its social potential manifest itself? In other words, what qualities should the perfect horse have? Certainly some breeds were more desirable than others, with Turkish and Barbary horses bringing fame and economic success for their owners by winning the popular *palii*, held in many Italian cities on feast days or during civic celebrations. And, from the beginning of the sixteenth century, the strong and elegant Spanish *gineta*[2] was highly praised and desired for its exaggerated movements and excellent skills in display.

To many people, a horse's provenance was just as important as its breed. Those rulers who owned stud farms would specialise in particular breeds, the most well-known being the Gonzaga of Mantua who, from the mid-fifteenth century, were producing race horses, war horses and *gineti* known throughout Europe for their high quality.[3] In addition to keeping detailed stud book records, owners used brand marks as an overt sign of provenance and also of quality. These permanent marks, burnt into the skin of the cheek, flank or shoulder of young horses served as

1.1. Ippolito Andreasi, Drawing of west wall of the Sala dei Cavalli, Palazzo Te, Mantua, 1567-8, showing 'Glorioso' with Federico Gonzaga's brand 'FE' surmounted by 'M' on the horse's flank.
Düsseldorf, Kunstpalast, Graphische Sammlung, Sammlung der Kunstakademie (NRW)
©Kunstpalast-Horst Kolberg-ARTOTHEK

equine 'assay' marks, giving proof of the horse's value in the same way that an artist's signature might indicate the value of a sculpture or painting. Certainly, the Gonzaga marks on the horses depicted in the Palazzo Te's *Sala dei cavalli* illustrate that these are home-bred horses: a chestnut horse on the east wall having a 'G' on its cheek, and another branded with an 'FE' in a lozenge surmounted by an 'M' on its flank. The latter is clearly depicted in Ippolito Adreasi's mid-sixteenth century drawing of the west wall (1.1). Similarly, interlaced 'Gs' shown on the flank of a horse in a fifteenth-century Ferrarese painting by an unknown artist, indicate that this was also a Gonzaga bred horse (1.2). Such identifying marks were also useful for sale and transit notes, as seen in a 1528 bill of sale for two Este horses, which included the brand marks sketched beside the horses' descriptions (1.3). By the mid-sixteenth century, mark books (*libri de marchi*) were being printed, listing many breeders throughout the Italian peninsula, and it is tempting to think that social standing increased if a breeder's brand mark was listed in this way.[4]

Unfortunately, it is not known who qualified to have their mark recorded nor if registration was required when horses were imported or exported – although in August 1524, a postscript from the Gonzaga agent in Venice mentions imported horses being recorded in the *Libro di San Marco*.[5] A mark book published in Venice in 1569 shows that women breeders and foreigners were amongst the kings, dukes, cardinals and monastic orders with registered marks.[6] The most

1.2 *The Adoration of the Magi*, 1450-1460, artist unknown. Rotterdam, Museum Boijmans Van Beuningen. Photo: Studio Tromp

1.3. Sale note for two Este horses to Giovanludovico di Botti, 24 July 1528. Modena, ASMo, AE, Amministrazione della Casa, Stalla, Carteggi diversi per cavalli e cose relative 1502-1789, b.2, fasc.2. Courtesy of Ministero per i beni e le attività culturali – Archivio di Stato di Modena, prot. N. 955

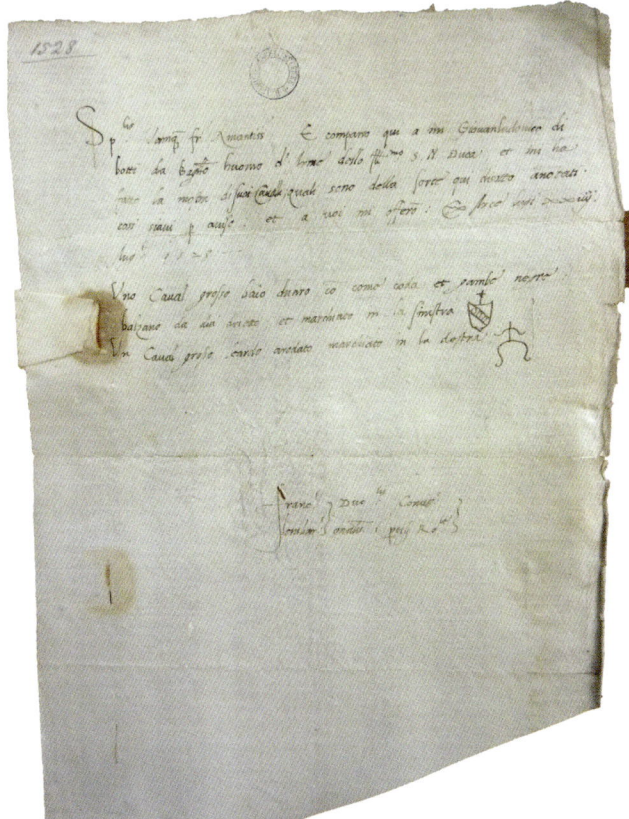

impressive horse breeder at this date was the Holy Roman Emperor; the *Libro* showing fifteen imperial marks, including those for his *gineti*. For these horses, the Emperor's mark was branded onto the right cheek of his Puglian breed and onto the left cheek of his Calabrian breed, with a secondary quality mark for *grandi*, *belli* and *gentili* put onto the right cheek – brands still valid in 1588 (1.4).[7] The same book shows that the Duke of Mantua owned two brand marks at this time, one for *corsieri* and the other for *gineti*. Whatever the reason for these brand books, there is no doubt that riding a horse branded with a Gonzaga or royal Neapolitan mark would have shown that the owner or rider could not only afford this precious commodity but also had the money to maintain it.

By the mid-sixteenth century both the French and English monarchs owned Mantuan horses, either exchanging them for home-grown breeds or receiving them as gifts. As such, Italian bred horses were deemed to have social potential by gaining their breeders a particular status in the highest echelons of Renaissance society. In fact, Mantuan and Neapolitan horses were exchanged between François I and Henry VIII at the Field of the Cloth of Gold in 1520, with Henry so admiring a Mantuan stallion ridden by François that the French king presented it to him. In return, Henry presented François with a Neapolitan courser[8] which, according to Soardino, the Mantuan ambassador to France, was of an inferior quality.[9] This association of royalty with Mantuan and Neapolitan horses not only confirmed the status and social potential of both breeds but also increased the prestige of their breeders and anyone fortunate enough and rich enough to own and ride one of their horses.

Appadurai rightly states that 'a commodity is valuable because it is difficult to acquire, not difficult to acquire because it is valuable'.[10] This is clearly the case for foreign horses imported by wealthy breeders such as the Bentivoglio, the Gonzaga and the Este. The Gonzaga not only dealt directly with the Sultan of Turkey but also sent agents to markets in the Iberian peninsula and North Africa to buy breeding stock. Such exclusivity gave their horses a particular type of social potential and gained the Gonzaga and their envoys access to the highest courts in Europe through their horse-breeding programmes. Both Francesco Gonzaga and his son, Federico II, exchanged horses with the King of England, sending him *gineta* and Barbary horses in exchange for English hobbies (*ubini*).[11] The social potential of a Mantuan bred horse is also shown in the English King's flattery of the Marquis when, in addition to praising his military and personal qualities, the King refers to him as his 'dearest friend'. Thanking Marquis Francesco for four 'most beautiful, high-bred and surpassing horses' Henry continues,

> And although we have long ago honoured you, in no small degree, for your well-proved nobleness of mind, your skill in war and virtues; now, however, when we discern your Excellency to be so singularly affected towards us, we receive and number your Excellency, with your most noble children, among our dearest friends, and we hold all belonging to you in the very highest esteem.[12]

Sometimes, equine gifts could also have a hidden agenda, as when an Este horse was used for a political purpose. In his history of Ferrara, Antonio Frizzi records that Duke Alfonso d'Este sent one of his grooms, Girolamo Sestola, to England with a superb horse together with gold trappings, three trained falcons and a leopard, with the object of inducing Henry VIII to persuade Pope Leo X to restore Modena and Reggio to the Duke.[13] In addition to the 'social potential' attached to these international gift horses, the racing ability of the Turkish and North African Barbary horses also brought owners and breeders a particular status and renown amongst their own

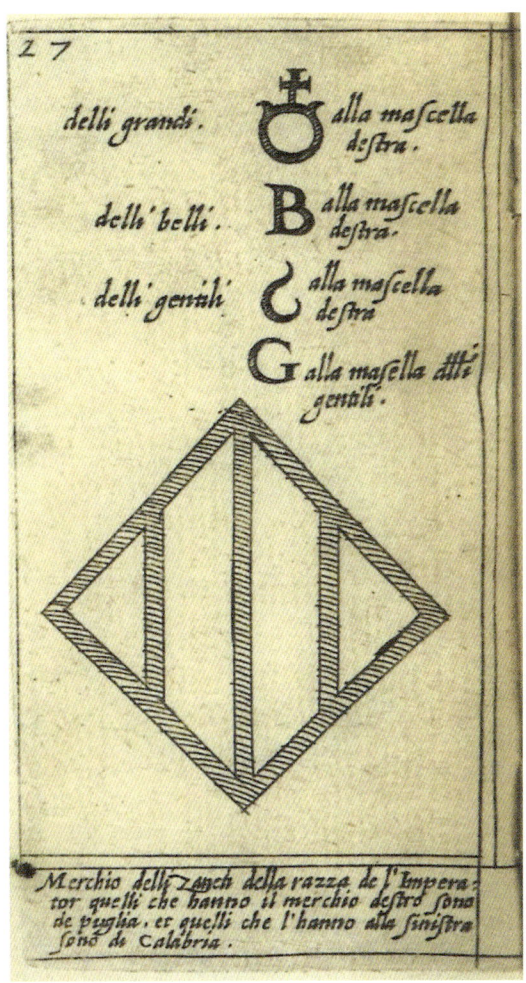

1.4 *Libro de marchi de cavalli con li nomi de tutti li principi e privati signori che hanno razza di cavalli*, Venice, 1588. Branding marks of the Holy Roman Emperor's Spanish *gineti*

people. This is particularly evident between 1484 and 1519, when Francesco Gonzaga's racehorses (*barbari*)[14] won him 314 of the 320 Italian *palii*, ninety per cent of the races in which they competed, most of them bred at the Gonzaga's Governolo stud on the left bank of the river Po[15] – many of them commemorated for the Marquis in a small illuminated book.[16]

Acknowledging then that the well-bred horse was a valued Renaissance commodity with 'social potential', what qualities brought it to be noticed in the Renaissance or made one horse more desirable than another? As for other commodities, such as jewellery, extravagant clothing and tapestries, the theory of cultural biography is also relevant for the horse. In the horse's case, the 'biography' starts with its provenance (the origin of its breeding) and continues with its appearance (conformation and colour) and its character and performance (training) – all of which contributed to its overall value. In this respect, a horse's 'cultural biography' could well be compared to that of a roughly hewn gemstone. Whether the young horse is the offspring of a good stallion and mare, or the gem is mined from a respected source, the base product is subsequently transformed into a more valuable and desirable commodity; in the case of the horse by a skilled trainer and for the gemstone, by a jeweller or gem-cutter. Each is then bought or sold at profit or presented as a valued gift according to its appearance and character. Once acquired, it is kept in a secure and often beautiful container – the Renaissance stable in the case of the horse, a jewellery casket for the gemstone. If the owner of either of these commodities was a person of note, this added to its social potential through its provenance, causing it to be admired and envied by outsiders, who would desire something similar and go to considerable lengths to acquire or imitate it. It could be said that here the analogy ends, with the horse eventually reaching the end of its useful life, whilst the gemstone continues to increase in value. However, it should be remembered that many of the horses admired in the Renaissance were stallions siring offspring, which carried their parents' genes and, in turn, were valued for their respected and often well-documented progeny.

An analysis of the different qualities that made the horse desirable can, therefore, be found in the three different stages contributing to the horse's cultural biography: the base product, the perfecting or training of the horse and the final valued commodity. The base product, in this instance the young unbroken horse, needed to have certain qualities which could be transformed into the desirable court horse. Various equestrian treatises describe the qualities required in the 'perfect' horse – that is to say the ideal conformation and the perfect colour – both of which come from successful breeding programmes. As will be seen, whilst Renaissance writers found conformation relatively easy to define, they found colour more problematical, as specific colours were believed to indicate particular traits in the horse's temperament or a tendency to certain medical problems. The aesthetic value of the horse was of considerable importance for two main reasons: first, because correct conformation meant fewer health problems or injuries and second, because the best-looking horses drew attention to the owner and rider. The second stage, the training of the horse, was written about at length in equestrian texts, with schooling dependent on discipline from an early age and authors varying in the amount of force recommended to achieve their goals. Some followed Xenophon's theory that the horse should act in partnership with man and willingly perform his tasks, whilst others preferred to dominate. But, whatever their methods, they aimed to produce a horse which would benefit both the courtier and his court.

In *De equo animante*, Alberti describes the various qualities deemed necessary for a stallion, listing fifteen essential points formed from a synopsis of earlier Greek, Roman and medieval Italian treatises. At no point in his treatise is a particular breed specified for the ideal horse, nor is its character analysed, but Alberti does warn the reader that

> Nature has not given [all horses] the same capabilities. Some shine more at war work; others are inclined to win Olympic crowns; others are adaptable for domestic use, civilian duties and farm work.[17]

It is possible the perfect horse that Alberti is describing is the horse he envisaged for the equestrian statue of Niccolò d'Este, for which he had been asked to judge a competition.[18] Nevertheless, many of his ideals for conformation would be relevant to any breed and are consistent with those of earlier writers – particularly Virgil, Varro and Columella; some ideals are relevant to the strength and stamina of the horse, others are purely aesthetic. This emphasis on conformation can be found as early as the fifth century BC, when Simon of Athens advised, 'whether we are dealing with small or large horses, the essential point . . . is that the animal is properly proportioned and symmetrical for such are always the best'.[19] Xenophon also advised that the only quality to be judged in an unbroken horse was its conformation as 'no clear signs of temper are to be detected in an animal that has not yet had a man on its back'.[20]

Alberti is strongly influenced by Virgil's *Georgics* in every aspect of the horse's conformation; an indication that ideals must have remained unchanged in the intervening centuries.[21] He starts by defining the overall impression a horse should make, stressing that it should have a substantial body and that the legs 'apart from their intrinsic beauty,' should be 'built, as far as possible, for strength'. Amongst the attributes believed to make a horse handsome are: a medium head, slim well-placed ears, an ample brow between the eyebrows, healthy black eyes of 'great purity', a tufted or wavy mane, which should fall to the right of the neck 'in controlled streams' and a tail, which is 'thick and flowing but solid, strong and sinewy'. He then continues with the aspects of the horse's body that would contribute to its overall strength and appearance. He recommends 'flared nostrils' and a mouth which should be able 'to open widely',[22] primarily to assist the horse's breathing when it exerts itself but also to present a fierce and powerful impression when on the battlefield, as clearly illustrated in some of Leonardo da Vinci's drawings.[23] Other characteristics contributing to health and stamina are a long straight neck, bony shoulders, a backbone that is neither prominent nor hollow[24] and a 'broad chest capable of great effort', leaving space for the lungs and heart. Alberti then explains that, although 'the ancients liked the stomach if it was a modest size', he writes that his contemporaries considered it should be 'more ample, with the area between the haunches full and prominent', adding that the stallion's 'testicles should be neither bloated nor hanging to excess but well-balanced and equal'.[25]

A further five points describe the necessary requirements for the thighs, legs and feet – aspects of a horse's conformation which, together with the depth and strength in the chest, are the most important for maintaining stamina – as a horse with badly formed legs might well have a tendency to go lame. He writes, 'the thighs should be perfectly proportioned' without 'distracting from the grace of the rest of the body' and the knees 'should not be bowed or swollen but firmly articulated around the kneecap', no doubt because such distortion could be an indication of poor breeding or care, or even overuse. The cannon bones, which support the knees and hocks, should be 'light and elegant', 'not too vertical, like those of a goat, nor spindly, nor leaning to one side or the other'.[26] Here Alberti might appear to focus on the horse's visual impact but the front legs and knees take much of the strain when a horse is being ridden or jumped, and the rear legs, together with the thighs, contribute to the horse's power. For these reasons the quality of the cannon bones is extremely important, as any malformation could render the horse useless. Finally, Alberti writes about the hoof, which 'must be well-formed', its wall at a 'slight slope', made of 'good horn, well hollowed out, with a hollow sound and of a dark colour'.[27] Great importance was attached not only to the form of the hoof but also to the care of the feet, with later writers, such as Fiaschi, stipulating remedial shoes for particular problems.[28] Alberti follows his detailed description of the perfect stallion with a brief description of the ideal breeding mare which, he writes, is more worthy of value 'if her character and appearance is similar to the stallion'. She should also have an 'open chest and shoulders', with her legs well developed and muscled and, with an eye to carrying a foal, he suggests that the mare 'should not become gigantic, excessive or fat, but graceful and, above all, [have] a large stomach' with 'her limbs sound and mature'.[29]

A century and a half after Alberti's treatise, similar ideals were defined in both poetry and in a treatise on painting. In a 1590 poem on hunting, the Mantuan nobleman Erasmus of Valvasone would describe the necessary qualities for a hunt horse. These included a double backbone – a ridge of muscle running either side of the spine[30] – rounded ribs, short flanks, a wide chest and full croup with arched withers,[31] a short head which should be held high, bright eyes and rounded nostrils from which fire should emanate.[32] And, in 1604, the Dutch painter Karel van Mander explained how painters should depict the perfect horse in his treatise, *Den grondt der edle vry schilder-const* [33] – an indication that the classical values of Virgil and Simon of Athens remained constant throughout the Renaissance.

1.5. Leonardo da Vinci, *A horse's left foreleg, with measurements*, c.1490-92. Inscribed 'Ciliano di messer galeazo'.
Royal Collection Trust
©Her Majesty Queen Elizabeth II, 2019

This Renaissance interest in equine conformation mirrors attempts to define the natural proportions and to understand the structure of the human body. An analysis of the horse's proportions is found in drawings, where artists searched for a logical method to define the perfect horse in painting and sculpture. Whilst some would seek to draw ideal specimens, others would analyse how the natural proportions of the horse gave it perfection. In his late fifteenth-century preparatory drawings for Francesco Sforza's monumental equestrian sculpture in Milan – a project that was never completed – Leonardo da Vinci drew on particular aspects of different horses in order to create an ideal 'whole' for his project – a method of finding perfection that has been compared to Apelles using the most beautiful girls of Athens 'as multiple models for his image of Helen'.[34] Two drawings in the British Royal Collection in Windsor show that Leonardo used Sicilian and *gineta* horses belonging to Ludovico Sforza's son-in-law, the great Milanese captain Galeazzo Sanseverino, to make precise anatomical studies. In the first, which is inscribed *Ciliano di messer galeazo*, Leonardo noted down the exact measurements of the horse's foreleg (1.5). In the second (1.6), he took the head measurement, from tip of muzzle to base of ears, and divided it into sixteenths in order to discover the exact proportions of the whole body. He also sketched the head and neck of a black Florentine horse owned by Mariolo

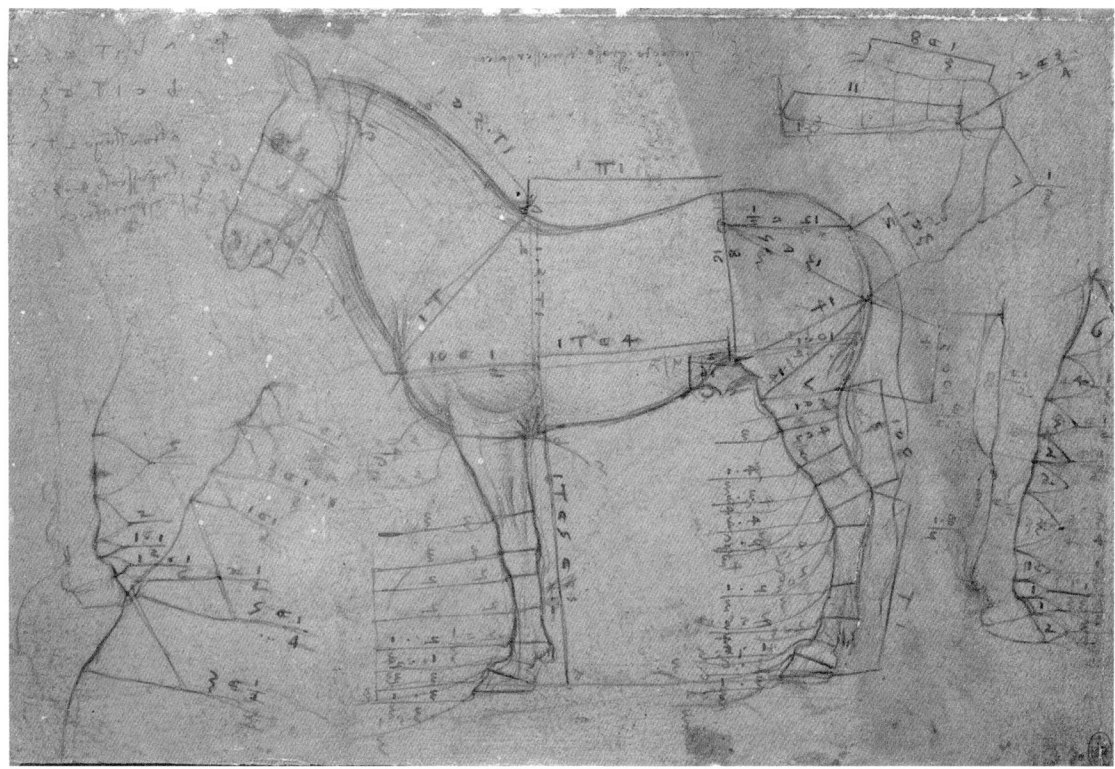

1.6. Leonardo da Vinci, *A horse in left profile, c.*1490. Inscribed 'gianecto grosso di messer galeazo'.
Royal Collection Trust ©Her Majesty Queen Elizabeth II, 2019

de' Guiscardi[35] as well as the hind quarters of a white stallion belonging to Ludovico Sforza's falconer.[36] In the same decade, Leonardo's master, Andrea del Verrocchio, had also attempted to discover a system of natural proportion in the horse, his drawing noting the precise measurements and fractions of the horse's body in relation to the size of its head, probably in preparation for his equestrian statue of Bartolomeo Colleoni (1.7).[37] Others, such as Raphael used classical precedent to depict ideal proportion by studying the antique sculptures on Rome's Quirinal hill and adding measurements to his sketch (1.8). By the end of the sixteenth century, the Bolognese nobleman Carlo Ruini had made a comprehensive study of the horse's anatomy, the *Anatomia del cavallo*,[38] in which immaculate woodcuts of the musculature, skeleton, veins, nerves and internal organs of the horse explained its structure and form in much the same way as Vesalius had depicted man's anatomy half a century earlier.[39]

Even so, some believed that conformation played only a small part in the horse's perfection. The Neapolitan horseman Caracciolo first listed three principal elements that made a horse perfect: beauty, agility and courage; he then sub-divided beauty into good overall conformation, correct proportion of the legs, and colour.[40] And, for Caracciolo, it was colour that was the most important, as it is 'the first detail our eyes register when we open them' and it is this element

1.7. Andrea del Verrocchio, Measured drawing of a horse facing left (recto), c.1480-88
New York, Metropolitan Museum of Art, Frederick C. Hewitt Fund, 1917. 19.76.5 (recto)

that 'informs us whether something is beautiful or ugly'.[41] The importance attached to colour led Renaissance theorists to analyse what determined it, using the analysis to explain a horse's character and its propensity to illness. Such theorising had not been considered in preceding centuries and can be understood as evidence of the Renaissance desire to understand nature. In fact, Simon of Athens believed that 'the good qualities of a horse [could] not be determined from its colour' only advising that, in his opinion, 'whole colours were best'.[42] And although Virgil wrote briefly in *The Georgics* that bay and grey were the best colours and white and sorrel – a bright golden chestnut colour – the worst,[43] neither Xenophon, Columella nor Varro, all of whom wrote extensively on the horse's conformation, included any advice on colour. Even in the fifteenth century, Alberti's wide ranging synopsis had only described three colours – two roans and a grey – as being recommended by the 'ancients': 'the colour of ash with a dark line down the back from the withers to the tail' and 'the colour of soot – that is to say red mixed with black'.[44]

By 1562, Claudio Corte would include eight chapters on the horse's coat:[45] two on the condition of the hair and how it grows, four on specific colours – bay, grey, sorrel and black, one on various mixed colours and one on the different white markings on the legs and head. In the same decade, Caracciolo admitted that he found himself in 'a tempestuous sea'[46] on the subject, probably because he attempted to link the horse's colour to planets, elements, humours and

1.8. Raphael Sanzio, *A marble horse on the Quirinal Hill*, c.1513.
Washington DC, National Gallery of Art, Woodner Collection, 1993.51.3a (recto)

zodiac signs in addition to the significance and interpretation of a horse's white markings on its face and legs; an analysis which takes sixty pages of his treatise. However, when discussing the humours, he makes the observation that together with the elephant, horse and man 'are the only animals which are by nature hot and humid, making them closer than any other [animal] to having a perfect temperament'.[47] Even though Corte's analysis of colour is more concise than Caracciolo's, it is nevertheless still complicated. Amongst other theories, he explains that heat (*cholera*) in the horse's body produces the sorrel (bright golden chestnut) horse, which is linked to fire; blood (*sanguine*) mixed with air produces the bay (chestnut with black mane, tail and legs); phlegm, corresponding to water, produces the grey and melancholia, linked to the earth, produces the black. He concludes that the horse with a mixed coat colouring must, therefore, have a mixture of humours and, depending on which humour dominates, the associated colour will be more prominent but, he warns 'in the whole world you will not find a horse composed of one pure humour'.[48]

With bay and grey possibly the best colours, what was thought to be the worst? Corte's least favourite colour appears to be black (*morello*) which he associates with a melancholic humour, corresponding to the element of Earth and making the horse 'ponderous, vile and of the worst character'.[49] On the other hand, while agreeing that the black horse has a melancholic complexion, Caracciolo believes this makes the horse gallant and brave, despite it being 'irritable, unreliable, bizarre, vile, fearsome and difficult to train'. But, he adds, if the black coat is mixed with another colour, the black characteristics are tempered by the humour and the planet associated with the secondary colour.[50] As a result he is full of praise for any horse that has black legs, mane and tail, especially the bay – known as *cavezza di Moro*[51] – and the dapple-grey horse – sometimes described as *stornello*.[52] Nevertheless, it seems there were notable exceptions, with Caracciolo mentioning the legendary Bressian black horse, Savoy, which Charles VIII rode at the Battle of Fornovo in 1495.[53] Even if Savoy was an exception, another black horse, Federico Gonzaga's stallion, Morel Favorito, had already been commemorated on the south wall of the *Sala dei cavalli* in the Palazzo Te in the 1530s. Indeed, amongst the twenty-one stallions recorded at their Mantuan San Sebastiano stables in 1521, the Gonzaga had six black horses,[54] all of which had the prefix *morello*, one being Morel Favorito. It is unlikely this stallion would have been commemorated, nor would it have been suitable for breeding, if it had conformed to Corte's or Caracciolo's theoretical melancholic characteristics: 'ponderous', 'vile' and 'unreliable' (1.9).

Further complications in defining ideal colouring arose from theories associating certain traits with the white markings (*balzane*) on a horse: the white leg markings (*calzane*) and the various stars and blazes on the horse's face. Although not mentioned in early treatises, by the late-sixteenth century these markings were often discussed at length, with Caracciolo dedicating two pages to the subject. His theories conclude that it is better and luckier to have white markings on the back feet than the front, that white markings on both right legs, or both left legs, known as *travato*, was a bad sign, although worse if on the left, and that a white sock on the right back leg, *arzeglio*, should be avoided at all costs because, even if the horse appears excellent in his work, he will be a disaster in battle. His most bizarre theory is reserved for white markings on diagonally opposed legs, *trastravato*, which he believed indicated that the foal's legs were tangled up in the womb and that this would become a natural instinct, the adult horse being liable to stumble or fall down, consequently endangering its rider's life.[55] In contrast to Caracciolo' various interpretations of these markings, Corte warns that there are many unproven theories for which he has never found any practical or probable reason, concluding that most early writers were very wise to pass over the subject in silence. He does, however, mention Apsyrtus' view that a completely white mouth and muzzle were indications of perfection and, if the horse's whole head was white, it had even more value as it would age more slowly. Explaining that it is phlegm 'a cold and humid humour' 'which is the cause of whiteness', Corte suggests that many contemporary theories have more imagination than truth.[56] This seemingly Italian obsession with a horse's colour was dismissed by the Spaniard Luis Zapata de Chaves, who, writing at the end of the sixteenth century, explained that he would not dwell on colour because when a horse is 'covered in silks and brocades [its] colour is not revealed as much as when it is out walking', adding

> even when parading on city streets, the colour is of the least importance, although they say that within a year the horse and its master look alike, so it would be beneficial and felicitous for the horse to be of a good colour.[57]

This need to define perfection reflects an increasing desire to create the perfect horse, with many Renaissance horse breeders cross-breeding their own stock with imported foreign horses. This added a sumptuous exclusivity to some of the Italian horse breeding programmes, by creating desirable commodities out of the more exotic breeds, such as the Syrian, Persian, Turkish, Barbary and Spanish horses – an example of the Western taste for 'the other'. In addition, the

1.9. The Gonzaga stallion Morel Favorito, Sala dei cavalli, Palazzo Te, Mantua, Giulio Romano *et al*, *c.*1527.
Courtesy of Comune di Mantova, n. 12657/2019

specialised knowledge associated with caring for these horses and the often complex and arduous methods of their acquisition added to their social history and, inevitably, to their value.

By the mid-sixteenth century authors were writing about the qualities associated with different breeds so that some horses would, by blood alone, be more highly valued than others. This resulted in the characteristics connected to particular breeds being defined particularly clearly by Marco de Pavari in his 1581 treatise, *Escuirie de M. de Pavari venitien*. Printed in Italian and French and published in Lyons, Pavari concentrates on the schooling of young horses and the re-schooling of badly-trained or ill-treated horses and he is at pains to point out the different qualities he associates with the known breeds.[58] Unlike Corte and Caracciolo, he does not consider conformation or colour of primary importance, focusing instead on character and the breed's ability to learn; a method of analysis which has been described as a form of 'primitive equine psychology'.[59] Pavari shows a dislike for the north European breeds, dismissing the German horses as the vilest – not only lacking in heart but becoming worse after training – and he criticises the Friesian horses for holding their heads too low. But following Italian fashion, he praises Spanish horses, describing them as genteel and responsive to commands with the simplest of bridles, so that the whip and spur are not necessary – only the hand and the touch of the rider's heel.[60] It was this responsiveness to training which made the Spanish *gineta* so popular as the classic performance horse in the European courts.

Having established the horse's breeding, conformation and colour, it was skilled training and meticulous care which transformed this raw equine material into a desirable and respected commodity. As one contemporary, Ottaviano Siliceo explained, whilst Nature gave the horse the right proportion, sincerity of heart and beauty, it was Art which gave it muscle and good discipline.[61] Helped by an understanding of the horse's character, it was this art or schooling which enabled it to perform elaborate displays of high school dressage in front of a selected audience. Following the Spanish occupation of Naples, academies of horsemanship had been established in Italy, the earliest founded in 1532 by Federico Grisone in Naples followed two years later by Cesare Fiaschi's academy in his home town of Ferrara. Together with Mantua, the cities of Naples and Ferrara would dominate equestrian culture throughout sixteenth-century Europe, through both horse breeding and the teaching of horsemanship. Whilst the Gonzaga thoroughbreds were highly prized throughout Europe, both Grisone and Fiaschi taught Italians and foreigners at their academies, their schooling methods highly respected and imitated – so much so that it became fashionable for foreign courts to employ Italian riding masters. Fiaschi's 1603 treatise, *Trattato dell'imbrigliare, atteggiare & ferrare cavalli*, first printed in 1556 under a slightly different title,[62] is particularly noteworthy as it contains seventeen chapters on training horse and rider, six of which use music. So that the rider could associate specific musical rhythms with the horse's paces, Fiaschi first describes the *maneggio* movement and then illustrates it, showing horse and rider with a stave of music at the top of the page, suggesting that the rider sings 'ah ah ah' in the same rhythm as clearly seen in his diagram for learning the *capriola* (1.10).[63] This musical exercise would not only have helped the rider relax; it would have encouraged horse and rider to move in harmony.

Through the many printed Italian treatises and the various riding academies, the interest in Italian academic horsemanship spread into the rest of Europe.[64] This evolution of equestrianism can be traced through certain trainer-student relationships starting with Fiaschi and Grisone, both of whom may have trained Giovanni Battista Pignatelli.[65] In turn, Pignatelli trained many foreign riders at his own academy in Naples: Salomon de la Broue, who wrote *Le cavalerice françois* (1602) and was riding master to the French king, Henri IV, and la Broue's contemporary student, Antoine de Pluvinel who, *c*.1566, had been sent to Naples at the age of ten. Pluvinel subsequently opened his own Parisian riding academy in 1594, where he instructed Louis XIII and wrote two books on horsemanship: *Maneige royal ou l'on peu remarquer le defaut et la perfection du chevalier*[66] and *L'instruction du Roy en l'exercise de monter à cheval*.[67] In addition, Pluvinel trained the German Fayser and the Spaniards Vargas and Paolo d'Aquino as well as St Antoine[68] – equerry to James I and Charles I with whom he is depicted in a Van Dyck equestrian portrait now in the British Royal Collection.[69]

Concurrent with Italy becoming the centre of academic equestrianism in the sixteenth century was the increased desire to understand the horse and the correct way to look after it or as Appadurai describes it 'the specialised knowledge as a prerequisite for appropriate consumption'– in this case equestrian expertise. Four of the five attributes which Appadurai suggests might turn a commodity into 'a luxury,' can be applied to the Renaissance court horse. In addition to specialist knowledge he lists: 'restriction by price to elites', 'complexity of acquisition, which may, or may not be the result of scarcity' and the 'capacity to signal social messages'.[70] The first two attributes could be said to relate to purchase and breeding, which has already been discussed, while the capacity to signal social messages will be covered in the chapter on magnificence. This belief that a specialised knowledge was required for 'appropriate consumption' is reflected in the flourish of Italian hippological treatises, some of which have already been mentioned, and the demand amongst the elite for Italian horse trainers. As early as 1514, when Francesco Gonzaga's head groom, Giovanni Ratto, had delivered and presented four stallions to Henry VIII, the English King had been so impressed by the performance of the Marquis's horses that he had asked for Ratto to remain at the English court 'promising good pay'; an offer that was subsequently refused.[71] But a few years later, Henry was employing Giovanni Antonio Scaticia, 'the most skilful rider in Italy . . . to teach their manage', who had come to England with a gift of horses from Alphonso Trottus of Ferrara.[72] According to William Cavendish, first Duke of Newcastle, Henry also sent for two of Grisone's pupils[73] one of whom, Robert Alexander,

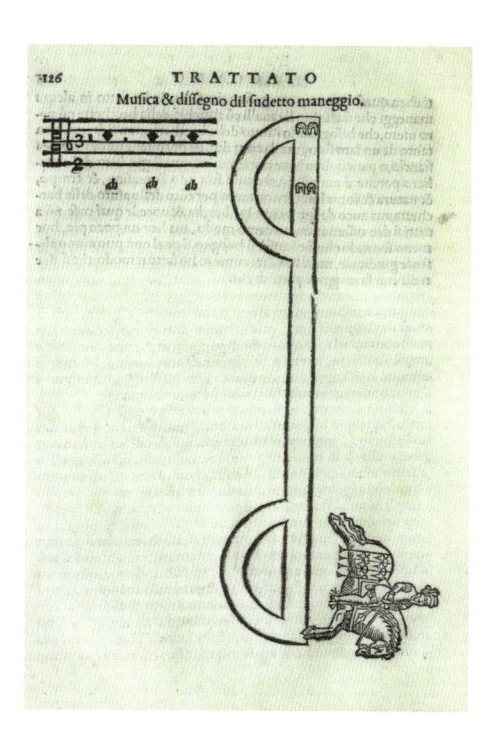

1.10. Cesare Fiaschi, *Trattato dell'imbrigliare, atteggiare & ferrare cavalli*, Bologna, 1556. Book II, ch. XVI, music and diagram for learning the *capriola*

brought the proudest coursers to his becke, and with his hand, spurre, voice and wand, did tame the stately steeds.[74]

By the end of the sixteenth century Italian-bred horses and those skilled in *maneggio*, especially the Spanish *gineta*, became valued commodities; commodities which not only had a monetary value but which, through their cultural biography, might also have social potential. The inaccessibility of the more exotic breeds had given them a particular exclusivity which only the richest of Renaissance princes could afford. Surrounding these commercial and social benefits there was a quest for knowledge about the horse and the culture surrounding it, resulting in an analysis of the many factors that contributed to an ideal temperament or to producing the most beautiful horse. Breeders sought to breed the perfect horse, while painters and sculptors searched for the ideal proportions of the horse's conformation, working both from nature and from classical ideals. The curiosity to find out what elements constituted a perfect horse or how this powerful animal could be persuaded to perform difficult feats resulted in a considerable equestrian literature in the sixteenth century. In addition, Italian riding academies and riding masters, highly valued throughout Europe, spread the required knowledge for shaping and 'polishing' these animals into obedient, biddable and desirable objects. As will be shown, this valuable commodity would be used by man as an extension of, and a means of displaying, his magnificence both within the confines of the court and in the more public pageants and parades.

1 Appadurai, *The Social Life of Things: Commodities in cultural Perspective* (Cambridge, 1992), 'Introduction', pp. 3, 6.
2 The origin of the word *gineta* comes from the Arabic berber tribe, Zanâta, famous for its horsemen and first mentioned in Spain in the tenth and eleventh centuries. See Noel Fallows, J*ousting in Medieval and Renaissance Iberia* (Woodbridge, Suffolk, 2012), p. 272, in which he discusses the different spellings: Portuguese, *gynet*a; Spanish, *gineta*; Italian, *zineta* or *jineta*; English, *jennet*. For this book the Spanish spelling, *gineta*, will be used.
3 Although Marquis Francesco II (1466-1519) and his son Federico II, first Duke of Mantua (1500-40) are remembered for their horses, it was Francesco's grandfather, Ludovico Gonzaga (1412-78), who had established the foundation of their stock.
4 For example, *Libro de marchi de cavalli con li nomi di tutti li principi & privati signori* (Venice, 1569 and 1588).
5 Mantua, ASMa, AG, b. 1458, 248r. The postscript is attached to Malatesta's letter dated 25 August 1524, 246r.
6 *Libro de Marchi* (Venice 1569). Women breeders: Bona, Queen of Poland and Duchess of Bari, Sra Barbara in Puglia. Sra Aurelia Sanseverina in Basilicata and Sra Victoria (consort of Sr Carlo Mormilio). Foreigners: French: Duke of Guise for two breeds, Henry IV of France and the Constable of France. Spanish: Alouigio Scangie [sic] is described as treasurer to the King of Naples – Philip II of Spain. Kings: Henry IV of France and the King of Naples, Philip II of Spain. Dukes: Duke of Mantua for two breeds. Cardinals: Cardinal of Lorraine and Cardinal Hippolito d'Este of Ferrara. Monastic orders: The Monastery of Santa Maria de Tremito, Abruzzo, Monastery of Santo Martino, Naples (Carthusians).
7 The Holy Roman Emperor's breeds can be found in the 1572-3 stud book for the Royal Maddalena stables which records horses born since 1566. Those listed are: P*iccola de Calabria, Grance [sic] de Calabria, Comune, Piccola de Puglia, Grande de Puglia, Imperiale, Reale, Gentile, Eletta, Ginetti reale, Ginetti fiumi, Ginetti di Calabria, Ginetti primi, Favorita* and *Mezana*. See Naples, ASN, Inv. N. 90-1. R. Camera della Sommeria, Patrimonio, b.1/39, fasc. 4, '1572. Conto de cavaliero Pyro Antonio Ferraro, cavalleriero delli cavalli de sua maiesta. Notamente de tutti li cavalli che restono ne la regia cavalleriza de la Madalena et de quelli de per ordine de sua Sig Illustrissima et Reverendissima si sono cacciati doppo l'ultimo de giulio 1572 insino al ultimo de presente mese de agosto 1573'.
8 'Courser' is a light cavalry horse.
9 Calendar of State Papers Venetian, III, 1520-1526, 62-3. For brief discussion on Gonzaga horse breeding see Andrea Tonni, 'The Renaissance studs of the Gonzagas of Mantua' in Edwards et al., *The Horse as Cultural Icon* (2012), pp. 261-78.
10 Appadurai, *The Social Life* (1992), p. 3.
11 Hobbies, known as *ubini* in Italy, were small horses bred mainly at the royal stud in Ireland. They were known for their sure-footedness, suitable as saddle horses with a comfortable walk and trotting pace.
12 London, British Library, Harley MS 3462, 147r (123), 16th July 1514, letter from Henry VIII at the Palace of Eltham. For a description of the exchanges of horses between Italy and the English court see J. P. Hore, *The History of Newmarket and the Annals of the Turf*, 3 vols (London, 1886), pp. 71-81.
13 Antonio Frizzi, *Memorie per la storia di Ferrara*, 6 vols (Ferrara, 1791-1809), IV (Ferrara, 1796; reprint, 1848), p. 278, *Meno giovarono di Enrico VIII Re d'Inghilterra, a cui, per cattivarselo, il Duca [Alfonso] mandò in donon per mano di Girolamo Sestola suo famigliare un superbissimo cavallo co' fornimenti d'oro, 3 dimesticati falconi, ed un leopardo.* Frizzi gives the date as 1516 but does not give a source for this reference.
14 According to Nosari and Canova, the term 'barbary' was used by the Gonzaga to signify one of their racehorses, not necessarily a horse from the Barbary coast. See G. Nosari and G. Canova, *Il palio del Rinascimento: i cavalli di razza di Gonzaga nell' età di Francesco Gonzaga, 1484-1519* (Reggiolo, 2003), p. 6. It is not clear whether other breeders used this term for their racehorses. However, Corte uses the lower case 'b' (*barbari*) for racehorse and the upper case 'B' (*Barbari*) when writing of North African horses. See Corte, 1562, II, 98r, ch. 52, 'De i cavalli, per correr palij, & de' Barbari massime.'
15 Nosari and Canova, *Il palio* (2003), p. 320.
16 See Chapter 3.
17 Alberti, CV, p. 39. Videtta, pp. 116, 118.
18 In the event, two separate sculptors were chosen: the Florentine, Niccolò Baroncelli for the horse, Antonio di Cristoforo for the rider. See 'Introduction'.
19 Simon of Athens (fl. 430 BC). English translation from Smith, *The Early History* (1976), I, pp. 7-8.
20 *On Horsemanship*, 1962, p. 297.
21 Virgil, Georgics III, trans. H. R. Fairclough, *Eclogues, Georgics, Aeneid I-VI* (Cambridge, MA & London, 1999), p. 183, 'His neck is high, his head clean-cut, his belly short, his back plump, and his gallant chest is rich in muscles . . . should he but hear afar the clash of arms, he cannot keep his place, he pricks up his ears, quivers in his limbs, and snorting rolls beneath his nostrils the gathered fire. His mane is thick and, as he tosses it, it falls back on his right shoulder. A double ridge runs along his loins, his hoof scoops out the ground, and the solid horn gives it a deep ring'.
22 Alberti, CV, pp. 17, 19 Videtta, pp. 98, 100.
23 See in particular Leonardo da Vinci, *Heads of horses, a lion and a man*, c.1503-4. Royal Collection Trust, RL 12326.

24 Others writers refer to this as a 'double backbone' or 'double spine', ie. the backbone has a ridge of muscle running down either side of its length. This was especially important for the rider's comfort, before the use of a saddle. See n. 21 above for Virgil. See also Columella, *On Agriculture*, Books 5-9, trans. E.S. Forster, E.H. Heffner (Cambridge, MA and London, 1968), VI, ch. 29, p. 199; Varro, *On Agriculture*, trans. W.D. Hooper, H. B. Ash (Cambridge, MA and London, 2006), II, ch. 7, p. 385.

25 Alberti, CV, p. 19. Videtta, p. 100.

26 Alberti, CV, p. 21. Videtta, p. 102.

27 Ibid. Alberti does not specify if the hoof is shod when making the hollow sound. However, Simon of Athens, writing for an unshod horse, wrote that, 'the sound [the hoof] makes when coming in contact with the ground will enable its character to be determined, for the hollow foot rings like a bell'. See Smith, *The Early History*, p. 8.

28 Fiaschi, 1603, III, pp. 137-9.

29 Alberti, CV, p. 23. Videtta, p. 104.

30 See note 24.

31 The raised part of the spine at the base of the neck and in front of the saddle.

32 Erasmus of Valvasone, *La caccia poema di Erasmo di Valvasone* (Milan, 1808), II, vv. 132-3, see p. 80.

33 Karel van Mander, *Den grondt der edel vry schilder-const* (Haarlem, 1604) and quoted in H. Miedema, *Karl van Mander: Den grondt der edel vry schilder-const* (Utrecht, 1973), I, pp. 222-3. Miedema's modern Dutch translation trans. into English by B. P. J. Broos, 'Rembrandt's portrait of a Pole on his horse', *Simiolus: Netherlands Quarterly for the History of Art*, VII: 4 (1974), pp. 192-218. The extract is pp. 202-3. 'Taking note of the horse's shapely figure, make sure the horn of his hooves glistens like jet- dark, slick and high and rounded at the edges. The shanks must be short, and not too bent or straight. The forearms long, and show them looking slender, sinewy and veined should the knees be modelled, the muscles lean, so that they do resemble the legs of a deer more than anything else. You can make the breast nicely broad and padded. The same goes for the shoulders and the crupper. The flanks round, the belly short, the back unbent, the trunk big; along the spine a groove should run. The neck must look long and thick and full of folds; A long mane should hang down on the right-hand side. The tail when dangling should fall right to the ground. Either that, or else tied in a pretty knot. While the buttocks should shimmer with fleshiness, the head must be on the small, thin and dry side. We prefer a forehead of nothing but bone and pointed ears, which should never be quite still, a large mouth, large nostrils and each of the eyes large and protruding'.

34 M. Kemp, Leonardo da Vinci: *The Marvellous Works of Nature and Man* (Oxford, 2006) p. 193.

35 This drawing is in London, Victoria and Albert Museum, National Art Library, Codex Forster III, 88r.

36 I.A. Richter, *The Notebooks of Leonardo da Vinci* (Oxford and New York, 1980), p. 315.

37 This work was once owned by Giorgio Vasari, who attributed it to Verrocchio. See W. Liedtke, ed., *Royal Horse and Rider* (New York, 1989), p. 165.

38 Carlo Ruini, *Anatomia del cavallo, infermità et suoi remedi; opera nuova degna di qualsivoglia prencipe, & cavalierie, & molto necessaria à filosofi, medici, cavallerizzi & marescalchi* (Venice, 1598). The book was published posthumously. A later edition, Venice, 1618 is used here.

39 Andreas Vesalius, *De fabrica corporis humani* (Basle, 1543).

40 Caracciolo, 1589, V, p. 463, *La bellezza si richiede in tre cose: nella taglia della persona, nella proportione delle membra, e nel color del mantello*.

41 Ibid, IV, p. 251.

42 Simon of Athens, MS 251 (III.3.19). English translation from Smith, *The Early History* (1976), I, p. 8.

43 Virgil, *The Georgics* (1999), III, p. 183.

44 Alberti, CV, pp. 21, 23. Videtta, p. 102.

45 Corte, 1562, I, chs 10 to 17.

46 Caracciolo, 1589, IV, p. 249.

47 Ibid, III, pp. 145-6.

48 Corte, 1562, I, ch. 11, 23v.

49 Corte, 1562, I, ch. 15.

50 Caracciolo, 1589, IV, pp. 272-3.

51 'Cavezza di Moro' suggests that this horse also has a black muzzle.

52 Caracciolo, 1589, IV, p. 274.

53 Ibid. I, p. 24.

54 Mantua, ASMa. AG, b. 2500. From the horses' names it is possible to ascertain that there are also four bays with the prefix *baio* and four greys with the prefix *liardo*.

55 Caracciolo, 1589, IV, pp. 297-298

56 Corte, 1562, I, ch. 17, 28r-v. A comprehensive list of the terms for white markings is given in the Glossary.

57 Luis Zapata de Chaves, 'Del justador' (1589-94), Madrid, Bib. Nacional, MS 2790, 182r-188v. 'Del justador' is ch. 125 of 255 chapters forming an eclectic work by Zapata de Chaves, *Miscelánea, ó varia historia*. It was edited by Corrasco González and published in 1859. Cited by N. Fallows, *Jousting in Medieval and Renaissance*

Iberia (Woodbridge, 2010), p. 387.

58 M. de Pavari, *Escuirie de M. de Pavari venitien* (Lyons, 1581), ed. P. Arquint, M. Gennero (La Veneria Reale (TO), 2008). None of the original Italian editions are known, but the French king's Lyonaise printer, Jean de Tournes, translated and printed the text in Italian and French. The 53 pages of Pavari's text are printed in two parallel columns; the original Italian text printed in Italics on the inner side of each page and the French translation in 'gotico bastardo' on the outer side.

59 Carlo Girardi, President of the Centro Internazionale del Cavallo, La Veneria Reale in Pavari, Escuirie (2008), p. 9. The Centro Internazionale del Cavallo is in La Veneria Reale, Piedmont.

60 Pavari, *Escuirie* (2008), pp. 28, 38, 29 and 50-51.

61 Ottaviano Siliceo, *Scuola de' cavalieri di Ottaviano Siliceo. Gentilhuomo troiano* (Orvieto, 1598), Book I, ch. 1, p. 1.

62 Fiaschi, *Trattato dell'imbrigliare, maneggiare, et ferrare cavalli* (A treatise on breaking, schooling and shoeing horses) (Bologna,1556).

63 Fiaschi, 1603, II, see especially pp. 100-111.

64 For example, Corte was employed in England and France; Pignatelli, taught by the Neapolitan Federico Grisone, instructed Antoine de Pluvinel, the first French riding master and instructor to Louis XIII.

65 André Monteilhet, 'A history of academic equitation' in J. & L.P. Froissard eds *The Horseman's International Book of Reference* (London, 1980), pp. 97-116, p. 99.

66 Antoine de Pluvinal, *Maneige royal ou l'on remarquer le defaut et la perfection du chevalier,en tous les exercises de cet art, digne des princes, fait et pratiquée en l'instruction du Roy* (Paris, 1623).

67 Antoine de Pluvinal, *L'instruction du Roy en l'exercice de monter à cheval, par messire Antoine de Pluvinal, son Sous-Gouverneur, Conseiller, en son Conseil d'Estat, Chambellar ordinaire, & son Escuyer principal etc.* (Paris, 1625).

68 Monteilhet, 'A history of academic equitation' (1980), pp. 99-100.

69 London, Royal Collection Trust, Anthony Van Dyck, *Charles I with Seigneur de St Antoine* (1633).

70 Appadurai, *The Social Life* (1992), 'Introduction: commodities and the politics of value', p. 38.

71 *Calendar of State Papers Relating to English Affairs in the Archives of Venice*, Volume 2 1509-19, ed. Rawdon Brown (1867), 'Venice, June, 1514', pp. 170-5, 438, 30 June, 1514, London, Giovanni Ratto to the Marquis of Mantua.

72 'Henry VIII: April 1519', *Letters and Papers, Foreign and Domestic, Henry VIII*, Volume 3:1519-1523, ed. J. S. Brewer (1867), pp. 58-72, 181, 12 April, 1519, Alphonso Trottus to Henry VIII.

73 William Cavendish, *A New Method and Extraordinary Invention, to Dress Horses, and Work Them According to Nature: Which was Never Found Out, But by the Thrice Noble, High and Puissant Prince, William Cavendish, Duke of Newcastle* (London, 1667), p. 2.

74 N. Morgan, *The perfection of horse-manship, drawne from nature; arte, and practise. By Nicholas Morgan of Crolane, in the countye of Kent*, Gent (London, 1609), 'Preface'. See Worsley, 'Design and development', 1989, pp. 248-9 for Italians working at the English royal stables.

Chapter 2

The Horse and Magnificence at the Renaissance Court

> I would like our courtier to be an accomplished horseman in every style of riding and, as well as having a knowledge of horses and all matters to do with riding, he should put every effort and diligence into surpassing everyone else just a little in everything, so that amongst others he is always the best informed in such a way that he will always be superior . . . so that our courtier should outstrip all others.
> Baldassare Castiglione, 1528.[1]

During the Renaissance the horse was important for logistical, diplomatic and military purposes and, as seen in the previous chapter, it was also valued as a commodity. However, beyond these qualities, the horse could be appreciated for the many other ways in which it might be of benefit. It was, for example, a means of projecting man's image, the most conspicuous methods of which were the public parades and pageants or the large gatherings of cavalry horses such as those witnessed by the Bolognese in peacetime and war in the 1490s. In such displays, wealth, status and power were exhibited through the quantity and quality of the horses as well as in the extravagant clothing for both horses and horsemen. In more private surroundings, courtiers and distinguished visitors might watch a display of *maneggio* or admire strings of court horses as they were paraded and exhibited at their stud farms. In addition, the horses' stabling – a category of architecture frequently overlooked by historians – was another means by which a Renaissance prince could exhibit his magnificence and power.

This chapter considers the ways in which the court horse and the culture surrounding it could benefit the Renaissance ruler's image in military conflict and in peacetime – both of which required the horse to be well-disciplined and responsive to its rider's commands. Military manoeuvres, like hunting, public processions and displays of *maneggio*, required horse and rider to be in perfect harmony both for safety and for aesthetic purposes, adding prestige to the rider through his ability to control and use the horse to the best advantage. Consequently, owners employed a well-trained staff to maintain and train their horses correctly, with a significant amount of advice and guidance found in the many sixteenth-century equestrian treatises. Furthermore, as a status symbol, the Renaissance court horse can be compared to the Venetian gondola, another 'object' which was used for self-promotion or self-definition.

During the fifteenth century, the appropriate use of wealth and power, together with the concept of 'magnificence', had been a popular subject for public debate. Centuries earlier, both Aristotle and Cicero had commented on the public display of wealth; Aristotle suggesting that magnificence was connected to spending money tastefully; Cicero explaining how much the Romans had loved public magnificence whilst hating private wealth.[2] Even in the 1420s, when sumptuary laws were being implemented in Florence, magnificence had been encouraged as a civic and moral virtue, although only for those for whom it was deemed appropriate. Fra Antoninus Pierozzi (later St Antoninus) would include secular architecture such as private palaces as being worthy attributes of the magnificent man, as these would benefit the city.[3] However, this positive attitude to public displays of wealth would be curtailed in the 1470s by Lorenzo de' Medici's sumptuary laws and by the Dominican preacher Savonarola a decade later, who considered them to be expressions of vanity not of virtue. In the same period, two writers from different sides of Europe – the Portuguese king Dom Duarte, who had spent six years at the English court,[4] and the Perugian born Giovanni Pontano – would suggest ways of using wealth wisely within the court. Dom Duarte's fascinating and instructive treatise, *Livro da ensinança de bem cavalgar toda sela* (The Art of Riding on Every Saddle), which concentrates on jousting and horsemanship, also includes advice on general etiquette for the wealthy owner, emphasising the importance of knowledge in order to spend money wisely.[5] Pontano's treatise, *De splendore*, explains how magnificence can be divided into private and public display.[6]

Written in the mid-fifteenth century, and unfinished at his death in 1438, Duarte's equestrian treatise stresses the importance of being knowledgeable when spending money on horses. He divides the 'power [which] every horseman must have' into two parts – the 'power of the body' and 'the power of wealth'.[7] He then explains that the 'power of wealth' should be assisted by knowledge for three reasons: first, when buying horses, a knowledgeable buyer can choose good ones or refuse them if they were too expensive; second, having bought them, he can 'improve their qualities and value' through training; and third, such knowledge can also save the owner money as, when caring for his horses, he can do so correctly.[8] Although a Portuguese text, Duarte's treatise is particularly important for two reasons: his royal status and his text's similarity to Italian Renaissance theory. While it was not unheard of for a head of state to write on hunting – his father Dom João I of Portugal had already written the *Livro da Montario* on the subject and Charles IX of France would write *La Chasse Royale* in the sixteenth century[9] – it was rare for a king to write on horsemanship. But of more significance is that some of Duarte's views are reflected in later sixteenth-century Italian treatises on horsemanship and the court, showing that they were consistent over the intervening years. Certainly, both the Portuguese king and the Italian courtier Castiglione would praise the ability of those who could ride in different styles, as illustrated by the title of Duarte's treatise. The possibility of riding in different styles is recorded in a 1521 inventory for the Este stables, in which at least ten different styles are recorded amongst the many saddles in one of their saddlery workshops.[10] These include saddles for jousting and leisure, a lady's saddle and military saddles (*ala stradiote*) for an adult and a child, one that is silvered and another with disc-shaped wings, as well as saddles described as Turkish, German, Sardinian, Japanese, *alla gineta*[11] and one for a mule. Another Este inventory lists saddles in the French style.[12] Caracciolo's treatise also described saddle styles both for war and peacetime. His list includes Stradiot, Turkish, German and French but adds four other styles: *alla Bastarda*,[13] Mantuan, Castilian and *alla Caramana*,[14] and he explains that there were innumerable styles at this period, with a saddle to suit every breed, as well as traditional regional varieties and imaginative designs thought up by inventive people.[15]

The Florentine preachers' and Duarte's theory on the appropriate use of wealth endorsed Aristotle's belief that magnificence is one of the two moral virtues associated with money, the other being generosity.[16] In Book IV of *Nichomachean Ethics*, the Greek philosopher associates magnificence with wealth – both self-made and inherited – high birth and reputation; qualities found in most Renaissance patrons. However, Aristotle writes that although 'the magnificent man is generous . . . the generous man is not necessarily magnificent'. To achieve magnificence the patron should be 'like an artist, [so that] he can see what is fitting and spend large sums tastefully' for only then will the result 'be worthy of the expense and the expense worthy of the result'. But he makes the condition that the patron must have either the suitable means to start with, acquired by his 'own efforts or from ancestors or connections', or he must be of 'high birth or reputation'. Only then will such great expenditure 'bring with [it] greatness and prestige'.[17] Aristotle's definition as to who is worthy of indulging in great expenditure, and possibly also of magnificence, would cover not only the ruling classes in the Renaissance but also bankers and military *condottieri*, as well as the upper echelons of the Church. As will be seen many of these classes of men had their own courts; many would spend extravagantly on their stables and horses.

Centuries later Giovanni Pontano, who from 1448-90 was at the Neapolitan court, concentrated on what constituted magnificence and would expand Aristotle's theory on private expenditure by joining splendour and magnificence together. Whilst the Greek philosopher had suggested that the most appropriate private expenditure should benefit the 'whole city or the people of position within it', with money spent on weddings, the reception of foreign guests and gifts,[18] Pontano wrote that private expenditure was also justified for personal display

> it is appropriate to join splendour to magnificence because they both consist of great expense and have a common matter, that is money. But magnificence derives its name from the concept of grandeur and concerns building, spectacle and gifts while splendour is primarily concerned in the ornament of the household, the care of the person and with furnishings.[19]

Analysing Pontano's theory, it is possible to place certain aspects of equestrian culture into his categories of magnificence and splendour. For example, his theory of magnificence in building can be found in the grandeur of several Renaissance court stables, while 'spectacle' was to be seen in the great cavalcades, military parades and hunting parties witnessed in Renaissance Italy, as well as in the gifts of horses, hunting hounds and falcons exchanged between rulers and princes. But, in addition to this magnificence associated with equestrian culture, it is Pontano's definition of 'splendour' that can be found in the elegant horse trappings and the ornamental architectural detail of some Renaissance stables. It is decorative elements such as carved capitals, frescoed walls and elaborate stucco work, which should be understood as an extension of 'splendour . . . in the ornament of the household'. More relevant, perhaps, is that the privileged viewing of a collection of thoroughbred court horses equates to splendour through 'the display of different things'.

In the same decade another Neapolitan, Giuniano Maio,[20] would associate magnificence with majesty, dividing it into two distinct categories: the first concerning the power displayed through horsemanship and the second noting the importance of hunting with beautiful hounds and falcons. In his dedication to Ferdinand I, King of Naples, Maio writes of

> works of magnificent extravagance used in the household: cloth, drapery, pictures, sculpture, rich clothing, vessels of gold and silver and other materials . . .[21]

Explaining that 'where sumptuous magnificence can make such an excellent display . . . it creates a nobility of spirit from the greatness of virtue and the easy delight shown.'[22] Then, flattering the King, Maio adds,

> The first [magnificence] is that, seated in majesty on a horse, You are the most powerful Prince and the most mighty horseman amongst those who display horses, so that many

delight in the quantity and beauty of these superb horses; which are given such care and diligence both in their consistent breeding and good management.[23]

It is not difficult to appreciate Maio's concept of sumptuous magnificence through spectacle in many of the processions which threaded their way across the Italian peninsula. Richly caparisoned horses and mules were admired in town and country alike as they travelled between courts and cities, whether in baggage trains or part of elaborate and extensive hunting parties and processions. Evidence for these conspicuous displays of wealth is found in contemporary chronicles and letters, as well as in court accounts. Borso d'Este's retinue, when he travelled to Rome in 1471 for his investiture as Duke of Ferrara, is one example. According to the humanist historian Stefano Infessura, Borso, who was known to wear cloth of gold and jewels even when hunting, was more sumptuously equipped than any lord who had ever entered Rome[24] with 700 attendants, 700 horses and mules, 320 hounds and a number of falcons and leopards, which required a further eight huntsmen.[25] Twelve caparisons[26] of *panno d'oro cremexino* were made by the court tailor Nicolò da S. Severino for the heavy horses (destriers), in addition to thirty of silver brocade for the pages' horses.[27] Even the baggage mules for the journey were covered in woollen cloths in the Este colours of red, white and green, decorated with appliquéd coats of arms.[28] In addition, to protect the horses from being scratched by the leopards, which travelled sitting behind the saddle, fringed mats were made out of old carpet and laid over the horses' rumps. Such mats can be seen in Benozzo Gozzoli's mid fifteenth-century frescoes, *The Procession of the Magi*, in the chapel of the Medici palace in Florence and were also used by Ercole d'Este in 1472 (2.1).[29]

In the same year as Borso's journey to Rome, Duke Galeazzo Maria Sforza, who for his own personal use was known to travel with at least forty horses, had an entourage of 1,000 people for his month-long journey for a formal visit to Florence. He ordered 150 velvet coverings in the Sforza colours of white and dark red, and 45 gold and silver fittings for the horses and mules as well as new clothes in brocade or velvet for the servants accompanying him.[30] The magnificence of the ducal train, arriving in Florence on 16 March, was noted in a letter from an onlooker, who described the horse trappings,

> There was a livery for his greater *camerieri*, all dressed in crimson, and each one well mounted on horseback, with a greyhound on a leash. There were also sixty pages, all dressed in green velvet, on huge coursers, all with fittings of gold and silver, and saddles covered with brocade of various colours and crimson. In similar fashion they led sixty-five to seventy mules with coffers and carriages, all with covers of embroidered silk.[31]

Twenty-three years later, a description of nineteen-year-old Beatrice d'Este, wife of Ludovico Sforza, was written by a French courtier as she led a mounted procession of court ladies, during the visit of King Charles VIII to the Sforza court.

> When she arrived she was on a horse with trappings of gold and crimson velvet, and she herself wore a robe of gold and green brocade, and a fine linen gorgette turned back over it, and her head was richly adorned with pearls, and her hair hung down behind in one long coil with a silk ribbon twisted round it. She wore a crimson silk hat, made very much like our own, with five or six red and grey feathers, and with all that on her head, sat up on horseback as straight as if she had been a man. And with her came many other ladies

2.1. Benozzo Gozzoli, *The Procession of the Magi*, 1459, Florence, Palazzo Medici Riccordi, Chapel, East Wall. Detail showing a hunting leopard on a protective mat. David Collingwood/Alamy Stock Photo

> as many as twenty-two, all riding handsome and richly apparelled horses, and six chariots hung with cloth of gold and green velvet, all full of ladies.[32]

Admiration for these displays of wealth continued into the sixteenth century, as shown in Castiglione's definition of the perfect courtier who

> should hold magnificent banquets, festivals, games and public displays; keep a great many fine horses for use in war or delight in peacetime, as well as falcons, hounds and all the other things relevant to the pleasure of great lords and their subjects.[33]

Towards the end of the century, in 1581, the French nobleman and essayist Michel de Montaigne described Pope Gregory XIII's 'ordinary equipage, consisting [of] a Spanish horse, a hackney and a mule followed by a litter all decked out in the same way' – the litter presumably offering the Pope an alternative form of transport. But on the Sunday after Easter – Low Sunday – these four modes of transport were preceded by twenty-five horses with 'caparisons and saddle-cloths in cloth of gold' and twelve mules 'similarly caparisoned' all led by grooms, followed by four horsemen carrying red hats on red velvet covered staffs with gilded handles, followed by the Pope on his mule and all the cardinals similarly mounted with their long robes hooked up by a cord to their mules' bridles.[34] In addition to these formal cavalcades and processions of Renaissance rulers and clergy, there were other opportunities for powerful dynasties to display their wealth. Throughout Italy, status and power could be witnessed in wedding celebrations, military manoeuvres and parades or extensive hunting parties, in which horses served as impressive showpieces for their owners. Often expensively clad with a silk bridle and fur or velvet-covered saddle, the Renaissance horse is comparable to the Venetian gondola, as both gave the owner the opportunity to display his or her magnificence in public.

A brief reference to a horse on *terra firma*, made by the Venetian historian Marin Sanudo, is mentioned by Dennis Romano in his article on the Venetian gondola as a marker of station.[35] The reference is worthy of examination as a comparison of horse and gondola illustrates that they could hold a similar status in the Renaissance; both useful in promoting an image for their owners. In his treatise, *De origine, situ et magistratibus urbis Venetae, ovvero, La Città di Venetia* written between 1493-1530, Sanudo had written that 'the cost of [a gondola] when it is new is fifteen ducats and still it is necessary to furnish it . . . so that the cost is very great, more than that of a horse'.[36] As Romano explains, Sanudo's comparison between the cost of a gondola and of a horse was made because the horse was the 'essential sign of *terra firma* status'.[37] Certainly, both gondola and horse were seen as status symbols and, as the principal methods of transport for privileged members of society, they distinguished their owners from ordinary citizens, who could only travel on foot or use public transport. But Romano's comparison between horse and gondola can be extended in several ways. In addition to being elite forms of conveyance, both offered ways in which status could be advertised through appearance – Pontano's definition of splendour through display. Sanudo's intentions may well have been to emphasise the importance of the Venetian gondola in his hometown but, in fact, gondola and horse had many similarities, not only in methods of displaying status but in their function and management as well. Both required a significant amount of upkeep and considerable expenditure on staff and shelter, as well as on luxurious furnishings and trappings. It is in care and display that horse and gondola held similar positions in Renaissance culture. Romano rightly points out that, in addition to being forms of transport, both were used for leisure – itself, a sign of status. But, although his article considers the role of the gondola as 'a marker of station', it should also be pointed out that more inferior gondolas and boats were used in daily life for logistical purposes, such as delivering foodstuffs and building materials – a role matched by that of the farm or carthorse.

What then were the similarities between the Venetian patrician's gondola and the court horse for their respective owners? Firstly, the specialist servants required and the social advantages accorded them through their skill and knowledge; secondly, the necessity for suitable mooring or stabling, which should be convenient and secure; and, thirdly, the use of gondola or horse as a means of displaying expensive accoutrements for the purpose of visual magnificence – such that which would lead to sumptuary laws. Elements of magnificence and splendour can be found in all three aspects and for these reasons it is worth extending Romano's comparison.

Whatever the purchase price of the gondola or the horse, this was just the beginning of an owner's financial outlay. Of primary importance was the employment of competent and trustworthy servants, whether gondoliers or grooms. Such men were required to maintain their charges in good and safe condition so that they were always available for use or, if idle, they had to make sure they were kept in a secure location. Maintenance was of the utmost importance. Gondolas needed to be seaworthy and kept clean with their rigging in working order; horses needed to be washed and groomed, their feet suitably shod and their tack kept in good condition.[38] But when comparing the work of groom to gondolier, the amount of work carried out by the different employees seems to have varied considerably. Those privileged enough to own a gondola employed a single gondolier although, according to the Venetian painter Cesare Vecellio, 'the nobles of Venice' employed two, 'one of whom has charge of the boat and is called the poop man, the other is occupied in other services to the master'.[39]

But Vecellio's subsequent criticism that much of the gondoliers' time was spent idly waiting to ferry their employers from one place to another, makes a sharp contrast to the grooms' days, which were exceptionally busy, one man held responsible for as many as four horses. Two chapters of Claudio Corte's *Il cavallarizzo*, which specify the grooms' daily responsibilities, show that there was little time for these stable boys to be idle. Each was required to groom and feed their charges both before and after they were exercised; stables needed mucking out and rinsing down and tack needed to be cleaned and checked for any broken straps or buckles.[40] Even at night, they were required to sleep in the stable to protect the horses from theft or fire. However, for both the conscientious gondolier and groom there was the chance to gain some social advantage from his work. It was possible for Venetian employers to bequeath their gondolier a boat or, if the gondolier was a slave, they might give him his freedom, both of which would allow him to earn an independent living. Romano gives several examples of such bequests, such as when Marin da Lezze left his servant, Antonio, a boat in 1538 so that 'he would have the means to live honourably'.[41] Social advancement was also possible for boys or slaves working in a stable: Corte explains that one of his stable boys, Giambattista da Cremona, had been promoted to 'the post of Rider in the Saddle and [that he had then become] Master of the Stable with provisions suitable for his status'.[42] A posthumous inventory for 1491 shows that two of the four black slaves working in a Neapolitan court stable had been granted their freedom by their late master, Count Onorato Gaetani.[43]

There is no doubt that members of elite Venetian society were using gondolas to mark their high position and prestige as well as to draw subtle distinctions of status amongst elite society itself but, as Romano explains, the richly appointed gondola could only symbolise status if it was rowed by a liveried and obedient gondolier.[44] Here again, the similarities between gondola and horse are clear as, on the mainland, the court horse would have played a similar role in promoting the status of its owner, with the horse's breeding and fitness reflecting the owner's equestrian knowledge, whilst the liveried *camerieri*, such as those accompanying Galeazzo Maria Sforza in 1471, signified his status. In both cases, the privileged owner would have been conspicuous amongst his compatriots for the quality of the commodity he owned. Once trained, harnessed and caparisoned a horse could be used in military displays or take part in the more public tournaments and public parades; once painted and richly furnished, the gondola became part of both private and public entertainment and pageantry in the Venetian republic such as taking part in regattas which, according to Romano, may have originated as military exercises[45] – as indeed had equestrian tournaments. With luxurious accoutrements, such as those made of velvet and silk, owners of both these Renaissance 'accessories' were able to exhibit their wealth, status and magnificence.

Both gondola and horse, therefore, gave the owner a suitable 'backdrop' on which to display his status amongst the general public as well as amongst his peers. But it seems that by 1562 competition between owners must have got out of hand, with the Venetian Senate passing a sumptuary law forbidding not only the silk awnings but also the carved, painted or gilded supports for them. In addition, gondoliers could no longer wear ostentatious livery; they had to be dressed plainly 'or in material of little value'.[46] And, in the Kingdom of Naples, a similar clampdown on excessive luxury is found in a sumptuary law concerning horse and rider, issued on 31 March 1533 on the orders of Charles V. The Viceroy Pedro de Toledo expressly prohibited 'gold or silver hangings in the embellishment of horses' with only the 'headpieces, pectoral and spurs [permitted to] be gilded'. In addition, the pectoral's leather straps should not be decorated with pulled gold or silver thread, nor should 'the stirrups be of gold or silver'.[47]

An element of magnificence can also be found in the ownership and stabling of large numbers of thoroughbred horses, the ability to house and care for them giving the Renaissance ruler or *condottiere* prestige amongst his people and his peers. It was not unusual, at a time when the horse was of major importance logistically and militarily, to see large numbers of horses passing through or parading in a city. The Bolognese diarist, Gaspare Nadi,[48] records several occasions in his diary when military or civilian horses were seen in Bologna. One occasion was the show of military strength for the private army of the Bentivoglio in 1493, when the *condottiere* ruler, Giovanni II Bentivoglio, celebrated his appointment as captain in the Duke of Milan's army. On 28 April, the diarist notes that Giovanni put on a military parade in which 1,800 horses took part. Although Nadi gives few details, he does describe it as a beautiful display (*una bela mostra*) and, with the quantity of soldiers and horses on parade, the power, wealth and status of the Bentivoglio must have been evident to the Bolognese onlookers.[49] Subsequently, in 1494 and 1495, the Bolognese would see a constant flow of horses through their city, as part of the Milanese support for the French king's advance on Naples. According to Nadi, 500 of the French brigade's horses passed through on the 27th of August, followed by another 500 two days later, then 60 horses under the standard of Duke Ludovico, 'Il Moro' and 50 more French on the 1st of September.[50] The following year, 1495, there would be a similar number of horses retreating through the city as the French withdrew from Italy, with extra Italian horses being sent to support the Milanese before the Battle of Fornovo on 6 July.[51] In between these cavalry movements, horses were to be seen in civilian entourages, which passed through Bologna. The cavalcade accompanying Piero de' Medici and his brother Cardinal Giovanni (the future Leo X),[52] as they fled to Venice from Florence in November 1494, Nadi describes as consisting of 8,500 people, of which 1,500 were on horseback.[53] It was not, therefore, unusual to witness these displays of power and magnificence, whether from large armies or from the numbers of horses required in moving a court from one city to another. And, whilst large numbers might impress, it was often the caparisons and quality of clothing that caught the eye of spectators.

Even without expensive caparisons and richly clothed riders it was still possible for a herd of beautiful horses to bring out the crowds. In April 1495, the Venetian public had the opportunity to witness the sight of fifty Croatian horses being transported from San Nicolò del Leone to Mantua. Bridled and saddled, they were taken down the Grand Canal via the Rialto on eight rafts and were, according to the Gonzaga ambassador,

> a beautiful sight for the great multitude of people, who were seen, unexpectedly, turning up from place to place, until [the horses] reached the Signori Procuratori of Saint Mark's.[54]

Similarly, half a century later, a letter shows how transferring a herd of Este brood mares could be entertaining. Having delivered the healthy horses safely to the Garfagnana valley, north of Lucca, Meschino Domaschino informed Duke Ercole not only of the condition of the horses but of the crowds that came to see them,

> I arrived in the Garfagnana, with your herd of mares safe and sound... marvellously fat and beautiful and grown, that You would not recognise them, so much so that they became a show, as they passed on the road from Pisa to Lucca, drawing the people's admiration who ran to see them.[55]

Like the Este herds, the Gonzaga horses were often moved across the countryside, no doubt drawing admiring glances as they were herded more than 60 kilometres to the open pastures of Monte Baldo and often as far as the borders with the Tyrol, to avoid the summer heat of the Po valley.[56]

Within the confines of a court, horses played a major role not only in equestrian entertainments but also in everyday affairs. Taking Lauro Martines' definition of the court as being both the environment and the personnel around a prince or ruler, it is possible to understand the importance of the horse's role. When the prince 'made laws, received ambassadors, dispatched letters, gave commands, decided cases, made appointments, took his meals, entertained and proceeded through the streets',[57] five of these nine regular occupations involved horses. Ambassadors arrived on horseback or by horse-drawn carriage; letters were sent by mounted courier; ingredients for the prince's meals were harvested and delivered with the help of horses; equestrian entertainments consisted of falconry, hunting, jousting or elaborate shows of *maneggio* and *carrousels* within the court and of street processions and parades amongst the general populace. These different roles for the horse partly explain the quantity of animals required by a court, but there were additional reasons, such as the increasing interest in importing and maintaining different foreign breeds in addition to the cavalry requirements of the mercenary general (*condottiere*). This might also explain the large size of many court stables, which often housed over one hundred horses. But whilst many of the court horses and mules must have been appreciated for their everyday chores, as the sixteenth century progressed it was the ability to *manege* to a high standard, which contributed to the magnificence and *sprezzatura* of the courtier and his ruler. Within the court, courtiers and professional court horsemen were expected to entertain by executing elaborate *maneggio* movements and jumps, without any apparent effort, despite requiring a high degree of fitness and agility on both the rider's and horse's part.

Comparing such horsemanship to other court entertainments, such as tilting and jousting, Castiglione's Count Lodovico says that he thinks

> no less highly of performing leaps on horseback, even though it is very exhausting and difficult because, more than anything else, it serves to make a man wonderfully agile and dextrous; and apart from its usefulness, if this agility . . . is accompanied by gracefulness, in [his] opinion it makes a finer spectacle than anything else.[58]

This belief in the value of skilled horsemanship is complemented by the many sixteenth-century treatises which explain how to train the horse in *maneggio*, such as Corte's *Il cavallarizzo*, the first treatise to have a title dedicated specifically to the riding master. Like Castiglione, Corte believed that man himself could benefit from equestrianism by achieving 'great prestige' and 'enhancement', which made him more superior and noticeable if he rode 'better quality and more beautiful horses'.[59] But Castiglione also advises the courtier should be suitably dressed with 'appropriate mottoes and ingenious devices' and his horses 'beautifully caparisoned' so that they 'attract the eyes of onlookers'.[60] As the sixteenth century progressed, groups of professional court riders and courtiers performed various *maneggio* displays to music, a form of equestrian ballet known as the *carrousel*. Performed on important court occasions, this intricate display joined together two of the major arts necessary for a courtier – riding and music. But just as Xenophon had set a classical precedent for a studied form of horsemanship, it was believed that the *carrousel* also had its origins in classical mythology, with many Neapolitan treatises including the myth of Sibarite horses dancing to the sound of music as a legitimisation of the antiquity of the cult of the horse in the Neapolitan kingdom.[61]

If displays of horsemanship were seen as giving a court prestige and splendour through the skills of professional horsemen, it was the chivalric tradition of hunting, a pastime for the whole court, which displayed a ruler's magnificence. Both in the medieval period and in the Renaissance, hunting was not only considered as a sport; it had been viewed for many years as a suitable training for warfare. Even Xenophon had recommended 'the practice of horsemanship by hunting... where the countryside is suitable and big game to be found', but had suggested that, if the conditions were not correct, two horsemen could benefit from their combined efforts, one playing the hunted animal and the other the hunter.[62] In this way a horseman would not only learn to pursue the enemy over all types of ground, he would also learn to handle his weapons correctly while doing so. In 1513 Machiavelli's prince is advised that, as part of his military training, he should 'always be out hunting, so accustoming his body to hardships and also learning some practical geography'.[63] And a few years later, Castiglione would concur with Xenophon and Machiavelli that hunting was the closest sport to warfare as it required the direct use of weapons and demanded a great deal of manly strength.[64] But, just as importantly, Castiglione added that hunting was 'the true pastime of great lords' and 'a suitable pursuit for a courtier, and we know that it was very popular in the ancient world'.[65] The importance of hunting within court life should not be underestimated as, in addition to benefiting both horse and rider for military purposes, its exclusivity offered a means for the elite classes to carry out business discreetly, whether for political or familial purposes.

It is, therefore, not surprising that many powerful rulers and princes pursued this 'pastime of great lords' and, in order to conserve a suitable amount of game for their sport and maintain privacy, they enclosed large areas of land which they then stocked with prey. These private hunting parks, such as those in Mantua, Ferrara and Milan, whilst protecting purpose-bred and imported quarry, also increased the exclusivity of this courtly sport. More publicly, there was also hunting in the open spaces of the mountains and plains of Italy, with the type of game varying according to the environment. It is known, for example, that Galeazzo Maria Sforza hunted bear at Varese, wild boar at Cusago and wolves at Villanova, in addition to the more widespread hunting of wildfowl, hares and deer.[66] Borso d'Este, who has already been noted for wearing cloth of gold and jewels when hunting, also had a wide range of parks in which to hunt. But his successor and brother, Ercole, seems to have been the first European to include a jumping course in one of his enclosed parks: the enclosure known as the Barco, close to Belfiore.[67] Here, over a three-mile spiral circuit of hurdles, he not only raced his Barbary horses against those owned by other ruling families but he also raced his leopards against one another in the privacy of his park.[68] Whilst the public races, *palii*, could be watched from houses and other vantage points in the city of Ferrara, this was not the case in the enclosed park and, in 1499, Ercole would order two stands to be made for the court ladies to watch these private races.[69] In the south of Italy, the Duke of Calabria (from 1494, Alfonso II of Naples), who is said never to have let a day pass when he did not ride or watch some of his many horses race,[70] had a wide choice of quarry in his Neapolitan hunting grounds: wild boar in Arnone, Eboli, Pianura, Marianella and Giuliano; deer in Quarto; foxes and hares in Foggia and Cerignola; quail in the plains; and 'various other prey' in Cuma, Pozzuoli and Monte di Procida.[71]

Hunting on this scale gave the prince an additional way to display his wealth and magnificence through the quality of his horses, hounds and falcons. Large numbers of horses were required for hunting, with more than one needed per man per day, although this depended on how hard and how far a horse was ridden. Certainly, King Henry VIII of England would sometimes require as many as eight horses for one day's hunting. In addition, copious stabling was required for resident court horses and those of visitors, such as at Leo X's hunting lodge, La Magliana, where the 225 feet long stables could hold as many as 160 horses. But even this capacity would not have been capable of housing Galeazzo Maria Sforza's entourage when he was Ludovico Gonzaga's guest at Mantua and Gonzaga for a month in 1471. On this occasion, the Milanese ruler advised his host that he wanted 'to live in my own way and as I do every day at home' and was expecting to bring over 500 horses in his entourage, amongst which were 200 for his wife, Bona of Savoy, 100 for himself, 40 for his brothers, 30 for his chancery and 60 for his falconers.[72] Not only was magnificence evident in this princely Sforza retinue but also in his host's generosity, as Ludovico would have stabled the visiting horses at his own expense.

Even in the confines of a city horses could play their part in promoting a ruler's status, in, for example, the etiquette required of dignitaries when making their formal entry into republican Florence. The most important guests were greeted at one of the city gates before proceeding to the Piazza della Signoria. Here, members of the ruling Signoria would be seated on the dais, *ringhiera*, in front of the Palazzo Vecchio, as the visitor approached them on horseback. Depending on the status of the visitor and the amount of respect he wanted to give the Signore, he would dismount at an appointed distance from the platform. As he did so, the members of the Signoria (the *Priori*) would rise and walk to meet him at a designated point. In this ceremony, therefore, the horse was an additional sign of the rider's status, carrying the more privileged guest closer to the Florentine seat of power. When, for example, the Duke of Milan, Galeazzo Maria Sforza and his wife visited Florence in 1471, they dismounted their horses, eighty yards away, although twelve years earlier the fifteen-year old Galeazzo Maria had ridden half way down the length of the Loggia dei Lanzi, before dismounting forty yards away. And, in 1465, Don Federigo of Naples had horrified spectators by riding right up to the platform – a privilege certainly not considered due to him as he was neither king nor first-born son of a king.[73]

The Florentine people, like the citizens of other cities, had the chance to witness great processions of visiting high ranking churchmen and rulers, such as that of Galeazzo Maria above, which consisted of 1,250 richly dressed courtiers and over 1,000 horses. But, in addition, they also had the opportunity to see the magnificent cavalcades of confraternities, such as the *Compagnia de'Magi*, in which the Medici were prominent members, and which enacted the story of the three kings in early January. The confraternity's procession, which in 1429 had included as many as 700 horses, displayed a wealth of magnificent fabrics on both riders and horses; the costumes thought to have been inspiration for Benozzo Gozzoli's frescoes in Cosimo de' Medici's private chapel in their Florentine palace (see 2.1). With the city being divided into four parts, one for each of the three kings and the fourth for Herod, the whole Florentine population would have had the opportunity to be entertained by this extravagant display.

In 1469, Cosimo's grandson, Lorenzo de' Medici celebrated his marriage with an elaborate joust in the city but, two years later, following the ostentatious cavalcade accompanying Galeazzo Maria to Florence, Lorenzo, the *de facto* ruler of Florence, would, like the Republic of Venice, introduce sumptuary laws affecting behaviour, not only in public spaces but within the confines of the Florentines' homes as well. These laws, and the preaching against luxury and extravagance by the Dominican Savanarola, resulted in a reduction of private wealth being displayed for public benefit in Renaissance Florence. As one of Lorenzo de' Medici's critics remarked, '[Lorenzo had] eliminated all those things that had traditionally won support and reputations for the citizens, such as marriage feasts and dances, *feste*, ornate dress. He [had] damned them all, both by example and by words.'[74] Even so, the young courtiers in the Medici circle would become increasingly exempt as time progressed. On going to Rome as a cardinal, Lorenzo's son, sixteen-year-old

2.2. Vigevano, Aerial view of the Castello Visconteo Sforzesco. 1. Falconry; 2. Galeazzo Maria Sforza's stables *c.*1470; 3. neo-Gothic archway; 4. Galeazzo Maria Sforza's stables, 1470s; 5. Ludovico Sforza's stables, 1494; 6. Area for grooming horses; 7. Blacksmiths' workshop.
Universal Images Group North America LLC/DeAgostini/Alamy stock photo

2.3. Castello Visconteo Sforzesco, neo-Gothic doorway leading to Galeazzo Maria Sforza's second stable, *c.*1470. Wikimedia commons/Tempo61

Giovanni had been advised by his father to spend his money on keeping a 'well-appointed stable and a well-ordered household' rather than on magnificence.[75] But, while following his father's advice on stables, the future Leo X used his horses for hunting which, now outside Florentine jurisdiction, he saw as an excuse for pomp and show; endorsing Giuniano Maio's theory that hunting was the second form of magnificence.[76] And, in 1510, three years before Giovanni became Pope, the apostolic protonotary, Paolo Cortese, would suggest that cardinals should not only live in splendid palaces but that, contrary to canon law, they should also 'take up riding and hunting'.[77]

It has already been noted above that Pontano, like Aristotle, had associated magnificence with buildings at the end of the fifteenth century and that Maio had praised King Ferdinand's magnificence in the quality of his horses and in the care he lavished on them.[78] And there is no doubt that the princely courts in Renaissance Italy would have stables which reflected the magnificence of their patron. Location, size, layout and ornamentation of these court buildings contributed to an overall impression of magnificence, as did the quality and quantity of the horses within them. However, only in exceptional cases could rulers house 300 horses in the privacy of their court, as may have been the case at the beautiful Sforza stables in Vigevano. Even stabling for 200 horses at the Medici villa at Poggio a Caiano was sometimes allocated on a first-come, first-served basis, with courtiers rushing to get a space rather than having their horses farmed out several miles away. But magnificence could also be found in the quality of a building's design, as in Rome, where the wealthy papal banker Agostino Chigi may have stabled as many as a hundred horses beside his villa on the banks of the Tiber. In this case, it was the extravagance of Raphael's design for the stable's façades which gave this building the appearance of a small Roman palace and contributed to its magnificence.

In 1470 Galeazzo Maria Sforza moved his court to Vigevano from Milan and the following year he commissioned Maffeo da Como to build two stables in the castle compound: one adjacent to the falconry and the second attached to the first by a large red-brick neo-Gothic archway, which led via the Piazza Beato Matteo to the city (2.2, 2.3). Both stables are said to have had the capacity for a hundred horses – although this seems unlikely[79] – with accommodation for staff or militia leading off a central passageway on the first floor.[80] To the rear of the first stable was a large covered area – possibly for grooming or washing the horses – whilst behind the second stable were the blacksmiths' workshops for shoeing horses and repairing metalwork. Following the murder of Galeazzo Maria in 1476 and the brief regency of his wife, Bona of Savoy, Ludovico 'il Moro', Galeazzo, Maria's younger brother, took over as *de facto* ruler of Milan and regent for his nephew Gian Galeazzo, with the intention of making Vigevano into a dynastic city. In 1494, Ludovico added a third stable as part of his continuous embellishment of the city and its castle. However, either the stables were not complete by October that year or they were not capacious enough for visitors' horses, as they are not mentioned in Pierre Desrey's account of the visit to Vigevano by Charles VIII of France. Only the beautiful castle where the retinue stayed is mentioned (*chasteau qui est un beau et agréable lieu de plaissance*).[81] Instead Desrey describes the double stables at the Sforzesca, a mile and a half from Vigevano,

> Firstly, there is a large fort with a spacious courtyard, around which, amongst other [buildings], there is a large stable, pleasantly constructed and well-planned, with tall columns and substantial foundations. On one side are the heavy horses and racehorses and on the other side are the brood mares.[82]

2.4 Castello Visconteo Sforzesco, Vigevano. Stable of Ludovico Sforza, *c*.1494

Ludovico's stable in Vigevano is slightly wider than Galeazzo Maria's two earlier buildings and about fifty per cent longer.[83] However, all three have the same interior lay out: a cross-vaulted stone roof covering a basilica plan, that is to say three aisles divided by monolithic columns of *serizzo* granite, with the wider central aisle used for services and access and the two side aisles for the horse stalls (2.4). Once the third stable was built, completing the enclosure of the five-sided courtyard, the façades of every building facing into the courtyard – castle, falconry and stables – were given a unity, their façades painted with a polychrome *diamante* pattern reminiscent of Ferrara's Palazzo Diamante, built for Sigismondo d' Este in the same decade (2.5, 2.6).

At Vigevano remaining traces of decoration show that the imitation *diamanti* were interspersed with *trompe l'oeil* scrolls, fluted Corinthian columns, garlands and various other devices, giving the courtyard a refined elegance. The overall impression would have been particularly impressive when the stables were approached from the fourteenth-century covered road (*La*

2.5. Vigevano, Castello Visconteo Sforzesco. Stable of Ludovico Sforza, *c*.1494, details of exterior wall painting

2.6. Palazzo Diamanti, Ferrara. Biagio Rossetti, 1493-1504. Wikipedia/Nicoló Musmeci

Strada Coperta) on the opposite side of the courtyard, a 167-metre-long passage which linked the old fortress to the castle. Inside the stables, it is easy to imagine the lines of tethered Sforza horses framed by the pale grey *serizzo* columns, the rough stone sparkling with light from the sun or from lanterns. But in addition to this architectural display, it is likely that the privileged visitor would have seen a considerable amount of colour and luxury in the horses' personalised head collars and rugs, and even the tack hanging up temporarily at the foot of their stalls. The stables would surely have matched the luxury afforded Galeazzo Maria's falconry, which also faced the courtyard and in which, according to Bernardino Corio,

> the perches of his hawks, falcons and other birds of prey were adorned with velvet, embroidered with the ducal arms in gold and silver.[84]

Approximately twenty years after the Vigevano stables were completed, one of the richest men in Europe, Agostino Chigi (1466-1520), employed Raphael to design his magnificent stables on the banks of the river Tiber in Trastevere. The villa, now the Villa Farnesina, and the stables can clearly be seen in Giuseppe Vasi's 1765 extensive panoramic map of Rome. The map's legend gives 295 as the 'Palazzina Farnese' while Chigi's stables, 296, are incorrectly labelled as 'Palazzo di Agostino Ghigi' (2.7, 2.8). Unfortunately, almost nothing remains of these stables – just a broken wall, some sixteenth-century drawings and Raphael's sketched plan (2.9, 2.10, 2.11).[85]

2.7. Giuseppe Vasi's Panorama of Rome, 1765. Detail showing Agostino Chigi's villa (295) and stables (296)

2.8. Detail of above showing Agostino Chigi's stables.
Both courtesy of the Rijksmuseum, Amsterdam

But these remaining artefacts and some anecdotes give an idea of the building's original appearance. As papal banker, the Sienese Chigi had employed Peruzzi to design his villa – bought by the Farnese in 1579 – close to the Vatican and outside Rome's city centre. However, for the stables he chose Raphael, who had worked on the decoration of the villa. The stables, which date from *c.*1512, were 12 metres wide by 40 metres long. They were, therefore, considerably smaller than those at Vigevano but their interior plan was similar with the basilica form divided by three aisles. The elegance of the façades with their elaborate carved *peperino* mouldings and classical orders which define the four levels, must have given the building an exceptional elegance – worthy of the banker who had earned the accolade '*Il magnifico*'. According to Chigi's seventeenth-century biographer, his great nephew Fabio Chigi,[86] the stables could hold one hundred horses. If this is true, some horses must have been housed in a semi-basement, as the ground-floor level would only have had capacity for forty. This raised ground-floor level was defined on the exterior by double Doric/Tuscan columns interspersed with areas of plain wall, the remains of which can still be seen in the Via della Lungara (2.12, 2.13). Above these two levels were a further two floors for accommodation: the *piano nobile* for guests, with square

2.9. Franco-Flemish drawing of Agostino Chigi's stables, elevations, 16th century. Anon. New York, Metropolitan Museum of Art

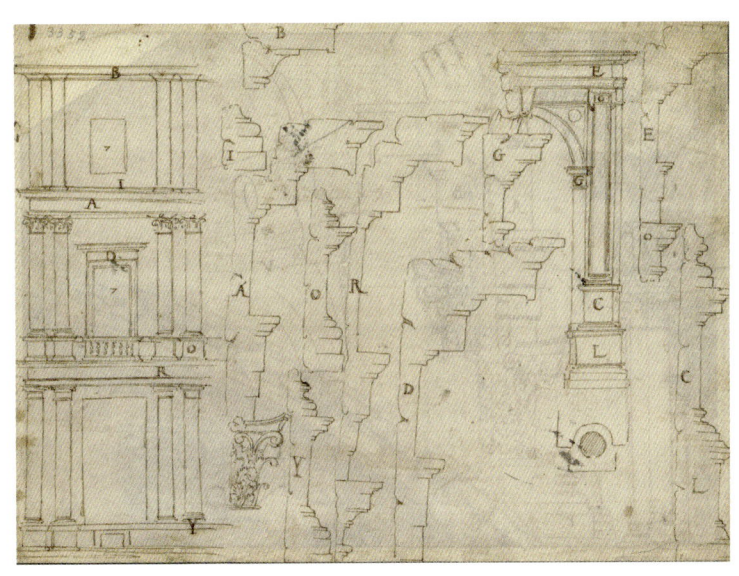

2.10. French, Agostino Chigi's stables, 16th century. Anon. Stable façade, entrance door and other details. Berlin, Kunstbibliothek ©bpk-Kunstbibliothek, SMB/Dietmar Katz

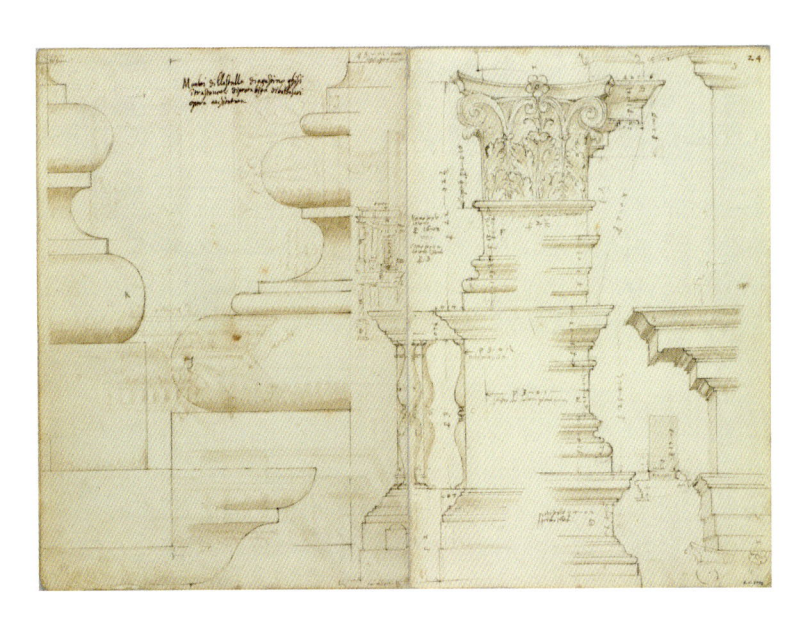

2.11. Cherubino Alberti, inscribed 'Membri di la stalla di agostino Ghisi in trastevere di preta di baldasari opera architetura', 16th century. Rome, Instituto centrale per la grafica. Courtesy of Ministero per i beni e le attività culturali

57

2.12. Rome, remains of Agostino Chigi's stables, detail of pilaster

2.13. Rome, remains of Agostino Chigi's stables. Façade on Via della Lungara

windows and balustrades interspersed with double Corinthian columns and the upper level, below the roof space, for staff. This latter floor had smaller windows placed above an architrave and, like the stable level, had double Doric/Tuscan columns. There is a similarity in the exterior wall surfaces of the villa and the stables – the areas of plain wall interrupted by the pillars – and it is known that, on the villa, these surfaces were once painted with decorative frescoes. Was the stable's exterior similarly decorated? It seems a possibility as, in addition to the stable having the form of a small Roman palace, the true purpose of the building is known to have confused some of Chigi's contemporaries. On April 30, 1518, the flamboyant banker held a banquet at which he entertained his employer, Pope Leo X, fourteen cardinals and several foreign ambassadors, following a day's hunting organised for the pope by the Cardinal of Aragon. Chigi spent lavishly; the banqueting room was hung with rich tapestries, silver plate was on show and extravagant dishes were served. When the Pope remarked to Chigi that he thought he and his banker had established a less formal relationship than the magnificence of the banquet implied, Chigi pulled on cords, allowing the tapestries to fall, revealing the stalls and mangers of his new stables and remarking that this was, in fact, only a humble building.[87]

In considering Aristotle's theory on the appropriate use of wealth and by extending the subsequent Renaissance theories on splendour and magnificence, it is evident that equestrian culture allowed many opportunities for the wealthy patron to display his status. Parades, whether in republican Florence or for princely pleasure, whether for a confraternity or for military prowess, hunting parties and diplomatic ceremonies not only gave the horse a central role in public life, it allowed the rider and owner the chance to exhibit his magnificence to those who could only watch and admire. This was achieved not only through the display of extravagant horse trappings, but more importantly in the quality and quantity of horses owned or controlled by any one court. The culture surrounding these well-bred thoroughbreds also gave their owners further opportunities to display their magnificence – the great court stables built both to protect and to exhibit these valuable commodities. These stables were not farm outbuildings but significant additions to the palace or villa complex, often designed by established court architects, with expensive materials used for their construction and elaborate ornamentation decorating their façades and interiors – all of which gave these buildings an eye-catching and, at times, palatial status.

As a result, both the horse and the culture surrounding the horse offered ways for a ruler or prince to project his image amongst his subjects and peers. However, for the horse to impress it needed to be fit and well disciplined – cared for by an attentive staff dedicated to bringing out its best qualities. To achieve this goal many sought to understand and explain the horse's character in order to train it appropriately and maintain its health. As will be seen, this required treating the animal with a considerable amount of respect, according it courtly adjectives, flattering epitaphs and lasting memorials.

1 Castiglione, *Il libro del cortegiano* (1528), ed. V. Cian (1947), I, ch. XXI, lines 24-31.
2 G.B. Pio, *Annotamenta* (Bologna, 1505), 2v, Cicero, 'Oratio pro L. Murena', 36.76: 'Odit populus Romanus privatum luxuriam, publicam magnificentiam diligit'.
3 Howard, 'Preaching magnificence', p. 355.
4 Dom Duarte (1391-1438). Aged 14 Duarte had been sent to the English court on the advice of his mother, Philippa of Lancaster, granddaughter of Edward III.
5 Duarte, *Livro da ensinança de bem cavalgar toda sela* (c.1438). There is only one known original manuscript of this work held in Paris, Bibliothèque Nationale de France (BNF), MS Portuguese 5, 99-128. It was copied in 1843 by a copyist from the King's Library in Lisbon and published as *Livro da ensinança de bem cavalgar toda sela, escrito pelo Senhor Dom Duarte, Rei de Portugal e do Algarve e Senhor de Cueta, transcrito do manuscrito existente na Biblioteca Real de Paris* (Lisbon). The work was unfinished at the time of Dom Duarte's death in 1438. I have used the following translation: *The Royal Book of Jousting, Horsemanship and Knightly Combat: a translation into English of King Dom Duarte's 1438 treatise Livro Da Ensinança De Bem Cavalgar Toda Sela, The Art of Riding on every Saddle*, trans. A.F. & L. Preto (Highland Village, TX, 2005).
6 Giovanni Pontano, *De splendore* (1498).
7 Duarte, *Bem cavalgar* (2005), II, ch. 1, p. 13.
8 Ibid. ch. 2, p. 14.
9 Charles IX of France (1550-1574), *La Chasse Royale* (pub. 1625).
10 Modena, ASMo, AE, Camera Ducale, Amm. della casa, Stalla Note-spese-inventori, 1521-1713, b. 2, fasc. 3, '1521 Selleria'. 'Inventario di le robe pertinente ali mano di M Signor g Aligueri quale sone intro note ō la quarta robe et la salari de lo Illus[trissimo] S[igno]r Nostro'. This inventory consists of eighteen pages.
11 Ibid, *Sela da giostre, - ala lezura, - de dona, - ala stradiote* and *- da puto ala stradiote, - arzonada, - alata discha, - ala Turchischa, - ala Todeschi, - ala sardische, - ala cipanose, - ala Zanete*.
12 Modena, ASMo. AE, Camera Ducale, Amm. della casa, Stalla, Note-spese-inventori, 1521-1713, Selleria b. 2, fasc. 3, Maestro Domenicho (saddler), 2 January, 1554, '*sela ala Francesca*'.
13 *Alla Bastarda* may be named for 'Il Gran Bastardo' also known as 'Monsignore lo Bastardo' or 'The Bastard of Burgundy'. This was Antoine (1421-1504) the illegitimate son of Philip the Good by his mistress, Jeanne de Presles, and half-brother to Charles the Bold. See G. Lubkin, *A Renaissance Court: Milan under Galeazzo Maria Sforza* (Berkeley, Los Angeles and London, 1994), p. 211.
14 *Alla Caramana*, possibly a Persian saddle style named after Caramania, the ancient name of Kerman, a province of Persia. See D. Brewster, *The Edinburgh Encyclopædia*, 18 vols (Edinburgh, 1830), XII, p. 446, 'Kerman'.
15 Caracciolo,1589, V, p. 363 '*innumerabili altre foggie, secondo le diverse specie di i cavalli, e secondo l'usanza delle Provincie, & varie fantasie delle persone, che producono ogni di nuove inventioni*'.
16 Aristotle, *Nichomachean Ethics*, 10 Books (350 BC), trans. D. Ross, notes by L. Brown (Oxford, 2009), see p. 224, notes for IV.1, where Brown uses the word *liberality* rather than *generosity*, explaining this is an alternative translation.
17 Aristotle, *Nichomachean Ethics* (2009), pp.65-66, IV.2, 1122a line 29 to 1122b, line 36.

18 Ibid. p. 66, IV.2, 1122b, line 36 – 1123a, line 4.
19 Giovanni Pontano, 'De splendore' (Naples, 1498), translation from E. Welch, 'Public magnificence and private display: Giovanni Pontano's '"De splendore" and the domestic arts', *Journal of Design History*, 15:4 (2002), pp. 211-21, p. 214.
20 Giuniano Maio (Naples, 1430-1493), knighted by Ferdinand I in 1480, from 1490 he was tutor to the royal children and, like Pontano, was a member of the humanist Accademia Pontaniano.
21 Paris, BNF, MS. it. 1711, Giuniano Maio, 'La opera de maiestate composta da Iuniano Maio, cavaliero neapolitano', Naples, 1492, 57v, *Sono et altre opere de magnifico sumpto apparate in lo culto domestico; panni, drapparie, pincture, sculture, veste ricche, vascelli de oro de argento et de altre materie . . .*
22 Maio, 'De maiestate', 1492, 58r, *'dove de pomposa magnificentia fai atanta et si excelsa demonstratione che non manco laleza del animo per la magnitudine del opera che la virtute per la delectosa commodità gia dimonstri'.*
23 Ibid. 58r, 'La Prima sié che sopra un cavallo in tua Maesta sedenco siei lo più possente cavalero de homo che manegia cavalli dove tanto te dilecti in multitudine et la bellecza de tanti et si generosi cavalli; con tanta cura et diligentia de continuo multiplicata et si ben posseduti'.
24 Stefano Infessura, *Diario della città di Roma*, ed. O. Tommasini (Rome,1890), p. 73, ' . . . venne cosi sontuosamente quanto venese signore mai'.
25 Modena, ASMo, AE, Cred. e Deb.1471, 74r, cited by L.A. Gandini in 'Viaggi, cavalli, bardature e stalle degli Estensi nel quattrocentro', *Atti e memorie della regia deputazione di storia, patria per le provincie di Romagna*, 3 (Bologna, 1892), vol. 10, pp. 41-94, pp. 47-5, n. 2.
26 Modena, ASMo, AE, Guardaroba 95.44: 'testiere, redene, pectorale, pendante e gropera' (headpiece, reins, pectral, pendant and crupper). These five items form the caparison.
27 Francesco Ariosto, 'De Fortunati felicisque illustrissimi Ducis Borsii in Urbem Roman ingressus Dieta', Vat. Chigi, I, vii, 261, ed. E. Celani, 'La Venuta di Borso d'Este in Roma', *Archivio della società romana di storia patria* (1890), pp. 361-450, p. 401.
28 Gandini, 'Viaggi' (1892), p. 50.
29 Modena, ASMo, AE, Tapezaria 10.12: '*un tapeda cum frapuni e fodrata de uno pezo de tapedo vechio . . . per portare in suxo la gropa de cavallo sotto li piede de uno lionpardo quando van in campagna*'.
30 Milan, ASMi, Registri delle Missive, letters no. 97 and 98; ASMi, Archivio Sforzesco, *c*.898, 4r. Codex of 'Le Liste de landata del Signor Duca de Milano a Fiorenza con altre liste aligate, 4 Mar., 1471. Cited in Lubkin, *A Renaissance Court* (1994), pp. 98-9 and p. 312, nn 76 and 77.
31 Lubkin, *A Renaissance Court* (1994), p. 100 and p. 312, n. 81 in which Lubkin cites C. Paoli, L. Rubini, P. Stromboli, eds *Della venuta in Firenze di Galeazzo Maria Sforza, Duca di Milano, con la moglie Bona di Savoia nel 1471: lettere di due senesi alla Signoria di Siena* (Florence, 1878), pp. 37-8, B. Dominici to the priors of Siena, 16 March 1470 [1471], Florence.
32 D. Godefroy, *L'Histoire de Charles VIII* (Paris, 1684), pp. 709-10, extract from a letter to Anne, Duchess of Bourbon. English translation taken from J. Cartwright, *Beatrice d'Este, Duchess of Milan (1475-1497):A Study of the Renaissance* (London, 1903), pp. 235-6.
33 Castiglione, *Cortegiano* (1528), IV, ch. XXXVI, lines 29-33.
34 Michel de Montaigne, *The Complete Works:essays, travel journals, letters*, trans. D. M. Frame (London, 2003), p. 1173.
35 Dennis Romano, 'The gondola as a marker of station in Venetian society', *Renaissance Studies* 8:4 (1994), pp. 359-74, p. 360.
36 Marin Sanudo, *De origine situ et magistratibus urbis Venetae, ovvero, La Città di Venetia (1493-1530)*, ed. Angelo Caracciolo Aricò (Milan, 1980) pp. 21-2.'
37 Romano, 'The gondola' (1994), p. 361.
38 The word 'tack' represents the bridle, saddle and other accoutrements necessary for riding the horse.
39 Cesare Vecellio, *De gli habiti antichi, et moderni di diverse parti del mondo libri due* (Venice, 1590), 122v – 123v.
40 Corte, 1562, I, ch. 37, 'Dell' officio de' garzoni di stalla'; ch. 38, 'Del governo de' cavalli in istalla'.
41 Romano, 'The gondola' (1994) pp. 367-8 and n. 35, citing Venice, Archivio di Stato di Venezia, Notarile, Testamenti, b.192, protocol, testament 156.
42 Corte, 1562, I, ch. 37, 'Del officio de' garzoni di stalla', 48r.
43 The posthumous inventory of Count Onorato II Gaetani, who died on 24 April, 1491, includes 12 black (*nigro*) slaves of whom 4 were working in the stable, 2 of whom said they had been freed by the Count. See *Inventorium honorati gaetani: l'inventario dei beni di Onorato II d'Aragona, 1491-1493* eds. S. Pollastri and C. Ramadori (Rome, 2006), p. 34 (29r of MS), 'Li schiavi'. The slaves are listed immediately before the horses in the inventory.
44 Romano, 'The gondola' (1994) p. 373.
45 Ibid. p. 369. Romano writes 'These maritime contests perhaps began in the fourteenth century as military exercises involving large ships with many oarsmen'.
46 The sumptuary law is printed in Giulio Bistort, *Il magistrato alle pompe nella republica di Venezia* (1912; reprint Bologna, 1969), pp. 391-2.
47 D. Salazar ed., 'Racconti di storia napoletana', *Archivio storico per le provincie napoletane* 34:1 (1909), pp. 78-117, p. 101.
48 Gaspare Nadi (1418-1504), *Diario bolognese di G. Nadi,* eds C. Ricci, A Bacchi della Lega (Bologna, 1886; reprint 1981), See 'Introduction', p. x-xii, where the editors explain that Nadi was a stonemason and not, as previosuly thought, the Bentivoglio's court architect.
49 Nadi, *Diario* (1981), p. 172, 28 April 1493. The eighteen hundred cavalrymen were in addition to the rest of the Bentivoglio army, amongst which were three hundred spearmen and three hundred bowmen.
50 Ibid. p. 182.
51 Ibid, p. 191.
52 Piero de' Medici (1472-1503) known as 'Piero the unfortunate' and his younger brother Giovanni (1475-1521) were the sons of Lorenzo the Magnificent.
53 Nadi, *Diario* (1981), p. 185, 17 November 1494.
54 Mantua, ASMa, AG b. 1435, 222r, 5 April, 1495. Letter from Antonio Salimbeni to the Marquis of Mantua, '*Heri domino Alexio insiemme cum la compagnia et cavalli partirono da Lio cussì li cavalli furono posti suso octo piatri cum le selle et forni-*

menti suoi et passarono per Canale grande facendo la via de Realto: che veramente fu bella cosa a vedere per la grande multititudine de gente che gli sopragionse de loco in loco, essendoli comparso sino li signori Procuratori de Sancto Marco'. Cited in Malacarne, *Il mito dei cavalli gonzagheschi: alle origini del purosangue* (Verona, 1995), p. 58.

55 Modena, ASMo, AE b. 2, fasc. 2, 'Stalla'. Meschino Domaschino to Duke Ercole II d'Este, 15 May 1543. *arrivai in Garfagnania cu' la raza del sue cavalle salve e sane [. . .] a maravaglia grasse e belle e grâ che sio grando & foc' le vedessa certo non li recognercera tanta sono diventate sfoggiate tal che nel passar da Pisa o Lucca lo strade si coprivano de giente chi correveno à verderle.*

56 C. Cavriani, *Le razze gonzagheschi dei cavalli nel mantovano e la loro influenza sul puro sangue inglese* (Mantua, 1974), p. 19, n. 15. 'Durante l'estate il Signore mantovano mandava le sue cavalle al libero pascolo del Monte Baldo per schivare i solleoni della Pianura Padana'.

57 L. Martines, *Power and Imagination: City-states in Renaissance Italy* (New York, 1979), p. 221.

58 Castiglione, *Cortegiano* (1528), I, ch. XXII, lines 14-18.

59 Corte, 1562, 1, ch. 4, 13r, *Grande ornamento, & quasi accrescimento è quello, che fa all'homo, recandolo superiore alli altri homini; & riguardevole tanto più, quanto più belli, & migliori cavalli cavalca.*

60 Castiglione, *Cortegiano* (1528), II, ch. VIII, lines 35-8.

61 The myth of the Sibarite horses is discussed in more detail in Chapter 3. The myth is described in Aelian's *On the Characteristics of Animals* (3rd century), XVI and in Athenaeus of Naucratis' *Deipnosophists* (3rd century), XII.

62 *On Horsemanship*, 1962, p. 339.

63 Niccolò Machiavelli, *The Prince*, trans. G. Bull (London, 1999), xiv, 'How a prince should organise his militia', pp. 47-8.

64 Castiglione, *Cortegiano* (1528), I, ch. XXII, lines 1-3.

65 Ibid. lines 4-6.

66 Lubkin, *A Renaissance Court* (1994), p. 90.

67 Ercole d'Este had enclosed the Barco in 1484 following the Venetian wars. See Tuohy, *Herculean Ferrara: Ercole d'Este (1471-1505) and the Invention of a Ducal Capital* (Cambridge, 2002), p. 243 and n. 49.

68 Ugo Caleffini, *Cronica della ill.ma et ex.ma et ex.ma Casa d'Este*, in ed. A. Cappelli, *Atti e memorie della Reale Deputazione di storia patria per le province modenesi e parmensi*, II (1864), pp. 267-312. See 16 December 1484, *Zobia a dì 16 el Duca andò in lo barcho e qui secondo el designo principiò a fare fabricare e fare una seve longa tre meglia, che andava in forma di lumaga cum stegati per fare correre suoi barbari a suo modo*. Cited in Tuohy, *Herculean Ferrara* (2002), pp. 243-4. For reference to the leopards see Tuohy, pp. 245-6.

69 Tuohy, *Herculean Ferrara* (2002), p. 244.

70 Naples, ASN, *Documenti per la storia, le arti e le industrie delle province napoletane*, 6 vols (1883, reprint Naples, 2002), I, lxx, 'Egli poi non v'era quasi goirno che non cavalcasse e non vedesse correre i suoi cavalli, che in gran numero avea'.

71 Naples, ASN, *Documenti per la storia, le artie* etc., I, lxxi.

72 Mantua, ASMa, AG, b. 1624, see Z. Saggi to L. Gonzaga, 14 May and 30 June 1471, Milan; see also letter of 27 Feb. Milan, and M Andreasi to L. Gonzaga 5 Mar. Milan. Cited in Lubkin, *A Renaissance Court* (1994), p. 101 and p. 312, n. 85.

73 For the Duke and Duchess of Milan's visit to Florence in 1471, Don Federigo's behaviour and the etiquette associated with the Signoria, see Trexler, *Public Life* (1980), pp. 314-18.

74 Filippo Rinnuccini, *Ricordi storici di Filippo di Cino Rinuccini dal 1282 al 1460*, ed. G. Aiazzi (Florence, 1840), cxlviii. Cited in Trexler, *Public Life* (1980), pp. 409-10 and p. 410, n. 197.

75 Lorenzo de' Medici to his son Cardinal Giovanni in Rome, March 1492, 'I advise you on feast days to be rather below than above moderation, and would rather see a well-appointed stable and a well-ordered . . . household than magnificence and pomp'. A. Fabronius, *Laurentii Medicis Magnifici vita*, 2 vols (Pisa, 1784), II, 308-12. The letter is translated in full in J. Ross, *The Lives of the Early Medici as told in their Correspondence* (London, 1910), pp. 332-35.

76 Maio, 'De maiestate' (1492), 58v.

77 Paolo Cortese, *De cardinalatu, libri tres* (Rome, 1510), pp. lxiii-lxvi. Cited in D. Chambers, 'The economic predicament of Renaissance cardinals', *Studies in Medieval and Renaissance History*, 3 (1966), pp. 287-313, p. 293.

78 Maio, 'De maiestate' (1492), 58r

79 The stables are 50m and 56m long and can accommodate two lines of horses. Housing 100 horses in each stable seems unlikely, as it only allows a metre width per horse.

80 Restoration work in the late-twentieth century uncovered earlier buildings corresponding to these two stables. The earlier buildings had narrow lancet windows and 'oculi'. The old masonry was used for flooring the new stabling. See G. Bombi *et al.* eds, *La biscia e l'aquila. Il Castello di Vigevano: una lettera storico-artistica* (Vigevano, 1988), p. 137.

81 Pierre Desrey, 'Relation du voyage du Royal Charles VIII pour la conqueste du Royaume de Naples par Pierre Desrey de Troyes', *Archives curieuses de l'historie de France depuis Louis XI jusqu'à Louis XVIII*, Series 1 (Paris, 1834), p. 215.

82 Desrey, 'Relation du voyage' (1834), I, pp. 215-6, *Le lundy treizième jour d'octobre, le noble Roy alla aux Granges à demie lieue du dit Vigeve; ces Granges appartiennend au duc de Milan . . . Premièrement, il y a une forte grande et spacieuse cour, auprès de la quelle est entr'autres une grande estable, qui est agréablement construite et ordonnée à haut pilliers et grand soubassemens ou d'un costé sont les grand chevaux et coursiers de prix, e l'autre les haras des jumens.*

83 The stables are 50m, 56m and 90m long respectively.

84 Bernardino Corio (1459-1519?), *Storia di Milano* ed. A.M. Guerra, 2 vols (Turin, 1978), II, 1408-9, p. 307, n. 15.

85 Florence, Uffizi Gallery, Gabinetto Disegni e Stampe, 1474 E v Raphael, 'Progetto per le stalle Chigi'. The drawing is very faint; New York, Metropolitan Museum of Art, Inv. 49.92.44v and Inv. 49.92.50r; Berlin, Kunstbibliothek, HDz. 3267/83 70r; Rome, Instituto centrale per la grafica, F.N. n. 7988, Cherubino Alberti 'Membri di la stalla di agustino Ghisi in trastevere di preta di baldasari opera architectura'.

86 Fabio Chigi's 'Chigiae familiae commentarij' (1618) is in Vatican City, Biblioteca Apostolica Vaticana (BAV), MS Chigi a.I.1. The manuscript consists of 182 folios.

87 For a description of the banquet see Vatican City, BAV, MS Chigi, a.I.1, 'Chigiae familiae commentarii', 34r-v. See also J. Shearman, *Raphael in Early Modern Sources (1483-1602)*, 2 vols (New Haven and London, 2003), I, pp. 335-7, '1518/30'.

D on the cheek. Brand for the stud farm of Signore Pietro Aloisio Farnese, Duke of Parma

Chapter 3

Second only to Man: The God-given Virtues of the Renaissance Horse

> Not only is a horse pleasant to the lover of horses and a spectacle to the lover of sight but . . . in the same way, just acts are pleasant to the lover of justice and in general virtuous acts to the lover of virtue.
> Aristotle, fourth century BC[1]

During the Renaissance, the horse and the culture surrounding it would become interwoven with court life. This is reflected in the courtly adjectives that were used to describe the horse's character: glorious, generous, intelligent, obedient and noble – all of them attributes that the courtier himself was expected to have. The horse was also credited with the human qualities of wisdom, temperance and patience,[2] Renaissance writers even suggesting that these virtues were God given.[3] These ways of defining equine character by human attributes have been described as a form of humanisation,[4] and this may be true. And there were further ways that equestrian and human culture mirrored one another in the Renaissance. For example, the similarities in equestrian and human medical literature, especially in the detailed anatomical studies of man and horse and in the ways that the horse's physiognomy was used to define certain human characteristics. Favourite horses, like many great men of the period, were commemorated in painting, statuary and poetry. It was perhaps because of their assumed similarities and man's affinity with this highly valued animal, that many writers sought to define the close bond between man and horse. Whether through humanisation or commemoration, it is evident that at this period the horse was the animal with which man was most closely compared.

In 1562, Claudio Corte went to considerable trouble to explain the belief that the horse had more intelligence, judgement and memory than any other animal, concluding that it was the horse's similarity to man in thought, intelligence and reason which made it so pleasing. Although he briefly mentions Aristotle's view that both horse and man are subordinate to the same 'passions of the mind', unusually Corte supports his theory by referring to mythology and suggests that man had had to invent the myth of the Centaur in order to explain his love for, and closeness to, the horse: the story in which Centaurus mates with the mares on Mount Pelion, resulting in the birth of the half-man, half-horse. Corte writes,

> it is under the veil of a fable demonstrating the similarity of horse and man [that] we are taught we are naturally inclined to love [the horse] . . . and become united with him almost as one single body.

The upper human part of the Centaur, Corte explains, resembles the intelligence and reasoning of man and, consequently, controls the lower equine part, 'making it do as he wishes'.[5] Of course, there had been other mythical human/animal relationships, with Plutarch describing men who 'had attempted to consort with goats and sows' as well as mares, while women had lusted after 'male beasts', relationships which resulted not only in centaurs but also in 'minotaurs, aegipans and . . . sphinxes'.[6] However, Corte's theory of the Centaur appears unique as there is no evidence to suggest that any other myth was used to support man's love for a particular animal during this period.

Rather than mythology, Pasqual Caracciolo would explain that it was natural similarities that brought man and horse together.

> It is not surprising that the horse resembles Man in many things, being animals subject to all the same feelings and diseases that we have, and they dream as we do, and like us in their old age, more than any other animal, they also become white-haired . . . and moreover, like us, even lose their teeth . . . And whereas all other animals follow their species by having one form and colour, horses are varied like men. And although horses share this and other conditions, such as faith, love and memory, with dogs, they unashamedly show that, more than anything else, they not only share but match our character. This similarity is perhaps the reason that they are such good friends of humans, as many examples show: beyond which, as a rule, there has never been a horse, which has willingly harmed the human race (unless he fell into a rage because of sickness).[7]

On the surface, Caracciolo's account seems to be pure adulation, praising the horse for its resemblance to man in both appearance and in character. Further analysis of the extract reveals attitudes to and beliefs about the Renaissance horse, particularly with regard to feelings, disease and memory. As regards 'feelings', it seems Caracciolo gives the horse the human characteristic of 'emotion' which, for an animal, is best described as memory or possibly a physical reaction to memory. Other writers were convinced that some equine behaviour was a response to the horse's treatment in earlier life. In 1562, Claudio Corte would explain how a 'good and pleasant horse', which had been regularly ill-treated, had reacted by pushing its master over before biting and kicking him to death.[8] Nineteen years later, Marco de Pavari's 1581 treatise, *Escuirie*, would explain how to re-train a horse that had been ill-treated or badly taught. Pavari very much concentrated on the psychological characteristics associated with different breeds, first finding the cause of the horse's behaviour and then adapting his schooling methods accordingly. This has resulted in Pavari's treatise being described as a form of 'primitive equine psychology',[9] a method of training that reflects the sympathetic methods advocated by Simon of Athens and Xenophon.

Caracciolo's theory that man and horse shared the same diseases was not new – it had been put forward by Pliny as early as the first century.[10] But in the Renaissance, there were also similarities in methods of diagnosis and treatment, as well as in the supposed causes and the measures taken to prevent sickness. For either man or horse to remain healthy, it was considered important to keep the four humours in balance. This is reflected in the amount of trouble to which writers would go to analyse how the horse's colour reflected the humours it contained. In the case of surgery or bloodletting, for both man and horse zodiac charts were consulted and recipes for medicines and ointments show that expensive imported ingredients were often used. And, as for man, preventing disease in the animal was of primary importance; clean stables with good drainage systems were seen as major factors in preserving the horse's health, in the same way that clean houses and cities would be recommended for man.

As regards Caracciolo's belief that a horse's dreams are similar to man's, this is of course impossible to verify and again it seems that he is proposing an imaginary similarity of horse to man. Whatever questions might arise over a horse's 'feelings' and 'dreams', Caracciolo illustrates the strong sentiment held for the horse in Renaissance culture. More importantly, he suggests that, during the Renaissance, man *wanted* the horse to be similar to himself in character, virtue and emotion as a means of understanding its perceived devotion to man. Such belief was repeated by several writers throughout the Renaissance period; some not only describing mythical and actual equestrian stories at the beginning of their treatises but also including examples to support methods of training and care. Caracciolo himself would go to considerable lengths to describe legends and stories behind notable men and their horses, including fifty-two pages on the subject at the beginning of *La gloria*.[11]

This adulation for the horse was not a Renaissance phenomenon; it was, like other Renaissance characteristics, a way in which earlier theories were endorsed or 'reborn'. Even in the seventh century a humanisation of the horse is found in the writings of Isidore of Seville, who described the horse as 'the only creature that weeps for man and feels the emotion of grief'.[12] In the twelfth-century, Albertus Magnus, had written that horses, like men, have the traits of 'knowledge, [good and bad] habits, fear, boldness . . . lust, desire and anger'.[13] As Salvatore Tramontana has rightly pointed out, by the thirteenth century the horse had been

> placed in a social context and in a cultural system in which [it] was not only instrumental for the solutions of various practical problems, but fundamentally instrumental for the representation of an interior world and a way of thinking.[14]

It has been suggested that this use of animal terminology could signify that, in the late Middle Ages, man was considering animals as 'elements of nature which [he] wishes to subjugate'[15] but it was actually continuing a long-established tradition with no evidence that this was the case. As early as the fourth-century BC, Aristotle had used the horse's qualities to explain 'virtue as a state of [man's] character'. In the *Nichomachean Ethics*, he suggested that virtue or excellence in either man or horse brings excellence to the things they do or produce.

> The excellence of the horse makes a horse both good in itself and good at running and at carrying its rider . . . Therefore, if this is true in every case, the virtue of man also will be the state of character which makes a man good and which makes him do his own work well.[16]

Such use of the horse in Aristotle's theory not only anticipates a particular understanding of equestrian values on the part of the reader but also indicates the importance of the horse's 'presence' within everyday parlance. In the same way that the horse was present in texts concerning man, in equestrian texts many of the horse's qualities would be compared with those of its master. Caracciolo would even describe the horse as having 'many of the qualities of feeling' and 'similar affections' as man himself.[17] Then, having described the horse as 'the most beneficial animal produced by nature', he concludes that 'it was always held dear in life' and like many famous Renaissance men, 'honoured by great people after death'.[18]

In addition to written terminology, the science of physiognomy allowed a further way for horse and man to be compared. In 1586, Giambattista della Porta's study of physiognomy, *De humana physiognomonia*, was printed. The work contained various human images alongside those of animals, with their respective features compared and analysed.[19] But in della Porta's treatise, the animals are not being 'humanised'; it is man who is being de-humanised, with his

3.1. Giambattista della Porta, *De humana physiognomonia*, Naples, 1586. Book II, p. 83. A comparison of man's and horse's features

features compared to different species in order to discover his character. Considered as a science, physiognomy has been described by Juliana Schiesari as 'an interpretive grid for understanding human character' and as 'a systematic decoding' in which behavioural characteristics of animals were connected to man's physical features.[20] According to Paula Findlen, this increased interest in physiognomy in the sixteenth century should be viewed 'as the sublime example of the obsession with nature's propensity to imitate', an obsession in which the 'human body became a repository of all the images of the natural – and frequently unnatural – world'.[21] Certainly, this seems to be the case, with della Porta using many different animals to ascribe their characteristics to man: lion, donkey, pig, eagle, monkey, ram, bull and greyhound. However, it is the three identical images in which man's features are compared to those of a horse, which are of interest here (3.1). These depict flared nostrils, a straight back and the ability to walk in a straight and upright manner. The flared nostrils, so admired in the Renaissance horse, were said to indicate a tendency to be quick tempered – a characteristic which della Porta relates to the 'handsome horse'.[22] He supports his belief first with Adamantius' theory that flared nostrils are 'evidence of ferocity and anger', and then by Suetonius' description of Caesar, who had a frothing mouth and damp nostrils and was known to have had a fierce and quick temper.[23] Regarding the second image, della Porta writes that man's straight upper back, corresponding to the horse's back, indicates boastfulness and ignorance – adding Aristotle's theory that if the back was 'supine and concave' it signified weakness and madness with the result that man, 'like the horse, which has a hollow upper back, [would go] crazy at the time of coitus'.[24]

The third man-horse image is used to represent the characteristic of walking upright, with a high head carriage. In his explanation, della Porta describes the horse in terms that could be valid for a successful *condottiere*: 'glorious and ambitious',[25] qualities, he adds, which had caused Aelian[26] to write that the horse had a 'haughty and elevated nature' and that, when lifting up its neck, made itself 'insolently puffed up and proud'. Della Porta then describes how to deal with such unwanted pride, giving an example which 'humanises' a mare by associating her with the human feelings of humiliation and subjugation. Here, (although not acknowledging him), he again quotes Aelian explaining that if a mare refuses to mate with a donkey in order to conceive a mule foal, she should be humiliated by having her mane and tail cut very short as a punishment for being too proud. Feeling 'ashamed', she is then made to suffer by allowing the 'ignoble' donkey stallion to mate with her[27] – a treatment which suggests that della Porta was unsympathetic towards horses and may not have liked animals at all. Findlen correctly assesses that physiognomy, or the 'mirror of nature', worked both ways, with one side having 'the lower creations serving as repositories of the higher ones' and the reverse side with man 'the most perfect of all natural creations' becoming the ultimate freak.[28] This may be true in physiognomy, but contrary to being considered as a 'lower creation', most Renaissance writers would consider the horse as man's equal. It was, as Caracciolo's text shows, thought to have human characteristics such as intelligence, memory and reason, many of which were reflected in the understanding of a horse's training and care.

Of course, it was the horse's memory and obedience in training which helped man control it and benefit from it. Reading *De equo animante* alongside Alberti's *Della famiglia*, Schiesari has concluded that Alberti saw horse training as a paradigm of man's domination over lesser beings in the Renaissance, 'an elaborate allegory of easy-going dominance over a physically superior animal that is also the highest ranking being after man himself'.[29] Schiesari is right that, during the Renaissance the horse was believed to be a high-ranking animal but she is wrong in describing Alberti's treatise as an 'allegory of dominance'. When Alberti briefly compares man and horse it is to help him explain the equine character;

> Each citizen, in order to follow the example of his companion in arms, to win his share of glory, to obey his superiors, or simply trained by chance or by the necessity of the moment – even if he is a beginner or a simple conscript – can, in the space of a moment, become a terrific soldier and rush into combat . . . It is the same with horses.[30]

Certainly, some would use character analysis to practise dominance over the horse, examples of which can be found in Grisone's *Gli ordini*, where he describes some of the cruel methods of the age. But in contrast to Schiesari's theory, Alberti's sympathy for, and understanding of, the horse shows he is enthusiastic for a partnership with, rather than dominance over, this proud animal. This is evident when he writes on the suitable training of a young horse, advising 'to put all one's care into persevering so that the colt is gentle, kind and sociable, obeying fair orders and gladly submissive to his master'.[31] This sympathetic approach followed Xenophon, who believed that the 'horse must make the most graceful and brilliant appearance in all respects *of his own will*[32] with the help of aids'.[33] Such attitudes to training emphatically did not use domination and were expected to result in the most complicated exercises looking effortless, fulfilling Castiglione's belief that, for the courtier 'true art is what does not seem to be art'.[34]

As Corte would later explain, obedience was one of the three specific ways in which the horse could give man pleasure,[35] the other two being its depiction or celebration, and its characteristics

3.2. Pirro Antonio Ferraro, *Il cavallo frenato*, Naples, 1602, Book III. *Natura non artis opus* (Naturally, not by force)

in common with man. However, it is obedience, which Corte lists first, explaining that it was a valued and necessary characteristic for everyone but especially for the nobility, who expected their servants and subjects to obey them.[36] It is not possible here to analyse the different Renaissance methods for schooling the horse, for which a considerable bibliography on training can be found in two books of essays: *The Culture of the Horse* and *The Horse as Cultural Icon*.[37] Nevertheless, it is possible to note various aspects of care associated with training and the responsibility of the *cavallarizzo* or riding master who oversaw all aspects of schooling including the work of the professional riders. Suffice to say that obedience in the horse can also be described as its domination by man. And, despite the perceived similarities between man and horse, or possibly because of them, it seems that in the Renaissance, man was prepared to school the animal in accepting his will – an attitude which can be seen as part of the desire to first understand and then control nature. If needed, justification for this attitude could be found in major religious texts such as the Bible[38] and the Qu'ran, both stating that animals were created for the benefit of man. But more significant is the fact that the verbs *frenare* and *domare* were used for horse training – both being verbs that can mean 'to crush', 'to control' or 'to make subservient' – an indication of man's desire to dominate. Even the English translation, 'breaking in', reflects a similar attitude. According to the many treatises written on horse training, domination was both physical and psychological and for this purpose the horse's character needed to be understood. Even so, only in a few cases was punishment recommended; most Renaissance writers advocating a sympathetic breaking in and training of the young horse, with at least one, Pirro Antonio Ferraro, including an illustration of horse and rider surmounted by the words 'Natura non artis opus' ('Naturally, not by force') in his *Il cavallo frenato* (3.2).[39] This follows Simon of Athens' and Xenophon's gentle and persuasive approach, with Xenophon's warning that, what the horse does under constraint, as Simon says, he does without understanding, and with no more grace than a dancer would show if he was whipped and goaded. Under such treatment, horse and man alike will do much more that is ugly than graceful.[40]

The desire to understand the horse's character also acknowledges that the horse was considered, as Elizabeth LeGuin has suggested, 'an independent intelligence, an Other, someone to be negotiated with, rather than something to be deployed'.[41] Even so, a wide variety of tactics were used to discipline the horse in addition to the voice, whips and spurs, with Xenophon, who had understood horses so well, stressing that a disobedient horse was 'not only useless, but often behaves just like a traitor'.[42] But, whatever the methods used, neither domination, or even co-operation, was easy for everyone and the horse's independent spirit meant that some praised it as an equaliser for any level of society, with Erasmus explaining that the only skill royal sons could learn properly was riding,

> because in all other things, everybody humoured and flattered them, but, since a mere horse doesn't know whether he is being ridden by a nobleman or commoner, rich man or poor man, prince or private individual, he throws off his back anyone who rides him incompetently.[43]

Nevertheless, a successful understanding of, and co-operation with, the horse was believed to bring man many benefits. These are particularly evident in four of the first five chapters of Corte's *Il cavallarizzo*: 'How the horse surpasses all base animals in serving and pleasing man', 'The advantages of the horse', 'The honour and prestige that the horse gives to man' and 'The delight given by the horse'.[44] Corte explains how the horse brings honour, adornment and delight as well as benefiting man's health both spiritual and physical – all contributory factors in a courtier's appearance and self-esteem. Corte praises the horse for 'listening to man very patiently', crediting it with the human virtues of 'infinite wisdom, temperance and patience' and, in its own way, he sees the horse as mirroring the kindness of God because it can benefit both the spirit and the soul. From all the 'noble roles' and services which it performs for man, whether in a 'meek' domestic environment or in the fierce conditions of war, the horse brings man pleasure, honour and benefit. Thus Corte asks, 'Should we ourselves, therefore, not serve the almighty Lord, our God' in the same way as horses serve us, and should we not therefore 'render them [our] infinite gratitude?'[45]

In Corte's chapter on the honour and prestige the horse gives to man, he explains how the best horses can make up for man's weaknesses by giving riders both physical strength and courage, thereby contributing to the rider's image in public and in private

> Great prestige, almost enhancement, will come to man, making him superior and so much more noticeable to other men when he rides better and more beautiful horses. Similarly, great honour is brought to man, substituting his own weakness; and by means of the horse [a man], even of miniscule strength, would be of great daring and, because of this, he will not be frightened by a greater strength. [The horse] gives honour, not only in combat, in war, assaults, duels and other similar things, but extending to magnificent festivals, public and private games, such as jousts, tournaments, running and breaking the lance and such as: running *palii*, the ring, quintain,[46] *carrousels*, games of canes,[47] killing bulls, fighting lions, bears and leopards, in hunting and performing *maneggio*, either with or without fancy dress, in front of lords and crowds of people ... The good

horse gives much esteem to a gentleman who rides well.

Corte continues: 'It is really true that happiness in this world is found in the substance of the body, of luck and the soul and that to possess good horses shows these three well.'[48] Such praise for a horse's benefits was not novel. In his fifteenth-century manuscript the Portuguese king, Dom Duarte, had already listed seven primary benefits resulting from owning and competently riding good horses: readiness to assist his master – taking care of many duties that bring him honour and benefit, to be at ease, to be respected, to be protected, to be feared, to be light-hearted and to have a bigger and better heart. He added that good horsemanship could also be seen as beneficial to the elderly who, as long as they did not get fat, could keep their riding skills into old age, something 'which does not happen with most arts'.[49] Corte too, described riding as 'a very noble and moderate exercise for all the limbs almost equally'. In addition to these physical benefits, riding was also believed to be good for mental health. Reflecting Dom Duarte's sixth benefit of 'light-heartedness', Corte goes a step further in suggesting that 'Riding increases a light humour and banishes serious melancholia. And this can easily be seen; that any great sorrow will be relieved in some way by riding a horse.'[50] He adds, 'There is no doubt that by chasing away melancholia, the horse necessarily brings exhilaration, and consequently pleasure.'[51]

Nevertheless, with Castiglione writing that the accomplished and versatile horseman was 'superior and more noticeable to others', it is difficult to believe that this rather than his physical and mental health was not the priority for the Renaissance courtier. In effect, the benefits of an equestrian education were, as Roche has summarised,

> an integral part of a whole, [involving] the skills of the body as well as those of the mind. At the same time [transmitting] behaviour, gesture and political metaphor, . . . the rapport of aristocrats and kings [and] the possibilities and limits of a social mobility.[52]

The horse's many perceived benefits in peace and war must have been a major factor in the need to understand not only its 'independent intelligence' but also the structure of its body in order to maintain its health. And, in many ways, this aspect of equestrian culture offered another opportunity for man and horse to be juxtaposed. In 1564, Corte's contemporary, the physician Giovanni Filippo Ingrassia, known as the Sicilian Hippocrates, had published a medical treatise with the informative but lengthy title translated as, 'Veterinary Medicine is formally one and the same with the better-known Human Medicine, differing simply in the dignity or nobility of the subject'.[53] Ingrassia, who is believed to have studied with Vesalius in Padua, dedicated his short treatise to the Viceroy of Sicily and, according to Frederick Smith, his fifteen chapters contain examples proving that 'veterinary medicine does not differ essentially from human medicine, and that both are subordinate to natural philosophy', with Smith adding that Ingrassia's unusual views were so advanced that even in 1910 they had not been accepted.[54] The fact that a second edition was printed in 1568 is evidence of a considerable readership and, indeed, many equestrian texts show that writers such as Corte and Caracciolo, would describe and give reasons for similarities and an affinity between man and horse.

In 2008, the many parallels found in veterinary and human medicine were illustrated by an exhibition at the United States National Library of Medicine in Bethesda, entitled *The Horse: A Mirror of Man*.[55] This showed that there were equivalent consultations of, and references to, ancient medical texts and that the designing and printing of astrological, bloodletting and disease charts together with the writing and illustrating of anatomical and physiognomical

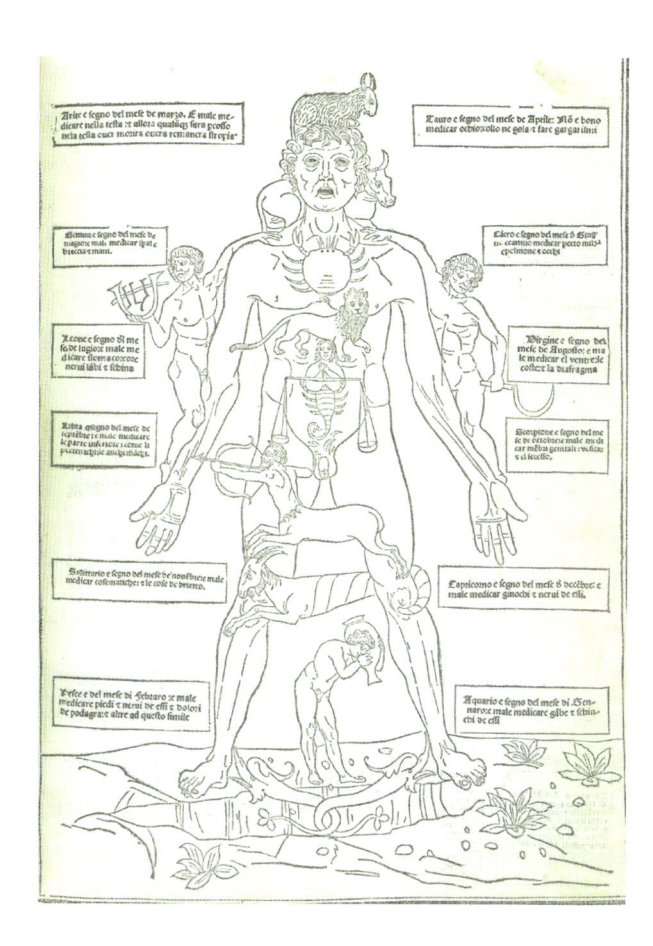

3.3. Johannes de Ketham, *Fasciculus Medicinæ of Jonannea Ketham*, Venice, 1494. The influence of the Zodiac on the human body

studies all contributing to an understanding of the human and equine body. It has already been noted that the equine humours were believed to affect not only the horse's colouring but also its health and, as for man, the four humours – sanguine, phlegmatic, choleric and melancholic – needed to be kept in balance to maintain health. As the works of Galen informed early physicians and surgeons, so the principal source for the *maniscalco* (farrier-surgeon) was the *Hippiatrica*; a collection of classical and Byzantine texts eventually printed in Latin in 1530, of which the six principal authors are listed by McCabe as Eumelus, Apsyrtus, Theomnestus, Hierocles and Hippocrates and Pelagonius.[56] By the end of the sixteenth century, two important medical works could also be closely compared for both their presentation and their medical advancement: Andreas Vesalius' *De humani corporis fabrica* and Carlo Ruini's *Anatomia dei cavallo*.

The *maniscalco* had always required a sound knowledge of the horse's anatomy and, from the medieval period, he was expected to understand the application of astrology to his work; a science in which zodiac signs and planets were not only thought to influence a specific part of the body but also affected where and when blood could be drawn and when surgery could be performed. If a comparison is made between two late fifteenth-century works – Ottolengo's untitled manuscript on equine sickness and injury, written *c.*1480,[57] and Johannes de Ketham's *Fasciculo de medicina*[58] on human medicine printed fourteen years later (3.3) – the following influences of the zodiac are notable for both horse and man: Taurus rules the neck, Gemini the arms or forelimbs and articulation, Leo the heart, Virgo the stomach and intestines, Scorpio the genitalia, bladder and buttocks, Sagittarius the thighs or haunches, Capricorn the knees, Aquarius the legs and Pisces the feet. But if, in turn, these two theories are compared with the uncomplicated but imprecise illustration in Filippo Scaccho's *Opera di mescalzia*,[59] written one

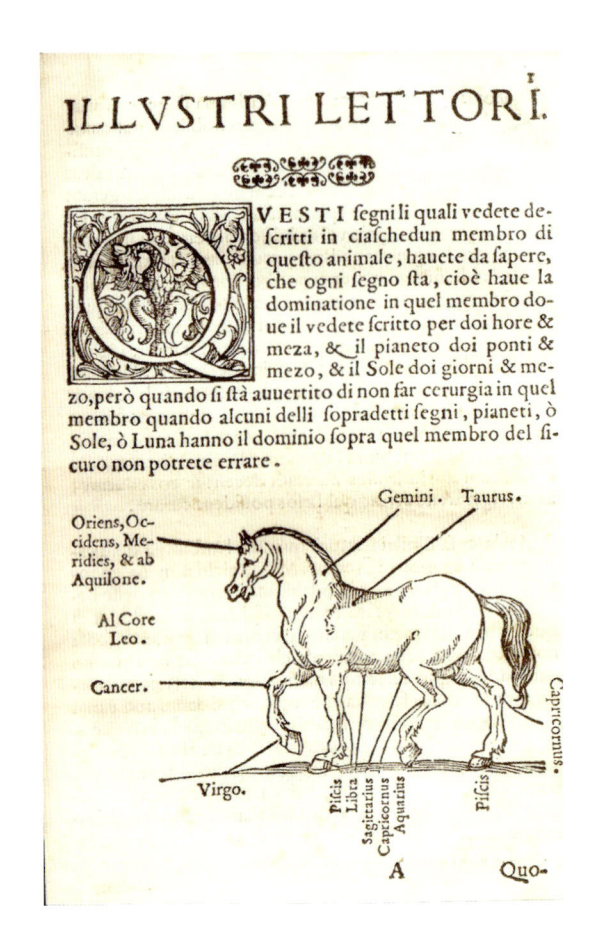

3.4. Filippo Scaccho da Tagliacozzo, *Opera di mescalzia*, Rome, 1591, Book I, p.1. The influence of the Zodiac on the horse's body

hundred years later, few of the zodiac references appear the same (3.4). For example, Taurus rules the withers, Gemini the neck or withers, Virgo the fetlocks, Sagittarius the genitalia and Capricorn the hocks and knees. Scorpio is not represented by Scaccho and only Leo, Aquarius and Pisces are listed in similarly controlling the heart, legs and feet. Bearing in mind that all three authors recommend not performing surgery or bloodletting from the named area if the moon is in the corresponding zodiac sign, it seems that charts could alter considerably over time and that both physicians and *maniscalchi* needed to keep up with new theories. Nevertheless, similarities between man and horse are evident in the amount of detail they were afforded by various medical authors, with comparisons possible in the details in bleeding charts, in which the bloodletting points are indicated, and in disease charts where the many different afflictions and diseases are listed and then 'attached' to the different parts of the body. By the end of the sixteenth century, such aids for the *maniscalco* would be assisted by comprehensive studies of the horse's skeletal and muscular structure as well as diagrams of the veins, nerves and internal organs.

By 1598 a comprehensive anatomical study of the horse had been published: Carlo Ruini's *Anatomia del cavallo*,[60] making the horse the first species to be accorded such attention after Andreas Vesalius's analysis of the human body, *De humani corporis fabrica*, in 1543.[61] However, there was one way in which Ruini's work would set a precedent. Although both physicians and *maniscalchi* were interested in development of the embryo, it was his anatomical images of a horse's foetus rather than that of a human child which first appeared in print, detailed studies of the foal before and after birth as well as of its internal organs (3.5, 3.6). In his introduction to

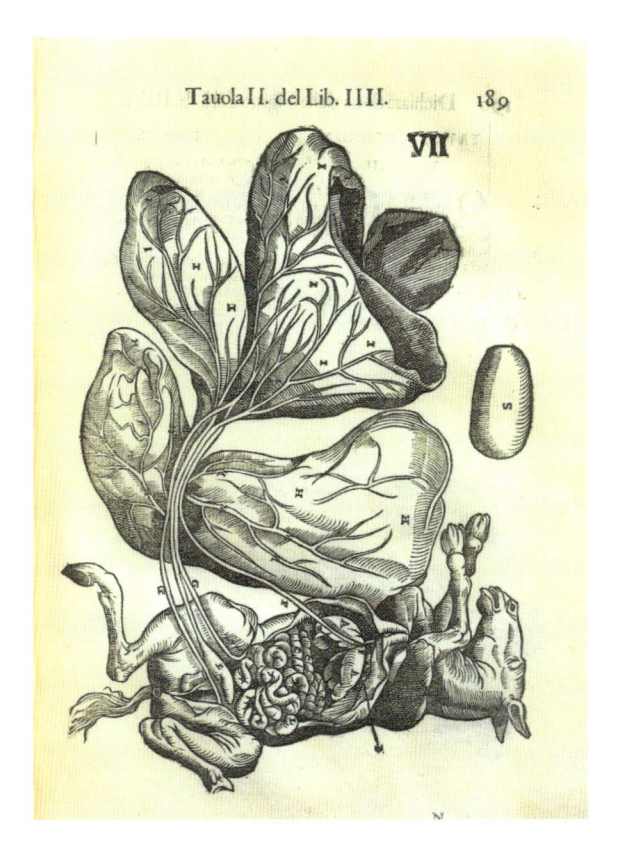

3.5. Carlo Ruini, *Anatomia del cavallo*, Venice, 1618, vol. I, IV, tav. II, fig. VII. An unborn foal shown open along the length of its stomach

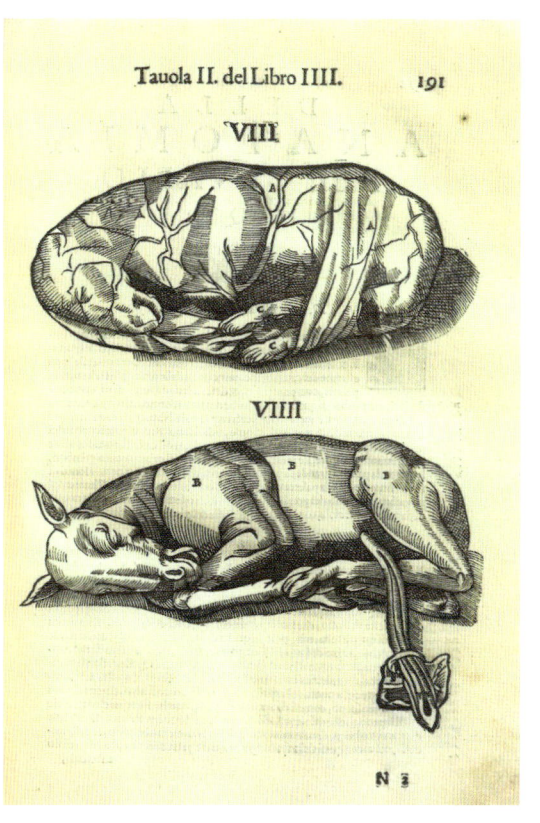

3.6. Carlo Ruini, *Anatomia del cavallo*, Venice 1618, vol I, IV, tav. II figs. VIII and IX. A new-born foal shown in its membrane and with membrane removed

volume one, Ruini explains that Nature had given the horse a 'great love towards man' together with 'a docile nature', which enabled man to teach him the 'things he can learn'. Consequently, the horse is loyal, benefiting man not only in war but also at home when he was 'hunting, racing, jousting, [or performing in] tournaments and other games of arms', all of which provoked 'enormous happiness'. Ruini concludes that, without the horse, man's life would be considerably harsher and more tiring. It is because of these benefits, and the fact that horses had 'delighted and served [Ruini] from a tender age', that he has written his discourse in order that 'this generous animal . . . so useful to the world' can be relieved from sickness. From well-studied and precise anatomical drawings and his analysis of the horse's ailments with their prescribed treatments, Ruini hopes this 'deserving and noble animal' can be kept healthy.[62]

Whilst the second volume of the *Anatomia*, 'Infirmità del cavallo et suoi rimedii', is concerned with ailments, it is the first volume, analysing and illustrating the anatomy of the horse, that is particularly notable for its extraordinarily detailed illustrations, many of which follow the format of Vesalius's treatise printed half a century earlier.[63] While the equine and the human skeletons are depicted from several different aspects in order to create a comprehensive understanding of the bone structure, both treatises show the musculature of horse and man depicted against landscape; with Ruini's composition showing the horse's foreleg raised and Vesalius's depicting the man's arm extended upwards to illustrate how muscles function (3.7, 3.8). However, whilst

3.7. Carlo Ruini, *Anatomia del cavallo*, Venice, 1618, vol. I, V tav.V. The horse's musculature

similarities can be found in many of the anatomical images, the structures of the two studies differ considerably in the way the chapters on anatomy are divided. Vesalius divided his study into seven books covering: the bones, ligaments and muscles, veins and arteries, nerves, nutrition and reproduction, heart and organs and the brain. In contrast, Ruini divided his section on anatomy into five books:[64] the head, brain and eyes – the vital parts formed by Nature (*parte animale*); those parts which make the horse active (*parte spiritale*); nutrition, reproduction and the limbs[65] – all of which include details on bones, veins and muscles, according to the body part considered. And, in contrast to Vesalius's nine chapters on the human brain at the end of his treatise, Ruini's first book, on 'parte animale', consists of forty-four chapters analysing every aspect of the head and brain and is by far the longest section, being followed by twenty detailed annotated images.

It would seem that Ruini's intense interest in every aspect of the horse's head, from its skull to its eye muscles, reflects the belief that this was the source of many equine illnesses and problems. Indeed, many equestrian treatises included treatments for illnesses believed to result from problems in the head, some of which were thought to affect the animal's behaviour. Corte summarises these problems in a very short chapter dedicated to the horse's brain in which he makes a comparison between the human and the equine brain and the problems arising if it is kept at the wrong temperature:

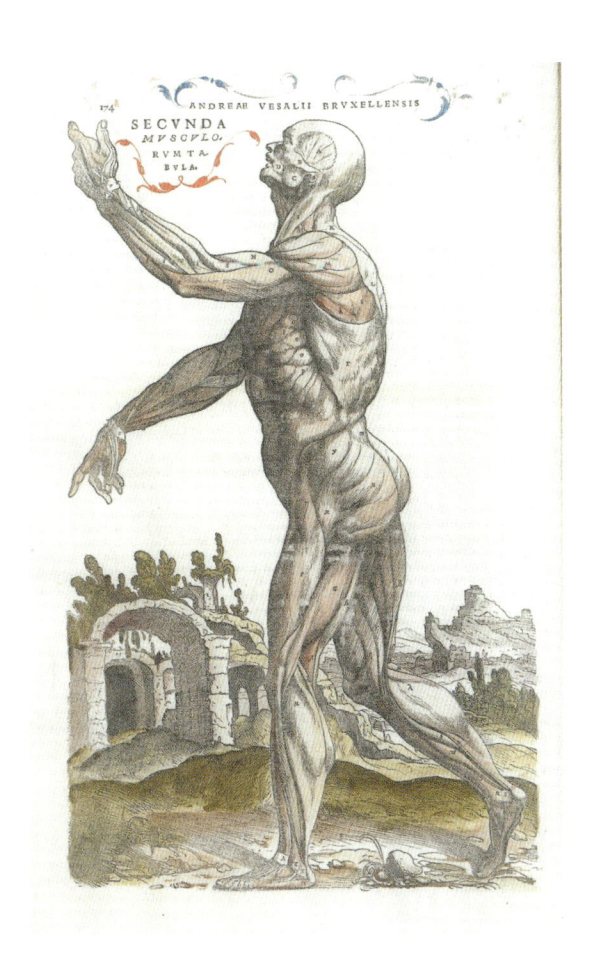

3.8. Andreas Vesalius, *De humani corporis fabrica*, Basle, 1543, Book II. Human musculature

The man's brain must not be too hot, because it causes instability, nor too cold because it causes inflexibility and, in some ways, stubbornness, but must be a moderate temperature in order to be good; it should also be so for horses, because if the horse has a hot brain, he will be docile, and immediately learn that which he is taught by his master and trainer; nevertheless it will often develop into another fantasy and will not be remembered . . . If [the brain] is cold, he will learn slowly and with difficulty, but that which he is taught once, he holds well in his memory. It would, however, be horribly slow and hard.[66]

This belief in the horse's intelligence and sensitivity is alluded to in Pavari's treatise, *Escuirie*, printed twenty years after Corte's work. As already mentioned, Pavari suggested gentle and sympathetic training, taking into account the horse's psychological characteristics, with its character analysed and its origins determined in order to give it the correct training or, if badly disciplined, re-training. Believing that bad behaviour results from ill treatment or, possibly, incompetent schooling, he recommends stroking and praising the horse rather than beating it, writing that 'pleasantness achieves more than despair'.[67] This very much follows the advice of Simon of Athens and Xenophon; the latter comparing the negative effects of ill treatment of a horse to that of a dancer, concluding that neither will perform gracefully if they have been 'whipped and goaded'.[68]

Unfortunately, the intelligence and sensitivity of the horse were ignored by incompetent horsemen, who mistreated their horses in order to dominate and control them. Some practices are related by Grisone when describing how to deal with resistance or obstinacy and, although considered as a last resort, some methods are cruel, others bizarre. They include hitting a horse on top of the head between the ears – a punishment repeated at least three times in Grisone's treatise,[69] putting a hedgehog (or any biting animal) under the tail, tying a vicious cat to a rope and throwing it between the horse's back legs so that it bites and scratches the victim, and stabbing the horse with an iron nail to make it move forward.[70] Even the long rowel spurs which were worn for ceremonial occasions and sometimes used in battle, jousting, hunting or racing, could cause considerable pain and injury to the horse's flanks. Such occasions required the horse to move forward, the horseman using every means possible if it was reluctant to do so. On occasions when the rider's hands were occupied with weaponry and reins or with his desire to win a race, the temptation to use the spurs becomes evident. And, when riding bareback in a *palio*, it would have been even more difficult for jockeys to control the spurs' pressure against the horse's side.[71] Giovan Battista Ferraro's instructions in his treatise from 1560,[72] and included as the first part of his son Pirro Antonio's *Cavallo frenato* (1602), show that such misuse must have occurred, as the Neapolitan *cavallarizzo* – riding master – advises the stable master to check whether the horse has been damaged due to negligence or rough riding. He writes that, if the horse has been 'overwhelmingly battered by spurs, [the stable master should] clean the wound with vinegar, or with oil, and salt and rub it down well', adding that it was usual to put on ground up glass in exchange for salt.[73]

Any physical harm to a horse, whether inflicted deliberately or by accident, might well stay in the horse's memory for life and many theorists wrote on its ability to learn and remember. Corte warns the reader not to be deceived into believing that the horse only has a little intelligence, then lists similarities in the way man and horse use memory.[74] Three of his anecdotes are worth considering, as Corte was not alone in his views. His first example explains how the Greek Sibarite[75] and Cardiani horses were trained to the rhythm of music in order to learn and perform jumps and dance patterns to the trumpet or *zampogna* – a form of bagpipe – sometimes standing on their hind legs, to entertain at feasts and festivals.[76] This anecdote would not have seemed particularly strange to a horseman who understood *maneggio* at the end of the sixteenth century. Cesare Fiaschi had already used music for training at his Ferrarese riding academy and his 1556 treatise associated particular rhythms with specific *maneggio* movements in the belief that, 'without the rhythm and beat of music', it was not possible to perform *maneggio* well.[77] In fact, his theory that the rider should sing 'ah ah' to the horse's rhythm would have been beneficial to both horse and rider, as it relaxed a nervous rider and, in doing so, also relaxed the horse being ridden (see 1.9). Later in the century, Caracciolo would also write at length on the different rhythms he associated with the horse's natural gaits, explaining that the horse was 'an animal of miraculous sensitivity taking great delight in music' and naturally moving to the rhythm of it with every pace.[78] However, whilst both Fiaschi and Caracciolo seem to be impressed by the horse's ability to recognise and react to musical rhythm, Corte dwelt on the ability of the horse to remember dance patterns through music in the same way as man might do.[79]

Corte's second example concentrates on the horse's skills of recognition by describing various tricks he had seen performed by a pair of German-taught horses in Rome.[80] Here he praises what he believes are horses' retentive memories as, when faced with a crowd of people, they were able to pick out a 'gentleman from a villain', a 'master from a servant' as well as singling out a youth and an old man and remembering other choices such as colours. And Corte seems particularly impressed with an entertainment in which the horses spread themselves out on the ground as if they were 'sleeping or dead' and then 'jump up . . . with great skill', a movement which had been developed for warfare, when a horse would lie down either for cover for its rider or so that the rider could mount it more easily. In his third example, he suggests that the horse's memory is, in some ways, better than man's and can be used to positive effect in wartime, such as the Tartars leaving their mares' foals behind when they go on military exercise. He explains that, even after several days away from their young, the mares can return to their 'abandoned foals' in the dark because they 'hold [them] in their memories longer than man remembers the way home'.[81] In fact, none of Corte's examples is particularly startling. As both Fiaschi and Caracciolo suggested, horses do react favourably to music, often moving together in harmony to the rhythm of a drum beat or when harnessed together as carriage horses. But although many animals can remember and perform tricks if they are rewarded, or take revenge if they frightened or harmed, this is part of their survival instinct. And, of course, the Tartars' mares would have had a strong maternal instinct to return to their herds and to their foals as these would be the places they felt most secure. This is not to demean Corte's views on the horse's memory which concur with other writers' views; proof that during the Renaissance men who understood and worked with horses wanted to place animal and man on equal footing.

Because of the high esteem in which some Renaissance horses were held, their owners followed classical precedent by celebrating them with significant equestrian memorials. These horses were not only depicted, or remembered, as mounts for their illustrious owners, they were also celebrated for their own achievements or beauty. In many cases, the locations given to these monuments are indicative of the political or social status of the horse's owner, with Ruini writing that 'wise kings' and 'great emperors' had commemorated the illustrious deeds of horses not only in statues but also in

> pyramids, and sepulchres [and by] naming peoples and lands after [horses] which had become well-known and immortal. And excellent poets, with cultured verses and poems, celebrated them, almost lifting them to the heavens.[82]

It is likely that three renowned statues from ancient history would influence these Renaissance memorials. First, that of Alexander the Great's one-eyed horse, Bucephalus,[83] often mentioned by Renaissance writers for which, according to Pliny, Alexander headed the funeral procession before building the city of Bucephala around the horse's tomb.[84] Like Bucephalus, Savoy, Charles VIII's black horse, was blind in one eye[85] and, although twenty-four years old at the Battle of Fornovo in 1495, was praised for its bravery and excellence by Caracciolo who explained that, at the end of its life, the horse was similarly buried with great ceremony.[86] Three early warhorse commemorations are worth mentioning here: Simon of Athens' horse; Julius Caesar's Spanish bred Astorcone; and Babieca, the horse of Rodrigo Diaz de Vivar ('El Cid'). According to Xenophon, a bronze statue of Simon of Athens' horse, had been erected in the Eleusinium Temple with a record of the Athenian's 'feats in relief on the pedestal'.[87] Caesar's Astorcone was described by Suetonius as having 'feet that looked almost human – each of its hooves . . . cloven in five parts, resembling human toes'.[88] Bred, reared and ridden by Caesar, this horse was commemorated by a statue in front of the Temple of Venus Genetrix. And, in the 11th century, Babieca was buried in front of the gates to the Monastery of San Pedro de Cardeña near Burgos in Spain, where an elm tree was planted to mark each end of the grave.

There were, and still are, many equestrian monuments to Renaissance leaders and *condottieri* but examples of a few of them show how much the horse contributed to the status of its rider.

3.9. Santa Maria Gloriosa dei Frari, Venice. Monument to Paolo Savelli, *c.*1408.
Image Didier Descouens/ Wikimedia Commons 2016

Both the Venetian generals, the Roman patrician Paolo Savelli (d.1405) and Bartolomeo Colleoni (1400-75) have memorials in prominent Venetian locations with Savelli's life-size painted and gilded wooden monument depicting him sitting astride his dapple-grey horse, as if progressing towards the high altar of Santa Maria Gloriosa dei Frari (3.9).[89] Seventy years later, Colleoni left a significant amount of money to the Venetian Republic to pay for a gilded equestrian memorial to himself, once destined for the most prominent Venetian square, the Piazza San Marco. No longer gilded and now outside the Scuola Grande di S. Marco and the basilica of SS. Giovanni e Paolo, it is Verrocchio's modelling of the horse, rather than Vellano da Padova's depiction of its rider, which now dominates the composition (3.10). But perhaps the most ostentatious of these images is the life-size fourteenth-century equestrian memorial to the Milanese ruler Bernabò Visconti, once poised over the high altar of the palace church of S. Giovanni in Conca in Milan.[90] In all three statues, the horses could be said to be supporting their riders both physically and mentally, their riders using them both in life and death as an essential part of their public image. And it was because of this that the horse's depiction was considered every bit as important as the rider's. As noted above, Leonardo da Vinci took great trouble to create the perfect horse for the proposed memorial to Francesco Sforza and, on at least two occasions, it is known that two sculptors were employed on a monument – one for the rider and one for the

3.10. Campo SS Giovanni e Paolo, Venice. Monument to Bartolomeo Colleoni, Andrea Verrocchio and Vellano da Padova *c.*1480-83

horse – presumably so that each figure was shown to its best advantage.[91]

There were also other ways in which horses were commemorated for their own qualities and achievements, such as in painting or poetry, which Corte believed brought men pleasure indirectly through delightful memories not only of the horse's obedience but also of its similarity to man. No doubt the painted images of Federico Gonzaga's six favourite stallions in the Sala dei Cavalli of the Palazzo Te gave him and his guests great pleasure when they entered this principal reception room. Extraordinarily realistic, these titled portraits were drawn by Giulio Romano and according to Vasari, painted *c.*1527 by two of his pupils, Benedetto Pagni and Rinaldo Mantovani.[92] It has been suggested by Malacarne that one horse, Morel Favorito, had been painted posthumously although this may not have been the case.[93] Certainly, records show that a favourite horse of the Marquis's, bearing this name, died in 1524.[94] However, by the time the Sala was being painted, there was another stallion also called Morel Favorito which sired at least three foals listed in the Gonzaga stud book for 1540. The entry shown here describes the dark bay filly foal born in 1539, sired by *Morello Favorito* out of a mare called Salvadiga (3.11).[95] Whether they were alive or dead, Federico was celebrating these horses in the same way that other rulers commemorated great men, each horse identified by its name, some with the Gonzaga brand mark and others with colourful head pieces. Standing alone, the horses have no handlers or jockeys; they are

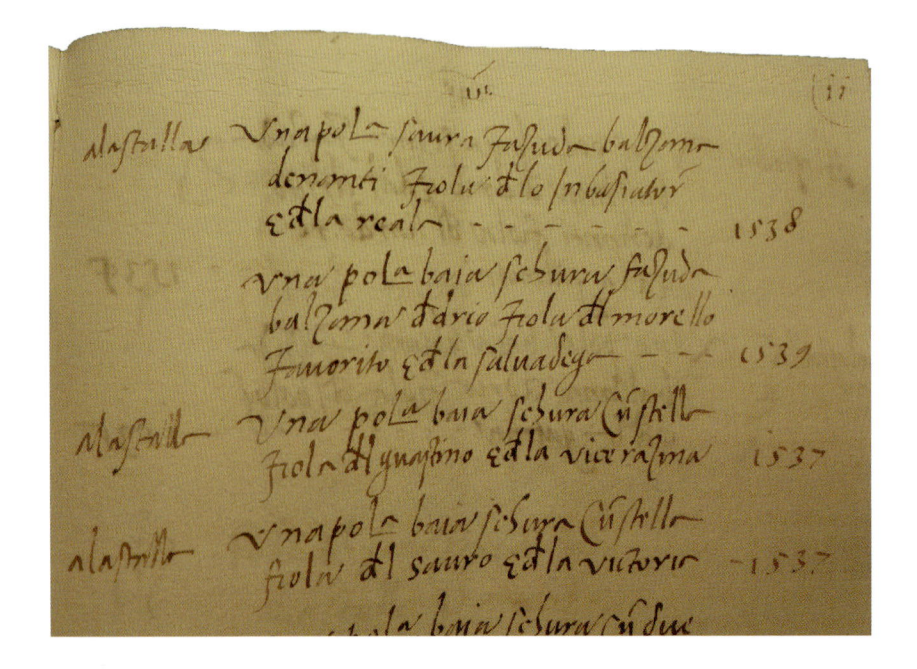

3.11. Gonzaga stud book, 1540. A record of one of Morel Favorito's foals born in 1539. 'Ala stalla. Una poledra baia schura fazunda balzana di drito fiola d'il morello favorito e de la salvadiga,1539'. Mantua, ASMa AG b 258 D.IV no 4, 1540. Courtesy of Ministero per i beni e le attività culturali–Archivio di Stato di Mantova

depicted in front of *trompe l'oeil* windows, while improbably positioned on top of door lintels and friezes. Even if Vasari was incorrect in describing them all as Turkish and Barbary breeds – at least one, the war horse Bataglia, resembles an English cob (3.12). Nevertheless, these were the Marquis's favourite horses and would have been a topic of conversation for any visitor to this impressive hall built on the foundations of Federico's father's stables.[96] Certainly, the two white Turkish horses[97] are particularly impressive with their henna-dyed tails: an expensive dye imported through Venice (3.13). Letters show that Federico was asking his agents to buy this expensive commodity, *archenna*, on a regular basis for dying the manes and tails of his Turkish horses, with as much as twelve pounds requested in 1529.[98]

The portrayal of favoured and important horses was not unusual in a Renaissance court. In fact, precedents for the Palazzo Te decoration were to be seen in two other Gonzaga properties: the palazzina at Gonzaga where at least 125 horses were kept and the stud farm at Marmirolo, both of which had a Sala dei Cavalli. In 1494-5 Francesco II Gonzaga, Federico's father, had commissioned the paintings at Gonzaga[99] and, in 1518, he paid Benedetto Ferrari for renovating frescoes at Marmirolo. One wall of the Marmirolo *sala* was painted in a *trompe l'oeil* composition, dividing it into four bays, framed by columns, pilasters and festoons, in each of which were depicted horses in a landscape, as if seen from a loggia in the villa.[100] But the Gonzaga were by no means alone in their love of equestrian subjects on their palace walls. In 1469, at the Sforza's Pavian court, a fresco of horses was planned for a wall at the top of a staircase outside the Duke's apartments. Although never executed, this *trompe l'oeil* painting was to have depicted Galeazzo Maria Sforza's stable master, Spagnolo, standing with grooms and horse – probably a pleasant reminder of a moment either before or after hunting, as it is known that the duke and his guests were able to ride up this staircase to their apartments.[101] In other courts records show that hunting scenes were known to be popular, many, no doubt, bringing back pleasant memories of a day's sport and stimulating topics for courtly conversation. Closer in style to the Sala dei Cavalli horse portraits are those painted for several rooms in Count Enrico Pandone's castle in Venafro. Painted in the 1520s, this cycle of magnificent commemorative life-size portraits were described by Carac-

3.12. Palazzo Te, Mantua. Sala dei Cavalli. Bataglia, Giulio Romano *et al.*, *c.*1527-30, detail

3.13. Palazzo Te, Sala dei Cavalli. Grey horse with hennaed tail, Giulio Romano *et al. c.*1527-30. Paolo Perina/Alamy stock photo

ciolo as of the most perfect and admired horses which had been painted from life.[102] Although named, these horses, unlike those at the Palazzo Te, are saddled and bridled, each portrait including information on the horse's breeding and character as well as the name of the person to whom it was given or from whom it was received by the Count.

In addition to these frescoes, three written 'portrayals' of horses – a funeral oration and two charming poems celebrating horses' achievements – illustrate other ways horses could be commemorated.[103] The first is found in a collection of funeral sermons for animals. Written by a variety of authors, the 1548 *Sermoni funebri de vari authori nella morte de diversi animali* includes eleven euologies to animals and birds as well as to a cricket.[104] The five-page eulogy

81

written by Bertolaccio for his horse Passamonte describes the horse as 'the most perfect animal that nature had ever produced' and 'the best bloodline that ever carried a saddle'. As if affirming this, he names the horse's parents – both stallion and mare – as well as going into significant detail on the horse's conformation and declaring that it had won 500 *palii*. Considerably shorter than Bertolaccio's eulogy is the epitaph written by the Florentine humanist and bureaucrat Bartolomeo Scala, in memory of Pierfrancesco de' Medici's champion racehorse Rondine (Swallow).[105] Pierfrancesco (1430-76), nephew to Cosimo il Vecchio, lived at the Castello of Trebbio in the Mugello valley. He is known to have had a great affinity with his horses, which he bred and traded, sometimes supplying them to Cosimo's grandson the young Lorenzo de' Medici. Entitled, 'Poem in praise of Pierfrancesco's horse', it seems likely that the Latin epitaph was to be attached to a lost commemorative statue.

> Of him to whom the swift swallow (*Rondine*) gave its name,
> See, nothing now remains but immovable marble.
> Once he was able to fight with the fleet winds,
> And he was able to run as swiftly as the rapid rivers,
> He, who many times won the prize in the glorious race
> By easily running passed other horses.[106]

If this epitaph was attached to a commemorative statue, such an accolade for an animal was not unique. In 1536, Federico Gonzaga would ask Giulio Romano to produce two designs for a tomb for a favourite dog which had died having a litter, stipulating that, 'We want her to be buried in a beautiful marble tomb with an epitaph'.[107] However, Federico's father, Francesco, owned a longer eulogy to one of his racehorses, which was included in a private record of his many racing achievements (see Appendix One). Written in Italian, rather than Latin, the poem celebrates one of his most famous horses, the chestnut Turkish horse Il Dainosauro – known as Sauro. The poem forms part of the small "Codice dei palii gonzagheschi",[108] commissioned by the Marquis from his debt collector, Silvestro da Lucca, in September 1512.[109] The vellum book lists the achievements of the Gonzaga racehorses, *barberi*, between 1499 and 1518 and contains miniatures of 35 of them, as well as a note of each horse's victories. As in the horse portraits in the Palazzo Te and Castello Pandone, most of the horses are depicted without their jockeys such as in the frontispiece, which depicts Il Dainosauro standing in front of some architecture. Only one horse, Isdormia Secondo, is shown being held by a groom. From a letter to Marquis Francesco, it is known that Lauro Padovano was commissioned to paint the horse portraits but the author of the poem remains anonymous.[110] The poem celebrates the chestnut's victory in the *palio* on the feast day of San Giovanni Battista in Florence – although it had also won several other *palii*.[111]

> Neither deer, nor leopard nor fugitive beast,
> nor arrow shot in fury from a bow
> nor lightening from the sky through darkened air
> morning or evening, ever passed so fast.
> Neither Phoebus, with his charger in the heavens
> whose speed has never been surpassed,
> nor wind which has defeated every storm
> has ever shown such fiery force,

> As nimble Sauro did,
> racing through Florentia
> to win the Baptist's golden prize.
>
> Glory of my Francesco, eternal honour
> for him, and for his merit, Gonzaga's fame
> resounds from the Indian Ocean to Mauritania.
>
> With wings and feathers on your back
> you have proven yourself so well, Sauro,
> that from the Indian Ocean to Mauritania
> under one sky and the other
> you will always be remembered.
>
> At first, you did not move so fast
> to gain yourself the golden prize,
> if you are true glory and satisfaction
> for the Mantuan Duke I cannot say.
>
> Racing, you were the honour of all the herds
> and when racing without a rider,
> certainly you vanquished the winds.
>
> The virtue which God entrusts in you
> resounds among so many,
> that all of Italy cries 'Turcho, Turcho'.[112]

In the poem, the author's comparison of Dainosauro to the mythical winged horse, Pegasus, equals the way many great men were compared to, or named after, classical gods during the Renaissance. But the most important aspect of this poem is that it is addressed to the horse itself and, by the writer declaring God has entrusted virtue to the horse, it anticipates Corte's belief that the horse had the human qualities of wisdom, temperance and patience.[113]

But was there a particular reason behind this curiosity about the horse or a need for its humanisation? There is no doubt that an analysis of the horse's body and mind not only informed the way the horse was portrayed and commemorated, it also assisted in helping to understand its character and its health – all factors that benefited the owner and rider. Indeed, most equestrian memorials were for man's benefit, not only commemorating the rider's past glories but also his status in society through the quality of the horse he was riding. Second, understanding the horse's character through various forms of analyses, such as astrology, the humours, its colour and its breeding, was thought to assist in its training and make it more biddable to the rider's commands, thereby enhancing the appearance of horse and rider. Third, maintaining the horse's health preserved both its beauty and its usefulness to man. In other words, each aspect of humanisation helped promote man's image in some way.

Elements found in both the visual arts and literature show that, by attributing it with particular qualities, the horse can be said to have been humanised by man. This was partly due to the desire to understand how and why the horse had developed such a strong bond with man and how it had achieved its elevated status in the animal kingdom. In their explanations, writers identified the qualities they believed existed in both man and horse, the horse being attributed with many of the virtues admired in a Renaissance courtier, such as obedience, nobility and glory. Alongside this curiosity to understand the horse's status, it seems a natural progression to desire an understanding of the horse's anatomy and how its body functioned, especially its brain; an investigation and understanding that had previously only been accorded to man. However, there is no doubt that men such as Alberti, Corte, Caracciolo and Ruini felt an affinity with the horses they had known, suggesting that they wrote their treatises not only to assist man but also so that the horse was treated sympathetically. The qualities they attributed to the horse and the ways in which they associated it with human virtues is evidence that, for them, the horse was a special animal worthy of both respect and love in return for the dedicated service it gives. As shown in the next chapters, this sympathetic approach is reflected in the considerable attention given to the horses' stabling, not only in the design of the building itself but also in finding a suitable location.

1 Aristotle, *Nichomachean Ethics* (2009), I, 8, ix-xii, p. 14.
2 Corte, 1562, I, ch. 3, 11v.
3 'Codice dei pallii gonzagheschi' (*c*.1512), 6r-v, anon. poem praising Dainosauro. Private Collection.
4 E. Tobey, 'The *Palio* horse in Renaissance and Early modern Italy', in Raber & Tucker eds., *The Culture of the Horse* (2005), p. 80.
5 Corte, 1562, I, ch. 5, 14v.
6 Plutarch, *Moralia*, 15 vols, trans. H. Cherniss and W.C. Helmbold (London & Cambridge, MA, 1957), XII, 'Beasts are rational', pp. 521, 523. Plutarch also writes of the comparable love between animals and humans: an elephant which rivalled Aristophanes for the love of a flower girl, a serpent that fell in love with an Aetolian woman, a goose that loved a boy and a ram which loved Glauce. See Plutarch (1957), XII, p. 399.
7 Caracciolo,1589, I, pp. 7-8.
8 Corte, 1562, I, ch. 6, 16r.
9 Pavari, *Escuirie* (2008), 'Introduzione', p. 9.
10 Pliny, *Natural History*, VIII-XI, trans. H. Rackham (Cambridge, MA & London, 1997), p. 117, 'The horse has nearly the same diseases as mankind'.
11 Caracciolo, 1589, I, see pp. 52-124.
12 Isidore of Seville, *The Etymologies* (7th century), Book XII, 'On animals', v. 43, 'Horses have a high spirit; for they prance in the fields, they scent war . . . some recall their own masters . . . when their masters are slain or are dying, many shed tears. The horse is the only creature that weeps for man and feels the emotion of grief', trans. in E. Brehaut, *An Encyclopedist of the Dark Ages: Isidore of Seville*, 2 vols (New York, 1912), I, p. 224.
13 Albertus Magnus, *On Animals. A Medieval summa zoologica*, trans. K.F. Kitchell and I.M. Resnick (Baltimore, 1999), p. 606.
14 Salvatore Tramontana, *Il Regno di Sicilia: uomo e natura dall' XI al XIII secolo* (Turin, 1999), ch. 5, pp. 69-70.
15 M.G. Arcamone, 'Il mondo animale nell'onomastica dell'alto Medioevo', *L'uomo di fronte al mondo animale nell'alto Medioevo: 7-13 aprile, 1983*, 2 vols (Spoleto, 1985), I, pp. 138-9, cited in Tramontana, *Il Regno di Sicilia* (1999), p. 66.
16 Aristotle, *Nichomachean Ethics* (2009), II, 6, xix-xxi.
17 Caracciolo, 1589, 'Sommario de' dieci libri', Summary of book 1, unpaginated, *Nel primo si è atteso a dimostrare come il cavallo sia glorioso, per essere il più giovevole animale di' quanti per uso dell'huomo siano stati prodotti dalla Natura; & per essere in molte qualità di sentimenti, & di affetti somigliante, & conforme a l'huomo istesso.*
18 Ibid. Summary of book 1.
19 Giambattista della Porta, *De humana physiognomonia libri IIII* (Sorrento, 1586). The translations in this book have been made from M. Cicognomi's Italian trans. *Giovan. Battista della Porta: della fisonomia dell'uomo* (Parma, 1988).
20 J. Schiesari, *Beasts and Beauties: Animals, Gender, and Domestication in the Italian Renaissance* (Toronto, Buffalo & London, 2010), p. 56.
21 P. Findlen, 'Jokes of nature and jokes of knowledge', *Renaissance Quarterly*, 43:2 (1990), pp. 292-331, p. 313.
22 Della Porta, *De humana* (1988), II, p. 83.
23 Suetonius, 'Divus Claudius', *The Twelve Caesars*, trans. R. Graves (London, 2007), p. 198, 'Claudius . . . had several disagreeable traits. These included an uncontrolled laugh, a horrible habit under the stress of anger of slobbering at the mouth and running at the nose, a stammer, and a persistent nervous tic'.
24 Della Porta, *De humana* (1988), II, p. 146.
25 Ibid. II, p. 181.
26 Aelian (Claudius Aelianus), *c*.170 *c*.235, *De natura animulium*.

27 Della Porta, *De humana* (1988), p. 181. Here Della Porta is quoting Aelian almost word for word from *De natura animalium*, II, ch. 10, 'The horse is generally speaking a proud creature, the reason being that his size, his speed, his tall neck, the suppleness of his limbs and the clang of his hooves make him insolent and vein. But it is chiefly the mare with a long mane that is so full of airs and graces. For instance, she scorns to be covered by an ass, but is glad to mate with a horse, regarding herself as only fit for the greatest (of her kind). Accordingly those who wish to have mules born, knowing this characteristic, clip the mare's mane in a haphazard fashion anyhow and then put asses to her. Though ashamed at first, she admits her present ignoble mate'. Translation from A.F. Schofield, *Aelian on the Characteristics of Animals*, 3 vols (Cambridge, MA and London, 1958), I, p. 101.
28 Findlen, 'Jokes of nature', p. 313.
29 Schiesari, *Beasts and Beauties* (2010), pp. 44-53, ch. 3, 'Alberti's *Cavallo vivo* or the 'Art' of Domination', p. 52.
30 Alberti, CV pp. 41, 43. Videtta, p. 120.
31 Alberti, CV p. 43. Videtta, p. 120.
32 The author's italics.
33 *On Horsemanship*, 1962, p. 355.
34 Castiglione, *Cortegiano* (1528), I, ch. XXVI, line 29.
35 Corte, 1562, I, ch. 5, 14r 'Del diletto che dà il cavallo'.
36 Ibid. 14v.
37 Raber & Tucker, eds., *The Culture of the Horse* (2005); P. Edwards *et al.* eds., *The Horse as Cultural Icon* (2012).
38 Genesis, I, v. 26, 'Let us make man in our own image, after our likeness: and let them have dominion over the fish of the sea, and over the fowl of the air, and over the cattle, and over all the earth . . . '
39 Qu'ran, *The Koran*, XVI, 8, trans. N. J. Dawood (London, 2006), p. 38, 'And [he has created] horses, mules and donkeys for you to ride and use for show'.
40 *On Horsemanship*, 1962, p. 355.
41 E. LeGuin, 'Man and horse in harmony', in K. Raber & T. J. Tucker eds, *The Culture of the Horse* (2005), pp. 175-96, p. 177.
42 *On Horsemanship*, 1962, p. 311.
43 Erasmus, *The Education of a Christian Prince* (1516), trans. N.M. Cheshire & M.J. Heath (Cambridge, 2002), p. 56.
44 Corte, 1562, I, chs 2, 3, 4 and 5.
45 Ibid. I, ch. 3, 11v, *Dandoci dunque il cavallo da speculare per mezzo suo nella bontà di Dio*.
46 Quintain: A quintain was used to help train a knight to use a lance effectively. It consisted of a shield or dummy, which was suspended from a swinging pole. When a charging horseman hit the shield/dummy, the whole apparatus would rotate. The horseman's task was to avoid the rotating arms and not get knocked out of the saddle.
47 The game of canes (*canna*) was imported to Italy from Spain as 'juego de las cañas'. It involved teams of horsemen hurling cane javelins at one another. *Canna* is thought to be similar to the Northern European game of *béhourd*, where combatants used canes instead of swords to train for tournaments and war. See Duarte, *Bem cavalgar* (2005), II, p. 7, n. 4.
48 Corte, 1562, I, ch. 4, 13r.
49 Duarte, *Bem cavalgar* (2005), IV, p. 9.
50 Corte,1562, I, ch. 3, 11v.
51 Ibid. ch. 5, 14r.
52 D. Roche, 'Le livre d'équitation du XVIe au XVIIIe siècle: esquisse d'une réflexion', *Le Livre et l'Historien: Études offertes en l'honneur du Professeur Henri-Jean Martin*, ed. F. Barbier *et al.* (Geneva, 1997), pp. 187-96, p. 187.
53 Giovanni (Gian) Filippo Ingrassia (1510-1580), *Quod veterinaria medicina formaliter una eademque cum nobiliore hominis medicina sit, materiae duntaxat nobilitate differens* (Venice, 1564). A 1568 edition is bound with three other medical treatises by Ingrassia, each with its own pagination. The four-part volume is entitled *Ioannis Philippi Ingrassiae Quaestio de purgatione per medicamentum atque de sanguinis missione Ducis Terraenovae casus enarratio et curatio, e quibus tum penetrantis in thorace vulneris, tum fistulae curandae methodus elucescit Quaestio utrum victus a principio ad statum usque procedere debeat subtiliando an potius ingrossando Quod veterinaria medicina formaliter una eademque cum nobiliore hominis medicina sit, materiae duntaxat nobilitate differens Omnia nunc primum in lucem edita, etc.*
54 Smith, *The Early History* (1976), I, p. 149.
55 *The Horse: A Mirror of Man: Parallels in Early Human and Horse Medicine*, U.S. National Library of Medicine, National Institute of Health, Bethesda, Maryland (2008), curated by Michael North. There is no catalogue for this exhibition.
56 A. McCabe, *A Byzantine Encyclopaedia* (2007), pp. 13 and 49.
57 Ottolengo, 'Proemio', pp. 11-12.
58 Johannes de Ketham, *Fasciculo de medicina* (Venice, 1494), p. 15. Johannes de Ketham was a German physician living in Italy at the end of the fifteenth century. His *Fasciculus medicinæ*, was translated into Italian by Sebastiano Manilio and first printed in 1491.
59 Filippo Scaccho da Tagliacozzo's *Opera di mescalzia* was first printed in Rome, 1591. A later edition is sometimes used here, *Trattato di mescalzia di M. Filippo Scacco da Tagliacozzo, Diviso in quattro libri; Ne' quali si contengono tutte le infermità de' cavalli così interiori come esteriori, & li segni da conoscerle, & le cure con potioni, e untioni, & sanguigne per esso cavalli* etc. (Padua, 1628).
60 The first edition of the *Anatomia* was printed two months after Ruini's death in 1598. Ruini (1530-98) was a near contemporary of Vesalius (1514-1564).
61 Andreas Vesalius, *De humani corporis fabrica* (Basle, 1543).
62 Ruini, *Anatomia* (1618), I, 'Proemio', p. 2.
63 The five books in Ruini's first volume concentrate on 1. The head, 2. The bones, muscles, veins and nerves of the body, 3. The digestive system, 4. The reproductive system, 5. The extremities.
64 Ruini, *Anatomia* (1618), vol. I, I, p. 3, ch. II, 'Del capo del cavallo', 'Dividesi adunque il cavallo, come in maggiori, & principali sue parti in quattro; cioè, nella parte animale, nella spiritale, nella nutritiva, & nella generativa, alle quali s'aggiungono gli estremi.'

65 Ibid, vol. I, II; III; IV and V
66 Corte, 1562, I, ch. 19, 'Del cervello', 29r.
67 Pavari, *L'escuirie* (2008), p. 42.
68 *On Horsemanship*, 1962, p. 355.
69 Federico Grisone, *Gli ordini di cavalcare et modi di conoscere le nature de' cavalli, emendare i vitii loro, Et ammaestrargli per l' uso della guerra & commodità de gli huomini* 3 Books (Venice, 1551), I, 59, II, p. 127, III, pp. 156, 158. The first edition of Grisone's work was published in Naples, 1550.
70 Grisone, *Gli ordini* (Venice, 1551), III, p. 186.
71 Giovanni Toscani's *cassone* panel, *The Race of the Palio in the Streets of Florence* (1418) depicts jockeys riding bareback with spurs. Cleveland Museum of Art, Holden Collection, 1916.801.
72 Giovanni Battista Ferraro's treatise published as *Delle Razze, disciplina del cavalcare, et altre cose pertinenti ad essercitio cosi fatto* (Naples, 1560), is included in his son, Pirro Antonio Ferraro's *Cavallo frenato* (Naples,1602). The four books of G. B. Ferraro's treatise occupy the first 159 pages of *Cavallo frenato*. Pirro Antonio's treatise starts on the next page but with a new pagination. The two books will therefore be distinguished by the author's initials and date – either G. B. Ferraro (1560) or P. A. Ferraro (1602).
73 G.B. Ferraro (1560), II, p. 83 in P. A. Ferraro, *Cavallo frenato* (1602).
74 Corte, 1562 I, ch. 6, 'Dell'intelletto, overo intelligentia del cavallo', 14v-16r.
75 Sybaris is an ancient Greek city in the south of Italy.
76 Corte, 1562, I, 14v. Here Corte appears to base his information on Book XVI of Aelian's *On the Characteristics of Animals* (3rd century), where the Sibarites are described as training their horses to pipe music as entertainment and the subsequent consequences. Aelian explained that this musical training caused the Sibarites to lose a war against the Crotonians as when the [Crotonians] were within range of the [Sibarite] archers, their pipers started playing dance music. The Sibarite horses shook off their riders and started to dance as if they were at a bacchanalia, throwing the Sibarites into confusion and causing them to lose the war. See A.F. Schofield, *Aelian on the Characteristics of Animals*, 3 vols (London and Cambridge, MA, 1959), III, pp. 294-5. See also Book XII of Athenaeus of Naucratis, *Deipnosophists* (3rd century), trans. C.B. Gulick, 7 vols (London and New York, 1933), V, pp. 343-4.
77 Fiaschi, 1603, II, ch. 1, pp. 75-6.
78 Caracciolo, 1589, V, p. 421.
79 For further information on the horse and music see E. LeGuin, 'Man and horse in harmony', in K. Raber & T.J. Tucker eds, *The Culture of the Horse* (2005), pp. 175-96.
80 Corte, 1562, I, 15r.
81 Corte, 1562, I, 16r.
82 Ruini, *Anatomia* (1618), I, 'Proemio', p. 1.
83 Corte,1562, ch. 7, 17r, '*Questo famosissimo cavallo fu d'un occhio solo per natura secondo Pellagonio*'.
84 Pliny, *Natural History* VIII-XI, (1997), p. 109.
85 Caracciolo, 1589, pp. 23-4, where Caracciolo gives De Commynes as his source. In B.E. de Mandrot ed., *Mémoires de Philippe de Commynes*, 2 vols (Paris, 1903), II, 1477-1498, p. 267, Book 8, ch. X of De Commynes' memoirs describes the Battle of Fornova. He writes, 'On Monday morning, around seven o'clock on the 16th of July 1495, the king mounted his horse and called for me several times: I came to him and found him fully armed, mounted upon the best horse I ever saw in my life, called Savoy. Some say it is from Bresse: Charles, Duke of Savoy had given him [the horse], which was black with only one eye and of average height but a good size for him who rode it'.
86 To date, the author has not found any record confirming the ceremonial burial of Charles VIII's horse, Savoy. However, Thomas Blundeville, citing Grisone, suggested the horse was Spanish; 'And the Kynge would afterwards many tymes saye of the valient courage of his horse, was the occasion of that victory. Which horse after that, he came to the city of Molina besides then was no more travelled, but well fed and tenderly kepte, so long as he lived; he was also solemnly buried when he dyed by the appointment of the Lady of Burbon [Duchess of Bourbon], sister unto the Kinge', see T. Blundeville, *The Arte of Ryding and Breaking Greate Horses* (London, 1560: reprinted Amsterdam and New York, 1969), see 'Examples recyted by Gryson' – 'Longe continuance'.
87 *On Horsemanship*, 1962, p. 297.
88 Suetonius, *The Twelve Caesars* (2007), 'Divus Julius', p. 29.
89 Savelli's monument is attributed to Rinaldino di Francia.
90 The statue is now in the Museo del Castello Sforzesco, Milan.
91 For Niccolò d'Este's monument in Ferrara, c.1445, for which Alberti had been a judge, Niccolò Baroncelli sculpted the horse, Antonio di Cristoforo, the figure. For Bartolomeo Colleoni's monument, c.1479, Andrea Verrocchio sculpted the horse, Vellano da Padova, the figure.
92 Vasari, *Vite* (1966), V, 'Giulio Romano', pp. 66-7. According to Lorenzo Bonoldi, *Palazzo Te: la Sala dei Cavalli* (Bergamo, 2010), p. 3, there were another four artists involved with the decoration of the room: Anselmo Guazzi, Agostino da Mozzanica, Fermo Ghisoni and Luca da Faenza.
93 Malacarne, *Il mito* (1995), pp. 152-4.
94 Mantua, ASMa AG, b. 2505, 223r, letter dated 19 October 1524 to Marquis Federico, describing the horse's death. The relevant extract is printed in Malacarne, *Il mito* (1995), p. 153. See also pp 150-4 where Malacarne discusses the horse's illness.
95 The 1540 Gonzaga stud book shows three foals sired by a stallion also called Morel Favorito. Two out of Turkish mares; one born in April 1538 out of Volpe, another born 3 March 1540 out of Inperiala. The third foal out of a Barbary mare, Salvadiga, was born in 1539. See Mantua, ASMa AG, b. 258, 'D. IV no 4, 1540. Note delle razze dellle cavalle, 1540', particularly ch. III, fol. ii of the book for Salvadiga's foal, '*ala stalla. Una poledra baia schura fazuda balzana di drito fiola d'il morello favorito e de la salvadiga, 1539*'.
96 See Chapter 5 for a discussion on the Te stables.
97 The assumption that most Turkish horses are white was made by Francesco Liberati, who describes the different breeds,

writing that *Cavalli Turchi sono per la più parte bianchi, forse aviene dal clima di quei paesi.* See Liberati, *La perfettione del cavallo, libri tre di Francesco Liberati Romano* (Rome, 1639), Book III, ch. I, p. 76.

98 Mantua, ASMa AG, b. 2932, l. 298, 107v in which henna is requested on 2 June, 1529, '*Volemo che ne mandati tre ò quattro libre d'Archeña da tingere le code à cavalli Turchi . . .* ' and 142v in which eight pounds are requested on 3 July 1529 '*. . . vogliate mandarmi fina ad otto libre de archenna cioe de quella herba con che si tingono in rosso le doce e le crine alli cavalli Turchi*'.

99 For a discussion on the frescoed decoration at Gonzaga, see C.M. Brown, '"Concludo che non vidi mai la più bella casa in Italia": The frescoed decorations in Francesco II Gonzaga's suburban villa in the Mantuan countryside at Gonzaga (1491-1496)', *Renaissance Quarterly,* 49:2 (1996), pp. 280-1.

100 E. Verheyen, *Federico Gonzaga and the Palazzo del Te in Mantua: Images of Love and Politics* (Baltimore and London, 1977), p. 64, n. 88.

101 The planned fresco is discussed at length in E. Welch, 'Galeazzo Maria Sforza and the Castello di Pavia, 1469', *Art Bulletin,* 71:3 (1989), pp. 352-67, p. 361.

102 Caracciolo, 1589, p.15, 'A tempo di nostri maggiori Arrigo Pannone Conte di Venafro e Duca di Boiano, in molte parti delle sue Roche fè dipignere del vivo i più perfetti è più graditi cavalli, che della sua scelta Razzi gli avvenivano'. The frescoes are discussed by Della Ventura and Ferrara in '"Fe dipignere del vivo i più perfetti e più gradite cavalli'. Enrico Pandone e il ciclo affrescato nel Castello di Venafro' in *Dal cavallo alle scuderie: Visioni iconografiche e architettoniche* (Rome, 2014), pp. 65-80.

103 Another commemoration is also mentioned by Gaspare Codibò, who records that Filippo Beroaldo (1453-1508) had written an epigram commemorating Giovanni II Bentivoglio's horse, Civetone. Gaspare Codibò, *Diario bolognese dal 1471 al 1504 con note e cronotassi dei priori e cappellani di Santa Maria Maddalena in Bologna,* ed. A. Macchiavelli (Bologna, 1915), p. 59, cited in C. Ady, *The Bentivoglio of Bologna: a Study in Despotism* (London, 1937), p. 191.

104 *Sermoni funebri de vari authori nella morte de diversi animali* (Venice,1548). A copy is held by the Bayerische Staatsbibliothek, Munich. The animals commemorated include a cat, dog, donkey, owl, magpie, cockerel and a cricket.

105 For more information on Pierfrancesco de' Medici, see A. Brown, 'Pierfrancesco de' Medici, 1430-1476: a radical alternative to elder Medicean supremacy', *Journal of the Warburg and Courtauld Institutes (JWCI),* 42 (1979), pp. 81-103.

106 Florence, Biblioteca Nazionale, MS Conv. Soppr. G8. 1438, 20v, Bartolomeo Scala (1430-97), *Carmina in laudem equi Petrifrancesci de Medicis: Ex re cui dederat pernixbene nomen hyrundo/ Aspice quam nihil est nunc nisi marmor inhers/ Et poterat quondam levibus contenere ventis/Et par cum rapidis currere fluminibus/ Qui totiens claro tulit certamine palmas/Cum longe ante alios cursibus iret equos.* Cited in A. Brown, *Bartolomeo Scala, 1430-1497, Chancellor of Florence: the Humanist as Bureaucrat* (Princeton, 1979), p. 272, n. 50.

107 The note is printed in A. Luzio, 'Isabella d'Este e il sacco di Roma', *Archivio storico lombardio,* Ser. 4, 10 (1908), pp. 5-107, p. 37, n. 2, Federico Gonzaga to Giulio Romano, *M. Julio, Ni è morta una cagnolina di parto, la qual voressimo far sepelire in una bello sepultra di marmore con uno epitaphio, perhò volemo che faciati dui dessegni che siano belli che li faremo fare di marmore, et fatti essi dessigni mandatenili or portateneli voi quanto più presto poteti bene valete*, Marmirolo, 15 October 1526.

108 'Codice dei palii gonzagheschi' c.1499-1518. The poem is on 6r-v. Private Collection. The poem is also printed in Malacarne, *Il mito* (1995), p. 229.

109 Mantua, ASMa, AG b. 2485. Letter from Silvestro da Lucca, dated 10 September 1512, saying that he remembered the Marquis would like to have an illustrated record of his racehorses, (*far un libro di carta di capretto et in quello ritrar li Barbari dal naturale et poi subsequentamente scriver li palii per loro habuti*), cited in D. Chambers & J. Martineau, *Splendours of the Gonzaga* (London, 1982), p. 147, catalogue entry n. 75. The *Codice* is 24 x 16 cm and was illustrated by Lauro Padovano. For a full transcript of the manuscript listing the horses and their achievements see Malacarne, *Il mito* (1995), pp. 88-93.

110 Mantua, ASMa, AG, b. 2485. Letter dated 20 September 1512.

111 Il Dainosauro had also won the *palii* in Ferrara and Mantua. The dates for his victories are not given, although those for other horses are.

112 'Turcho' – this accolade probably refers to the horse's breeding although Francesco's grandfather, the *condottiere* Ludovico Gonzaga, was known as 'Il Turcho' for his victory against the Turks and it is possible that Francesco, himself a soldier, had inherited the title.

113 Corte, 1562, I, ch. 3, 11v.

PART TWO

The Court Stable

Introduction

> When a man has found a horse to his liking, bought him and taken him home, it is well
> to have the stable so situated with respect to the house that his master can
> see him very often . . .
> Xenophon, fourth-century BC.[1]

If the service given by horse to man was considered important, the reverse was also true: that is to say the necessary care and support that man was expected to give to the horse. The reliance by the court on its horses meant that these animals required suitable housing and care, whatever their role might have been. As Giles Worsley explains, the stable is not necessary for the survival of a horse as, in the wild, the horse shows little need for a shelter. It was as part of man's domestication of the horse that the stable – like the bit, saddle or harness – became a necessary part of horse ownership.[2] The stable not only gave this valuable court commodity safety from predators, it also benefited his health and appearance whilst housing him conveniently close to the court. Inside the stable, there is no need for the horse to use his energy growing a thick coarse coat as protection against the cold; he maintains his short sleek silky coat, easy to groom in preparation for any event. Safely tethered in his stall, he is less likely to damage his legs or feet and become lame, his food can be rationed and his health monitored. The stable, therefore, contributed to the appearance, management and efficiency of the horse whilst keeping it secure and readily available. In short 'the stable guarantees the most efficient return of horse power to food consumed'.[3]

    Exotic and highly valued Renaissance thoroughbred horses were not housed in service buildings as many of their medieval predecessors had been. Their stables, often located in primary locations, became places of display in which not only the equestrian knowledge but also the magnificence of the owner could be shown through the quality of his horses; the stable acting as an equine gallery, comparable to similar spaces within the ruler's palace in which he could show off his other various collections. As a painted *cassone* would protect extravagant clothing, the stable would protect the horses. And in the same way that a frescoed hall served as a backdrop to elaborate entertainment and dining, an elegant stable interior would exhibit horses to their best advantage. Apart from its role as protective housing and background 'scenery', the autonomous stable would develop a status and magnificence of its own, with carefully designed interiors and richly painted or decorated walls, making it worthy of consideration as a significant court building. There were, in fact, several ways in which the stable building itself could impress: through its capacity for holding large numbers of cavalry horses such as at the late fifteenth-century stables at Vigevano and Urbino, where up to three hundred horses are said to have been housed at any one time; through the elegance of exterior decoration, such as the frescoed decoration at Vigevano and Ponte Poledrano or elaborate plasterwork on the walls of Agostino Chigi's stables in Rome; through the ingenuous use of an awkward space, which is to be found at Pius II's stables, constructed beneath the hanging garden of his papal palace at Pienza or Carlo Borromeo's three-storey decagonal stable, the *Rotonda*, in Milan and through the height and prominent location of Alessandro Farnese's sixteenth-century stables at Caprarola.

In 1615, Vincenzo Scamozzi would record many of the men who owned stables with enormous numbers of horses: 'the great dukes of Florence, Ferrara, Mantua, Parma and Urbino, as well as those of the princes and titled *Signori* in the kingdom of Naples'.[4] In some instances these great stables have survived owing to the versatility of their original design. The standard and most practical ground plan for a Renaissance stable replicated the basilica church, divided lengthwise into three aisles; the two outer aisles housing the horses, the wider central service corridor used for access and for walking the horses. Consequently, the suitability of these large spaces for modern-day use has resulted in structural surveys and historical studies being made before the buildings were restructured. The wide variation of such conversions – whether in the past or present day – illustrates the flexibility of these stables, with uses such as gallery, museum and exhibition area, library, catering and hospitality school, holiday accommodation, a student bar, medical research laboratories and hospital, as well as an earlier use as a forced labour camp or an abattoir.[5] Unfortunately, not many of these surveys and studies are widely available for research and although they often make it possible to understand the exterior appearance and internal layout of a particular stable, it is difficult to find any evidence of the original interior fittings or flooring. Even if still *in situ*, such fittings are unlikely to be original as stables were often remodelled in the intervening years. Consequently, the main source of evidence for items such as partitions, hayracks and mangers must come from contemporary architects' specifications and sketches, theoretical treatises and manuscripts. Additional information can be taken from stables depicted in Renaissance nativity scenes, whether sculpted or painted, in the same way that details of contemporary interior furnishings or patterns of planting might be illustrated in Renaissance annunciation scenes. Even so, caution must be observed in both cases as artists are depicting rustic, not court, stables and idealised rooms and gardens. Similarly, caution must be taken when describing original flooring. Although some stone and brick flooring or evidence of drainage and water supply might remain, wooden flooring in the form of planking has not survived and, unless documented in architectural specifications, the ideal type of wood can only be learnt from theoretical texts.

In Renaissance Italy, books dedicated to stable design did not exist; information, therefore, must come from a variety of treatises on architecture, horsemanship and animal health. Nevertheless, these works together with archaeological footprints, if combined with modern surveys, Renaissance paintings and drawings, contain sufficient information to envisage these important court buildings and understand how they were managed. Renaissance patrons may have fallen short of the Emperor Caligula, whose favourite horse, Incitatus, was provided with 'a marble stable, an ivory stall, purple blankets and a jewelled collar as well as a house, furniture and slaves',[6] but their stables would become elements of courtly magnificence, sometimes with extravagant decorative detail, and they had a large stable staff to look after them. As will be seen, Raphael's stables for Agostino Chigi, which in 1518 were furnished to entertain Pope Leo X and fourteen cardinals at an elaborate banquet, contributed to an overt display of the Sienese banker's wealth. This kind of extravagance did not end with the Renaissance. Two hundred years later in France, the Prince de Condé would entertain foreign dignitaries in Jean Aubert's magnificent Chantilly stables. But Chigi's stables were not exceptional; many other stables were also given the same attention to detail as the court palace or villa.

This part of the book explains some of the influences on Renaissance stable design by looking at various theories and practices during the period 1450 to *c.*1600. What, for example, influenced the various developments? Was it the advice given in newly published classical texts? Was it the emphasis on cleanliness for the benefits of equine health? Was it the requirement for a suitable space for a conspicuous display of consumption? The following three chapters consider theories for finding suitable stable sites; the theories and influences on exterior architectural design and the importance attached to the interior lay out of a stable to maintain the horses' health.

1 *On Horsemanship*, 1962, p. 313.
2 Worsley, *The British Stable* (2004), p. 4.
3 Worsley, 'The Design and Development', 1989, p. 8.
4 Vincenzo Scamozzi, *L'idea della architettura universale, di Vincenzo Scamozzi, architetto veneto divisa in X libri* (Venice, 1615), Part 1, II, ch. XXII, 'De Luoghi da munitionioni e vittovaglie & alloggiamenti de' soldati e da guarnigioni e stalle publiche da cavalli', p. 177.
5 Vigevano, Poggio a Caiano, Caprarola, Cafaggiolo, Bologna, Ponte Poledrano (Bentivoglio), La Magliana, Viterbo, Pienza.
6 Suetonius, *The Twelve Caesars* (2007), p. 174.

Brand for the *corsieri* of the Illustrious Signore Duke of Mantua

Chapter 4

Facing the Heavens: Choosing a Location

You know the story, how the king had met with a horse, but wished to give the creature flesh and do it without delay, so he asked someone, reputed to be clever about horses, 'What will give him flesh most quickly?' To which the other replied: 'The master's eye'. So too, it strikes me Socrates, there is nothing like 'the master's eye' to call forth latent qualities, and develop them to beautiful and good effect.
Xenophon, fourth-century BC.[1]

You must build the stable in a place as close as possible to the palace of the *Signore* and, if this is not possible for all of his horses, because of inconvenience that would arise, at least for the majority of them. But building it where you want, make sure that you build it in a place as convenient as possible for water, and that there is enough for the daily use of the horses.
Claudio Corte, 1562.[2]

Two priorities governed the choice of location for a stable, both of which were specified by Corte: accessibility for the owner and sufficient water. Proximity to the residence not only meant that the stables were more likely to be secure but also that they were conveniently situated for the owner and his guests when arriving at a castle or villa. Accessibility brought a third benefit, explained in Xenophon's dialogue and often mentioned by Renaissance theorists: the belief that horses thrived if the conscientious owner visited his stables regularly to oversee their management and training. Similar to the essential requirements for the site of a villa or castle, it was important that the stables were built in a dry location, with access to water but without the danger of flooding. And, although a variety of sites were chosen, whether in a city court complex or in the countryside where hunting and horse breeding took place, these two priorities prevailed. Having fulfilled the requirements of accessibility and water supply, other secondary reasons might influence the exact location, such as the desire to impress, the proximity to major roads or the avoidance of certain unhealthy environments. This can be seen at Poggio a Caiano where, for ease of access, it would have been possible to build the magnificent Medici stables facing any one of the villa's aspects, but a choice was made to position them on the south-east corner of the villa's grounds, making them visible from, and convenient for, the junction of three major routes connecting Florence, Prato and Pistoia. Making the stable easily accessible from major roads or a castle entrance would also have brought the building to the notice of visitors as they approached, evident at the Bentivoglio castle at Ponte Poledrano or within the Sforza castle courtyard at Vigevano when accessed via the covered street, the Strada Coperta. Whilst this might be convenient, it also gave the owner the opportunity to impress his visitors by the size of his stable or by the extravagance of its architecture and decoration. In essence, placing the Renaissance stable in a convenient location could also make it a means of displaying wealth and magnificence.

Early writers on husbandry sometimes defined the suitable location for a farmstead, with at least four giving details of the horse's stable: Xenophon, Vitruvius, Columella and Palladius. Xenophon's *On Horsemanship* included advice on the correct site for a stable with some details for the interior and, in the following centuries, Vitruvius, in his first-century BC *De architectura* and Columella[3] and Palladius[4] in their treatises on agriculture from the first and fourth centuries, also gave advice on aspects of stable design and horse management. Renaissance theorists, such as Alberti, Corte and Caracciolo, all refer to Xenophon's theory, emphasising the importance of the master keeping watch over his horses. This is seen in Claudio Corte's treatise in which he summarises earlier writers in order to create a pyramid of classical support for his theory that the stable should be 'under the master's eye'. After praising Xenophon, 'who has written most excellently on the horse', Corte quotes the Greek general's theory 'that the stable must be built in a place where the owner can conveniently and regularly see his horses' which, Corte explains, was an allusion to Aristotle's anecdote concerning a Persian, who had asked him what was the most important thing for fattening up a horse, to which Aristotle had answered 'the eye of the owner'. Corte then includes Plutarch's advice, found in *The Morals*, that 'nothing fats the horse so much as the king's eye'.[5] It is difficult to know why Corte felt the need to use these classical sources to support his theory as, even prior to the Renaissance, court stables had been easily accessible when in the subterranean level of a main residence, such as at the twelfth-century Vatican stables or the fourteenth-century Visconti stables in Pavia. However, as has been suggested for other Renaissance writers, it is possible that Corte wished to show off his knowledge on a specific subject as, in addition to his pyramid of classical support, he continued with his own explanation of how horses suffer if the master does not manage them well,

> And this is true. That whoever neglects building [the stable] in such a place I regard as having little love for himself, it being evident that the horse receives the body of the master who rides him, whether he is in the stable or being managed. Because if the horseman does not build his stable in a place where he can quickly and regularly see his horses, who will ensure that they can trust him? And so they become thin. Which reminds me of reading about a good humoured fat horseman who, riding a very thin horse, was asked what was the cause, and replied that he had pastured it and that he had taken care of it himself, when in fact the horse had been pastured and cared for by the servants. A truly shameful reply by the horseman, which displays much negligence on the owner's part.

On the other hand, for those owners who did keep a close eye on their horses, Corte was full of praise

> Blessed are those princes, *signori* and horsemen, who have total care of these thoroughbred animals,[6] so that it is not enough for them just to house [the horses] as comfortably as possible and see them every day in the stables but, in addition, they also settle them in their stalls.[7]

A few years later, Pasqual Caracciolo would also warn of the consequences of bad management:

> I can truthfully say this: that the *signore* who uses negligence on his horse, is also neglecting himself, because one clearly sees that, in dangerous situations, the horse takes on the persona of his owner, as if to repay his owner faithfully . . . [therefore] the diligent owner must often go into the stables.[8]

4.1. Castello Visconteo Sforzesco, Vigevano. South side of the courtyard. The Maschio is on the left and Ludovico Sforza's stable is on the right. Centre is the neo-Gothic arch between Galeazzo Maria Sforza's two stables.
SFM ITALY C/Alamy Stock Photo

Over one hundred years before Corte's advice, Alberti had also quoted *On Horsemanship*, 'one reads with Xenophon the old proverb that the look of the master fattens the horse'.[9] But in Book Five of *De re aedificatoria*, Alberti gives different advice when mentioning stud horses, suggesting that they should be kept further away in a place where they will not 'offend anyone inside the house with their smell'.[10] The problem of housing stud horses close to a residence remains an issue a century and a half later and is mentioned by Vincenzo Scamozzi in his architectural treatise, *L'idea della architettura universale*:

> Stables for valued stud horses should be sited in places which are easy to access, so that the master and those who oversee and school [the horses] can be pleased by the sight of them; but they should not be [built] too close to the living quarters or respectable places, because of the neighing, nausea and stench.[11]

Certainly, stud horses can make a considerable noise, particularly if stallions are allowed to attack one another or attempt to reach the mares, but good management would keep stallions in different stables or pastures to the broodmares and foals. This is evident from letters in the Gonzaga archives and was suggested in Vasari's description of Giulio Romano's work on the Isola Te in which, by using the plural of stables, *stalle*, he implied there was more than one stable and that the Gonzaga stallions and mares were probably housed separately:

> . . . where his Excellency had a property called Il Te and some stables, in the middle of a pasture, where he had the stud farm of his stallions and mares.[12]

At the great court stables at Vigevano, the possible 'neighing, nausea and stench' of up to three hundred court horses – even if not stud horses – must have become part of daily life at the Sforza court as the magnificent stables, which form three of the five sides of the castle's great service court, are directly overlooked by the main residence, *Il maschio* (4.1). The earliest of these stables

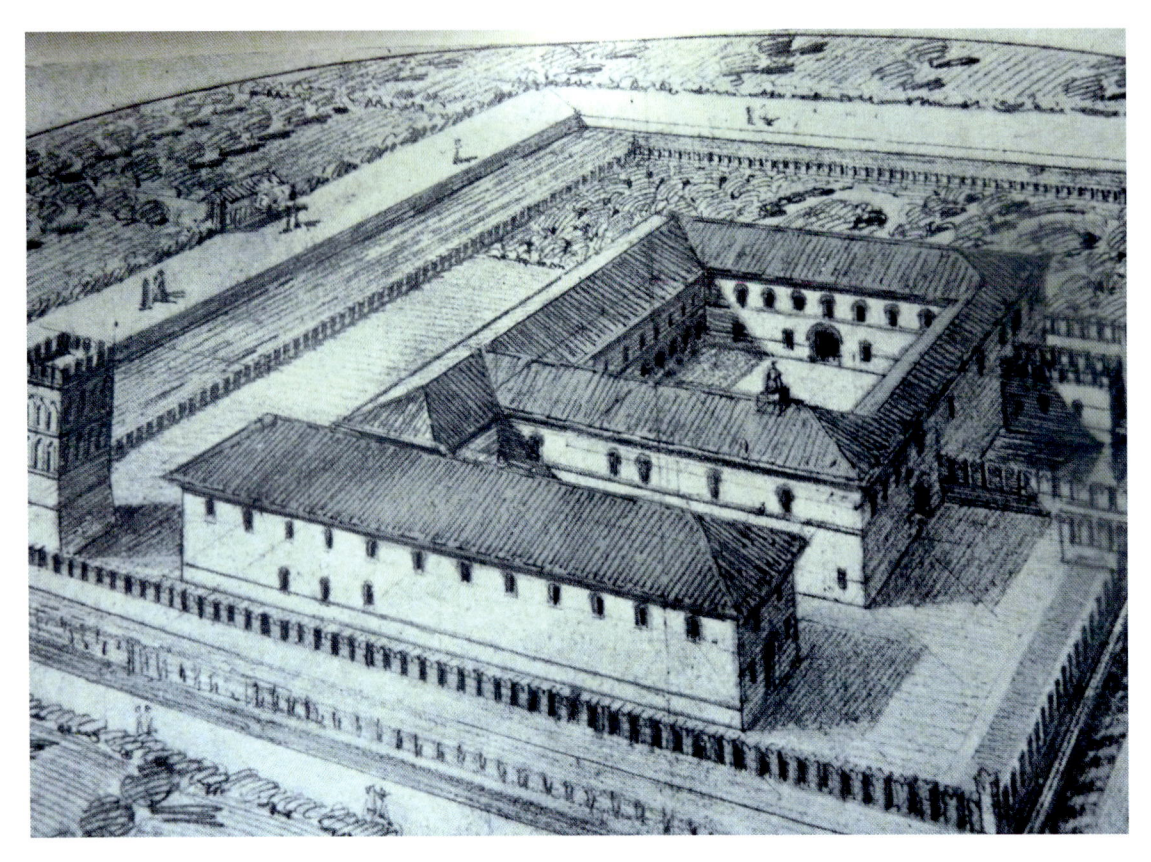

4.2. Bentivoglio (formerly Ponte Poledrano), the Bentivoglio Castle, *c*.1460 from the north-west. The stables are in the foreground. Image A. Rubbiani, *Il Castello di Giovanni II Bentivoglio a Ponte Poledrano*, 1914

had been renovated and rebuilt under Galeazzo Maria Sforza, who entrusted the project of a second stable to Maffeo da Como in the 1470s. The third and by far the largest stable at ninety-one metres in length,[13] was added by Galeazzo Maria's successor, Ludovico 'Il Moro' in the 1490s, filling the gap between the earlier stables and the entrance tower and thereby enclosing the courtyard (see 2.2). As Pellegrino later explained, having the stables close to the residence meant that 'the prince', in this case Galeazzo Maria or Ludovico Sforza, had the advantage of watching his horses when they were brought out of their stables – which must have outweighed the disadvantage of any noise or smell. On a much smaller scale, the Bentivoglio stables at their hunting grounds in Ponte Poledrano, north of Bologna, were built as a wing attached to the castle whilst, in Bologna, some of their horses were also stabled within the palace compound (4.2 and 4.3).

In earlier centuries stables were sometimes built at cellar level or as part of a walled castle complex, giving them security and allowing the owner private access from his residence. It is known, for example, that between 1368 and 1420, the papal stables at the Vatican were in the subterranean level of a twelfth-century tower, with the treasury and a chapel above them.[14] And although Federico da Montefeltro had Francesco di Giorgio's impressive stables, known as La Data, beside his palace in Urbino, he also had a large vaulted area, probably once used as stables and subsequently for saddling and unsaddling the horses, in the palace basement directly below

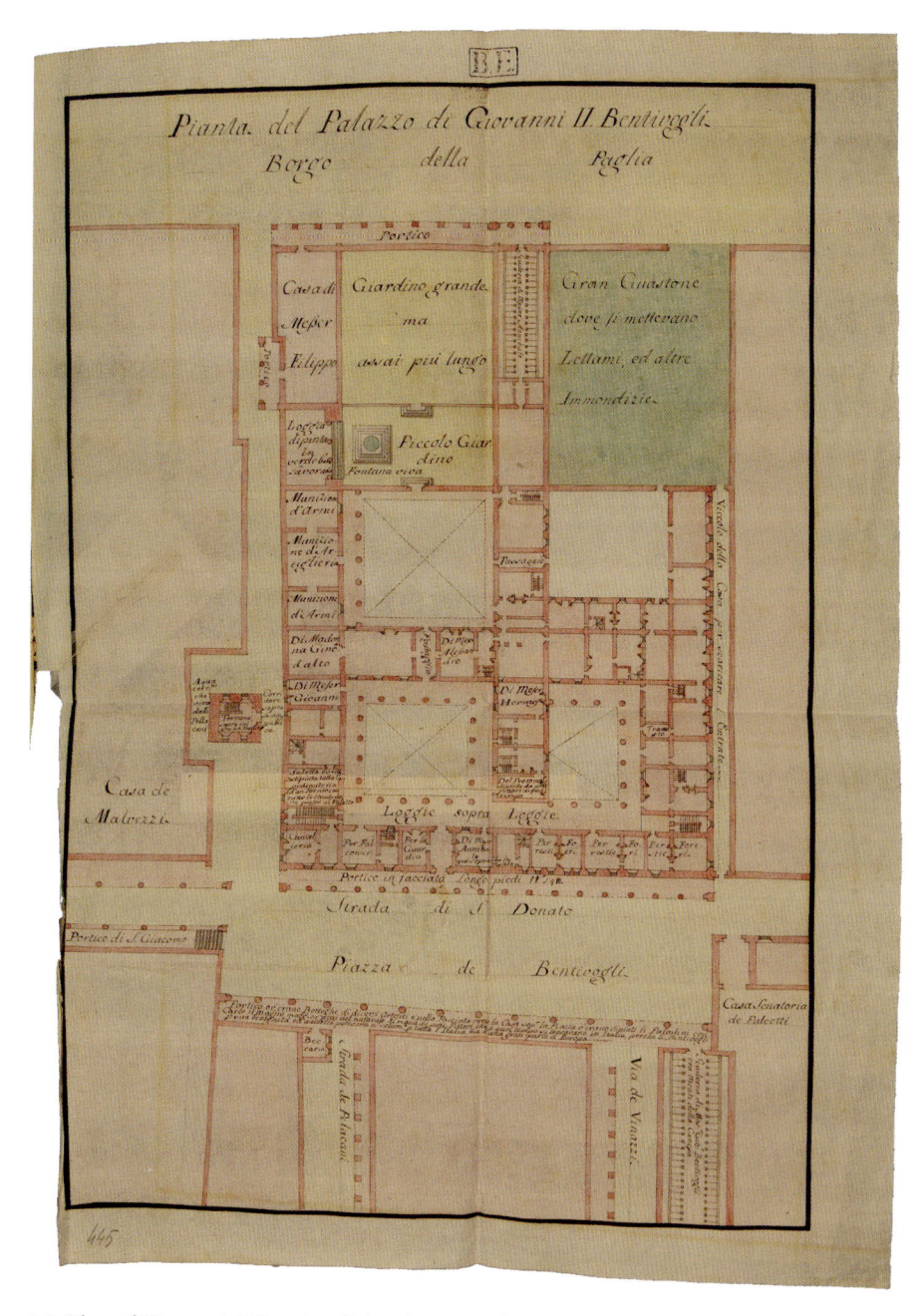

4.3. Plan of Giovanni II Bentivoglio's palace in Bologna. Top centre is 'Scuderia di Messer Annibale', bottom right 'Scuderia di Messer Giovanni Bentivoglio'. Modena, Gallerie Estensi, Bib. Estense Universitaria, MS a.J.8.1, Cherubino Ghirardacci, *Historia di Bologna*, 17th century, Part III, 1393-1509, 445r. With permission of Ministero per i beni e le attività culturali

4.4. Palazzo Ducale, Urbino. Federico da Montefeltro's subterranean stables

4.5. Castle of Crac des Chevaliers, Syria. Stables, *c.*1142-1271. Johnny Grieg Int/Alamy Stock Photo

the ducal apartments (4.4). Similarly, Galeazzo Maria Sforza had vaulted subterranean stables at Pavia, built by his ancestor Galeazzo Il Visconti in the fourteenth century alongside the cellars and prisons of the Castello Sforzesco. For both these *condottiere* rulers it was essential for their horses to be secure. These wide single-vaulted stables, which would have had lines of military horses tethered on either side, follow a design known for hundreds of years and which is still in evidence at the Knights Hospitallers' castle of Crac des Chevaliers in Syria, built between 1142

4.6. Palazzo Ducale, Urbino. Stepped ramp leading from the castle courtyard to the subterranean stables

and 1271 (4.5). Some underground stables had a secret passage or stairway to the main residence. This was for two purposes: first, so that great *condottieri* and rulers, who might have enemies either within or outside their states, could leave their residences discreetly in times of danger and second, as shown above, it was considered important that owners could easily oversee their horses being managed correctly.

In Urbino, Duke Federico could access his subterranean stables directly via a private staircase from the ducal apartments and could exit them on horseback via a stepped ramp leading directly to the courtyard (4.6). The Duke's later 'La Data' stable was also reached via a spiral ramp in a tower close by. Francesco di Giorgio writes that the ramp was

> reserved only for the *Signore*, by which [he] could, without being seen, see the entire stable and everything the staff and the master of the stable [were] doing.[15]

Other palaces and villas also had discreet access, more for convenience than for spying on the staff. Pius II's palace, designed by Rossellino c.1459, had access to the stables via a stepped ramp leading from a large doorway in the main courtyard and, whilst this allowed private access to a tunnel leading to the papal stables, it was also a means of avoiding some of the noise made by horses within the palace. A cross-section and an asymmetric plan of the palace clearly show the

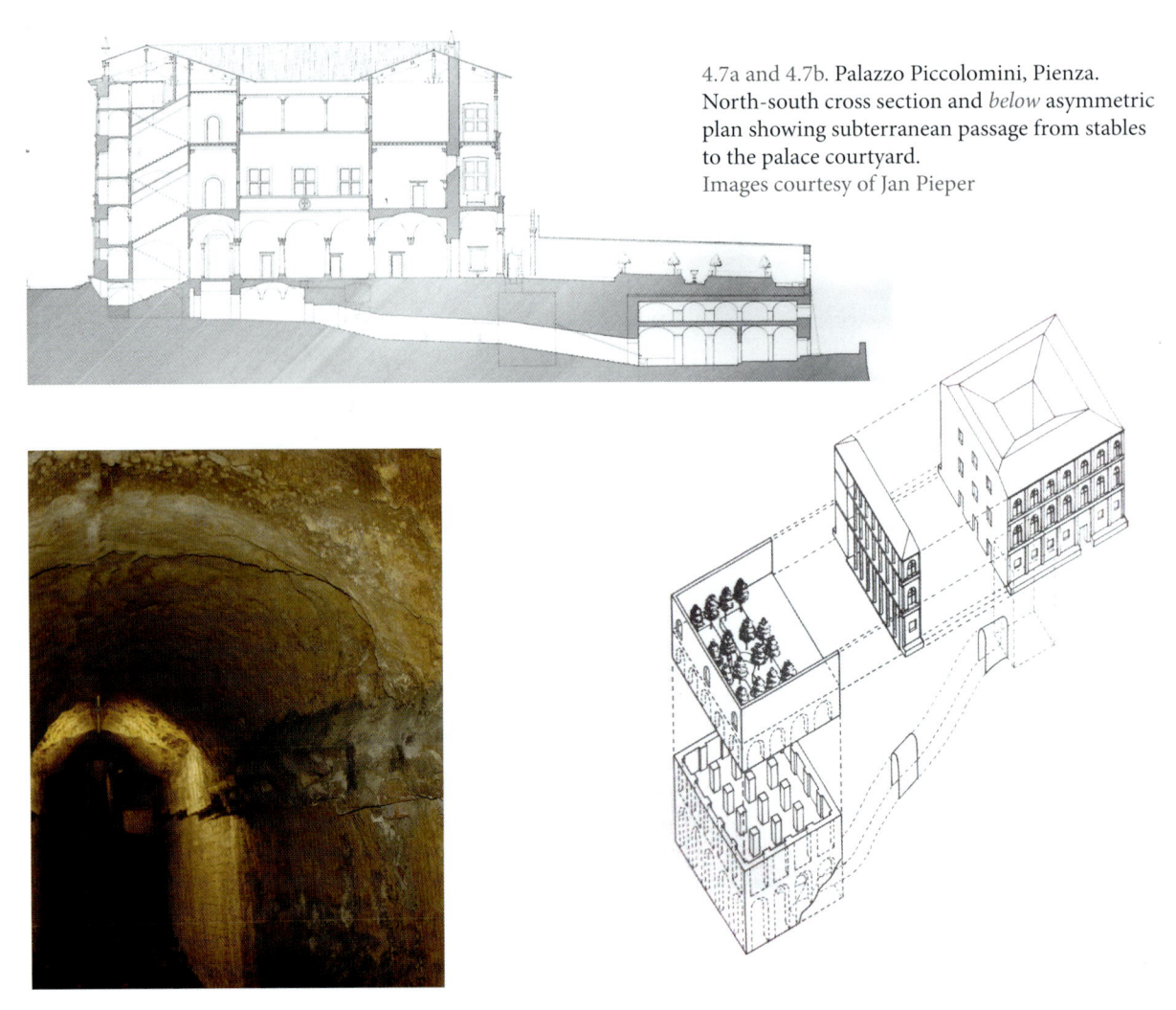

4.7a and 4.7b. Palazzo Piccolomini, Pienza. North-south cross section and *below* asymmetric plan showing subterranean passage from stables to the palace courtyard.
Images courtesy of Jan Pieper

4.8. Palazzo Piccolomini, subterranean passage leading to stables

narrow tunnel descending to the stables, which are situated beneath the hanging garden (4.7a, 4.7b & 4.8).

Like Pius's palace, both Giovanni de' Medici's villa at Fiesole and Duke Cosimo I's Uffizi building in Florence were built on slopes and had subterranean stables as part of their structure. Although Vasari names Michelozzo as the architect for the mid-fifteenth century Fiesole villa, recent research proposes that Alberti was responsible and that this design became an architectural prototype for the Renaissance villa.[16] A century later, Vasari's subterranean stables followed the Uffizi's U shape, the shortest wing running parallel with the Lungarno terrace. Despite the Duke's reservations, this space was used for stabling, one of the entrance ramps leading up from the river bank. Not surprisingly, when the river flooded in 1589, several horses drowned.[17] At least two other Medici villas had private access to their stables. At Cafaggiolo, evidence of a short underground passage has been found which may have connected the villa to the west end of the stables.[18] And, at Poggio a Caiano, plans show that Duke Cosimo emulated the discreet private passageway from the Uffizi to the Palazzo Pitti by having barrel-vaulted underground passages leading from underneath the main portico of his villa to the various annexes distributed

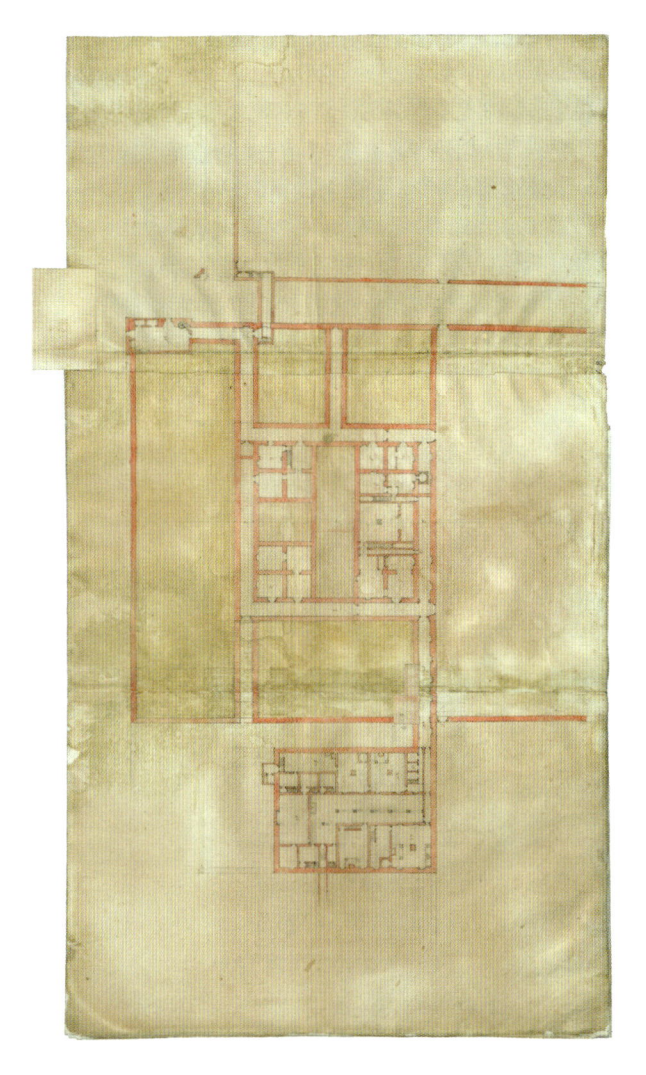

4.9. *left* Subterranean passages at Poggio a Caiano, c.1500-1510. The stables are at the top of the image. Florence, ASF, Miscellanea di Piante, F.323, c.6. Anon

4.10. *above* Poggio a Caiano, bridge linking the Medici stables to the Villa's gardens. In the sixteenth century the Prato road ran under it

around the gardens (4.9). This network also accessed the stable gardens via a circular staircase descending from the tennis court tower while, from the villa gardens, a bridge was built leading directly into a foyer on the upper level of the stables (4.10).

In the city, rulers tended to keep their horses stabled either inside the palace complex or at least within sight of the main residence. In Bologna, the impressive fifteenth-century Bentivoglio stables which face onto a large piazza, were positioned directly opposite the main façade of their magnificent palace. Now used as a student bar, the vaulted interior is greatly altered but the dividing octagonal columns remain and the building still dominates the piazza.[19] An eighteenth-century manuscript (see 4.3) shows these stables as having been for Messer Giovanni's horses (*Scuderia di Messer Gio. Bentivoglio*), whilst within the safety of the palace complex itself there was further stabling for about fifty horses[20] with more discreet access to the street behind it, the Borgo della Paglia (now Via delle Belle Arti). A contemporary description of these two stables, taken from 'Il Libro di ricordi' in the Gozzadini archives, explains that Giovanni Bentivoglio's palace is 'the most beautiful in all of Italy'. Having described the palace layout, it continues:

> Behind the garden were the sons' stables and the stable for Messer Giovanni's Barbary horses, with another large courtyard and his stable in front of the palace [facing] onto its piazza as can still be seen, always full of beautiful horses, and another stable for the carriage mules.[21]

Even within a private complex, the sculptor and architect Filarete makes it possible for an owner to view his horses secretly. In Book VIII of his *Libro architettonico*, concentrating on the ideal city of Sforzinda, he explains that, between the lord's gardens and his stables, Filarete has made provision for a street which is 20 *braccia* wide and 100 *braccia* long (*c.*12 x 60m). He explains, 'the reason for the street is this, when your Lordship wishes to observe the movements of a horse without being seen, he can do so easily'.[22] Like the Bentivoglio's palace in Bologna, Filarete's proposed stables have another entrance at the back leading onto a street. More suburban, but also sited next to the gardens, were the elegant stables of Agostino Chigi's Roman villa, which were designed by Raphael *c.*1512. Said to house as many as one hundred horses, the three-storey stables ran parallel to the Tiber with the villa's gardens separating them from the river bank. Sadly, due to poor foundations, the stables soon deteriorated and were finally pulled down at the beginning of the nineteenth century, leaving a section of wall facing onto the Via della Lungara (see 2.14).

Wherever stables were built the need for fresh water prevailed, not only for filling the large watering troughs and for grooming and washing the horses but also for cleaning the stables. Many Renaissance texts detail how often a horse should be washed (sometimes twice a day) and also place emphasis on the clean stable – with floors scrubbed and drains and mangers washed through on a regular basis. Research shows that water was supplied to the stables from various sources; some buildings having access to rivers, others needing wells or elaborate pipe work to service them with good quality water. In the first century, Columella had recommended that country stables should be positioned half way up a slope on a slight eminence, so that they were not washed through by rain but had access to a constant supply of fresh water from mountain rivers, a 'never-failing' spring or from rainwater if it was carried by clay pipes.[23] From Renaissance texts and letters, there is no doubt that suitable drinking water was of great concern both in the stable and in pastures. Corte writes that whilst clear fast-flowing cold water is suitable for horses in very hot weather, cloudy water is generally more suitable, and he emphasises the importance of salt to a horse's diet:

> It is true that drinking water for horses is best when it flows quietly, is a bit dirty and cloudy with a milky colour, as it is more likely to contain salt, than when it is fast-flowing and clear. Because this does not fatten up [the horses] nor cause good digestion but keeps them thin and underdeveloped, whereas the other kind makes them grow and warms them by giving the horse more nutrient and a better digestion.[24]

However, if such water cannot be found Corte suggests that *semola*, a finely ground cereal, should be stirred into the clear water in order to give the horse the same benefit. Alberti had also advocated the benefits of salt in the horse's water, especially after exercise:

> In order to make [the horses] take as much water as possible, you must encourage them to drink with salt; this quickly works to re-strengthen the legs.[25]

Provincia di Mantova Lombardia

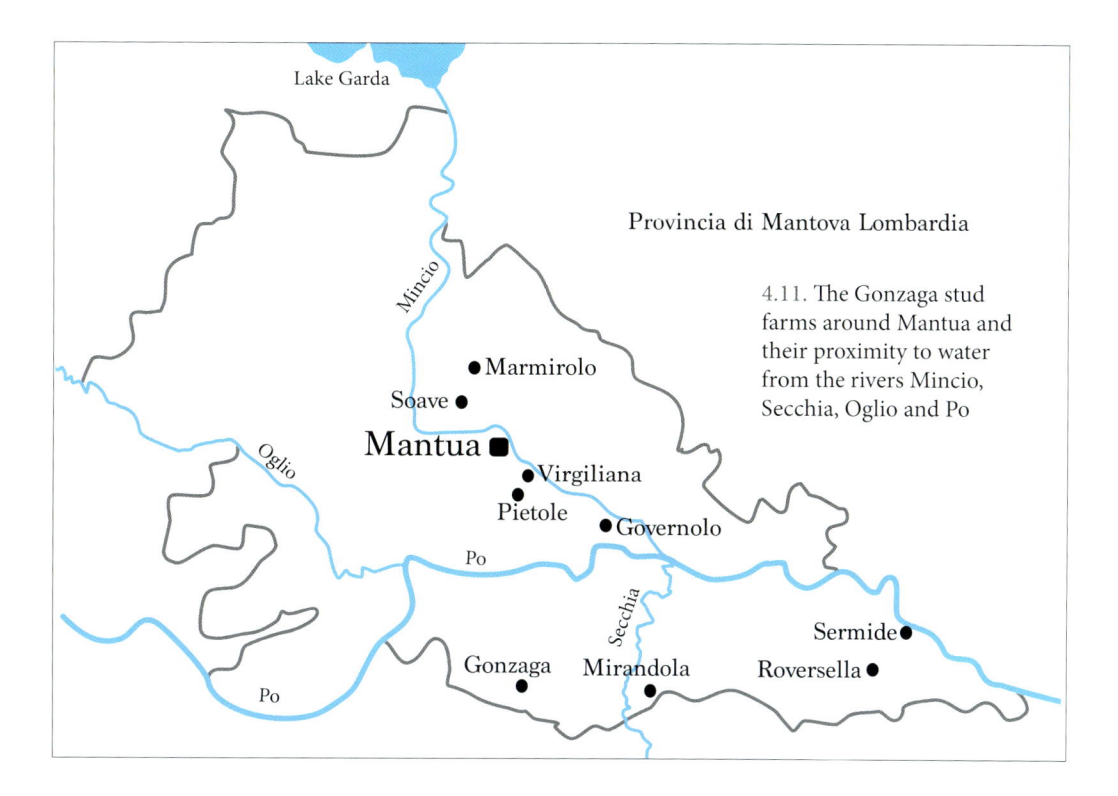

4.11. The Gonzaga stud farms around Mantua and their proximity to water from the rivers Mincio, Secchia, Oglio and Po

Good quality water was also essential in the pastures which sustained the stallions, mares and foals and, for this reason, most stud farms were situated within easy reach of a river or canal. In Puglia, the Venetian Republic's stud farm, La Cavallerizza, had pastures in the wide lush valley, the Canale di Pilo, served by several mountain streams; the Gonzaga stud farms around Mantua were located in the vicinity of either the Po river or its tributaries, the Secchia and the Mincio. Their stud farm at Mirandola is close to the Secchia, while the Margonara,[26] Virgiliana and Piètole farms are on the Mincio river and Soave was served by a canal (4.11). Although situated in the Po flood plain, it seems that the stud farm at Roversella was dependent on water drawn from wells which could give cause for concern. An undated letter from the late-fifteenth or early-sixteenth century, written by the Gonzaga agent, Lodovico Nonio, describes a lack of clean water around Roversella and his belief that this may be the cause of repeated sickness at the stud farm. Certain that this is not a sickness caused by fodder or water in good supply, he is convinced that the problem is fetid water brought from the bottom of wells in arid summers. Nonio writes that

> having observed that the grass is in abundance but the quality is very weak and that all the water has sediment, especially in those seasons which have been dry for many years, making it necessary to have such deep wells that it is not possible to lower the bucket deep enough without dirtying the water. This is very dangerous, because the fetid part of the water must find somewhere to settle: in the lungs, the diaphragm or even in the urinary tract.[27]

Nonio's concerns would appear to be justified as it is now known that the area south of the Po, the Sermide basin in which the Roversella stud was situated, has some wells with good water and others which, for no apparent reason, contain large amounts of minerals: calcium, magne-

4.12. *Il Castello di Cafaggiolo*, Giusto Utens, late-sixteenth century, showing stables and tributary on the left. Florence, Villa medicea della Petraia. The Picture Collection/Alamy Stock Photo

sium, sodium chloride and potassium, as well as various nitrates and traces of iron. Certainly, horses are very sensitive to changes in a water's quality and it may well have been these minerals that caused the horses to be sick.[28] Apart from the dangers of contamination, wells could also become blocked, as at the Aragonese Marcianise stables near Naples where, in 1489, specialist well cleaners were brought in (*mastri da cavare pucze per annecatre uno puczo che era asseccato*).[29] This cannot have been an easy job as it is known that at least one of these wells was fifteen metres deep.[30]

As for court residences, whether palace, castle or villa, different methods were employed to bring suitable and ample water to their various stables. An example where river water is channelled can be seen at Michelozzo's mid fifteenth-century stables for the Medici villa at Cafaggiolo in the Mugello valley. The late sixteenth-century lunette by Utens, painted for Duke Ferdinando I, clearly shows a channel or tributary from the Sieve running parallel to, and about ten metres from, the south side of the ninety-metre-long stables, between some kennels and a parallel line of trees (4.12, 4.13).[31] Water for the villa's moat was also taken from the Sieve but, due to the river's persistent flooding, this has since been filled in. It is likely that river water was also stored in a small reservoir close to the stable's south wall (4.14). This rectangular *pozzo* is three metres by two metres and approximately two metres deep and is surrounded by a forty-centimetre wide stone border. Together with stone drainage channels, intermittently covered with short wooden planks, running against the south wall of the stables (4.15), the small reser-

4.13. Cafaggiolo, south side of stables

4.14. Cafaggiolo, *pozzo* on south side of stables

4.15. Cafaggiolo, stone drainage channels on south side of stables

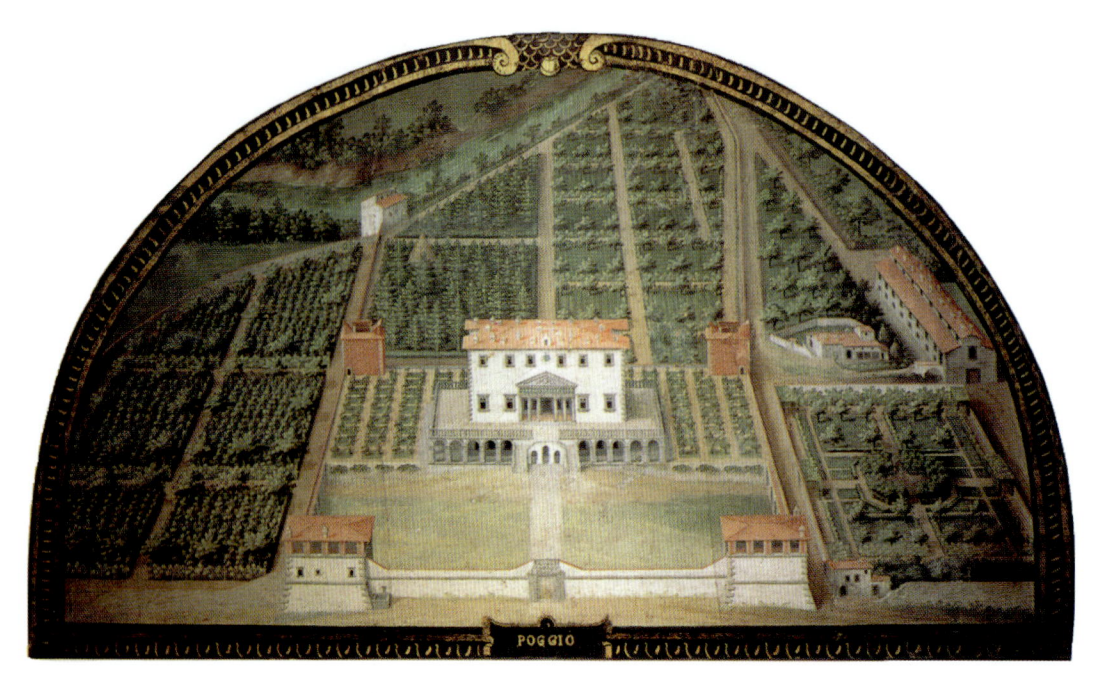

4.16. Poggio a Caiano, Giusto Utens, late-sixteenth century. Florence, Villa medicea della Petraia. Art Collection 3/Alamy Stock Photo

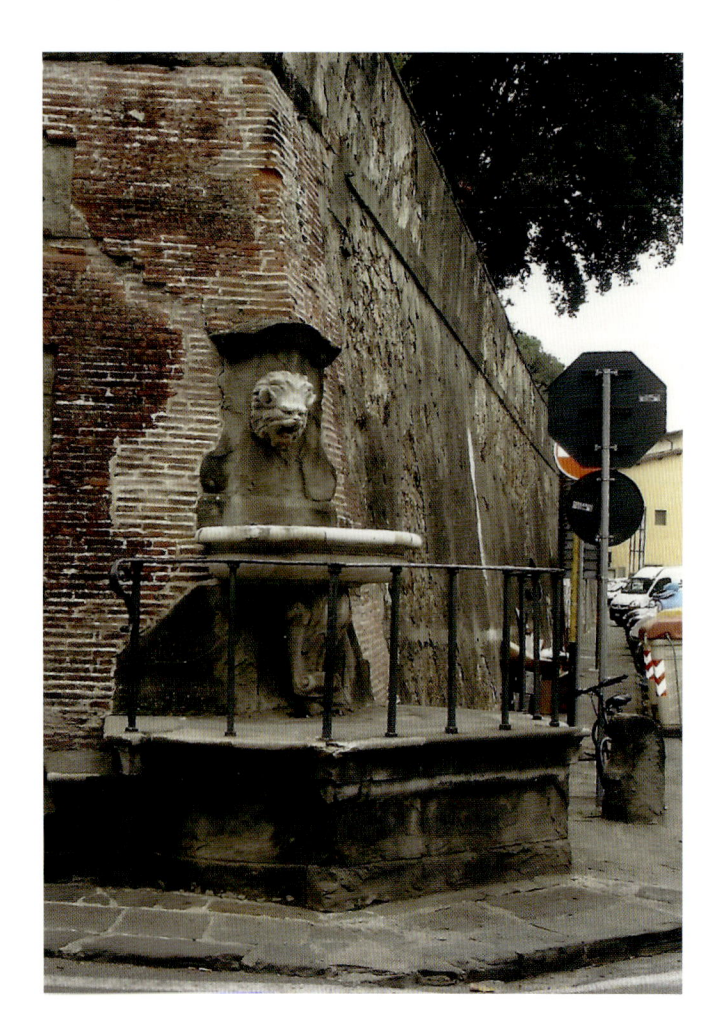

4.17. Villa Medici, Poggio a Caiano. A drinking fountain in the perimeter wall. The Medici stables can be seen to the right

4.18. Pienza (Corsignano). Pius II's palace is in the centre of the image with stables beneath the palace gardens

voir would have assisted the cleaning of the stables, with water from the adjacent channel.[32]

Another Medici villa, at Poggio a Caiano, drew water from the Ombrone river. The large stables, designed by 'Il Tribolo' for Duke Cosimo I in the 1540s,[33] could house as many as two hundred horses all of which would require water for drinking and washing. Flowing about fifty metres behind the west end of the stables, Utens' lunette shows the river passing alongside the villa's garden wall (4.16). Both the sluice gates in the retaining wall and payments in 1590 for a new channel leading underneath the gardens to the front of the stables show that water was supplied from this source.[34] In addition, the proximity of the river meant that it could be used for washing down or cooling and refreshing tired horses. However, drinking fountains on a wall beside the stables and a large drinking trough in the atrium indicate that spring water may also have been available for the horses to drink (4.17). The importance of a nearby river is confirmed in Scamozzi's treatise on architecture, where it is explained that the Borghese Pope, Paul V, had his guards' horses stabled very close to the papal palace in Rome, in order that they could easily be led into the flowing river to drink and splash about.[35]

Most stables were, in fact, situated close to rivers, canals, or lakes such as at the Gonzaga's stables in Mantua but, in some instances, architects and patrons were prepared to go to considerable trouble in order to supply water to stables built on what might be considered 'unsuitable' sites. Three stables are worth noting as they required extensive engineering to supply both the court personnel and the court horses with sufficient water: Pienza, where Aeneus Silvius Piccolomini, Pope Pius II, employed Bernardo Rossellino to transform his birthplace Corsignano into a Renaissance town; the ducal stables at Urbino; and at Caprarola, where Cardinal Alessandro Farnese completed the impressive pentagonal villa begun by his grandfather. In sharp contrast to the Medici villas at Cafaggiolo and Poggio a Caiano, there was no river available to serve the subterranean papal stables at Pienza. Although the small Tuscan town is situated on a rocky outcrop between two valleys, through which the Tuoma and the Orcia rivers flow, the town itself was dependent on wells and cisterns sunk into the rock (4.18). For the quantity of water required by the papal palace it was therefore necessary to construct an elaborate hydraulic

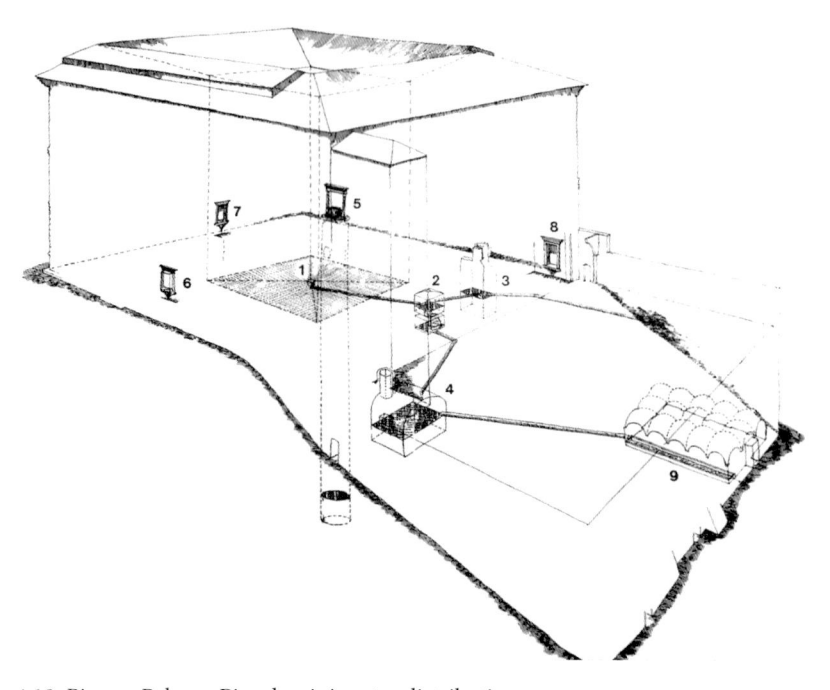

4.19. Pienza, Palazzo Piccolomini, water distribution.
   Key:
   1. Manhole in the paved courtyard and the first filter
   2. Purification room
   3. Spillway and cistern of non-drinkable water
   4. Cistern of drinking water, under the garden, for the hydraulic provision of water to the kitchens and the gravity feed to the stables
   5. Well on the piazza with further opening from the cellars for sampling water (see 4.23)
   6/7. Well fountains on the wall, fed by a cistern on the roof
   8. Wall fountain on the loggia overlooking the garden
   9. Drinking trough in the stables below the hanging garden

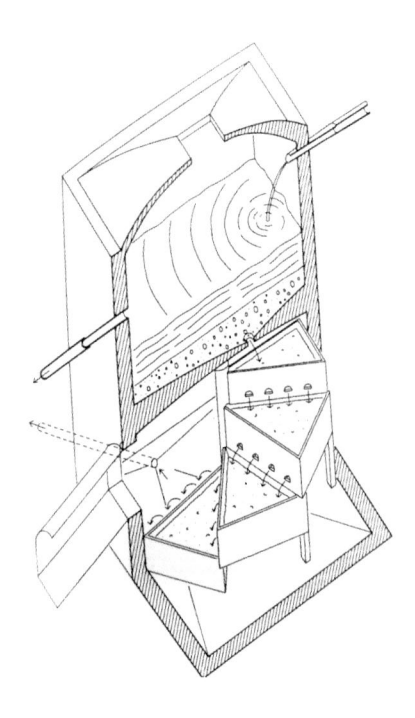

4.20. The water filtration under the main courtyard of the Palazzo Piccolimini.
Both drawings courtesy of Jan Pieper

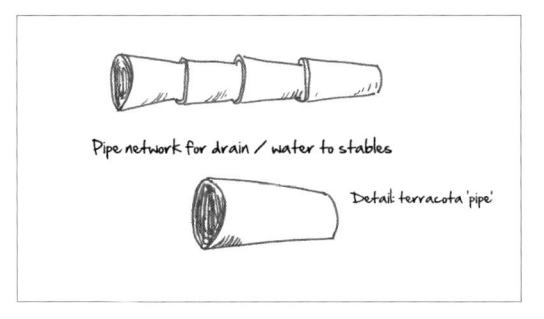

4.21. Palazzo Piccolomini, interlocking terracotta pipes

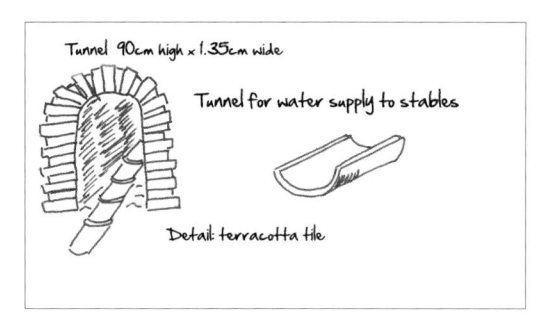

4.22. Shaped terracotta tiles forming the base to the tunnel supplying drinking water from the central cistern to the subterranean stables

system, connecting different water sources in order to supply the palace and the subterranean stables. The Pope's *Commentaries* indicate that the stables had developed as a means of supporting the garden:

> Here Pius had intended to plant a garden, but the ground was uneven and sloped sharply. Very thick walls were built on a stone base and between columns of brick and stone it had arched openings which could provide stabling for a hundred horses and workshops for blacksmiths.[36]

Together with the papal household, these one hundred horses would have required a considerable amount of water; water which was brought from a variety of sources, using both spring- and rainwater conveyed to the palace via an elaborate system of cisterns, wells and pipes. Rainwater was gathered in a reservoir on the palace roof and supplied to a large cistern under the main courtyard, purifying it via a system of sand filters in which the sand became increasingly fine. From here, it served the kitchens via an hydraulic system and was carried in clay pipes to the stables (4.19, 4.20). This system not only made use of the rainwater but the pipework also helped to keep the subterranean levels dry enough for storage space, stables and workrooms.[37] Pius writes,

> The reservoir on the roof carried off some of the rain outside, . . . and carried some down into the court, so that after being filtered through gravel, it might fill the cisterns, of which there were three: two in the palace and a third very large one in the garden . . . [38]

Beneath the garden, it is still possible to see the continuous system of conical terracotta pipes linked into one another which carried water along the east side of the stables, close to the roof level of the wide underground passage through which horse-drawn carts supplied the palace with goods and services (4.21, 4.22 and see 4.8). At the opposite side of the palace, a 'waterfall' of linked semi-circular terracotta tiles – reminiscent of an irrigation system – allowed a flow of water through a small passageway about one and a half metres high, ending in a large water trough or cistern in the stables (see 4.19. pipe between points 4 and 9).[39] In contrast to the width of the service tunnel, this passageway is only just wide enough and high enough to allow a small

4.23. East wall of the Palazzo Piccolomini, Pienza. Two well heads. The well to the right is 25 metres deep. It can be accessed half way down, from an inspection chamber in the palace cellars, in order to test the water's quality

man or boy to pass through it – presumably for maintenance. This complicated network of water distribution included an inspection chamber accessed from the palace cellars, which was located in a 25-metre-deep well under the piazza to the east of the palace, as well as a purification room below the hanging gardens through which the water was filtered (4.23).[40] According to Giannantonio Campano, Pius had intended to flood the Orcia valley creating a lake in front of his palace, but this was never completed.[41] Presumably if horses needed to be refreshed or washed they would have been taken down to the river Orcia two kilometres away. Alternatively, although this has not been verified, a large pool may have been built for this purpose, as was proposed by Leonardo da Vinci in the 1480s:

> Let a pool be outside the stable for [the dirt to be washed off] the horses so they can splash about after a journey. Let it be one and a half *braccia* deep and be paved, with thick sand and fine gravel over the base.[42]

An equally elaborate water system is found in the Ducal stables in Urbino. Bernardino Baldi's sixteenth-century description of Federico da Montefeltro's castle describes how the rainwater from the roof and the gardens was gathered into cisterns, which supplied the stables and the castle cellars, and that underground channels took water down to the Mercatale and the city walls to supply wash houses and horse troughs.[43] Water also had to be diverted to the late sixteenth-century Farnese villa, which overlooks the small town of Caprarola in the Cimini Mountains, thirty miles north of Rome.[44] Giuseppe Vasi's *Prospetto di Caprarola* clearly shows these impressive four-storey stables to the left of the villa (4.24). Known as 'Lo Stallone', these stables were probably designed by Vignola although the construction was overseen by Giovanni Antonio Garzoni da Viggiù, who had previously been chief stonemason.[45] Completed in 1585, these four-storey stables compete in size and status with the Farnese villa itself, standing twenty metres high from ground level to cornice, one hundred metres long and fifteen metres wide. Dominating the town alongside the villa at the top of the main street the stables could contain

4.24. Prospetto di Caprarola, c.1746-1748. The new stables, Lo Stallone, are at top left

4.25. The well head at the Villa Farnese stables

as many as one hundred and twenty horses on the ground floor.[46] Like Pius II's stables, those at Caprarola are built on rock, in Lo Stallone's case on volcanic *tufa*. According to Michel de Montaigne, who visited the Farnese Villa in 1581, the area was so barren and alpine that the Cardinal had to draw the water for his fountains from Viterbo, eight miles away.[47] And although the stables were not yet built at the time of Montaigne's visit, it is quite possible that the well on the upper side of the stables was supplied by the same source as the garden's fountains (4.25).

Once a site had been chosen and a water supply assured, the aspect for the stables had to be decided. Theoretical texts usually recommended that the stable should run east to west, enabling the majority of windows to be positioned on the southern and northern aspects. Much of course depended on the geography of the location and the space available, so that architects were not always able to pursue the perceived ideal. However, some examples do conform and although the Medici's Cafaggiolo stables were built a century before Corte's treatise, he might be describing them as having the ideal aspect. Corte writes that stables should be

> Well positioned and situated in such a way that, towards midday, it only lacks the northern light; so that in winter this part will be closed and shut and, in the summer, open.

He continues by describing how large doors should be placed opposite each other half way down the stable block, one facing 'the midday sun and the other the north', which would help to regulate the temperature inside the stable, as well as assisting with access for the horses. Corte then adds details of the windows, which should be 'from one aisle to the other' and 'large enough and numerous enough, as the beauty and use of the stable demands'.[48]

Corte's specifications were not new to the Renaissance. They, like many aspects of equestrian culture were following a classical ideal, in this instance the fourth-century Palladius, who had recommended that the stables should

> Look towards the southern part of the heavens, but let them not be without windows from the north, which being shut during the winter may not be hurtful [and] when opened in the summer they will be refreshing.[49]

Palladius also suggested that the courtyard should be

> open to the south and exposed to the sun, whereby it may more easily receive some warmth in the winter for the sake of the animals that are there.[50]

This advice still held good for Pasqual Caracciolo,

> Palladius wishes that the stables for either oxen or horses should face south, but so that they neither lack nor are deprived of north facing windows, so that being closed in the winter, nothing would harm them and, being open in the summer, would refresh them.[51]

The Venetian Vincenzo Scamozzi, whose *L'idea della architettura* was published in 1615, prescribed different aspects, varying them according to the local climate in order to keep the stables at a suitable temperature:

> If the area is cold, the [stable] should face south, towards the Garbino,[52] but if it is hot and humid then it is better that it faces the Levant, towards the Tramontana.

And he later adds:

> In temperate areas the stalls should be lit, at least from one side, and it would be better from two, but in those [places] which are hot, you should not have direct light, either from the south or the west because each one of them is harmful to the horse.[53]

Only in certain circumstances were Italian stables built running east to west with a southern aspect. This was more likely to be possible in the countryside where space permitted, as found at both Francesco Gonzaga's and Federico Gonzaga's later stables on the Isola Te;[54] the Bentivoglio stables at Ponte Poledrano; the Medici stables at Cafaggiolo and Alessandro Farnese's Lo Stallone at Caprarola. In addition to the correct aspect, the stables at Cafaggiolo have larger windows on the south side than on the north, indicating the concern with keeping the stable's temperature as constant as possible. In contrast, the great stables at Poggio a Caiano seem to have been built for the convenience of those arriving via the approach roads, so that they run north-south; and in the city of Vigevano, the three Sforza stables are positioned to surround the palace's five-sided courtyard with only the earliest of the three stables having an aspect that could be said to face south.

Evidence shows that Renaissance specifications for a stable's site very much followed those of earlier classical authors. Certainly, architects gave priority to the security of the horses, most specifying that the stable should be sited near to the main residence and under the watchful eye of the owner and, as for a palace, it was common sense for stables to be built close to good quality water. The water shortages that the Gonzaga's stud farm experienced in the Sermide basin may well have been precipitated by too many horses grazing on the available land, as barren pastures soon lead to sickness especially in the heat of summer when mares require lush grass to produce milk for their foals. Similarly, it is logical to expect that cold winter air blowing through north-facing windows could cause dangerous chilling to a sweating horse. However, the fact that specifications for a stable's ideal site remained the same for so many centuries should not be seen as Renaissance theory simply emulating earlier ideas; these well-practised ideals were tried and tested, requiring little or no innovation to securely house healthy, useful horses. As will be shown in the next two chapters stable architecture, both exterior and interior, would also be influenced by classical precedent. Thus the stable would become an elegant building, not only benefitting the horses but contributing to the magnificence of their patron.

1 Xenophon, *Memorabilia and Oeconomicus*, trans. E.C. Marchant (London and New York, 1923), XII, p. 23-4, (Ischomachus to Socrates).
2 Corte, 1562, I, ch. 36, 46r.
3 Lucius Junius Moderatus Columella, 'De re rustica', 9 Books (1st century AD), trans. as *On Agriculture*, Books 1-4 trans. H. B. Ash (Cambridge MA and London, 1941-55), Books 5-9 trans. E. S. Forster and E. H. Hefner (Cambridge MA, 1968).
4 Rutilius Taurus Aemilianus Palladius, 'Opus agriculturae' (4th century AD), trans. T. Owen as *The Fourteen Books of Palladius Rutilius Taurus Æmilianus, On Agriculture* (London, 1807).
5 Corte, 1562, I, ch. 36, 45v-46r. See *On Horsemanship*, 1962, p. 313; Aristotle, *Oeconomica* (4th century BC), trans. E. S. Forster (Oxford, 1920), I:6 1345a, 'The sayings of the Persian and the Libyan may not come amiss; the former of whom, when asked what was the best thing to fatten a horse, replied, "His master's eye" while the Libyan, when asked what was the best manure, answered, "The landowner's footprints"'; Plutarch, *The Morals* (c.100 AD), trans. A. R. Shilleto, 5 vols (London, 1898), I, 'On education', ch. XIII, p. 23.
6 Corte uses the word *generoso*, translated as 'well-bred' and therefore as 'thoroughbred'.
7 Corte, 1562, I, ch. 36, 45v-46r.
8 Caracciolo, 1589, VII, p. 569. (Note: the first edition of *La gloria* was dated 1566).
9 Alberti, CV, p. 89. Videtta, p. 166.
10 Alberti, *De re aedificatore*, trans. J. Rykwert, N. Leach, R. Tavernor, *On the Art of Building in Ten Books* (Cambridge, MA & London, 1988), V, ch. 17, p. 150.
11 Scamozzi, *L'idea della architettura* (1615), Part 1, III, ch. XVII, 'Le stalle per le razze de' cavalli', p. 301.

12 Vasari, *Vite* (1966), V, 'Giulio Romano', p. 65.
13 Galeazzo Maria's stables are 56 and 50 metres long.
14 L. Giordano, '"La polita stalla": Leonardo, i trattatisti e le scuderie rinascimentali', *Viglevanum: Miscellanea di studi storici e artistici*, XIX (April, 2009), pp. 6-15, p. 13, citing A. Monciatti, *Il palazzo Vaticano nel Medioevo* (Florence, 2005), p. 141.
15 Francesco di Giorgio Martini in ed. C. Maltese *Trattati di architettura, ingegneria e arte militare*, 2 vols (Milan, 1967), II, p. 340. In this work, Maltese has merged two copies of Francesco di Giorgio's treatise: Siena, Biblioteca Comunale, MS S. IV. 4e and Florence, Biblioteca Nazionale, MS Magliabechiana II. 1. 141.
16 Vasari, *Vite* (1966), III, 'Michelozzo', p. 236 and see D. Mazzini and S. Martini, *Villa Medici a Fiesole: Leon Battista Alberti e il prototipo di villa rinascimentale* (Florence, 2004).
17 See D. Mignani, 'Le scuderie granducale nei sotterranei del fabbricato degli Uffizi' in eds Benedetto and Padovani, Governare l'Arte, Oct. 2008 (Prato), pp. 224-234.
18 I am grateful to Marco Giardano and Fabio Soldatini for this information.
19 Designed by Pagno di Lapo Portigiani, c.1460, for Santo and then Giovanni II Bentivoglio. The Bentivoglio Palace was destroyed in 1507.
20 Another contemporary description confirming the location of these two stables is found in Bologna, Archivio del Convento di San Francesco, MS 35, Giovan Battista and Giangaleazzo Bottrigari, *Ricordi (700-1554)*, 300r-v, 'Haveva poi dal canto di drieto due grandissime stale fate in volta oltre la principale e magiore de tute, posta dinanzi al'opposito del palazzo, mediante la piaza', cited in Antonelli and Poli, *Il Palazzo dei Bentivoglio* (2006), p. 100.
21 Bologna, Biblioteca comunale dell'Archiginnasio, Archivio Gozzadini, I, b. 3, Libro di ricordi (1480-1590) di Alessandro Gozzadini, 47r-48r., cited in Antonelli and Poli, *Il Palazzo dei Bentivoglio* (2006), p. 76.
22 Filarete, Antonio di Pietro Averlino (1400-1460), *Libro architettonico* 25 vols (c.1464), VIII, 58r-v. For an illustration of Filarete's groundplan see 57v 'D'. See J. R. Spencer, trans. and ed., *Filarete's Treatise on Architecture*, 2 vols (New Haven and London, 1965), I, p. 100.
23 Columella, *On Agriculture* (1941), I, p. 59.
24 Corte, 1562, I, ch. 38, 49r.
25 Alberti, *CV*, p. 83. Videtta, p.158.
26 The Margonara stud farm was close to Governolo. The buildings no longer exist.
27 Mantua, ASMa, AG, b. 258, *Sì che per me stimo che tutti li mali che sono occorsi in queste razze per il passato e ch'occorrono di presente, intendomi di quelle che sono affatto incogniti, derivano da i cibi e dall'acqua, havendo io osservato che gl'erbaggi sono sì in quantità opulentissima, ma in qualità hanno troppo del morbido e che l'acque tutte hanno del feccioso, massimamente in quelle stagioni che sono andate asciutte per molti anni, atteso che rendono le sortie così basse ch'appena vi si può affondare la secchia senza intorbidar l'acqua; cosa molto dannosa, stante che quella parte fecciosa che fa l'acqua, è necessario che faccia la sua residenza, e nei polmoni, e nel diafragma, ovvero nei vasi dell'urina . . .*
28 For information on the findings in the Sermide valley, see G. Gozzi, 'Il territorio mantovano: studio di geologia', *Civiltà Mantovana*, 1:37 (1973), pp. 69-118, p. 111.
29 Naples, ASN, Sommaria, Dipendenze 1, 36, fasc, 2, *Cunto et libro de le dispese se fando a la cavallaricza de lo illustrissimo signor duca in Marczanise, per me, notario Monado scrivano de racione, in quella et primo per incasare paglia de fare mete de quisto anno VI indictione 1488*, 17r-50v. See 27r-v, 28v. See L. Gennari *Struttura e manutenzione della cavallerizza regia di Marcianise (1488-1493)* (Salerno, 2006), p. 21 and Appendix II, pp. 47-8.
30 Gennari, *Struttura e manutenzione* (2006), p. 21.
31 The Sieve is a tributary of the Arno. Although not certain, it is likely that this channel was man-made. The stream is now underground but exits a culvert level with the east end of the stables.
32 It should be noted that, until recently, the Cafaggiolo stables served as farm buildings. Over the years, alterations have been made and different uses adopted for the different areas. The 'reservoir' was covered and used as a weigh-station within living memory.
33 A recent article has named 'Il Tribolo' (Niccolò di Raffaello di Niccolò) as architect of the stables. They had previously been attributed to Baccio Bigio (Bartolomeo Lippi), a generation earlier, with later alterations by Il Tribolo. It is now believed that Baccio Bigio built and may also have designed the Medici San Marco stables in Florence. See Daniela Lamberini, 'Il Tribolo ingegnere e i lavori al Poggio a Caiano', *Niccolò, detto il Tribolo, tra arte, architettura e paesaggio*, eds E. Pieri, L. Zangheri (Signa, 2001), pp. 173-85.
34 Florence, ASF, *Guardaroba Mediceo*, F. 136, 434r-5v. Cited in F. Gurrieri and D. Lamberini, *Le scuderie della Villa Medicea di Poggio a Caiano* (Bologna, 1980), p. 19.
35 Scamozzi, *L'idea della architettura* (1615), Part 1, II, ch. XXII, p. 177.
36 Piccolomini, *The Commentaries of Pius II*, Books I-IX, trans. F. A. Gragg (Northampton, MA, 1936-7), IX, p. 600.
37 Even today, although in poor structural condition, the stables remain dry. This is partly due to the important methods of draining water away through pipes but also to the stable's 'double' ceiling. Above the roof of the stable is an empty ventilated chamber about a metre high, before a second roof, which supports the hanging garden.
38 Piccolomini, *The Commentaries* (1936-7), IX, p. 598.
39 The system of open semi-circular pipes is reminiscent of the Arabic *falaj* system of irrigation. Due to poor light, it was not possible to take photographs of these pipes. As an alternative, sketches have been made.
40 For a comprehensive study of water supply and storage in Pienza see Umberto Bindi, *Pienza, i luoghi dell'acqua. Dalle fonti della Pieve di Corsignano alla Bonifica della Val d'Orcia* (Montepulciano, 2002).
41 Giannantonio Campano, *Pii II vita* (before 1474) cited and translated in C.R. Mack *Pienza:the Creation of a Renaissance City* (Ithaca and London, 1987), Appendix 1, doc. 6, pp. 177-9, especially p. 179, '[Pius] had planned to . . . create a lake in the territory of Pienza after damming the river Orcia and diverting the same stream at the base of Mount Amiata'. See also Mack, *Pienza* (1987), p. 155 and Appendix 1, docs 3 and 4, in which the poems of Lodrisio Crivelli and Porcellio Pandomi also mention the Pope's intention to create a lake.
42 Paris, Institut de France, MS. B, 38v-39r. Pedretti (1977) II, p. 39. Taking the Florentine *braccia* as 58.36 cms. Leonardo's pool

would have been 88cms (35 inches) deep, enough to reach a horse's stomach.
43 Bernardino Baldi, 'Descrizione del Palazzo ducale d'Urbino di Bernardino Baldi da Urbino Abbate di Guastalla' (1586-7), ch. XVI, 'Artifitii del Palazzo'. See *Descrittione del Palazzo ducale d'Urbino,* ed. A. Siekera, *Studi e ricerche,* 87 (Alessandria, Italy, 2010), p. 565.
44 The villa was begun by Cardinal Alessandro Farnese in 1530, under the architect Antonio da Sangallo the Younger. When Alessandro was elected Pope in 1534, as Paul III, the project was halted until his grandson, also Cardinal Alessandro, continued the project under Giacomo Barozzi da Vignola *c*.1555.
45 When Giacomo Barozzi da Vignola died in 1573, Alessandro Farnese did not appoint a new architect but employed Garzoni, who had already been responsible for the Farnese hunting lodge, the Barco, the expansion of the *pescheria* and the Palazzina del Piacere in the gardens above the villa. See C. Robertson, *'Il Gran Cardinale', Alessandro Farnese, Patron of the Arts* (Yale, New Haven & London, 1992), pp. 87-8.
46 A survey by Sebastiano Cipriani, dated 26 June, 1704, following earthquake damage in January and February, 1703, stated that 'from the shape of its stalls' ('a forma delle sue poste') the stable could hold 112 horses, but later surveys suggest that it held 120 horses. See Enzo Bentivoglio, 'Le scuderie di Palazzo Farnese a Caprarola. I 'remedi' proposti da Giovanni Battista Contini e Sebastiano Cipriani dopo il terremoto del 1703 (dai MSS. 34 K13 e 34 K14 della Biblioteca Corsiniana di Roma', *Quaderni del Dipartimento di Patrimonio Architettonico e Urbanistico,* Anno XIV, 27.28, pp. 181- 90, p. 184.
47 Montaigne, *The Complete Works* (2003), p. 1254.
48 Corte, 1562, I, ch. 36, 'Della stalla & sue pertinentie', 47r-v.
49 Palladius, *The fourteen books* (1807), I, ch XXI, 'Of stables and ox-stalls', p. 32.
50 Ibid. I, ch. XXII, p. 32-3.
51 Caracciolo, 1589, VII, p. 573, 'Palladio vuole, che la magione sì de' cavalli, e sì de' Buoi, guardi al Mezo giorno: ma che nõ haggia bisogno, nè sia priva de i lumi del Settentrione, i quali nel verno chiusi niente offenderanno, e la state apperti rinfrescheranno.'
52 The 'Garbino' is a south-westerly wind also known in Italy as the 'Africo' or 'Libeccio'. It is known for bringing heat, and sometimes Saharan sand, from Africa.
53 Scamozzi, *L'idea della architettura* (1615), Part 1, II, ch. XXII, pp. 177, *se il regione sara fredda, si volterà l'aspetto à mezo dì, à Garbona, mà se fosse calda, e stemperata, all'hora sarà meglio à Levante, à Tramontana.* The Tramontana is a cold northerly wind.
54 In documents referring to stud farms and stables on and near the Te island, both the San Sebastiano and the San Biagio stables are mentioned. From a 1628 plan of Mantua, it appears that the San Sebastiano stables were to the west of the San Sebastiano palace (built between 1506-8), and that the stables situated further away on the Island may have been called San Biagio. For this book, the stud farm stables on the island will be referred to as the Te stables.

For *gineti* on the cheek. Brand for the Brothers of Santa Maria de Tremito, this stud farm is in Abruzzo, the brand goes on the right flank

Chapter 5

The Stable as Spectacle

> The stables of a prince should be close to his courtyard, so that whether all or some of the horses are brought out to eat, joust or do anything else, the prince, being in the gallery of his palace, can see them; and when foreign princes visit him, they can be suitably lodged.
> Pellegrino Tibaldi (sixteenth century).[1]

As with any valued commodity the Renaissance court horse required suitable and secure housing. But, in designing and constructing the court stable, there was often another important aspect for the architect to consider: the deliberate and ostentatious display of the horses themselves. Consequently, a significant amount of thought and expense went into stable design, complementing the attention given to a suitable location and access to good quality water. This chapter considers the factors that influenced a stable's appearance and the ways in which the stable developed into an autonomous building within the court. Research shows that the stable's exterior appearance was influenced by established architectural forms such as the Greek temple, the basilica or the cloister, sometimes adapted to suit a specific site. Architects also had to consider the ideal ground plan for the horses' welfare and the various requirements of each patron, often adding elaborate decorative details to a stable's façades. In doing so the Renaissance stable became a specific space in which horses could be exhibited to select members of society, often displaying a owner's magnificence. Such displays were, as Giles Worsley writes, 'a critical function of stable design [and] at least as important as [the horses'] practical management'.[2]

That the ostentatious display of horses in a stable could be described by Worsley as a deliberate act of self propaganda,[3] suggests that Renaissance princes were showing off their collections of horses in much the same way as they showed off other collections such as paintings, books or antiquities. Like other valuable commodities, horses required a suitable space in which to be viewed, and, for them, it was the elegant well-lit architectural background and tidy surroundings of their stable that contributed to their display. Ownership of a valued collection of any kind indicated not only a specialist knowledge in acquiring it, but also for maintaining it in good condition; a collection of horses was no different. Moreover, evidence shows that while the central court stable might be used for viewing the horses, it was principally stud farm stables in the countryside that were used for equine displays, some even having special stands for spectators, such as in Ferrara and Mantua.[4] Letters indicate that Gonzaga stud farms were visited both by court staff and by important visitors for whom displays were arranged. For example, in 1515 the Gonzaga factor at Marmirolo advised Marquis Francesco that the Cardinal of Aragon, natural brother of King Alfonso I of Sicily, had been pleased by his visit to the *palazzina* and that, after dinner, he had been entertained by a display of the *gineta* stallions which he had praised highly, followed by a parade of the *gineta* and Turkish mares with their foals.[5] In November that same year, Marquis Francesco would take his brother, Cardinal Sigismondo Gonzaga, to the island of Te, where they watched colts 'of every breed' from the San Biagio stables[6] – no doubt in the specially designated showing area with the Mantuan lake as a backdrop. A letter from the Gonzaga agent, Aurelio Recordati, dated 10 May 1538, illustrates first hand the delight provided by a beautiful stable of horses. Even allowing for flattery, Recordati appears genuinely impressed when writing to Marquis Federico in Mantua,

> Yesterday, for amusement, immediately after dining, I went to Gonzaga to look at Your Excellency's horses, which, as they were all in the stable, I caused to be brought out under the portico one by one, which made a good display and, in a word, all of them were superb. Also, as many of them have become so beautiful, they deserve to be named, so I asked what they were called. My short memory brings them to mind so that I can write [about]them . . . Amongst those that I remember are Campagna, the barbary, which has become as beautiful as a *ginetto*; those two barbaries that are guelded, . . . Migono [and] Favorito . . . [and] especially [the barbary] Aquila, which has not only developed a magnificent body . . . but shines like a mirror and dances over the ground.[7]

Apart from such open-air displays of horses, guests also had the opportunity to see the horses when they were lodged above stables, which had accommodation on the upper floors, often of significant elegance. This was the case at three sixteenth-century stable-guesthouses, *foresterie*, which are particularly notable: Agostino Chigi's stable on the west bank of the Tiber, designed by Raphael, Duke Cosimo de' Medici's stable for his villa at Poggio a Caiano, designed by Il Tribolo[8] and Vignola's stables designed for Alessandro Farnese's villa at Caprarola. In 1741 it was claimed by the Caprarola superintendent, Leopoldo Sebastiani, that Pope Gregory XIII's entourage had stayed in these impressive Farnese stables in September 1578 and that a triumphal arch was built over the Viterbo road joining the stables to the Farnese gardens.[9] In fact, Sebastiani's anecdote must have been fabricated as records show that Lo Stallone – referred to in archives as the new stables (*stalla nova*) – were still having foundations laid five years later in 1583.[10] It seems more likely, therefore, that the papal entourage stayed at the old stables (*stalla vecchia*), which records show had been refurbished.[11] Exactly where these 'old' stables were situated is difficult to ascertain but a topographical drawing of Caprarola by Jacques Lemercier (1608) shows a stable, almost identical to Vignola's design, standing to the left of the circular court (5.1). However, the legend in a slightly later map by Villamana (1617) explains that this building, together with an almost identical one designed by Vignola as servants' quarters, was built in a different location alongside the Villa's gardens.[12] Despite this explanation, two buildings remain either side of the circular court. It is possible that the left-hand building was the stable in which the papal entourage lodged, although it is now precariously close to a precipitous drop and there would be no room for the exercise yard depicted by Lemercier. Just as impressive as Vignola's design is Bramante's plan for what may have been a three-storey stable as part of Julius II's renovations for the Vatican, a theory put forward by Henry Dietrich Fernández.[13] A drawing in Florence, made in Bramante's workshop and dated 1505-7, clearly shows the location and outline for the Pope's stables with a ramped staircase (5.2).[14] According to Frommel, Bramante's design was following Nicholas V's mid fifteenth-century stable plans with a library on the first floor.[15] Either way, Bramante's stable building would have been unique had it been built.

Renaissance stables, therefore, were not simply protective buildings for the horses, they became exhibition spaces, places of entertainment and sometimes formed part of the guest accommodation. As such, they not only played a significant role in court life, they were buildings

5.1. Jacques Lemercier, *Scenografia generale del Palazzo di Caprarola*, 1608. The old stables are left foreground.
Biblioteca Apostolica Vaticana – Disegni. VcBA 10008202 ©BAV. All rights reserved

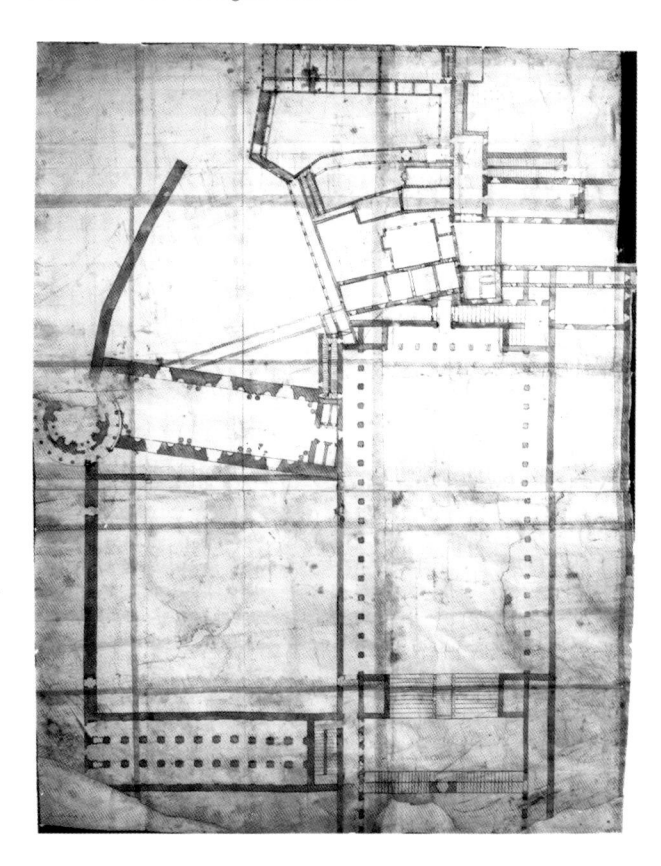

5.2. Antonio da Sangallo the Younger for Bramante, 1505-7, project for the renovation of the Vatican. The stables are left foreground.
Florence, Uffizi, Gabinetto dei disegni e delle stampe. Courtesy of Ministero per i beni e le attività culturali, Galllerie degli Uffizi

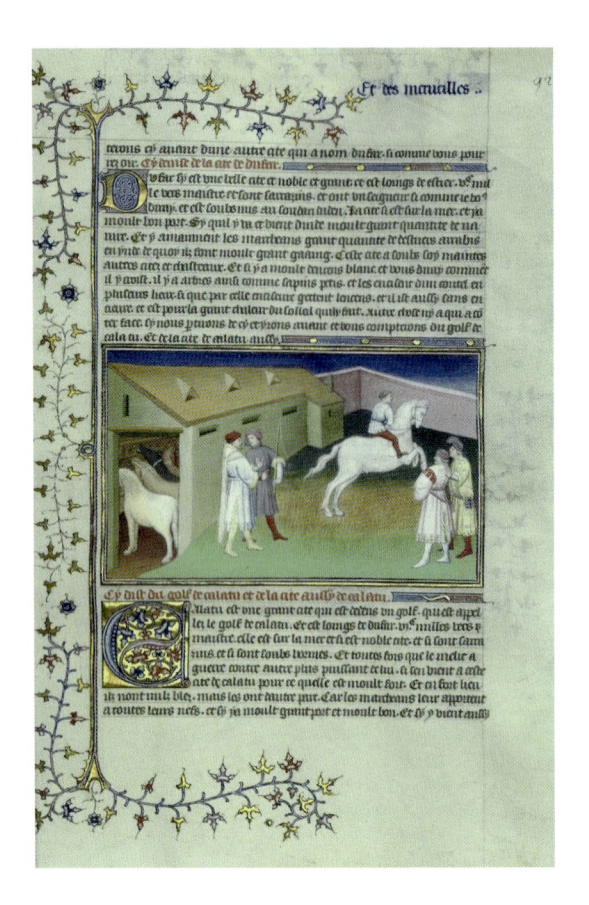

5.3. Stone built stables. Master of Mazarine, 'Sale of Arab horses' in Marco Polo, *Livre des merveilles*, c.1430. Paris, Bibliothèque nationale de France, fr. 2810, 92r © BnF

for which renowned architects made designs and on which patrons could lavish money. Those considered here were built between 1450 and *c*.1600 and include a variety of patrons: royalty,[16] aristocracy,[17] popes,[18] cardinals,[19] bankers and the Venetian Republic. Although the latter two categories might not be thought of as having princely courts, the bankers, the Medici family and the Pope's Sienese banker Agostino Chigi[20] were amongst the richest men in Europe and were equal to the Renaissance princes of the time in their spending on stabling for horses. From 1495-1530, the Venetian Republic would have the use of Alfonso of Aragon's[21] stables near Alberobello in Puglia. Known as La Cavallerizza,[22] this valuable breeding and training area for the Republic's military horses[23] is worthy of consideration because of its unusual Puglian architecture and magnificent schooling ground and pastures in the Canale di Pilo.[24] It should also be noted that in the most powerful courts, rulers' wives sometimes emulated European queen consorts by having their own stables run separately to those of their husbands. There is no evidence to indicate if there was any difference in design or management of these female-owned stables. In Mantua, Isabella d'Este had her own riding and hunt horses as well as racehorses running under her name, as did her mother, Eleanora of Aragon, Duchess of Ferrara, who employed ten stable staff supervised by Donato da Milano.[25] Letters between Isabella and her husband, Francesco Gonzaga, show that in 1492 when Isabella's Barbary stallion Safinato won a *palio* in Gonzaga, Francesco asked her to return the horse to him – a request she declined.[26] Records show that in 1476, Bona of Savoy, wife of Galeazzo Maria Sforza, ordered a seneschal to 'assign half the stable

5.4. Brick and wood stables. Liévin van Latham c.1460, *Les Miracles de Notre Dame*. Paris, Bibliothèque nationale de France, fr. 9199, 65r ©BnF

facilities at Galliate Castle to her own court',[27] indicating that she wanted control over her own horses and mules.

Wherever the stables were situated, whether at the main court complex or in the countryside, the stable staff and professional riders required accommodation and important trades such the *maniscalco*, the bridle maker and saddler needed conveniently placed smithies[28] and workrooms. In addition, the horses' fodder and bedding required dry storage and the often extravagantly decorated caparisons and tack needed secure housing. It is often difficult to ascertain where these service quarters were situated and few medieval stables remain to help analyse what developments there might have been in Renaissance design to change the stable's layout. However, two fifteenth-century manuscripts and an Italian fourteenth-century court stable serve as rare evidence for the medieval period. Firstly, an early fifteenth-century depiction of a stable by the French Master of Mazarine shows horses feeding from hayracks and mangers in a stone-built structure (5.3). The stable appears to have vents in the thatched roof, indicating that either this space was used for fodder storage or as accommodation, while a chimney at the far end suggests that this section may have been a farrier's workshop. This illuminated manuscript also gives useful information on feeding stations, the horses depicted in a single line with no dividing rails between them. In contrast, a late fifteenth-century Flemish manuscript clearly depicts a two-storey brick and wood structure with a tiled roof and exterior staircase (5.4). Here, the horses also stand in a single line but are separated by poles attached by rope to wooden pillars at the

5.5. Castello Visconteo, Pavia. The stables are in the wing to the left. Wikimedia Commons/Tempo61

5.6. Castello Visconteo, Pavia. The west-wing subterranean stables, fourteenth century. Image courtesy of Musei Civici del Castello Visconteo, Pavia

end of the stall. There is, nevertheless, no evidence that either of these styles of stable was built in Italy, and despite them being free-standing buildings they seem distinctly rustic when compared to the magnificent court stable in Pavia dating from the fourteenth century (5.5, 5.6). Built for Galeazzo II Visconti, these stables occupy the entire west side of the Castello Visconteo at subterranean level. The 720 square-metre floor area, is broken into nine bays by eight Gothic arches, which are 5.35 metres at the highest point and which span the wide floor space (5.6). The outer walls have feeding troughs indicating that there could be twenty horses tethered in each bay, giving a capacity for at least 180 horses. These stables were still in use over a hundred years later when Galeazzo's descendent, Galeazzo Maria Sforza, was ruler of Milan and it can be assumed that they were still functioning efficiently. Certainly, the rectangular basilica outline was one of the most successful stable ground plans, which would continue throughout the following centuries.

5.7. The Ducal castle at Urbino, with the circular ramp to La Data stables in the foreground

The decision by some patrons to build stables in the subterranean level of their principal residence had two main advantages: it kept the horses secure and allowed convenient and discreet access for the owner. Both were necessary considerations for either a *condottiere* ruler, such as Federico da Montefeltro at Urbino, who might want to prepare his horses or join his troops inconspicuously, or Galeazzo Visconti, who faced several rebellions as ruler of Milan. Both the subterranean stables at Urbino (see 4.4) and at Pavia were made of brick and designed to have horses tethered in lines facing the outer walls, with a wide aisle running between them, a stable plan already established in the twelfth century – as at Crac des Chevaliers (see 4.5). In comparison, this ground plan was not used in the papal stables at Pienza where Pius II's subterranean stables are divided into five aisles, each with four bays. Here, circular columns support the double roof space between the stabling and the hanging garden above, a plan which the Pope's architect, Bernardo Rossellino, designed for keeping the stables dry – using the intervening vaulted space for fodder storage. However, in this case, as already shown in Chapter 4, the construction was also functional.[29]

These three subterranean stables, despite their size, were service buildings rather than part of any overt or ostentatious display of power or wealth. They were not the brightly lit spaces seen at Vigevano or Poggio a Caiano, where windows on either side of the building would flood natural light over the horses. When, in the 1480s, Federico da Montefeltro commissioned Francesco di Giorgio Martini to design his third stable,[30] now known as La Data, this building, reputed by the architect to have held as many as 300 horses, was evidence of the Duke's wealth and power not simply from its size but from its location (5.7).[31] To maintain his private access from the castle, the Duke had a majestic circular ramp built to reach his new stables, which stretched along the edge of the city as part of the perimeter walls below his private apartments and which are now partially restored. Francesco di Giorgio speaks with considerable pride of

5.8. Federico Barocci, *Crucifixion*, 1604 (detail). The damaged La Data stables are seen centre left.
© Photographic Archive Museo Nacional del Prado, Madrid

these stables in his treatise on architecture, giving one of the earliest detailed descriptions of a Renaissance stable. Although little evidence of it remains, research shows that this stable would set a precedent for certain aspects of stable design, with trap doors allowing for hay and straw to be thrown down directly from the upper floor into the stables. Having poor foundations, the roof soon collapsed, a detail that is visible in the lower left section of Federico Barocci's 1604 *Crucifixion* (5.8). In addition, the building suffered not only from earthquakes and landslides but also from considerable alterations over the intervening years. However, paintings and recent comprehensive archaeological studies, supported by contemporary documentation, help to build a picture of how spectacular they must have looked to any visitor, especially if approaching Urbino from the west (5.9).[32] Certainly, by 1506, the city had trouble finding sufficient stabling for Julius II's court. Elisabetta Gonzaga, Duchess of Urbino and wife of Guidobaldo da Montefeltro, would write to her brother, Francesco Marquis of Mantua, having received his list of those in the Pope's entourage who required accommodation. Explaining that Urbino was 'neither like Mantua nor Ferrara', she wrote that the small city would not be able to accommodate more than sixteen people and fifty horses for each of the thirty cardinals, senior prelates and ambassadors who, in addition to the foot and horse guards, were accompanying the Pope.[33] A temporary solution seems to have been used: there is evidence from existing iron rings that some horses were tethered to the outer walls of the Mercatale, although this area would not have given the horses much shelter.[34]

Fluctuations in horse numbers were regular occurrences for Renaissance courts and cities, both from extra cavalry horses and those of visitors. In 1450, the *condottiere* and Captain

5.9. La Data stables seen from the West: Gaspar van Wittel, 1652/3-1726. View of Urbino, detail. New York, The Morgan Library and Museum. 1956.10. Gift of Paul Fatio

General of Milan, Ludovico Gonzaga, was known to have kept 1,300 regular cavalry which he boosted to 3,000 in wartime.[35] Although it is not clear exactly where these 1,300 Gonzaga cavalry horses were stabled, it was not unusual for a ruler to have several stables close to his main residence. For example, as seen in Chapter 4, the Bolognese ruler, Giovanni II Bentivoglio, stabled his cavalry horses and his guards in a large stable opening onto the piazza in front of his palace, while the more elegant private stabling, Scuderia di Messer Annibale, was situated within the palace grounds (see 4.3). Even without military horses, stabling requirements increased considerably when a ruler accommodated his guests' horses as well as those of his court. As Pellegrino Tibaldi explained, a prince's stable should be close to the palace piazza so that 'when foreign princes visit him, [their horses] can be suitably lodged'.[36] Court or visiting horses which could not be housed in the main court complex, often had to be stabled further afield in surrounding estates or properties. As shown in Chapter 2, Galeazzo Maria Sforza's court had travelled to Florence with a vast entourage in 1471, but even his two Vigevano stables could not accommodate all the horses belonging to his court in 1476, which numbered over 1,000 – the total given by one of Duke Galeazzo Maria's officials, when drawing up a list of 'all those assigned to ride with the court . . . to whom one has to give lodgings'.[37] And it was perhaps for this reason that the Milanese duke issued his courtiers with ordinances on the management of their stables, as was the case for the ducal secretary, Cicco Simonetta.[38]

There were, of course, considerable advantages for a guest housed in his host's *foresteria* or to have his horses stabled close to the main residence, not only for the convenience in joining any court entertainments but also for his status; the more important guests or courtiers being

5.10. Villa Medici, Poggio a Caiano

5.11. Villa Medici, Poggio a Caiano. Arcading used as temporary stabling

entitled to the more convenient stabling. In practice this did not always happen. An exchange of mid sixteenth-century letters illustrates that there was a shortage of court stabling at Poggio a Caiano – the villa designed in the 1480s by Giuliano da Sangallo for Lorenzo de' Medici – which became one of the Medici's most popular country houses in the sixteenth century (5.10). The letters show that, prior to the completion of Il Tribolo's stables for Duke Cosimo in the mid-sixteenth century, there was insufficient stabling at the Medici villa. Francesco de Marchi, courtier and military architect in the service of Duke Alessandro de' Medici's wife, Margaret of Austria, wrote in his *Architettura militare* that the loggias around the villa 'could be used if there was a great quantity of horses' (5.11). Furthermore, anonymous documents from the first decade of the sixteenth century show that one of Sangallo's staircases was modified by adding three steps in order to make the loggia more accessible for the horses.[39] Certainly the arcaded loggias surrounding the Medici villa's lower floor are wide enough to shelter horses if tethered to the

5.12. La Cavallerizza, south and east sides. Image Piero Santoro, 1931

walls of the villa, although in bad weather it may have been necessary to give them more protection. Once this area was exhausted, it seems that horses and visitors were billeted amongst houses and farms on the Medici estate, such as La Cascina, the magnificent farm built by Lorenzo de' Medici in the 1470s, with such stabling allocated according to a precise hierarchical order. Or much to a courtier's inconvenience, the horse might be kept in the open – whatever his master's status – if his unfortunate servant arrived late. In October 1545 a letter from the ducal secretary, Lorenzo Pagni, pleads with the Duke's major-domo, Riccio, for the stable master to stop treating him so badly as, returning from ducal business in Siena, he found his stabling had been allocated to soldiers' horses.[40] It seems, therefore, that once any stabling close to the villa was exhausted, horses were sent further afield causing considerable inconvenience. No doubt, Il Tribolo's magnificent stables, built next to the Medici villa, went some way to solving this problem as not only could they hold over 200 horses, they could also accommodate visitors and staff in the twenty-six apartments on the spacious upper floor.

As the Renaissance progressed, the court stable became increasingly autonomous as a court building. And whether used to house a valuable collection of horses or to stable guests' horses on a temporary basis, the stable, like the palace or family chapel, would become an architectural category through which the prince could display his wealth. Apart from Vitruvius's use of the classical orders, early writers of equestrian and agricultural treatises had little impact on the exterior style of a stable's construction, only advising on the correct location and aspect, and only a few of them would write on the flooring and interior fittings – details which they believed affected the horse's health. However, Renaissance architects, such as Alberti, Francesco di Giorgio Martini, Leonardo da Vinci, Sebastiano Serlio and Vincenzo Scamozzi, as well as equestrian specialists such as Corte and Caracciolo, do suggest some exterior and interior details. For the exterior, architects often followed the regional style of architecture, whether the elaborate *peperino* carving for Agostino Chigi's Roman stables (see Chapter 2) or the conical *trulli* roofs for the Venetian stud farm complex in Puglia, La Cavallerizza (5.12). For the stable interior, there was a uniformity of design, with the conventional lay out evolving from the medieval barrel-vaulted stable, as seen at Urbino and Pavia, and developing into a pattern which mimicked the classical basilica form – a rectangular floor plan divided into three aisles – defined either by rows of columns or by heelposts. As in a church, the central aisle or nave, is slightly wider than

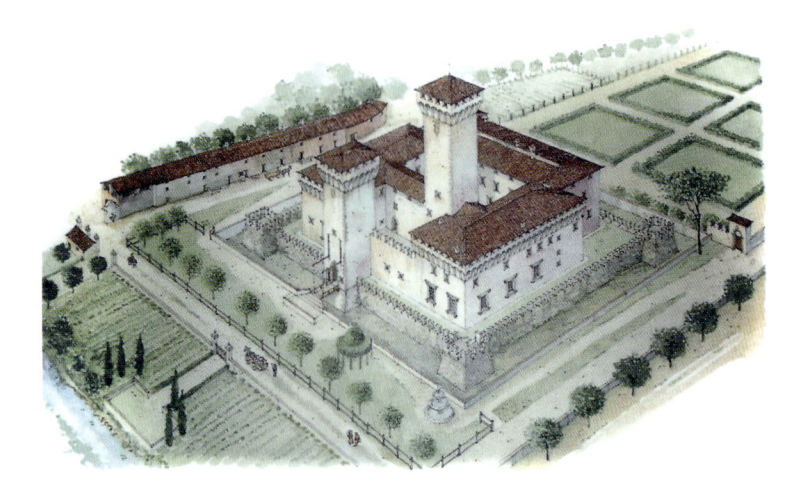

5.13. Cafaggiolo, reconstruction of 16th-century Medici villa and stables. Courtesy of Fabio Soldatini (2009)

5.14. Cafaggiolo, interior of Medici stables

the side aisles, with Corte suggesting that it should be at least two *canne* – about 4.5 metres or 15 feet – in width.[41] This central 'nave' was used for access, with the side aisles used for the horses, standing with their heads tethered to the outer walls and their tails towards the centre so that any manure or urine would drain into the gullies behind their back feet. A form of this ground plan was already in use in the mid-fifteenth century at Cafaggiolo – where the Medici stable is divided into bays – and has remained popular ever since (5.13, 5.14). The practicality of this layout usually meant that the horses could be seen from a single viewpoint; a factor which benefited both their care and their display.

All stables had at least one upper floor, some with as many as three. These levels served several different purposes: housing stable staff, militia or visiting guests in addition to storing fodder and straw. In some cases, there was a mixture of uses for these floors, as seen in Valvassori's plan of the four-storey Farnese stables at Caprarola where 100 horses could be housed on the ground floor. Here, the first floor was divided into a hay and fodder storage area (*fienele*), reached by a wide external ramp to the west end, with the remainder of this level and the upper floors used for staff and guest accommodation (5.15, 5.16). Both Giovanni II Bentivoglio's stables at Bologna and the Sforza's at Vigevano had militia on the upper floors; the latter housing

5.15. 'Lo Stallone', the Farnese stables at Caprarola.
Wikimedia commons/Medea

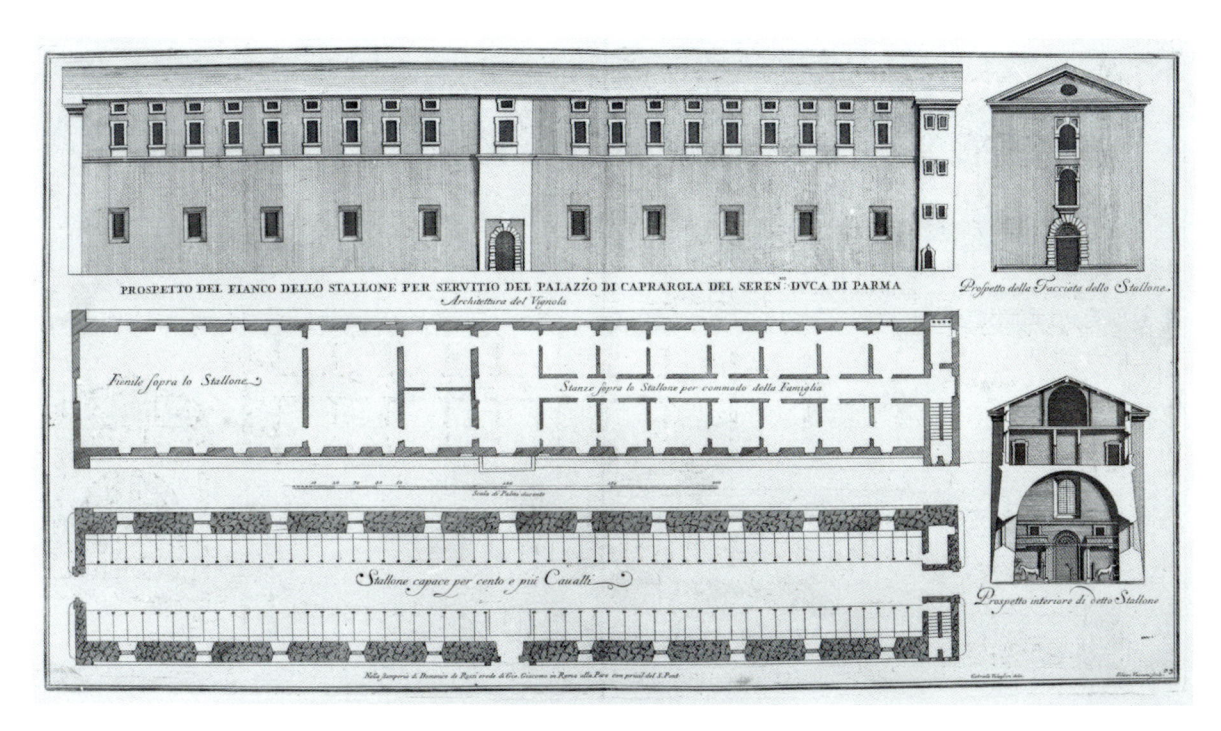

5.16. Farnese Stables, Caprarola. Elevation and plans of ground and first floor.
Domenico de' Rossi, ed., *Studio di architettura civile*, Rome 1702-1721, Plate 23. Gabriele Valvassori, engraved Filippo Nasconi. Rome, Istituto centrale per la Grafica, courtesy of Ministero per i beni e le attività culturali e per il turismo

top: elevations of the south façade and the main east entrance

centre: first-floor hay and fodder store is shown on the left, reached via an external ramp. To the right is the stable staff housing

lower: ground floor plan showing stabling for one hundred horses by marking out the stalls. The cross section indicates the height of the building with the barrel vaulted stable and the heelposts

5.17. Medici stables at Poggio a Caiano, principal façade. Wikimedia commons/Sailko

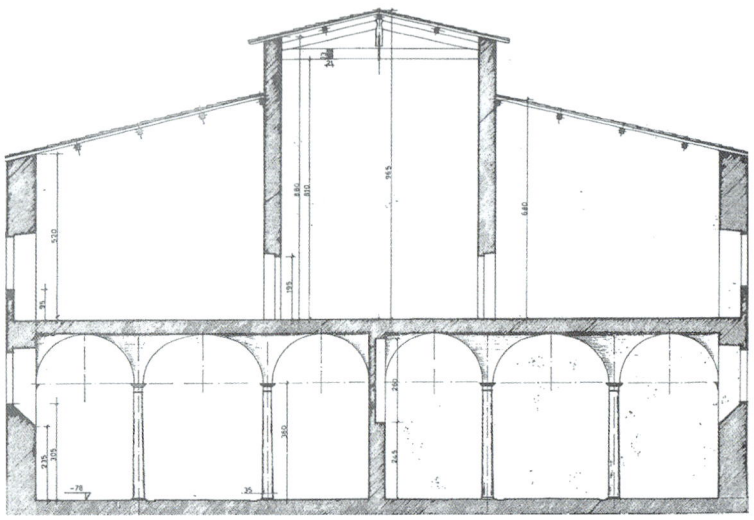

5.18. Cross-section of the Medici stables at Poggio a Caiano. Diagram Gurrieri and Lamberini, *Le Scuderie della Villa Medicea di Poggio a Caiano*

5.19. Medici stables at Poggio a Caiano, first-floor corridor with doorways to apartments

130

5.20. Tibaldi, La Rotonda from the Via delle Ore, Milan

Ludovico Sforza's guard had a central corridor on the first floor with rooms leading off it, each with a fireplace. The lay out at Vigevano was similar but not as elegant as the beautiful Medici building in Poggio a Caiano, where the twenty-six symmetrical apartments lead off the 15 feet-wide first-floor corridor, each having a fireplace on the interior wall, a window and a loft room in the roof space above it, presumably for a guest's servants (5.17).[42] A cross-section of these stables by Gurrieri and Lamberini shows Il Tribolo's original double-basilica stables with six aisles (5.18) – omitting the later ground-floor extension to the right of the building which would contain dog kennels. The diagram also illustrates the impressive height of the first-floor central corridor from which each apartment could be accessed (5.19).

An unusual variation of the basilica design was planned for the Spanish Neapolitan stables in 1584. A request from King Philip II's chief stable master (*caballerizo mayor*), Diego de Córdoba, resulted in a letter that year explaining that the two royal stables, known as La Maddalena and L'Incoronata were unsuitable for, and incapable of, keeping the 'mares and foals of His Majesty's royal breed comfortable'.[43] A new building was subsequently commissioned by the Viceroy, Pedro Téllez-Girón, 1st Duke of Osuna, from the military architect Giovan Vincenzo Casale in an area close to the city walls in the Via de Santa Maria della Stella. A sketch by Casale shows a low building of sombre classical design for both the exterior and the interior of the stable, which has three aisles, defined by Tuscan columns. But, unusually, the wide central aisle contains the stalls and mangers, while the side aisles were destined to house carriages and to be used for various services. Subsequently, the Spanish king halted the works and in 1592 instructed his Viceroy, the Count of Miranda, to maintain and alter the Maddalena stables instead. The stables were eventually completed in 1612, fourteen years after the king's death.[44]

There is a notable exception to the popular basilica ground plan: the beautifully proportioned three-storey decagonal stable designed by Pellegrino Tibaldi (also known as Pellegrini)[45] for Carlo Borromeo, which stands beside one of the main entrances to the Archbishop's palace in Milan and projects into the Via delle Ore (5.20). Known as 'La Rotonda', this relatively small stable housed eighteen mules on the lower level and eighteen riding horses on the main floor, with storage for fodder on the upper level.[46] The building follows classical precedent but is not based on a basilica; it is reminiscent of a Greek temple with access to the main floor through a *pronaos*, where four Doric columns support the pediment. The lower floor is reached via a cobbled path leading down from the Via delle Ore and via wide external steps from the principal

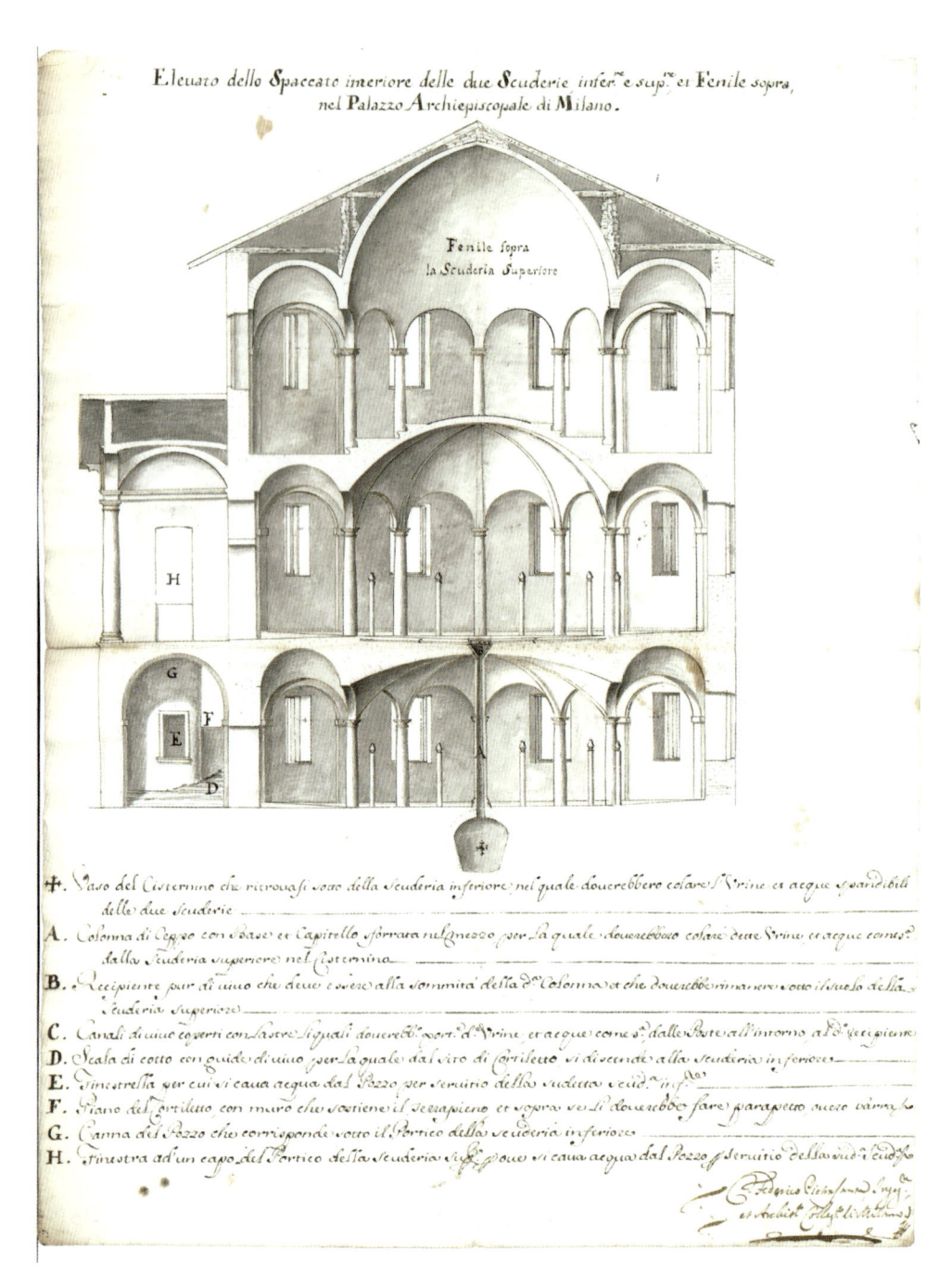

5.21. La Rotonda, Milan, vertical section showing the increasing height of the vaulted ceilings, entrance portico, well shaft, heelposts and pillars. C.F. Pietrasanta (1656-1729). Courtesy of Archivio Storico Diocesano di Milano, Mensa Arcivescovile, Palazzo Arcivescovile, cart. 3

level, while staff can access each of the three levels via a spiral staircase housed in a circular tower to the right of the *pronaos*. It is not known why the stable had such an unusual floor plan although, in the 1950s, Paredi put forward three suggestions:[47] the stable had been adapted from a deconsecrated baptismal church,[48] the ground plan was determined by the foundations of an earlier building, or simply that it was the solution to an awkward site. More recently, in 1987,

5.22. La Rotonda, main floor for 18 horses

5.23. La Rotonda, lower-ground floor for 18 mules, showing smaller windows

Both images courtesy of Fondazione Culturale Ambrosianeum, Milan

Richard Haslam concluded that the building was always intended as a stable.[49] But whatever the origins of this impractical design, the building does not allow for a central aisle. Instead it has a vaulted ambulatory on each floor, divided from the centre by ten pillars – those on the two lower levels have Doric capitals, those on the upper level are of the more elegant Ionic order. Certainly, Carlo Federico Pietrasanta's detailed drawings made at the turn of the seventeenth and eighteenth centuries, show some of the intricate detail of Tibaldi's unusual design (5.21). As can be seen, each floor is vaulted with the central section covered by a cupola, which becomes more acute on each level. In addition to showing the cupola's increasing height, Pietrasanta's vertical section shows a well shaft (G) with 2 access windows: (H) for horse stables and (E) for mule stables; the hollow central column (A), topped by a covered V-shaped receptacle (B), which takes urine and waste water from the horse stable, via the semi-basement to a cistern (✤). Some of these structural details remain visible today (5.22, 5.23). However impractical it may have been, it is certain from two records that La Rotonda was used as a stable. First, on a visit to Milan in 1595, Cardinal

133

Federico Borromeo wrote,

> on the site once occupied by canonical housing . . . two stables were built in the form of an octagon [sic], a lower and an upper one, with a well and storage space for hay and straw for the use of the horses and mules of the Illustrious Archbishop and his household.[50]

In a letter written at the beginning of the seventeenth century Federico Zuccaro reports that he had seen Tibaldi's stable in the Archbishop of Milan's palace, a stable which could be converted into an elegant temple.[51] Despite Tibaldi's clever innovations for keeping the stable clean, the animals would have been closely confined and the decagonal design may have made it awkward to manage. Even his own treatise, unfinished at his death in 1596,[52] makes no mention of the Rotonda's shape, instead he conforms to the basilica plan with

> two rows of columns that form three aisles; in two of which are the horses' stalls and mangers, [whilst the horses] can be walked in the central aisle.[53]

It seems, therefore, that Tibaldi's design may well have been developed through some form of constraint, as Paredi has suggested.

In order to create a more impressive building, some architects multiplied the basilica shape either by doubling it as in Florence and Poggio a Caiano, or creating another floor to gain the required capacity, as Raphael may have proposed for Agostino Chigi or Bramante had planned for Pope Julius II. At Poggio a Caiano, the architectural plan followed that of the Medici's Florentine San Marco stables, built and probably designed by Baccio Bigio (Bartolomeo Lippi) between 1515-16.[54] In both Medici stables, two 'basilicas' of identical width and length run parallel to one another, creating a stable 108 metres long by 31 metres wide, allowing for the horses to be stabled in four lines (see 5.18).[55] Like Tibaldi, both Bigio and Il Tribolo may have been restricted by the sites for their stables; the Florentine stable being in the centre of a city and the Poggio stable limited by its proximity to the Ombrone, where the position of the river did not allow for a single-width basilica stable to house 300 horses. Il Tribolo, therefore, designed the double stable in order to fit the site which, in turn, allowed for the elegant accommodation on the first floor. The similarity of these two Medici stables is apparent in late sixteenth-century depictions: Buonsignori's birds'-eye map of Florence and Giusto Utens' lunette painted for Grand Duke Ferdinand I. The late sixteenth-century map shows the buildings surrounding the San Marco stables (5.24), while Utens shows Il Tribolo's building as it would have looked on completion c.1550, with its main façade facing south and the Prato road running down the west side (5.25).

Drawings show that Raphael's early sixteenth-century stable-guesthouse designed for Agostino Chigi consisted of four floors: one at semi-basement level, which may have served as stables; the principal stabling on the ground floor; a first floor serving as a *foresteria* with several guestrooms (Frommel sugesting that there were seven guestrooms on the right side and a banqueting room to the left);[56] and a top floor probably reserved for less important guests, servants and stable staff. In his biography of the Siense banker, Chigi's great-nephew, Fabio Chigi,[57] referred to one hundred horses having been stabled at the villa – which seems unlikely. Excavations carried out by the Accademia dei Lincei and the Institute Centrale del Restauro di Roma in 1970, show that the stable was approximately 12 x 41 metres with a semi-basement, the grilled windows of which are seen in the late-sixteenth century drawing of the façade (see 2.12). The ground floor stabling, which follows the basilica plan, would certainly not have been

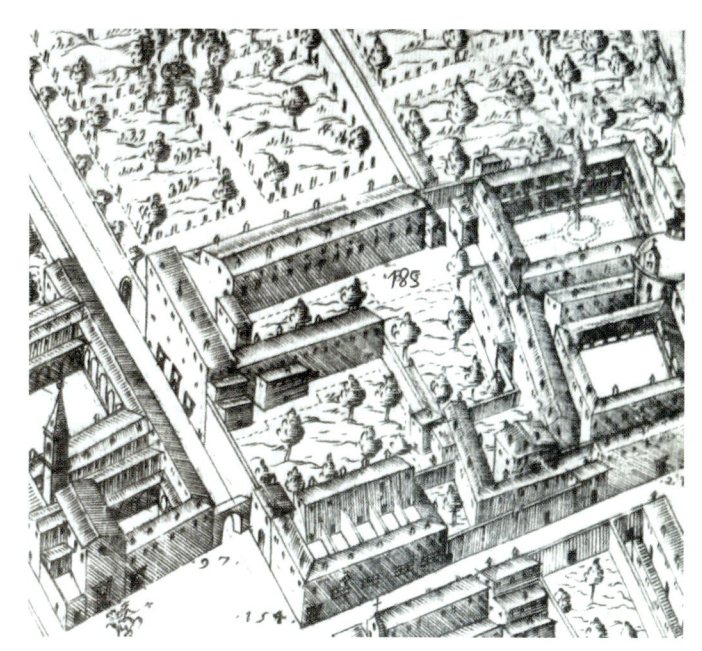

5.24. Medici San Marco Stables, Florence. Stefano Buonsignori, Map of Florence, 1594, detail. Stables marked '185'.
Wikimedia/ Sailko

5.25. Medici stables at Poggio a Caiano, Giusto Utens. Detail of 4.16 showing Prato road on the west side of the stables

able to accommodate the banker's one hundred horses; it would only have had a maximum capacity for fifty. To account for the further fifty horses, Frommel has concluded that the semi-basement level was also used as stabling. However, this would have been an impractical and unlikely solution as, with only the small grilled windows and one light shaft in the east wall for light, the dark, damp conditions would have created an unhealthy environment for the horses. Furthermore, the basement would be liable to flooding due to its proximity to the Tiber. It therefore seems more likely that the 'extra' fifty horses were stabled elsewhere and that Raphael's basement area was created to prevent any dampness or possible flooding coming into the ground floor stabling. A similar vacuum had been created below part of the Medici stables at Cafaggiolo, built alongside a stream, and at Francesco di Giorgio's stables in Raphael's hometown of Urbino. As already noted, little of Raphael's stables remain because of their unstable foundations built on the rubble of several earlier houses. Together with the frailty of the façade, which excavations show was not structurally attached to the basement, this poor workmanship contributed to the sad demise of these once beautiful stables, which started to crumble a few years after they were built.[58]

At the beginning of the seventeenth century the Venetian architect, Vincenzo Scamozzi (1552-

5.26. Brickwork under plaster, Medici stables, Poggio a Caiano

5.27. Palazzo Piccolomini, Pienza, stable vaulting

1616) suggested a novel way for housing large numbers of horses although his plan, like the basilica or temple, also followed an established religious format – the cloister. If there was enough space, he suggests garrison horses and servants should be housed in one wing of a quadrangle with fodder and wood storage in other wings and hay and straw stored on the upper floors. Each wing should have large windows and a doorway in the centre opening onto the large central courtyard,[59] in much the same way as monastic buildings were designed. Although this architectural concept is not dissimilar to the Neapolitan *cavallerizza* in which the stables, riding school and staff accommodation are housed in a single complex, the 'cloister' stable does not seem to have been adopted for other Italian court stables. However, further afield, a quadrangular stable complex had already been built at the royal courts of Henry VIII of England and François I of France, the former at Hampton Court in the 1530s and the latter at Fontainbleau, possibly designed by Serlio. According to Worsley, there were no non-royal quadrangular stables known from the sixteenth century in England and they remained exceptional in the seventeenth century.[60]

The most common material for building Renaissance stables was brick, usually rendered on both the exterior and the interior walls. Sometimes these walls were decorated with frescoes or carved ornamentation or the windows and doors might be given a rusticated surround or contrasting stone border. Records show that at Poggio a Caiano the bricks were produced in a nearby furnace, close to the River Ombrone.[61] For the interior, restoration work has shown that cavity walls were filled with rubble before rendering was applied (5.26). By contrast, in Pienza where a mixture of stone and brick was used on the stable's exterior, the internal arcading was made mainly of brick (5.27), and at the late-sixteenth century Farnese stables in Caprarola volcanic *tufa* was used to create the impressive four-storey, hundred-metre long building. Some cities, such as Ferrara and Mantua, had no stone or marble quarries nearby. If, as in the case of Vigevano's interior columns, stone was required for construction, it had to be imported at considerable expense. For roofing, evidence shows that most stables had terracotta tiling supported by wood beams. An exception is to be found at La Cavallerizza in Puglia, where the cone-shaped *trulli* as well as the stud farm's pitched roofs are made of traditional grey stone. Because of the fear of fire, most interior ceilings were constructed of rendered brick or stone,

5.28. Leonardo da Vinci, study for stables. Milan, Biblioteca Trivulziana, Codex 2162, 22r, c.1487-90. Copyright © Comune di Milano. All rights reserved

with the main floor, over the horses' stabling, either cross- or barrel-vaulted.

As explained above, one of the ways in which a Renaissance prince could display his wealth was in the decoration of his stables – the 'casket' in which he sheltered and displayed his collection of valuable horses. In the mid-fifteenth century, Alberti had praised architectural ornament, explaining that 'graceful and pleasant appearance ... derives from beauty and ornament alone' adding 'if this quality is desirable anywhere, surely it cannot be absent from buildings'.[62] But decorative façades were not new to Renaissance Italy and had existed in ancient Rome. According to Scamozzi, the fourth-century writer Flavius Vopiscus had mentioned paintings depicting the deeds of the third-century Emperor, Marcus Aurelius Carinus, in the arcades of the imperial stables.[63] Both archives and existing buildings show that many wealthy Renaissance Italians would follow Carinus' lead and Alberti's advice, using both fresco and elaborate ornamentation on their stable façades, the decoration varying both in design and materials as it would do on palaces and country villas. In many instances it is difficult to discover the overall impact such decoration might have had on any visitor, with frescoes having disappeared, stucco work fallen away and brick walls re-rendered. Nevertheless, for the stables at Mantua, modern technology has made it possible to reproduce the decorative effects given to a stable,[64] while drawings and archival records provide evidence of elegant façades for other Italian court stables, when powerful men such as the Sforza, Gonzaga and Bentivoglio ruled their vast estates.

The highly decorated wall surface, sketched in Leonardo da Vinci's Trivulziana Codex (5.28), is a good example of an ornamented façade if, as Pedretti has suggested, it was intended for the

5.29. Giulio Romano, Venus carries away Cupid in her Chariot, preparatory drawing possibly for the Palazzo Te stables. Paris, Louvre Museum. Photo © RMN-Grand Palais (musée du Louvre)/Thierry Le Mage

stable drawn on the facing page (see 6.15). Dismissing Geymüller's theory that the drawing was for a palace[65] and Firpo's that it was for a triumphal arch,[66] Pedretti describes the design as 'exquisitely Quattrocento in character'.[67] There is no doubt that Pedretti's belief is justified, especially when Leonardo's design is compared to other known stable façades such as Agostino Chigi's. From four drawings and a sketched outline,[68] made in the late sixteenth century, it is possible to imagine this elegant stuccoed façade for Raphael's most important private patron,[69] who was known for his extravagant displays of wealth (see 2.10-2.12). And, as noted in Chapter 2, it is quite possible that Chigi's stables were, like his villa, also decorated with frescoes. A similar combination of elaborate stucco work and painting may have decorated the walls of stables designed by Raphael's pupil, Giulio Romano in the 1520s. In 1958, Frederick Hartt suggested that four model drawings by Romano were intended for the interior walls for the new stables built for Federico Gonzaga on the south-west side of the Palazzo Te (5.29).[70] Unfortunately there is no remaining evidence of this decoration to prove or disprove Hartt's theory. However, given the evidence of earlier stable decoration, it is possible that the model drawings may have been for the exterior – rather than the interior – walls of the new stables giving them a similar appearance to the Chigi stables, which Romano would have known. As will be seen, Federico's father, Francesco had also had elaborately decorated stables on the Island of Te.

It has already been shown that the Sforza's Vigevano stables once had elaborate *trompe l'oeil* frescoes covering their external walls, the entire surface painted with a mix of geometric patterns, classical motifs and Sforza emblems (see 2.5). Similarly, Francesco Gonzaga's stud farm stables on the Te island[71] and at Pietole, south-east of Mantua, are known to have had overall painted decoration. Court accounts show that both stables were painted and expanded by Francesco between 1501 and 1514. Based on Vasari's account of the building of the Palazzo Te,

5.30. The Palazzo Te, Room of Ovid, fresco showing construction of the Palazzo from the north side. Image courtesy of Comune di Mantova

5.31. Giulio Romano, The Palazzo Te, north-west corner, 1525-35. imageBROKER/Alamy stock photo

it was believed that this stable, in which Andrea Mantegna may have had a hand, was partially pulled down to make way for the north wing of Giulio Romano's new palazzo for Marquis Francesco's son, Federico (5.30, 5.31).[72] This belief was confirmed when archaeological remains of an earlier building were found within the north wing, showing that the Sala dei Cavalli, the reception room containing life-size horse portraits, had been built on the stable's foundations. Notably, evidence of earlier walls, a pitched tiled roof and fragments of decoration from both the interior and the exterior of this stable remain inside the walls and roof space of the existing palazzo. Some pieces are in and above the two rooms adjacent to the Sala dei Cavalli[73] and a small section of frieze can be seen in the north-facing alcove (5.32). From this archaeological evidence, it has been concluded that both sides of the west and east end of the earlier stable

5.32. A section of decorative frieze in the north wing alcove, Palazzo Te, Mantua

5.33-35. Sections of frieze and a merlon from earlier stables now inside the roof space of the north wing of Palazzo Te

Images courtesy of Comune di Mantova

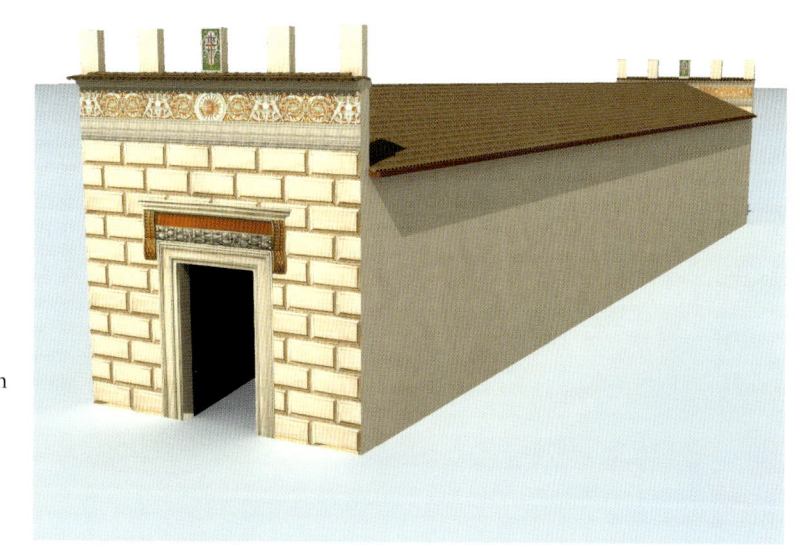

5.36. Hypothetical reconstruction of Francesco Gonzaga's stables. Courtesy of Ugo Bazzotti and Comune di Mantova

were painted with a Mantegnesque frieze in antique red and cream, surmounted by a painted egg and dart border. At the centre of the 85cm deep frieze is the Gonzaga emblem of the sun in a *tondo*, either side of which pairs of *putti* hold a bust placed on a *tabella ansata*, which is supported by dolphins (5.33-5). From the dolphins' heads swirling arabesques of leaves spring out across the width of the façade. The west wall frieze contains evidence of the building's patron and date of completion; below the left hand bust is the date 1502 and below that on the right the initials of the patron, Francesco Gonzaga, 'FMMIIII', who was the fourth Marquis of Mantua.[74] There are also traces of five merlons which surmounted the frieze at each end of the stable, the larger central one having a different Gonzaga emblem on both sides. Evidence of a large painted doorway at the east end shows that it was surmounted by a *trompe l'oeil* frieze, either end of which were scrolls supporting a cornice. With computer imaging Ugo Bazzotti has suggested how the elegant façades and doorway may have appeared (5.36). Certainly with surviving evidence of its pitched roof, a cross section of the Gonzaga stable may well have been similar to Sebastiano Serlio's stable design for a 'Royal Palace', shown in *Book VI* of his treatise on architecture a few years later (see 6.19).[75]

Bazzottti's theoretical reconstruction has led to a dismissal of any previous theories and to conclude that the original building was not a stable but a *palazzina* used by the Gonzaga family for entertaining on the island.[76] His hypothesis is founded on two assumptions: first, that the small fragments of decoration that remain are too elegant to have been part of a stable, and second, from evidence of an earlier hayloft in the roof space above the east wing of the existing palazzo, Francesco's stables were situated here rather than in the north wing. This second piece of evidence is based on Laura Fieni's research into the space above the east wing, which revealed a 'more rustic' construction with a hayloft over the top of it. This had seven vertical wall sections on both sides of the roof space, leading to her conclusion that the walls were pre-Giulio Romano and that the lower 'rustic' level must have been stabling.[77] However, both Fieni's and Bazzotti's hypotheses are flawed for two reasons. First, although the upper level may well have been a hayloft, it does not follow that the lower level was a stable as it is was not unusual for hay and fodder to be stored in a separate building to the horses. Second, and more importantly, accounts show that another stud farm stable, also belonging to Francesco Gonzaga, had elegant painted

5.37. West end of the Bentivoglio stables, Ponte Poledrano, Bentivolgio

5.38. The Bentivoglio stables: east end with terracotta frieze

decoration covering its façades. A letter, dated 3 July 1515,[78] which includes costings for painted decoration at the Pietole stables, indicates that these stables also had friezes painted on the interior and exterior, with *quadroni* or rustication covering all sides of the building and armorials over the entrance – an appearance which must have made it appear similar to the Te stable. Bazzotti mentions this letter but suggests only that the Pietole stables may have set a precedent for both the San Sebastiano palazzo and the later Giulio Romano Palazzo Te.[79] With Francesco Gonzaga's renowned interest in, and love for, his thoroughbred horses, it is more likely that this *palazzina* was indeed a suitable gallery for the Marquis's horses before it was replaced by his son's Palazzo Te twenty years later. Further investigation into the decorative effects applied to Francesco's other stud farm stables might, perhaps, show that these important buildings were being given a unifying and deliberately conspicuous appearance.

In the Bentivoglio's capital city, Bologna, the vast stables situated opposite their palace, which housed Giovanni II's private guard, are also known to have had their façades painted with colourful equestrian scenes.[80] Although the palace was destroyed in 1507, the stables still remain with the brickwork exposed and the interior much altered to serve as a student bar. Similarly, the Bentivoglio's seventy-metre long stables at their pleasure palace at Ponte Poledrano were painted decoratively (see 4.2). The once-moated castle, built for Giovanni II in the 1480s, is surrounded by gardens and a castellated brick wall with a fifty-horse stable wing attached to the north side (5.37, 5.38). The stable roof is slightly lower than the castle and, unlike the castle, does not have a terracotta cornice, only a short piece of decorative terracotta frieze above the east end doorway. However, the buildings do have some similarity in their architectural detail: both having arched windows on the first floor and square windows on the lower level. More importantly, according to Rubbiani, *gabella* accounts from 1643 show that the stable's exterior walls were once painted with the same design as the castle's, uniting them in the same way as the Vigevano courtyard would have been. The walls are recorded as having a white background, divided into lozenges framing the Bentivoglio *imprese* of joined and divided canes, with the mottos *Unitas fortior – divisio fragilis*.[81] In the castle's central courtyard, the white background was decorated with flowing green branches onto which red roses were attached by ribbons, displaying Giovanni's celebratory name for his castle, *Domus Jocunditatis*. Sadly, almost nothing remains of the painted decoration although ghostlike images are visible.

Sometimes, painted stable façades could serve a practical purpose. Writing in the mid-seventeenth century, Bocchi and Cinelli describe the great Medici San Marco stables as having frescoes on the wall of a covered area that was used for schooling horses when it was raining. Recorded as being by Alessandro Allori (1535-1607), the paintings are described as depicting six horses performing 'diverse stances and various movements'.[82] Although it is not known if similar paintings of *maneggio* movements were used to assist training in other riding schools of the period, it would seem quite possible. Certainly, it was not unusual for wealthy owners to have eye-catching stables façades. And whilst it might be argued that, in many instances, such decoration was to unify the buildings in a court complex, it should also be understood as elevating the stable's importance within Renaissance court society.

In addition to their decorative exteriors, many stables had impressive entrances: a covered external area or a lobby dividing the horses from the exterior. And whilst this may have been for security it also protected the horses from draughts or excessive heat or cold. The principal entrance into the stabling was, therefore, sometimes preceded by a portico or arcade, as at Pietole or the Borromeo stables in Milan, or it might lead into an atrium which could be ridden into and used for mounting and dismounting horses or for disembarking from carriages as at Poggio

5.39. The Bentivoglio stables, Bologna, principal entrance

a Caiano. With the Renaissance stable becoming an autonomous building, the main entrance was often accorded considerable attention by the architect, in the same way that a palace's principal façade or entrance had been. Some stables, such as those belonging to the Bentivoglio in Bologna, had a portico preceding the entrance (5.39). Here, the elegant circular brick columns with carved composite capitals are reminiscent of those in the central courtyard of the Bentivoglio's country residence at Ponte Poledrano. And, from a sixteenth-century drawing of the seignorial palace, it is possible to conclude that the design of the stable's portico may also have matched that of palace's façade on the opposite side of the large piazza, giving this important space a uniformity in the fifteenth century.[83] Certainly, the portico at the Gonzaga's stud farm stables at Gonzaga, mentioned in Recordati's letter, also served as a theatrical space in which horses could be displayed 'one by one' for the benefit and enjoyment of the Gonzaga agent.[84]

The decorated façades and doorway of the Gonzaga's Te stables, which included Marquis Francesco's emblems and initials, have already been described. Equally notable is the doorway into Agostino Chigi's Roman stables, where the arched entrance into the stables is larger and more elegant than that of the two openings to the right of it: one leading to stairs for the guest

5.40. Detail from Franco-Flemish 16th-century drawing of Agostino Chigi's stables, entrance façade and door. Anon. New York, Metropolitan Museum of Art, Inv. 49.92.50r

5.41. Francesco di Giorgio, doorway for San Bernardino, Urbino

accommodation on the *piano nobile* and also down to the semi-basement; the other to a small courtyard (5.40). Here, Raphael has placed partially recessed Tuscan columns on either side of the entrance, which support a cornice. And, similar to the Gonzaga façade, the name of the patron is above the entrance: 'AUG. GHISIUS. SENENSIS'. Fiori and Tafuri have suggested that this design was influenced by a church entrance in Raphael's birthplace, Urbino: Francesco di Giorgio's doorway for San Bernardino, which has fluted composite columns framing it in the same way, although, as Shearman has suggested, Raphael's inspiration for the recessed columns may have come from a Roman tomb (5.41).[85]

Two other impressive stable entrances have a more rustic appearance in tune with their rural settings. The Medici stable at Poggio a Caiano has a principal façade framed by brickwork quoins which run the full height of each of the two corners, reflecting the detailing of the Villa's ground floor (see 5.10, 5.17). This austere south-facing wall is only interrupted by the symmetrical setting of three doors and a large cruciform window,[86] all framed by grey *pietra serena* stone but with only the large central rectangular doorway heavily rusticated. The plain *pietra serena* surrounds are repeated on the first-floor interior, where the twenty-six entrance doors for the

5.42. First floor, Medici stables, Poggio a Caiano

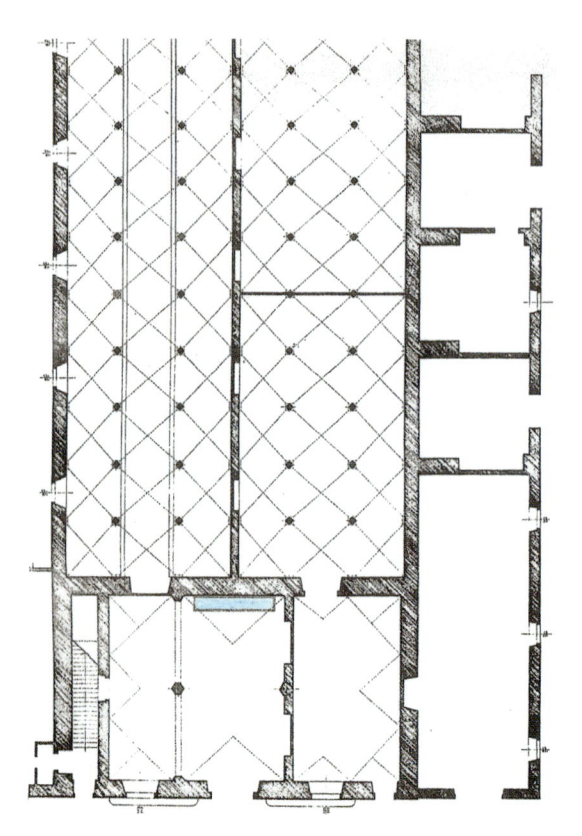

5.43. Southern end of the parallel stables at Poggio Poggio a Caiano with atrium. Drinking trough marked blue. Plan: Gurrieri and Lamberini, *Villa Medicea di Poggio a Caiano*

small apartments and small internal windows are also framed by the grey stone (5.42). Having entered through the rusticated entrance, the light vaulted atrium with its two large hexagonal *pietra serena* columns stretches across the width of the building and leads via two smaller rectangular doorways into the two parallel stables. Between these two doors, on the atrium's back wall there is a large drinking trough for refreshing the horses (5.43). In contrast, the north end of the building is considerably plainer with two wide arched doorways, allowing direct access for horses and personnel to the central stable aisles from the Prato road or, after washing the horses, from the river Ombrone (5.44). These two doorways are framed in brickwork, not accorded the same treatment as those to the south. However, unlike its doors, the north façade does have a *pietra serena* surround to its corresponding cruciform window at first floor level, which illuminates the first-floor corridor. The economical decoration, in which rendered brickwork forms a simplistic background to the *pietra serena* outlining of windows and doors, appears appropriate for the elegant, balanced design of this country court stable.

A similar but more exaggerated mannerist treatment was given by Vignola to the imposing entrance of Alessandro Farnese's impressive new stables at Caprarola, built in the 1580s and known as Lo Stallone (5.45).[87] Here the large east-facing arched door, which faces the Villa Farnese, has a heavily rusticated surround of alternating white *tufo* and *peperino*. The rustication is eye-catching, not only because the blocks of stone project from the smooth wall surface but also because of the variation in the stones' colouring. The keystone and the stones on either side

5.44. North façade of Medici stables at Poggio a Caiano.
Wikimedia Commons/ Giuseppe Faienza

5.45. The Farnese stables at Caprarola: principal entrance to Lo Stallone

of it break through the rhythm of the rusticated arch and thrust upwards to become part of a cornice forming an improbable support for the large first floor window This gives a playful effect to an otherwise austere façade, reminiscent of some of Giulio Romano's architecture at the Palazzo Te approximately half a century earlier. The Caprarola doorway leads into a wide passage with staircases on either side, before opening onto the long aisle between the two lines of sixty horse stalls under high barrel-vaulting.

Many large stables such as Caprarola and Cafaggiolo, also had doorways situated in their longer façades, allowing further access for stables and staff. As shown in Chapter 4, Corte had suggested that a stable should have 'two large doors at half way' with one facing the 'midday sun and the other the north',[88] probably to help regulate the temperature of the stable interior as well as serving as an entrance. But this could also serve as an escape route for horses and staff in the event of fire, a regular hazard when stable boys were required to light oil lanterns to keep the stable lit or carry candles if called to visit the horses during the night.

It is fair to say that both tradition and courtly display played a key role in how the court stables were designed, with many exterior façades accorded a significant amount of attention and decorative detail. Leading Renaissance architects designed stables which, although often built on restricted sites, were constructed according to established classical architectural forms: the basilica, the temple and the cloister. External frescoes, such as at Francesco Gonzaga's stables at Pietole and on the Island of Te, would have made these buildings dominate the surrounding pastureland; their *trompe l'oeil* friezes and fake rustication not only making them conspicuous but also reflecting the importance a princely owner attached to breeding and showing his horses. It could be said that the extravagant painted decoration at Vigevano and Ponte Poledrano – or the elaborate stucco work on the Chigi stables – was excessive, but it is notable that these stables were given a treatment comparable to other court buildings. As will be shown, a similar amount of attention was given to the stable interior, where established classical ideals were mixed with Renaissance theories of cleanliness for maintaining the horses' health.

1 Pellegrino Tibaldi (Pellegrino Pellegrini), 'L'architettura', Part I, ch. 19, 'Le stalle', p. 19, in G. Panizza, ed., *L'architettura/Pellegrino Pellegrini; edizione critica a cura di Giorgio Panizza*, in series *Classici Italiani di Scienze Tecniche 7:1* (Milan, 1990), p. 36. The exact date of the treatise is not known, although it was unfinished at Pellegrino's death in 1596.
2 Worsley, *The British Stable* (2005), p. 9.
3 Ibid. p. 18.
4 Mantua, ASMa, AG, b. 2914, 86v, letter, dated 3 November 1506, from Francesco II Gonzaga to Girolamo Arcari, *Hieronymo, volemo facci coprir quella bancha hai facto far ne la monstra de gli cavalli verso il laco* . . . Cited by M. Bourne in *Francesco II Gonzaga: The Soldier-Prince as Patron* (Rome, 2008), p. 452 (228), where she suggests that *bancha* might be a viewing stand.
5 Mantua, ASMa, AG, b. 2491, 165r. Letter dated 18 June 1515 to Francesco II Gonzaga, *Illustrissimo Signor mio etc aviso Vostra excellentia come il Reverendissimo monsignor Cardinale Ragona sia visto tuto lo palazo di Marmirolo alqual è piazuto sumamente ogni cosa et lo sito del loco. E dopo disnar glie sta facto la mostra di staloni zaneti li quali sono sta laudati da luj . . . E dopo se comenzo la mostra de le cavale zanete e turche menate denanti a luj in caveza ad una ad una cum li soi poledrinij dreto* . . .
6 Mantua, ASMa, AG, b. 2491, 27v. Letter dated 20 November 1515 to Federico II Gonzaga, *Partita Madamma dal Signore vostro padre che possena essere circa hore xxiiij, la sua excellentia insieme col Cardinale in caretta andorno sul Te: et lì il prefato Signore monstrò tutti li poledri de ogni sorte al prefato monsignore cardinale quali gli piacquino sumamente; et dicti poledri tutti erano ne la stalla di San Biasio.*
7 Mantua, ASMa, AG, b. 2526, 350v-351r. Letter dated 10 May 1538.
8 Opinions vary as to how much of the present-day stable was designed by Baccio Bigio (Bartolomeo di Giovanni Lippi). Articles describe Bigio, a master mason and builder, as working on the stables 1516-21, with the architect and engineer Il Tribolo (Niccolò Pericoli) employed by Duke Cosimo in 1548. Others attribute the entire building to Il Tribolo. However, Lamberini's convincing evidence seems definitive: Il Tribolo was responsible for the Poggio stables and Baccio Bigio constructed, and possibly designed, the Medici San Marco stables in Florence, in preparation for the formal entry of Giovanni de' Medici, Pope Leo X. See D. Lamberini, 'Il Tribolo ingegnere e i lavori al Poggio a Caiano', in E. Pieri and L. Zangheri eds, *Niccolò, detto il Tribolo tra arte, architettura e paessaggio* (Signa, 2001), pp. 173-93. For this book, the design of the Poggio stables will be attributed to Il Tribolo.
9 L. Sebastiani, *Descrizzione e relazione istorica del noblisssimo, e real palazzo di Caprarola* (Rome, 1741), pp. 118-9.
10 Rome, ASR, Carte Farnesiane, Cam. III, b. 518, *Libro delle misure della fabbrica del palazzo del Illustrissimo e Reverendissimo Farnese a Caprarola*, 17th *misura* (20 June 1581 – 5 February 1583), *A la stala nova*.
11 Rome, ASR, Cam. III, b. 518, 1st *misura*. The *misura* contains information on stable fittings.
12 Villamana, *Ichonografia generale del Palazzo di Caprarola dell'illustrissimo Signor Cardinal Farnese*, Legend n. 8, *Corpo di casa per servitio del cortile di sotto dall'Architetto in questo luogo disegnata, ma poi adoperati tutti due in uno verso l'angolo Seg.o . . . separati solamente della strada che in traversa per mezzo nell'istesso piano de i giardini.*
13 The late Henry Dietrich Fernández of the Rhode Island School of Design explained his theory in conversation with the author, 11 May 2009.
14 Florence, Uffizi, Gabinetto Disegni e Stampe, n. 287.A. See also C.L. Frommel, S. Ray, M. Tafuri eds, *Raffaello Architetto* (Milan, 1984), where the same plan is labelled *Antonio del Pellegrino, Bramante (?), Progetti per il rinnovamento del Palazzo Vaticano. Inchiostro e sanguina, aggiunte e matita, alternative incise 1340 c 1010 mm.*
15 Frommel et al. eds, *Raffaello Architetto* (1984), p. 361.

16 Alfonso I of Naples and Philip II of Spain.
17 Federico da Montefeltro, Duke of Urbino; Galeazzo Maria and Ludovico Sforza, Dukes of Milan; Borso and Ercole d'Este, Dukes of Ferrara; Federico Gonzaga, Duke of Mantua and Cosimo de' Medici, Duke of Florence
18 Popes Pius II and Julius II.
19 Cardinals Alesssandro Farnese and Ippolito d'Este, Archbishop Carlo Borromeo.
20 Agostino Chigi (1465-1520) left 400,000 ducats when he died. He had been banker to two Popes, Alexander VI and Julius II. From the revenues of banking and alum mines, he built an empire across Europe and the Near east, had offices in Alexandria, Constantinople, Cairo, Leon, London and Antwerp, employed over 20,000 people and owned 100 ships.
21 Alfonso I of Naples (Alfonso V of Aragon) (1396-1458).
22 *Cavallerizza*: in the north of Italy *cavallerizza* indicates a riding school; in the south of the country, especially in those areas ruled by Naples, *cavallerizza* indicates a walled complex, which included a training area or riding school, staff accommodation and stables.
23 The Venetians valued the Pugliese horses and wanted to cross-breed them with their own stock. See G. Notarnicola, *La Cavallerizza della Serenissima in Puglia* (Venice, 1933; reprinted Alberobello, 2008), p. 34.
24 The stud farm and supporting buildings included a training track in the form of a figure of 8. Situated between Monopoli and Alberobello, the Cavallerizza covers 335 sq. kilometres, faces south and stretches to the coast. The Aragonese King of Naples, Ferdinand II, allowed the Republic of Venice to occupy several Puglian ports and the surrounding Murghese countryside as part of his negotiations to secure the Republic's support against the French occupation. For a comprehensive history of the Venetians' occupation of La Cavallerizza, see Notarnicola, *La Cavallerizza* (2008) and F. Porsia, *I cavalli del re* (Brindisi, 1986).
25 Tuohy, *Herculean Ferrara* (2002), p. 40.
26 See ASMa, AG, b. 2108, 52r (Francesco to Isabella, 28 August 1492) and 199r (Isabella to Francesco, 1 September 1492). See C. James, 'Marriage by correspondence: politics and domesticity in the letters of Isabella d' Este and Francesco Gonzaga', *Renaissance Quarterly* 65 (2012), pp. 321-52, pp. 329-30.
27 Milan, ASMi, AS, 932r, Bona of Savoy to Giuliano da Varese, 6 November 1476. Cited in Lubkin, p. 227 and p. 356, n. 68.
28 Smithy: a farrier's or blacksmith's workshop both for working with iron and for shoeing horses.
29 Piccolomini, *The Commentaries* (1936-7), IX, p. 600.
30 See L. Fontebuoni & P. Refice, 'Verifiche documentarie', in ed. M. Bruscia, *La Data (orto dell'abbondanza) di Francesco di Giorgio Martini: Atti del convegno Urbino, 26 settembre 1986*, (Urbino, 1990), pp. 83-9, p. 83.
31 According to his treatise, Francesco di Giorgio's stables at Urbino were 28 '*piedi*' wide, 36 *piedi* high and 360 *piedi* long. Taking one Urbino *piede* as 0.353m (13.9 inches), this converts to 9.88m wide x 12.70m high x 127m long. If indeed the stables were to hold 300 horses, this would allow each horse only 85cm in width, meaning the horses would touch one another; 170cms would be more practical. It has been suggested that Francesco di Giorgio was 'rounding up the numbers' and more likely La Data would have held 220-230 horses. See M.A. Barone, S. Gennari, C. Giovannini, *Rilievi e indagine storica sulla Data*, in ed. Bruscia, *La Data* (1990), pp. 21-44, pp. 30-31.
32 See also G. Cialdieri, *The Assumption*, 1630. Museo Albani, Urbino where the stables are clearly visible.
33 Mantua, ASMa, AG, 'Lettere dei Conti e Duci di Pesaro e Urbino ai Gonzaga', b. 1068, 396r, 9 September, 1506, … *ma in lo tornar qui cum Sua Beatitudine seria impossibile venendo sua Santità cum vincti octo in trenta Cardinali molti altri prelati, Ambasciatori, et si pò dir cum tutta la Corte, et cum la guardia a piedi et a cavallo, sapendo la excellentia vostra che Urbino non è né Mantova né Ferrara. Et si è facto discriptione che non si può dare per Cardinale di allogiamente che per cinquanta cavalli, et sedici letti per uno.* Cited by L. Fontebuoni, 'Documenti', *La Data*, (1990), p. 88.
34 Similar rings, probably dating from the fifteenth or sixteenth century, are attached to the inside walls of the covered road (La Strada Coperta) leading into the courtyard at Vigevano. The rings are set at two different heights, indicating that mules were also tethered here.
35 Jean Le Bel in ed. and trans. P.E. Thomson, *Contemporary Chronicles of the Hundred Years War* (London, 1966), p. 70, cited in Hyland, *The Warhorse, 1250-1600* (1998), p. 53 and p. 227, n. 8.
36 Pellegrino Tibaldi, "L'archittetura", 1, ch. 19, p. 19 in Panizza ed., *L'architettura* (1990), p. 36.
37 Milan, ASMi, AS, 932r, *1476. Lista de li deputati acalcare dreto ala corte del nostro Illustrissimo Principe et Excellentissimo Signore ali quali se ha adare alogiamenti*, cited in Lubkin, *A Renaissance Court* (1994), pp. 265-70, Appendix 2.
38 Milan, ASMi, 'Ordini per il governo della famiglia di Cicco Simonetta', *c*.1476, printed in C. Magenta, ed., *I Visconti e gli Sforza nel Castello di Pavia e loro attineze con la Certosa e la storia cittadina*, 2 vols (Milan,1883), II, 'Galeazzo Maria Sforza CCCLXXXII, Arch. di Stato, Milan', pp. 371-5, see p. 373. No manuscript number is given by Magenta.
39 Florence, Biblioteca Nazionale Centrale di Firenze, (BNCF), Fondo Nazionale, II. I. 277, 77v, Francesco de' Marchi, *Architettura militare*, Book II, ch. 5, *Le loggie che sono intorno al Palazzo, le quali possano servire quando vi andasse gran quantità di cavalli, come io vidi in tempo di Duca Alessandro*, cited by Lamberini, 'Il Tribolo', p. 192, n. 63. See also Florence, Uffizi, Gabinetto Disegni e Stampe (GDS), 4013 A, 'a causa e Cavaglj possino j(n)ntrare più facilmente in dette Loggie', cited in Lamberini, 'Il Tribolo' (2001), p. 184 and pp. 192-3, n. 64.
40 Florence, ASF, Mediceo del Principato, F. 1170 A, ins, 3, 144v. Letter from Lorenzo Pagni to Pier Francesco Riccio, dated 28 October, 1545. Cited in Lamberini, 'Il Tribolo' (2001), pp. 173-93, pp. 185 and 193, n. 65 in which a section of the letter is quoted.
41 Corte, 1562, I, ch. 36, 47r. Taking the *canna* as *c*.2.25 metres.
42 The first-floor corridor is 6.30 metres wide (*c*.21 feet) and 9.30 metres high (30½ feet). Each apartment's floor area is 7.40 x 7 metres. An architectural survey from 2007 mentions the apartments having a sink, but does not give a date for this fitting. See *Analisi di prefattibilità per il project financing: Recupero delle Scuderie della Villa Medicea di Poggio a Caiano*, 3° (Comune di Poggio a Caiano, April 2007), 2.3 'Architettura', p. 6.
43 The Maddalena stables were in the swampy area near the Maddalena bridge over the Sebeto river; those of the Incoronata were on the road of the Incoronata. See F. Strazzullo, *Architetti e ingegneri napoletani dal 500 al 700* (Naples, 1969), pp. 138-9, cited in Hernando Sánchez, 'La Gloria del cavallo' (1998), IV, pp. 277-331, p. 300, n. 61.

44 For information on these stables see Hernando Sánchez, 'La Gloria del cavallo' (1998), pp. 284-5 and p. 300, nn. 61-3.
45 Pellegrino Tibaldi (1527-84), also known as Pellegrino de' Pellegrini.
46 Trapdoors cut into the flooring of the third floor indicate that hay and straw could be thrown down to the horses on the central level.
47 A. Paredi, *La Rotonda del Pellegrini* (Milan, 1950).
48 Either S. Giovanni alle Fonti, which had been octagonal or, more possibly, S. Stefano alle Fonti, which functioned until *c.*1500.
49 R. Haslam, 'Pellegrino de' Pellegrini, Carlo Borromeo and the public architecture of the Counter Reformation' in *Pellegrino Tibaldi: nuove proposte di studio: Atti del convegno internazionale Porlezza-Valsoda: 19-21 settembre 1987, Arte Lombarda*, New Series 3-4 (1990), pp. 17-30. See also Haslam's correspondence with the author December 2010-February 2011.
50 No reference is given for this quotation cited by Paredi, *La Rotonda* (1950), p. 14.
51 Federico Zuccari (1542-1609). Zuccari's letter to Lodovico Caracci, dated 7 August but the year is not noted by Bottari in G. Bottari and S. Ticozzi eds, *Raccolta di lettere sulla pittura, scultura ed architettura*, 8 vols (Milan, 1822), VII, Appendix xxxviii, pp. 516-9, p. 518, *Ho veduto nel palazzo dell'arcivescovo di Milano una scuderia di quest'architetto* [Pellegrino] *che potrebbe essere ridotta ad elegantissimo tempio . . .*
52 Two manuscripts of Pellegrino Tibaldi's treatise exist, neither of which is autograph: Milan, Biblioteca Ambrosiana, MS P. 246 Sup. and Paris, BN, MS Ital. 474 (formerly 7742).
53 Pellegrino Tibaldi, in Panizza ed. *L'architettura* (1990), Part 1, ch. 19, p. 19.
54 The suggestion that Baccio Bigio designed and built the San Marco stables is found in G. Belli, 'Alcune osservazioni sulla carriera architettonica di Tribolo', *Nicolo detto 'Il Tribolo'* (Signa, 2001), pp. 57-71, p. 57.
55 In the 17th century, the stables had an extension of 13 kennels attached to the east wall.
56 See Frommel, *La Villa Farnesina* (2003), p. 44.
57 Fabio Chigi, Pope Alexander VII, 1599-1667.
58 For a fuller account and explanation of the excavations, see C.L. Frommel, *La Villa Farnesina* (2003), pp. 42-45.
59 Scamozzi, *L'idea della architettura* (1615), Part 1, II, ch. XXII, p. 177.
60 Worsley, *The British Stable*, (2004) pp. 21-3. Worsley gives the earliest of these quadrangular stables in England as Henry VIII's Royal Mews at Hampton Court, 1537-8.
61 F. Purini, 'Ricostruire modificando le scuderie medicee di Poggio a Caiano', *Costruire in Laterizio 77* (September/October, 2000), p. 24.
62 Alberti, *On the Art of Building* (1988), VI, 'On ornament', ch. 2, p. 155.
63 Scamozzi, *L'idea della architettura* (1615), Part 1, II, ch. XXII, p. 177, *Nel Palatino furono le stalle con i portici, ne' quali (come dice Vopisco) erano dipinti de' spetacoli di carino imperatore.*
64 For Vigevano see G. Bombi *et al.* eds, *La biscia e l'aquila* (1988), p. 109. For Mantua see U. Bazzotti, 'Un luogo e certe stalle' (2006), pp. 154-5.
65 H. von Geymüller in J. P. Richter ed., *The Literary Works of Leonardo da Vinci, compiled and edited from the original manuscripts by J. P. Richter*, 2 vols (London, 1939), II, p. 52. See C. Pedrettii, *Leonardo da Vinci: the Royal Palace at Romorantin* (Cambridge, MA, 1972), p. 84 and n. 18.
66 Pedretti cites L. Firpo, *Leonardo architetto e urbanista* (Turin, 1962-3) in *Leonardo da Vinci* (1972), p. 84 and n.18.
67 Pedretti, *Leonardo da Vinci* (1972), p. 84.
68 New York, Metropolitan Museum of Art, Inv. 49.92.44v and Inv. 49.92.50r; Berlin, Kunstbibliotek, HDz. 3267/83, 70r; Rome, Gabinetto Nazionale delle Stampe, F. N. n. 7988, Cherubino Alberti, *Membri di la stalla di Agustino Ghisi in trastevere di preta biga di baldasari opera architetura*. For the sketched outline see Florence, Uffizi Gallery, Gabinetto Disegni e Stampe, 1474, E v, Raphael, *Progetto per le stalle Chigi*.
69 Raphael decorated two chapels and the Trastevere villa for Chigi, as well as designing his stables.
70 F. Hartt, *Giulio Romano* (New Haven, 1958), pp. 88-9.
71 In documents referring to stud farms and stables on and near the Te island, both the San Sebastiano and the San Biagio stables are mentioned. From a 1628 plan of Mantua, it appears that the San Sebastiano stables may have been to the west of the San Sebastiano palace (built 1506-8), and that the stables situated on the Island may have been named San Biagio.
72 Vasari, *Vite* (1966), V, 'Giulio Romano', p. 65.
73 Camera di Ovidio and Camera di Amore e Psiche.
74 FMM IIII (Franciscus Marchio Mantuae Quartus) Francesco II. The frieze is similar in character to that of the eight painted and gilded wood and stucco pilasters (Venetian, *c.*1500) made to frame Andrea Mantegna's *Triumphs of Caesar* in the Palazzo San Sebastiano, two of which are in the Stanza del Labirinto, Museo di Palazzo Ducale, Mantua.
75 Sebastiano Serlio, *Tutte l'opere d'architettura et prospettiva*, 7 books (1537-75), VI, 'On Habitations', 73r. Book VI (1537) remained in manuscript until the 20th century. See *Sebastiano Serlio on Architecture*, trans. V. Hart and P. Hicks (New Haven and London, 2001), pp. 152-3, 'The final details of the Royal Palace at number XXII'.
76 Ugo Bazzotti, '"Un luogo e certe stalle" sull' isola del Te prima di Giulio Romano', *Civiltà mantovana*, 3:122 (2006), pp. 144-61. The article gives a detailed description and hypothetical reconstruction of the building.
77 Laura Fieni, 'Palazzo Te a Mantova: indagine stratigrafica dei sottotetti. Preesistenze e trasformazione al progetto di Giulio Romano', *Archeologia dell'Architettura* VIII (2003), pp. 209-19, p. 218. Cited by Bazzotti, 'Un luogo e certe stalle' (2006), pp. 157-8.
78 Mantua, ASMa, AG, b. 2491, 166r, 3 July 1515, *frigi di dentro et intorno intorno alla stala da pietol; Armori via sopra la porta; Quadroni dal friso por zoso per tuta la fazada . . .*
79 Bazzotti, 'Un luogo e certe stalle' (2006), p. 151.
80 A sign attached to the stables by the Città di Bologna reads, *È questo il più conservato dei locali di servizio annessi al palazzo dei Bentivoglio distrutto nel 1507. Risale alla seconda metà del XV secolo . . . La facciata di questo e degli attigui edifici era, in età bentivolesca, decorata con coloratissimi affreschi di storie cavalleresche.*
81 A. Rubbiani, *Il castello di Giovanni II Bentivoglio a Ponte Poledrano* (Bologna, 1914; reprint, Bentivoglio, 1989), p. 35. Rubbiani writes that much of the information on the Castle's appearance comes from reports concerning the Naviglio, citing:

Bologna, ASBologna, Archivio del Comune, Carte della Gabella, 'Disegno e descrittione dei Canali et Edificii quali serveno alla Navigazione da Bologna a Ferrara e Pertinense et Adherenze du quella a commode et informatione dei Signori della Congregatione di Gabella. Fatto l'anno MDCXLIII'. The codex was made by F. Martinelli and Camillo Sacenti. See also a plan of the castle in Bartolomeo Castelli, *Equilibrazione delle acque* (17th century).
82 Francesco Bocchi & Giovanni Cinelli, *Le bellezze della città di Firenze* (1677), pp 16-17.
83 The Bentivoglio's Bolognese palace was designed by Pagno di Lapo Portigiani (1408-70), who had trained with Donatello and Michelozzo. The drawing of the palace's façade can be seen in Bologna, Convento di San Francesco, MS n.35, G. B. and G. Bottrigari, *Ricordi (700-1554)*, 300r.
84 Mantua, ASMa. AG, b. 2526, 350v-351r. Letter dated 10 May 1538. See also Malacarne, *Il mito* (1995), pp. 160-1.
85 J. Shearman, 'Raphael as architect', *Journal of the Royal Society of Arts* (*JRSA*), CXVI (April, 1968), pp. 388-409, p. 401.
86 Giusto Utens' lunette of Poggio a Caiano (*c*.1589) shows the stables with only the central door and large cruciform window breaking the plain façade. However, the two side doors are thought to be original. The plain *pietra serena* detailing is repeated at the first-floor level interior, where the apartment doors and windows are also framed by the grey stone.
87 It is probable that Giacomo Barozzi da Vignola (1507-73) designed the Caprarola stables, although he had died before they were completed. The construction was under the direction of Giovanni Antonio Garzoni (Maestro Giovannantonio), overseen by Farnese's major-domo, Bishop Alessandro Rufino. Garzoni had already been responsible for the Farnese hunting lodge, the Barco, the expansion of the *pescheria* and the Palazzina del Piacere at Caprarola, 1584-6. A letter in the Neapolitan State archives shows that the stables were still unfinished in March 1584 as they had only just started constructing the mangers. Naples, Archivio di Stato di Napoli (ASN), Carte Farnesiane (CF), 1358. 1, *La fabbrica della stalla va inanzi . . . et se sonno comincie a fare la mangiatore*. For more information on the building of these stables see C. Robertson *Il Gran Cardinale* (1992), pp. 87-8. The 'Stalla nova' is 100 metres long by 15 metres wide and held over 112 horses.
88 Corte, 1562, ch. 36, 47r-v.

64.

Merchio della razza del Cardinal di Ferrara Don Ippolito da Este.

Brand for the breed of Don Ippolito d'Este, Cardinal of Ferrara

Chapter 6

As Beauty demands: Inside the Stable

> Stables were not merely places for horses to live in, but also galleries where they
> could be displayed to advantage . . . their ostentatious display in stables . . .
> was a deliberate act of self-propaganda on the part of the owners.
> Giles Worsley, 1989.[1]

In the same way as ornate jewel boxes housed valuable contents, the decorative elements of a Renaissance stable's exterior were merely a prelude to the collection of valuable horses within. A practical and well-planned stable interior was a major factor for the owner – whether *condottiere*, prince or banker – not only for showing off his horses but also for maintaining their fitness and health. This chapter considers the interior planning of the Renaissance stable, looking first at the decorative elements and lighting within the stable; second, the methods used to contain and feed the horses and third, the floor surfaces and drainage systems – all details which were considered of the utmost importance for the horses' well-being as well as for their presentation.

Immediately upon entering the stable, a visitor would note the way in which the space was designed and furnished, in the same was as he might observe and scrutinise his host's palace – his eye observing the elegant columns and painted walls. Painted interior walls were not unusual, see, for example, the Mantegnesque friezes decorating the Gonzaga stables at Pietole[2] and Te. Whilst at Ponte Poledrano no evidence remains, the interior walls of the Bentivoglio stables were recorded by Rubbiani in 1914 as being painted with *trompe l'oeil* lozenges framing neighing horses.[3] If this was the case, the appearance of this stable interior may well have resembled one of the castle's main reception rooms, the *Sala degli stemmi*, on the *piano nobile*, where the lozenge-shaped designs on the walls enclose the Bentivoglio *impresa* of a saw, the *sega*. In addition, Vasari writes that Bramantino had painted horses being groomed on the interior wall of a stable outside the Porta Vercellina in Milan, in which one of the frescoes was so realistic that a horse had kicked out at it, believing it to be alive.[4] Although these stables were already ruined when Vasari wrote his *Vite*, such anecdotes serve as evidence that Renaissance stable interiors were colourful spaces. It may be that archaeological finds or archival research will uncover more examples of frescoed stable interiors, although to date nothing has appeared. Even if such interior decoration was exceptional, there is no doubt that many Renaissance court horses were stabled in elegant well-lit spaces, their stalls framed by classical columns with elegant carved capitals.

When, in 1487, the diarist Ugo Caleffini recorded the lavish interior of Ercole d'Este's stables at the Palazzo San Francesco with their marble columns and marble vaulted ceiling,[5] he inadvertently gave an example of how a visitor might be impressed by the quality of materials used in a stable's interior. It was certainly not unusual for architects to use elegant columns and expensive materials in stables as they would in residential and religious architecture – a extravagance of which Alberti approved,

6.1. Bologna: sixteenth-century arcade with hexagonal columns similar to those in the Bentivoglio stables

6.2. Pienza: circular pillar at the Palazzo Piccolomini stables

> There is nothing to be found in the art of building that deserves more care and expense, or ought to be more graceful than the column.[6]

Some patrons chose to emulate local designs. For example, in contrast to the slim circular columns and composite capitals of the portico (see 5.39), the interior columns of the Bentivoglio's Bolognese stable are closer to the more substantial octagonal shape of the city's sixteenth-century arcades (6.1). A local influence is also found in Julius II's early sixteenth-century stable in Viterbo, Bramante's Stallone del Papa, where 'twenty four vast columns of *peperino*, all in one piece . . . twelve in each section' of the stable divide the 100 horse stalls.[7] Documents from the early-sixteenth century show that these impressive *peperino* columns are identical to those in the loggia of the Rocca's inner courtyard.[8]

In Pienza, Pope Pius II's stables have a mix of square and circular columns – the latter similar to those in the Bentivoglio's stable portico – which support the stable's vaulted ceiling and the hanging garden two levels above it. However, unlike those in Bologna, the Pienza columns have simple Tuscan stone capitals (6.2). A stately simplicity is also found in Il Tribolo's double basilica plan at Poggio a Caiano, where the six aisles are defined by four rows of twenty-five monolithic Doric columns in grey *pietra serena*, which support the cross-vaulted ceiling, the spring arches ending in decorative grey stone corbels on the outer walls (6.3). Here, the contrast of rendered walls and austere grey stone continues to give this space a magnificence even without horses. At the earlier Medici Cafaggiolo stables, *pietra serena* had also been used for architectural detail but with more reserve as, having no columns, only the carved corbels on the outer walls and

6.3. Poggio a Caiano: Il Tribolo, the former Medici stables now the Museo Soffici. © Alberto Muciaccia

6.4./6.5. Cafaggiolo: details of corbel and arch in the Medici stables

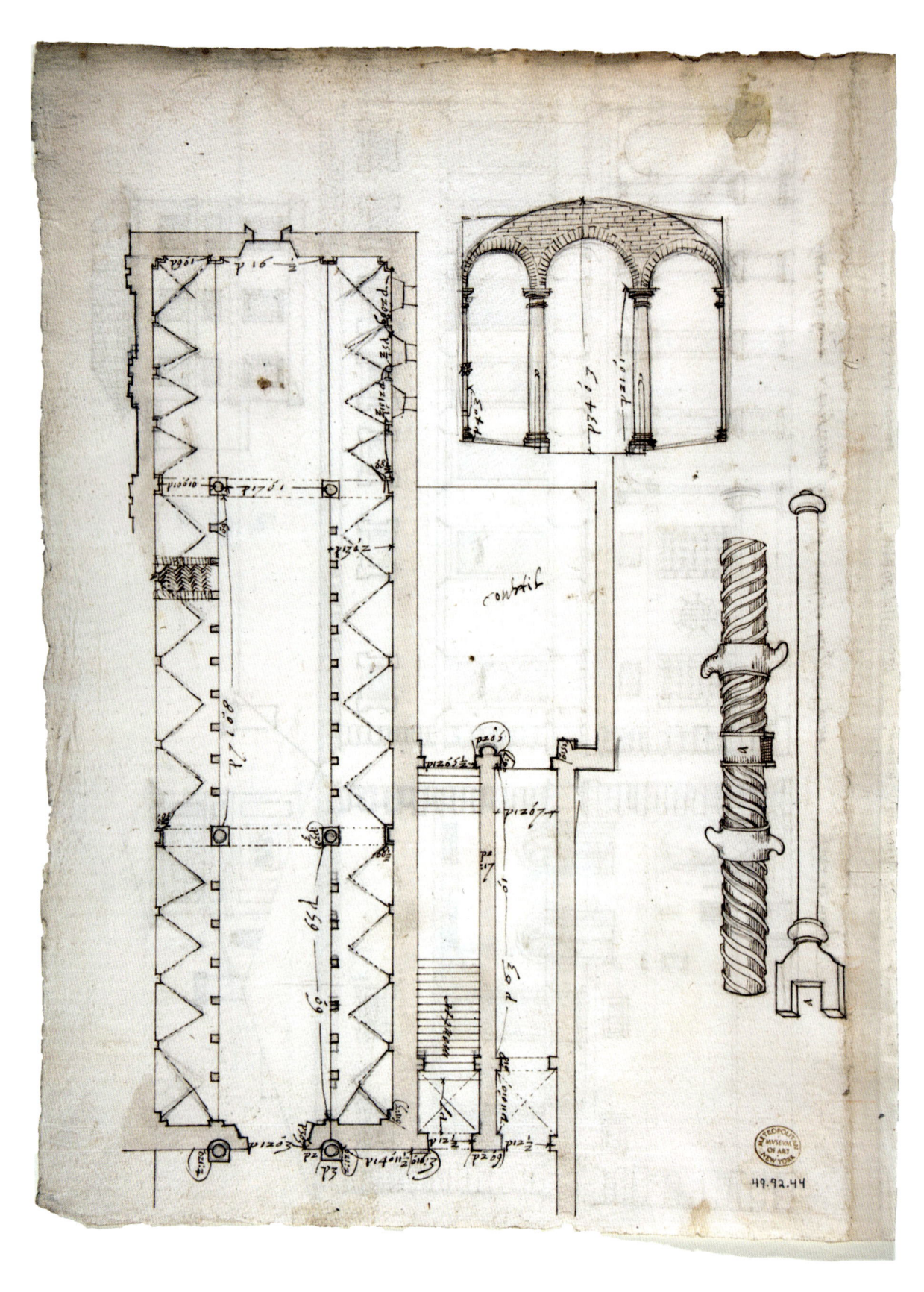

6.6. Mid sixteenth-century plan and cross-section of Agostino Chigi's stables. Anon. Courtesy of New York, Metropolitan Museum, inv. 49.92.44

6.7. Ludovico Sforza's stable at Vigevano, *c.*1490

the borders of the dividing arches are made of the grey stone (6.4, 6.5). The interior of Chigi's Roman stable must have projected a more sophisticated effect as, in 1518, the architecture had fooled Pope Leo X into believing it was a banqueting room[9] but, in this case, a plan of the stable's ground floor shows that Raphael had only used two pairs of Doric columns, positioned to divide the stable's length into three sections and supporting the long barrel-vaulted ceiling, shown in a later cross-section drawing as being made of brick (6.6). Here, there appear to have been three corbels between each pair of columns; each column having been matched by an identical column recessed in the outer wall which supported the barrel-vaulting over the horses' aisles.

A different, but unifying, effect is found in Vigevano, where the three Sforza stables all have rows of elegant monolithic *serizzo* columns dividing and defining the aisles. In each stable the grey columns differ slightly; those in the two earliest stables being slimmer and supporting more acute arches in their cross-vaulted ceilings than those in Ludovico il Moro's later stable (6.7). All three have Corinthian capitals with a shield carved into each of the four sides of the hard grey granite, which close observation shows have been incised with the Sforza *stemma*. In August 1489 Ludovico had ordered Ioanetto da Mandello to take as much *serizzo* granite as was necessary to Vigevano for the use of the stables[10] and, on 27 January 1490 requested Master Giovanni da Mandello and Master Antonio della Porta to transport the necessary amount of columns for the 'construction of our principal stables at Milan and Vigevano'.[11] He also ordered wood from the Sforza estates at Bellinzona and Lucarno, eighty kilometres north of Milan, and in April was employing three sculptors, Cristoforo Stucco, Giovanni Brogio and Erasmino da Castello, who had been given permission to leave their work on the Milanese cathedral to work for a month at Vigevano.[12] It is probably these men who were responsible for carving the Sforza emblems into the hard *serizzo* granite. Even if the extravagant use of stone for the Medici and the Sforza

6.8. La Magliana hunting lodge and stables (left) built c.1513, as they looked in the mid-nineteenth century. Eugenio Landesio, *Casale della Magliana fuori di Porta Portese: alle 7 miglia.* Lithograph, Weiller, 1835 Rome. Courtesy of National Central Library of Rome (BNCR, 18.B.VIII.62)

columns is exceptional, it does illustrate that some Renaissance princes were prepared to spend considerable amounts of money on their stable interiors as well as on the exteriors. As already mentioned, little evidence remains of Francesco or Federico Gonzaga's stables, as there is no doubt that these stables would have matched the elegance found at Vigevano and Poggio a Caiano or perhaps even surpassed it. Certainly, the *serizzo* and *pietra serena* columns and interior details added elegance to a stable interior but they were not the only way of dividing the interior space. At Julius II's and Leo X's vast hunting stables, La Magliana, a continuous wall divided two-thirds of the sixty-eight-metre building to form two separated lines of horse stalls (6.8). Now situated within Rome's suburbs, this large building serves as a hospital, the Ospedale San Giovanni Battista. Both Bramante's assistant, Giuliano Leno, and Giovan Francesco da Sangallo (Giuliano da Sangallo's nephew), worked on this austere building until 1521 and, although unfinished, the ungainly looking country stable, with its robust external buttresses, contrasts significantly with the elegance of Chigi's city stable.

Even more unusual are the internal divisions of Carlo Borromeo's Milanese stable, which are as difficult to understand as the decagonal floor plan if, indeed, the building was designed as a stable (6.9). Pietrasanta's later cross-section shows the positions for pillars, heelposts and tack room as well as two staircases, a well shaft (C), spiral staircase (D) and hay and fodder chutes from the top floor *fienile*, which are situated either side of the entrance door (E). In addition, dotted lines indicate the drainage channels meeting at the central drain (F), which

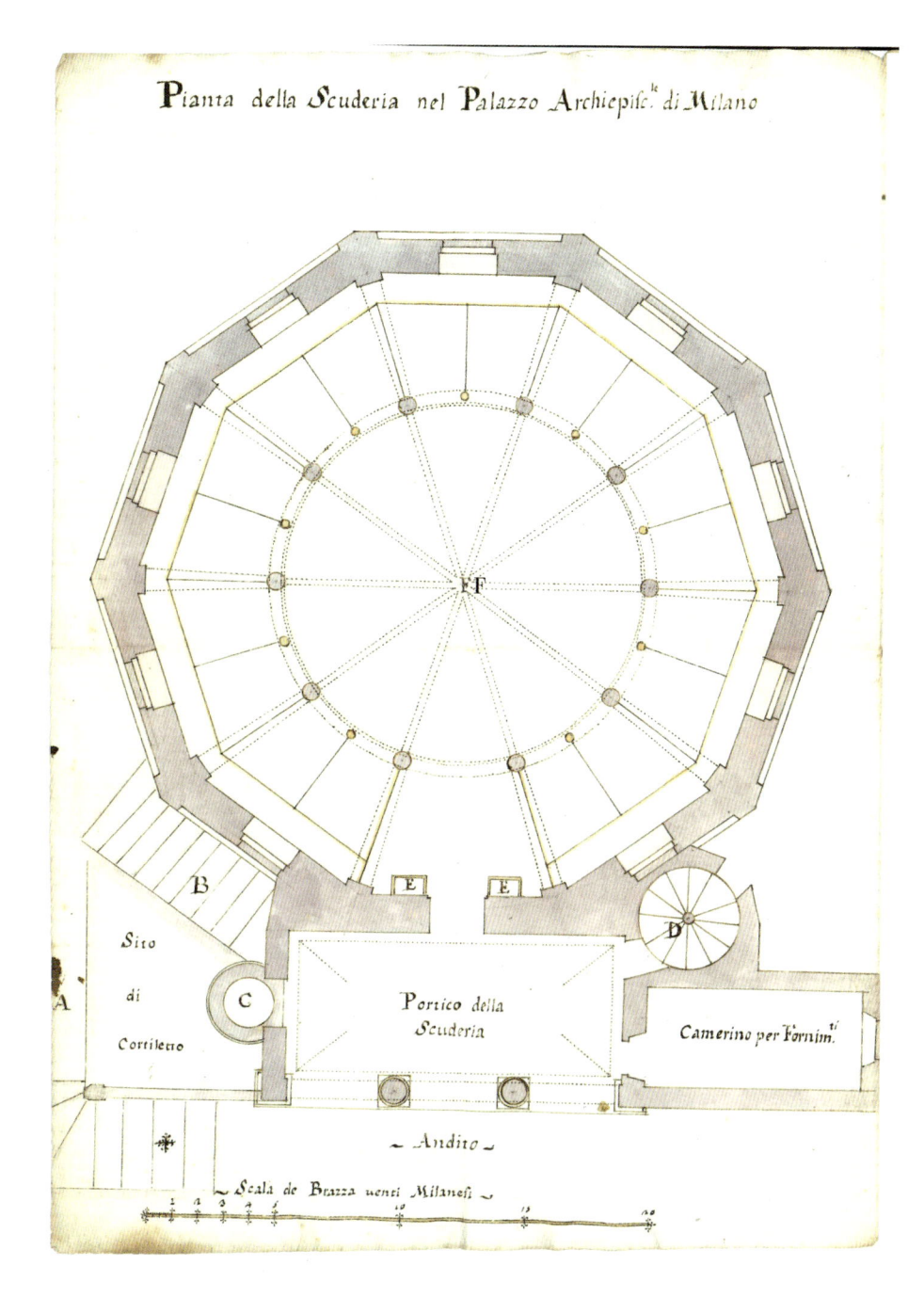

6.9. La Rotonda. Milan, cross-section of the principal level. C.F. Pietrasanta, (1656-1729). Courtesy of Archivio Storica Diocesano di Milano, Mensa Arcivescovile, Palazzo Arcivescovile, cart. 3

leads to a cistern under the mule stable at lower ground level. Certainly, Tibaldi has followed convention by having the Doric order on the lower floors and the more elegant Ionic columns on the upper floor. And, like the Medici and Chigi stables, the Doric order is used for the areas stabling the mules and horses. But why, if the building was always intended as a stable, were the more elegant Ionic columns placed in the hayloft, where only the grooms and stable boys would have seen them?

6.10. Giusto Utens, *Il Trebbio*, c.1590. The stables are centre-right. Florence, Villa medicea della Petraia. ©akg-images/Rabatti & Domingie

6.11. The stable building at Il Trebbio

6.12. Il Trebbio interior, brick vaulting

An alternative to columns for dividing the stable's internal space were heelposts made of wood or stone. In wide single-vaulted spaces, architects would install such posts to mark out the individual horse stalls, using adjustable divisions between the horses such as in the vaulted fifteenth-century Medici stables at Trebbio and the barrel-vaulted stables at Pavia, or possibly at Urbino's La Data stables (6.10, 6.11 & 6.12).[13] Most of these single-vaulted stables are considerably earlier in date than the Farnese stable at Caprarola, Lo Stallone, where the ground floor may be unique for late sixteenth-century Italy in having a fifteen-metre-wide barrel vault

6.13. The Farnese stables, Caprarola: the barrel-vaulted interior of Lo Stallone

spanning a stable of over one hundred horses (6.13). It is quite possible that this stable owes a debt to contemporary French architecture as, according to Worsley, the barrel-vaulted stable was the preferred option in France at that time.[14] Both the architect Vignola and Alessandro Farnese had spent time at the court of François I; Farnese as Papal Legate to the French court and Vignola when working for the French king at Fontainbleau between 1541 and 1543, and it may be that both men were influenced by French stables. There were advantages in having a stable of this design, especially if on a large scale: not only could it impress through sheer spaciousness but also, without columns, the interior remained uncluttered.

Whatever the ground plan, each horse required its own space, divided from its neighbour and with its own feeding trough and hayrack. To discover how the interior of a Renaissance stable functioned, Leonardo da Vinci's drawings and notes are of primary importance.[15] Although it is not certain whether Leonardo's drawings, dated by Kemp to the 1480s,[16] depict actual stables or designs for a future project, theories about their relevance abound. Amongst these, Firpo suggested that Leonardo is creating an 'ideal stable'[17] and Pedretti associated the sketches with the Medici San Marco stables, which he suggests were constructed under the supervision of Baccio Bigio.[18] These sketches have a significance as working models for the stable interior as they allow a comparison of Leonardo's often inventive ideas with existing buildings in order to form a picture of how the Renaissance stable might have appeared and functioned. Apart from archival evidence, design details can be gathered from Alberti's *De equo animante*, Federico da Montefeltro's *Ordini* and Corte's *Il cavallarizzo*.[19]

Leonardo's two cross-sections show a similar exterior appearance but very different internal layout, due to the different proportions of the aisles in both width and height (6.14, 6.15 *over*). Both the Parisian and the Milanese drawings would have been made during Leonardo's time at the Milanese court and the similarities between the Parisian Manuscript B and the Sforza stables at Vigevano – particularly in the spacing of the arcading on the side walls, the continuous mangers and the position of the windows – is interesting. However, in other respects the stables differ considerably. In Vigevano, for example, there is no space for, or evidence of, hay chutes for distributing hay directly from the loft into the hayracks, or of the intricate additional arches and recessed columns dividing horse stalls, suggesting that Leonardo may have been proposing improvements for these stables. In fact, either of the manuscript sketches could be showing intended plans for two other Milanese stables: those of Ludovico Sforza's son-in-law and captain, Galeazzo da Sanseverino, whose stable he is known to have designed, and those of the courtier Mariolo de' Guiscardi, for whom he is also thought to have designed a palace outside the Porta Vercellina in Milan – both men owning horses which Leonardo sketched in preparation for his equestrian monument of Francesco Sforza.[20] Whatever the case Leonardo's extensive hay store shown on the stable's upper level in Manuscript B (6.14), is unusual: in stables such as Vigevano and Poggio a Caiano several decades later, the upper floor is used for accommodation not primarily for fodder.

Nevertheless, if Leonardo's drawings are considered in conjunction with Corte's treatise seventy years later, several similarities arise. For example, Leonardo's detailed cross-section in Manuscript B, reveals a basilica stable with three aisles of equal width and height, while in the accompanying note, he writes,

> The way in which one must arrange a stable: you must first divide its width into 3 parts, its length matters not; and let these 3 divisions be equal and 6 *braccia* broad for each part and 10 high, and the central part shall be for the use of the stablemasters, the 2 side ones for the horses, each requiring 3 *braccia* in width and 6 in length . . .[21]

On the other hand, Leonardo's alternative design in the Trivulziana Codex contradicts the idea for three equal aisles and shows a central aisle one and a half times the width of the side aisles and considerably higher (6.15). Differently proportioned aisles are seen at Poggio a Caiano, where the central aisle is 4.20 metres wide and each of the two side aisles are 3.10 metres, a design characteristic which reflects Corte's theory that a stable's central aisle should be at least two *canne*[22] wide but preferably three or more, the extra width being mainly for effect but also for practicality. Corte emphasises the visual effects, explaining that the 'more beautiful [the central aisle] is to look at' the 'more magnificent and regal' it is.[23]

With the exception of Tibaldi's decagonal stable in Milan, all stables considered here had a central service aisle divided from the two side aisles either by columns or heelposts, or a combination of both. Apart from being supportive and in some instances decorative these columns and posts defined the horses' stalls by allowing a space for one or more horses between them. It should be noted that the capacity of a stable was sometimes exaggerated and probably only indicated the number of horses that could be stabled on a temporary basis. At Vigevano, the three stables are reported to have held 300 horses: one hundred horses stabled in each building. This is certainly credible for the largest 91-metre-long stable as, with 25 supporting columns on each side, it is likely that, using Leonardo da Vinci's allowance of 3 *braccia* or 1.75 metres per horse, two horses could be stabled between each pair of columns with a wooden divider (now lost) or poles between them. But the two earlier stables at Vigevano are considerably smaller, and would certainly not have had the capacity for 100 horses.[24] At Poggio a Caiano, Lamberini has suggested that three horses would need to be stabled between each pair of pillars if the full capacity of 296 horses and mules was to be achieved.[25] This also seems unlikely as it would make the Medici stalls uncomfortably narrow for the horses and it is more likely that only two horses stood between the pillars, making the actual number stabled at Poggio closer to 200.[26] It has already been noted that Raphael's stable for Agostino Chigi's was unlikely to have housed 100 horses on a single level[27] but it is notable for Raphael's unusually sparing use of full-length columns, with most horse stalls defined by heelposts. The ground plan shows the stable divided by only two pairs of Doric columns supporting the brick barrel vault, each matched by corresponding recessed columns on the outer wall which supported the arcades over the side aisles. The bay closest to the stable entrance is then divided into fourteen stalls by heelposts or short stone columns, while the larger central section contains twenty stalls. The third bay shows no divisions and may well have been used for washing and grooming the horses (see 6.6).

Whatever the capacity of the stable, each horse required a defined space. While the horses were kept in ordered lines by columns and heelposts, they also needed to be kept apart, both to prevent them stealing each other's food and to stop them biting and kicking one another. This was achieved in several ways: by tethering and hobbling them and by partitioning their stalls. Corte recommends that,

> In the middle of the wall, close to the head of the horse, should be a ring, so that you can attach the necessary rope, which is attached to the noseband of the horse's halter, ending at the said ring, with the evident use of such an attachment. There must be two iron rings for every stall, with one on the side and the other on the manger, plugged [securely] into the rails, and two and half *palmi*[28] apart from one another; these must be tied to the horse by two ropes, one attached to one ring and the other to the other ring; and this will make the horse have a firm, not soft, neck; not turning on one hand more than the other, as when a single rope is attached to him.[29]

Three centuries earlier, Giordano Ruffo, stable master to the Holy Roman Emperor Frederick II, had also recommended using two ropes for tethering a young horse, but only for specific purposes: to help tame him and to steady him when he is groomed.[30] Corte's method of tethering by two ropes might seem repressive, but he believed this method of restraint benefited the horse's development and conformation by strengthening the neck muscles. Presumably, like Ruffo, he is only recommending this tethering for specific periods in the day as, when describing the flooring, he mentions that the horse should be able to 'lie down, get up' and 'turn around',[31] – impossible if the horse was tethered on both sides. Similarly, Caracciolo recommended this two-rope method in order to prevent the horse's neck from becoming softer or harder on one side than on the other.[32]

In addition to tying up the horse, two methods were used to prevent him from biting or kicking his neighbour: hobbling, and posts and rails. The first, like tethering, restrained the horse by loosely tying one front leg to the corresponding back leg or the two front legs together. Caracciolo suggests this is done with wool, explaining that the horse 'cannot go forward in any way . . . [a] tradition, which, above all else, is good for the legs',[33] explaining that by spreading the horse's weight evenly over all four feet, its legs and shoulders will develop equally, which suggests it was as much for aesthetic value as for the horse's safety that these methods were

6.14. Leonardo da Vinci, sketch for an ideal stable, *c.*1485-1488. Paris, Bibliothèque de l'Institut de France, MS 2173-manuscrit B, 39r. Photo ©RMN-Grand Palais (Institut de France)/ René-Gabriel Ojéda

6.15. **Leonardo da Vinci**, Sketch of a stable, *c.*1487-9. Milan, Biblioteca Trivulziana, MS 2162, 21v. ©Comune di Milano. All rights reserved

6.16. Wooden dividing poles attached with rope. Detail of 5.4

6.17. Posts with hanging bales attached by chains, Dunster Castle stables, c.1617.
©William C. Rolf

6.18. Leonardo da Vinci, wooden dividing poles at two levels. Detail of 6.14

recommended. However, at the turn of the seventeenth century, Ferraro spoke out against hobbling, describing it as a Spanish custom which benefited the stable boys more than 'the poor horses' and adding that hobbling should only be done as a last resort.[34]

Having defined the length and breadth of a horse's stall, substantial divisions between horses were required – the flimsy wattle fencing depicted in early paintings of nativity scenes being unsuitable for horses if indeed they were ever used. This partitioning was created with wooden poles (6.16) or hanging bales suspended from leather straps or chains which were attached to wooden heelposts or stone columns, similar to those at Dunster Castle in Somerset (6.17). Possible evidence of rail fixings remains on the stone columns at Poggio a Caiano, which still have a number of iron rings attached to them. An idea of their appearance can be found in Leonardo da Vinci's Manuscript B, where he shows two sets of dividing rails – one rail level with the horse's flank and the lower heel rails at hock height, both clearly fixed on the inner, stall side of the columns (6.18). This is an unusually impractical detail for a man with such an inventive mind as it would be more convenient to have them attached to the outer side of the column, easily accessible from the central aisle. These heel rails running behind the horses' back legs prevented them from kicking out and, as Leonardo explained, stopped 'the horses from pulling out their tying', suggesting that they usually had a certain manoeuvrability whilst tied up. However, whilst Leonardo's rails are shown fixed, those hanging from chains would have had more flexibility and it would be relatively easy for a horse to kick its legs over them.

In stables where heelposts were used, Corte advises that they should be made of 'good wood, excellent quality, very straight [and] one and a half *canna* high (about 11 feet or 3.35 metres) and well secured in the ground'.[35] No doubt heelposts were installed in the fifteenth-century barrel-vaulted Urbino stables where the Duke's ordinances stipulate that either hanging rails or wooden planks should be used to separate the horses from one another.[36] Similarly, Alessandro Farnese's account books show that hanging bars attached to heelposts were replaced in the old stables at Caprarola in 1560.[37] Unfortunately, there is no remaining evidence of these posts and hanging rails but, although not specifying whether they are made of wood or stone, Serlio's mid sixteenth-century cross-section (6.19, *over*) shows them with a decorative ball crowning each post, and an idea of their appearance can be gathered from the early seventeenth-century examples at Dunster Castle (see 6.17). Corte's emphasis on the quality of the posts suggests they were part of the stable's aesthetic, giving the stalls an uninterrupted uniformity in the same way rows of stone columns would have done. It is difficult to decide whether or not the restriction of horses by double tethering and hobbling did benefit their conformation, as Corte and Caracciolo had claimed. Whichever is the case, the limitation of the horses' movements and their regimented lines indicated one way of displaying man's control over these powerful animals.

Even if tied up loosely, Leonardo's measurements for the stall – 3 by 6 *braccia* (1.75 x 3.50 metres)[38] – allowed the horse little manoeuvrability. Many years later, Corte recommended a larger space, 'two and a half man's paces wide' and 'four paces from the manger to the end of the column', suggesting it should be wide enough for the groom to turn the horse round from either side and manage him comfortably. Corte goes a step further and introduces a new concept, the *cassetta* or loose box.

> For the princes and riders who can, I would like them to place some looseboxes (*cassette*) at the end of the stable for their most favoured horses and for those that are ill but not with contagious diseases . . . These looseboxes or compartments can be made of planks, in such a way, that each favourite horse has its own [space].[39]

6.19. Sebastiano Serlio, cross-section of a stable (top right). *Tutte l'opere d'architettura et prospettiva*, VI, 73r, 'For the Palace of a King', detail

To date, the loosebox has been described both as 'English' and as 'the most significant innovation of late eighteenth-century stable design',[40] but the concept existed in Italy at least a century earlier and it is possible that Corte himself had introduced the idea to England, when working at the Elizabethan court in 1564-5. The loosebox had several advantages: it allowed the horse more freedom of movement, its fodder was protected, straw was not strewn around the stable and there was no need for the horse to be tethered unless being groomed. But it also had disadvantages: it was considerably more expensive to make than hanging rails, it occupied a larger area, reducing the number of horses in the stable and it could not keep the horses in line. As Corte's words explain, the loosebox was only for 'princes or those who can' afford both the space and the money for it.

For centuries, theories had varied on the correct height of mangers and hayracks but, as in justifications for tethering, authors often supported their theories with the perceived benefits for the horse. In the fourth century, Vegetius had recommended that each horse should have its own manger and that the height of the rack should be

> in proportion to the horse's stature, neither too high lest their throat be extended so as to do them hurt; nor too low, lest it touch their eyes and their head.[41]

Many years later, Ruffo had suggested that all fodder should be given to the horse as low down as possible, near to the horse's feet, whether it was 'hay, straw, barley or anything else', because while strengthening itself through nourishment the continuous use of its neck and head will make it more supple and make the horse easier to school. In addition, the horse's legs would become stronger and better proportioned.[42] A century and a half later, Alberti is giving similar advice:

> With barley and seed, make sure that [the horses] have to eat from the bottom of their trough. This will prevent them from gorging themselves or swallowing too much seed whole and, besides that, it will make their muscles and chests firmer and stronger.[43]

By the end of the fifteenth century, the *ordini* for Federico da Montefeltro's stables at Urbino acknowledges that there were 'many diverse opinions' on mangers, advising that whether the manger is shared or each horse has his own, it must be slightly wider at the top and installed at a height where the horse cannot knock into it with his shoulder or chest.[44] Unfortunately, as with other wooden fittings, no remaining evidence has yet been found of any wooden mangers although one is depicted in the wooden stable depicted in Figure 6.17. But stone mangers do survive at Vigevano and Pavia, running the full length of the stable walls and indicating that, by the late-fifteenth century, the manger's height had been raised from floor level to an accepted position at chest height for the horse (see 5.6). This height is suggested by Leonardo's drawing and in his recommendation that the manger should be two *braccia* (116 cm) from the ground,[45] and by Serlio in his mid sixteenth-century treatise (see 6.19, 6.20).[46] Like Vegetius, the partitioned manger is recommended by Leonardo, Corte and Caracciolo; Caracciolo suggesting that the manger should have wood or stone dividers

> so that each horse can eat his food in his own time, or later; not preoccupied with his neighbour ... [because] there are those that are naturally fastidious who are slower than others at eating, and if one does not protect their ration, in short, they will become thin.

Caracciolo also describes the physical and digestive benefits this style of manger would bring the horse,

> so that by arching his neck to take the food from inside, it will become supple; beyond which through this movement and work they will chew their fodder better and prepare it for better digestion.[47]

As to the actual shape of the manger, Corte suggests it should be in 'the shape of a boat or bowl' to prevent the horse throwing his food about.[48] This would have been similar to the boat-shaped mangers shown in Serlio's drawing and which remain at Pavia (see 5.6). It seems that mangers were made either of stone or of wood, despite the danger of the wood splintering and harming the horse. At Caprarola, the Farnese accounts record that the stable's stone mangers were given a coat of whitewash, *calce*.[49]

Cleanliness was also considered important, with Vegetius having suggested that both the 'bowl for serving [the horses] with barley and the manger, be always clean, lest any filth be mixed with their food, and be hurtful to them'.[50] To keep the mangers clean, both Francesco di Giorgio and Leonardo described a wooden cover for the stone manger. Leonardo explained it should be made so that 'it can be uncovered, as are boxes by raising their lids' and illustrates

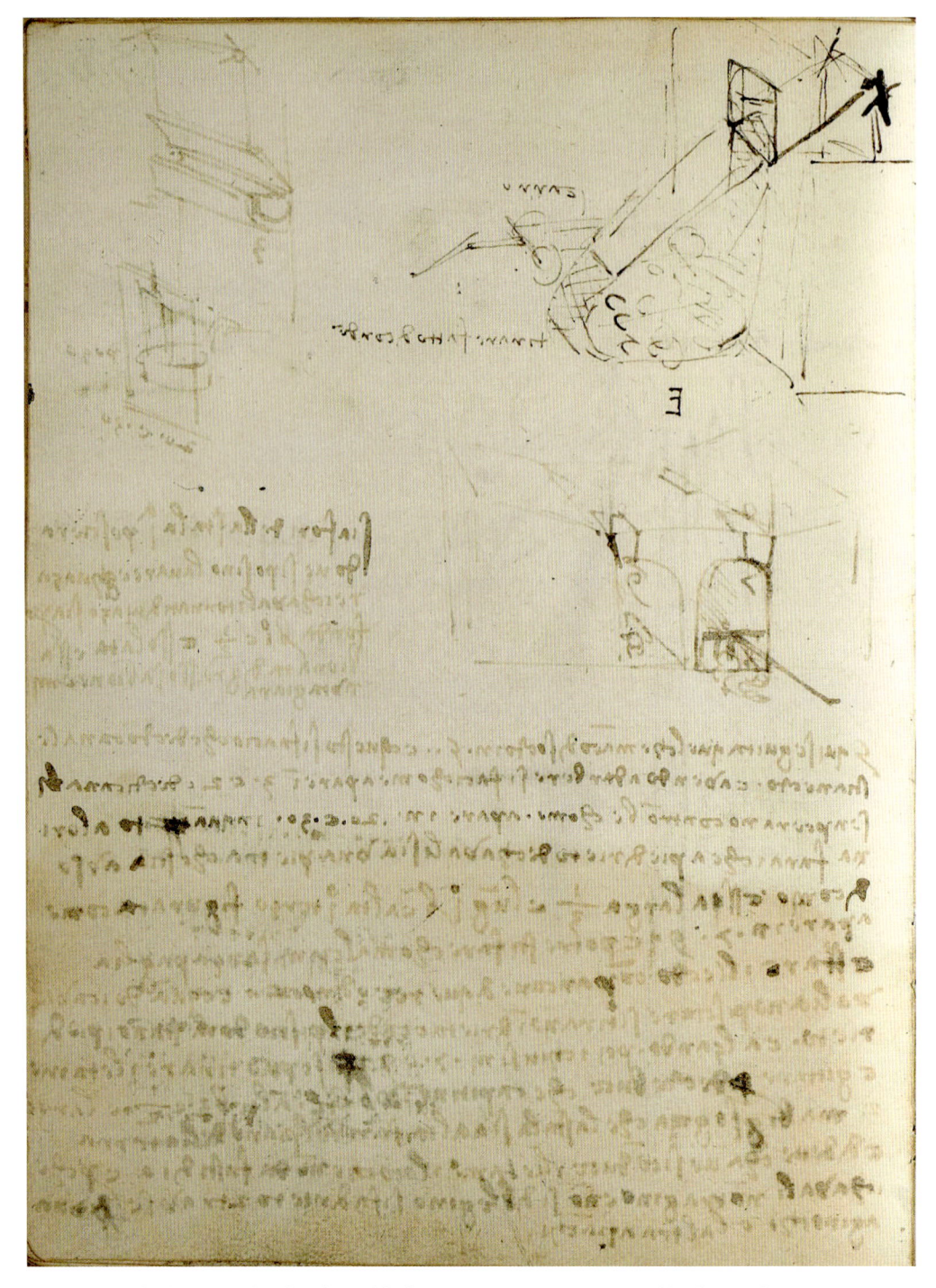

6.20. Leonardo da Vinci, sketches for stable fittings, *c.*1485-1488. Paris, Bibliothèque de l'Institut de France, Ms 2173-manuscrit B, 38v. Photo © RMN-Grand Palais (Institut de France)/ René-Gabriel Ojéda

top left: covered manger, with water/food bowl below it.
top right: hoist (*carro*) for lifting hay and straw
bottom right: a cross-section of the stalls' sloping floors and the stable's drainage system

6.21. Master of Mazarine, 'Sale of Arab Horses', c.1430, showing the position of the hayrack and manger. Detail of 5.3

this in his cross-section (6.20). In the same decade, the account books for the Duke of Calabria's Marcianise stables[51] show payments for one hundred individual wooden table-top covers fitted at these stud farm stables, describing them as attached to the individual mangers in four places[52] and, at Caprarola, repairs were made to covered mangers in the 1560s.[53] These covered mangers could also be used as water channels, with Francesco di Giorgio explaining that, at La Data, the water passing through the troughs not only cleaned them but could also be released from certain points to assist in washing down the stable.[54] Even so, despite their hygienic advantages, it seems that stone troughs were not in common use in the early seventeenth century when the Venetian architect, Scamozzi, explained that certainly for military stables, it was more usual to make a manger out of wood than of stone,[55] probably because stone was more expensive for large numbers of cavalry horses.

Like the manger, the hayrack was considered to strengthen the neck as the horse reached up to it. Several treatises, as well as Leonardo's sketch, suggest that the rack should run the full length of the stable wall, positioned above and parallel to the manger. This position was already established in the early-fifteenth century and is shown in the Master of Mazarine's miniature showing the sale of Arab horses (6.21). Contrary to this view, Alberti is unique in suggesting that the hay is put into hanging baskets,

> Hang up the baskets of hay sufficiently high that the horses, in order to reach it, must stand up, crane their necks, and expend some effort. This will ensure that their heads remain dry and their shoulders agile.[56]

The material for Alberti's basket is not specified, although probably of pliable wooden strips or rope, loosely banded together so that the hay can be pulled out by the horse. Placed at a height level with the horse's head it would, as Alberti writes, exercise the neck of the horse when eating the hay; the modern-day equivalent, the hay net, has the same effect. As usual, Leonardo is specific about the height of the hayrack, saying that it should be three *braccia* (1.75 metres)[57] to the base of the rack and four (2.33 metres) to the top, allowing a 1 *braccia* (58.3 cms) space above the manger.[58] However, another option is given in the Urbino ordinances which show concern that dust from a hayrack could fall into a horse's nose, causing it to cough. Instead, they advise putting the hay in the mangers with crossbars over them, presumably to stop the horse pulling out large wads and scattering hay on the floor.[59]

Almost a century later, Caracciolo still felt the need to rebuff Ruffo's theory of feeding the horse on the floor[60] which had, he wrote, been recently endorsed by Gioachino Camerario.[61] Explaining that this should only be done if there is nothing to distract the horse and you want to hurry him up,[62] Caracciolo repeats Vegetius' suggestion that the ideal height of the rack depended on the horse's size.

> The hayrack should be the correct height, according to the horse's disposition, not higher than necessary, so he is not breathless when he extends his neck, nor so low that it touches his head and eyes.[63]

He then explains that if the hay rack is incorrectly placed, the horse might not consume enough hay, or dust could cause problems in the nostrils and eyes or cover the mane with dirt. Such conditions, he adds, are more suited to a hostelry than to a riding school, and he dismisses the advice to put food on the floor even if it is said to make the horse 'more manageable and more beautiful'. Instead he writes that the hayrack should be high up to benefit the horse's appearance, so that

> young foals take their food [whilst] looking above them, and become accustomed to holding their heads up high, which is considered of great charm in a horse.[64]

Depictions of a hay rack can be seen in both Leonardo's manuscript and in Serlio's cross-section of a proposed palace stable (see 6.18 and 6.19).[65] Leonardo's drawing shows a continuous structure, partitioned for each horse, which is wider at the top to allow hay to be thrown down into it from the hayloft on the first floor. The rack, which projects over the covered manger, is shown with a series of parallel vertical rails, presumably held together with a cross bar at the top and the bottom, through which the horse could pull out mouthfuls of hay or straw. According to Worsley this sloping rack was a standard fitting in England, Germany, Spain and France as well as in Italy. But whether a basket or a hayrack, one of the principal advantages of these fittings was that less hay was wasted, as little fell onto the stable floor which might have been damp with urine. And of course by reaching up for the hay, the horse's neck was strengthened – enabling the high head carriage that was much praised in the horse. This very much reflects other Renaissance theories in stable design, which intended to create the correct environment and conditions for the horse to develop strong musculature and good head carriage, aspects which contributed both to its appearance and performance and, therefore, to its value as a court commodity.

It was, however, no use building up a horse's musculature if its legs and feet were not in the best condition. And it was for this reason that both the stable's flooring and its drainage were given considerable attention; poor quality or slippery surfaces affected not only the horse's feet but its general health. Xenophon had even compared the feet to the foundations of a building:

> Just as a house is bound to be worthless if the foundations are unsound, however well the upper parts may look, so a war-horse will be quite useless, even though all his other points are good, if he has bad feet; for in that case he will be unable to use any of his good points.[66]

In the mid-fifteenth century, Alberti would warn of the effects on the horse of a damp and dirty floor:

> the fetid smelling vapour of manure in the stable ... weakens everything that it moistens and is, more than anything, a true scourge for the legs and the feet of horses.[67]

Consequently, architectural and equestrian texts would not only emphasise the importance of suitable flooring and healthy environments, they would also advise on the most suitable methods for keeping the stable dry and clean. This should be seen as part of 'the culture of cleanliness', which Douglas Biow has described as one of the pre-occupations of the Renaissance: the 'pre-occupation with dirt and cleanliness'.[68] This was why Alberti had not only criticised the dirty stable but emphasised the importance of efficient drainage for maintaining human health. In the same way that he had written of 'the fetid smelling vapour of manure', he criticised Siena for being 'filthy and offensively vaporous' because the Tuscan city had no drains, he writes

> I need not stress here how important drains are in maintaining the sanitation of the city, the cleanliness of the buildings, public and private alike, and toward preserving the wholesomeness and purity of the air'.[69]

It was also, no doubt, why Leonardo had described a detailed drainage system for a stable[70] similar to the one he had designed for a model city.[71] In fact, throughout the Renaissance an emphasis would remain on the importance of cleanliness in all aspects of life, not only as a protection against the spread of disease but also as a form of cultural expression, with many writers including it as a topic in their books on economics and household management.[72] Torquato Tasso described cleanliness as 'not only pleasant to look at' but as conferring 'nobility and dignity on things that are base and mean by nature'.[73] Similarly, those who wrote on stable architecture would also concern themselves with the values and importance attached to cleanliness, suggesting suitable flooring and drainage systems to maintain the horses' health.

Of course, for the visitor to a Renaissance stable it would be the surface of the central aisle, running between the lines of horses, which would be noticed as he entered the stable, not the flooring beneath the horses which was probably covered with straw. But for those who advised on husbandry or stable design, the area under the horse was at least as important as the central aisle, if not more so. The construction and maintenance of the stable flooring was, therefore, a major factor in stable design both for the horses' health and for the visual effect. Unfortunately, few stables retain their original floor surface unless of brick or stone, the wood having rotted or the floor having been resurfaced, although at Poggio a Caiano there is clear evidence of drainage channels with grilles set at regular intervals at the base of the stalls (6.22, *over*). However, some more rustic country stables provide evidence of a flooring of bedrock filled with cobblestones and it may be that some of the rural court stables, such as stud farms, had this type of flooring. A summary of early works on husbandry shows that there had been a long-standing concern with keeping the stable dry, specifically the horse's stall. Xenophon, for example, mentioned the danger of a slippery floor, recommending drainage channels in a sloping cobblestone floor, each

6.22. Drainage system at the Medici stables, Poggio a Caiano, photographed through a protective glass screen

stone about the size of the horse's hoof, which, he believed, would also 'harden the feet of the horses standing on them';[74] a flooring rarely recommended in later texts. In the first century, Columella had suggested that the stable should be 'floored with boards of hard wood'[75] and in the fourth century Palladius recommended using 'boards of strong timber' to be

> laid at the bottom of the stalls of the stable with straw, that it may be soft for the horses when they lie down, and the boards may be hard for them when they are standing.[76]

Similarly, Vegetius had suggested that floors should not be made of soft wood but of 'solid hard lasting oak well put together; for this . . . hardens the horses' hoofs like rocks'.[77] At the end of the fifteenth century, Leonardo would also advocate the use of wood but, in his case, *in lieu* of straw, 'you could do, as some do, without straw and make the sleeping place of boards of oak or walnut'.[78] Conversely, in the same period the Duke of Urbino's *ordini* recommended wood or brick flooring but follows Xenophon's advice that it should slope, so that urine could drain away through pierced bricks to the drainage channel beneath the stable.[79]

Apart from removing wet straw from the stall, one of the principal ways to preserve a wood floor was to create a vacuum underneath it, so that air could circulate and keep the underside dry. Alberti gave a brief but clear description of the ideal stable floor and, although he suggested 'oxen need a stone floor to stop their feet rotting in their filth', like Columella, Palladius and Vegetius he recommended a wooden surface for horses, for a horse's stall, a trench must be dug and then covered with planks of holm or oak, to prevent the ground becoming damp with urine and the pawing of hooves from wearing down the floor and hoof alike.[80]

By the 1560s, Corte had dismissed brick flooring for being dangerous[81] and recommended planks of 'elm, oak or another strong wood' laid on joists, the area between the joists filled with coal (*carboni*) with a ventilated area under the stall. However, his advice for a temperate climate was different

If the floor is in a temperate country, it doesn't matter if you have floorboards, bricks or pebbles . . . and pebbles are better than brick because they keep drier and suit the horse's feet better and also they keep cool.[82]

Unlike Corte, in 1615 Scamozzi would not make an allowance for a change in climate, suggesting instead that a stable floor should be made of river pebbles or earthenware bricks laid in mortar, although never of flintstone or 'pietre felici' because these could bruise the horse's feet.[83]

The contradictory advice on this important aspect of stable design makes it difficult to ascertain which surfaces were actually used in Italian Renaissance stables. And yet it does suggest that writers were primarily concerned for the horses' welfare, finding advantages and disadvantages in most of these surfaces. Wood might be softer and warmer as a base on which to stand or lie but, without good care and maintenance, it would rot and require replacing. As for the long-lasting and colder hard surfaces, such as bedrock, stone and brick, these could wear down the horse's iron shoes or break the unshod hoof, unless the floor was covered with a thick layer of straw. Flat paving such as tiles or bricks could become slippery – although there is evidence that herringbone brick was used at Caprarola. In 1565, the use of hard stone flooring would be described by Thomas Blundeville as an 'unsuitable Italian habit'.[84] But evidence shows that such criticism was unjustified as, in reality, many Italian theorists, like Blundeville himself, favoured wood at this period.

Xenophon's suggestion of a sloping floor became an important factor for keeping the stable clean but, as with many aspects of Renaissance stable design, it also had an aesthetic value. Making the horse stand higher in front than behind was not only thought to help settle it but also contributed to its appearance, when standing in the stall. Ruffo's chapter on how to recognise the beauty of a horse explains that the horse should stand higher in front than behind[85] and, even in the late-seventeenth century, a similar view would prevail, with the Dutch born Balthazar Gerbier claiming that 'the higher a Horse stands towards the Manger, a better sight it is, especially when the Lights of the Stable strikes on the Horse[s'] . . . backs'.[86] He then explained the physical benefits for the horse, who by 'reposing more on his hinder feet than on the foremost [would] be more light and nimble in his gate and pace'.[87] The earliest evidence of an actual sloping floor is found in Francesco di Giorgio's late fifteenth-century treatise, where he describes his magnificent Urbino stables, La Data, as having a stall floor that would assist drainage as it was 'slightly sloping and lower in the centre', which he believed also settled the horses 'which like to stand higher at the front'.[88] The idea is also evident in Leonardo's note accompanying his stable sketch where he describes the stall half a *braccia* (*c*.30cm) higher in front than behind[89] – his sketch showing such detail as does his drawing in the Trivulziana Codex.[90] His detailed explanatory text to the first of these drawings is worth quoting in full:

6.23. Galeazzo Maria Sforza's stable at Vigevano, c.1470, showing convex central aisle with drainage gulleys at each side

6.24 and 6.25. the east end of Lo Stallone, the Farnese stables at Caprarola, showing herringbone flooring (*far left*) and detail of the drainage gulley (*right*)

As for the manure, you will see that the rear feet of each horse correspond to a wedge-shaped stone which should be one third of a *braccia*[91] wide, one *braccia* long and one third of a *braccia* thick ... and when the horses want to stale,[92] they should step back so that the manure would fall away where they are standing with their feet. And once the lids are lifted, one can collect the manure and throw it through such holes, which give onto vaulted cubicles three and half *braccia* high and two *braccia* wide, but the stable should be high above the ground level; and from the said cubicles the manure is carried away to a convenient place.[93]

As already stated, at Poggio a Caiano drainage channels and grilles remain through which water and urine once drained away, although any sign of the original flooring has disappeared both from the central aisle and from the stalls either side of it. Drawings of Raphael's Chigi stables and in Serlio's treatise (see 6.6, 6.19) also show stalls sloping down from the outer wall towards the central aisle, an idea continued by both Corte and Caracciolo and by Scamozzi at the beginning of the seventeenth century with the latter recommending the slope both for strengthening the horse and for its health.[94] In contrast, unlike the Italians and the Dutch-born Gerbier, the Englishman Thomas de Grey considered it cruel to make the horse put extra weight on its back legs, as it caused pain and resulted in lameness.[95] Nevertheless, in France, the tradition of a sloping stone floor was still being recommended by François de Garsault in his *Le Nouveau parfait maréchal* of 1741.[96]

A strange variation of the sloping floor, which had apparently become popular in Naples, is criticised by Corte as being awkward for the horses to stand on. He describes how Neapolitan horsemen were installing a hump-backed floor (*gobbo*) to the stall which, from Corte's description, must have been the shape of a cushion over which the horse straddled its legs,

> The floor base [is] humpbacked in the middle, making it low in front and also at the back ... the horses find it difficult to rest themselves, and difficult to get up if they lie down, the urine can only be in those areas running through the front feet.[97]

It seems, therefore, that variations of the sloping floor had become an accepted part of Italian stable design by the mid-sixteenth century. However, whilst good drainage was beneficial for the horses' feet and aided the cleaning of the stables, it should be remembered that the angled floor also contributed to the visual effect of the horse's conformation. Gerbier's reasoning behind the angled floor may well have been seen as beneficial to a horse's appearance in Italy as it would be in seventeenth-century England. But even if the apparent extra height added by the sloping floor to the horse's head, neck and shoulders helped display the horse's good breeding and conformation, most writers would emphasise the benefit to health rather than to the horse's appearance.[98]

What then of the central service aisles, some of which still survive in their original form? Corte had suggested that this wide aisle should be paved in brick or terracotta tiles,[99] although this contradicts his earlier advice that 'most dangerous and disastrous for the horse are those areas made of brick'.[100] Nevertheless most of these aisles had hard wearing surfaces, being made of stone slabs, bricks or cobblestones. The principal method for keeping the central aisle dry was its shape – usually slightly raised in the centre – which allowed any fluid to drain down to the gutters running between the central aisle and the horse stalls. This is seen from the convex grey stone aisle running down the centre of the earliest Vigevano stable (6.23) and at Caprarola, where the russet herringbone brickwork is visible in the east end of the stable entrance, with pale stone drainage channels on either side (6.24, 6.25). Beyond the 'regal magnificence' of a wider central aisle, Corte had added some practical benefits: it enabled the horses to be promenaded indoors if the weather was inclement, it was also useful for cooling down tired or sweating horses, drying them after being washed or gently exercising them if they were ill.[101]

In advising how to look after exhausted horses, Caracciolo recommended that the stable should shelter the horses in the same way that a cellar shelters wine: 'cool in the summer and tepid in the winter'.[102] In both *De equo animante* and *De re aedificatoria* Alberti had warned that a sweating horse should never be left in the shadows of a cold night nor in a strong north wind,[103] advising that the stable wall facing the horse's head should not be damp because 'the horse has

6.26. The Medici stables Cafaggiolo, vaulting under the west end

a thin skull, susceptible to moisture and cold'[104] and explaining that the moon's rays 'can cause cataracts and heavy coughs'.[105] But it was not only in the winter months that there was a fear of horses becoming chilled. In August 1492, the Gonzaga's riding master, Francisco de Mediolano, wrote that the stables at Gonzaga were very cold because they were not covered and that, if the horses remained there, he believed most of them would become ill.[106]

It was due to this fear of the cold that writers suggested stables should have extra warmth, with harness rooms, blacksmiths' forges, kitchens and even pottery kilns seen as possible heat sources, although sometimes with reservations. Corte recommended having fires in the harness rooms at either end of the stables and also that the smithy should be located close to the stables, supplying heat from the farrier's furnace;[107] certainly, several examples of these indirect sources existed. At Pienza, the subterranean stables are described as including several blacksmiths' workshops[108] while in Urbino, the subterranean area used for saddling, mounting and dismounting horses had two sources of heat: the large kitchen fireplace on the opposite side of the wall and Duke Federico's thermal baths – the latter presumably for the convenience of the Duke as well as for warming the stables.[109] Furthermore, the stables at Cafaggiolo may also have benefited from a form of under-floor heating beneath the west end. Now almost completely filled with rubble, a small excavated section has revealed brick vaulting that could have housed kilns, possibly used for the Fattorini's production of *maiolica* under Medici patronage in the sixteenth century (6.26).[110] Conversely, there was an established fear that too much heat was bad for horses. Vitruvius suggested that, although 'the stable, above all in the villa, should be built in the warmest place', the animals 'should not face the fire' as this would make their coats shaggy,[111] while Vegetius wrote that horse stables should be warm not hot, because although heat 'preserves their fatness . . . and may seem to refresh them, nevertheless it causes indigestion'.[112] Later, Francesco di Giorgio endorsed these views, writing that horses should not be housed close to a furnace as excessive heat, like extreme cold, could be bad for them.[113]

It was no doubt due to a desire to maintain suitable stable conditions that advice was given on the correct size and location of the windows. It is not certain when Italian stable windows were glazed although by 1565 Blundeville had recommended glazing in England.[114] However, there were alternative ways of keeping the heat in and the insects out. It is known, for example, that in July 1492, five days after they were constructed, thirteen windows at the royal Aragonese stables at Marcianise had canvas tied over them with tapes to prevent flies and other insects from entering the stable.[115] Of course, it may be that these windows were already glazed and that the canvas acted as a fly screen when the windows were open. Certainly, Gandini mentions that Este *selleria* records from 1478 show that it was customary to put old sheeting over the court stable windows[116] and, similarly, records show that cloth windows were part of the renovation of the Ferrarese San Francesco stables in 1535.[117] Nonetheless, in Poggio a Caiano it seems likely that the large mid sixteenth-century windows lighting the first-floor corridor would have been glazed, purely for the comfort of the people inside. But whether glazed or not, all windows were positioned above the horses' heads, sometimes as much as three metres from the ground. And whilst this height may have helped with the horses' security, it also produced aesthetic and health benefits for the horses. Not only did the height, and the downward sloping internal sills, allow wide shafts of natural light to illuminate the stable, they prevented cold draughts or hot sunrays from falling directly onto the horses' backs. Most windows were rectangular, although there is an exception at Vigevano where the arched windows contrast with the Gothic bipartite windows of the other courtyard buildings.[118] Corte would encourage as much sunlight as possible in his ideal stable, suggesting that from 'one aisle to the other' there should be numerous large windows 'as the beauty of the stable demands'.[119] Scamozzi's advice was more detailed as, like his advice on the stable's aspect, it varied according to the climate. In temperate areas the stables should be lit at least from one side, although 'better from two'; in hot places there should be no direct light 'from the south or west because each one of them is harmful to the horse'. In every case, he writes, the windows must be above the heads of the horses, because draughts can be dangerous especially if the horses are hot from exercise.[120]

The basilica plan lent itself to having windows on both the longer walls but the location did not always allow for this. Francesco di Giorgio, whilst describing the various details of La Data, made no mention of the large windows, which archaeological evidence shows were only on the valley side of this great stable. A similar problem arose at Viterbo, where one side of the early sixteenth-century Stallone del Papa was built against the Rocca's surrounding wall (6.27, 6.28). However, a different problem arose at Pienza where only three sides of the subterranean stable are pierced by small windows, due to the structural nature of the buttressed walls (6.29). Other stables such as Tibaldi's Rotonda had a rectangular window central to each wall on all three levels, with the exception of the entrance wall – those for the semi-basement being slightly smaller. And

179

6.27. Viterbo: La Rocca with the Stallone del Papa on the left, 1506-10. G Sisto Fietti, drawing for F Bussi, *Istoria della città di Viterbo*, 1742. Courtesy of The Warburg Insitute, London

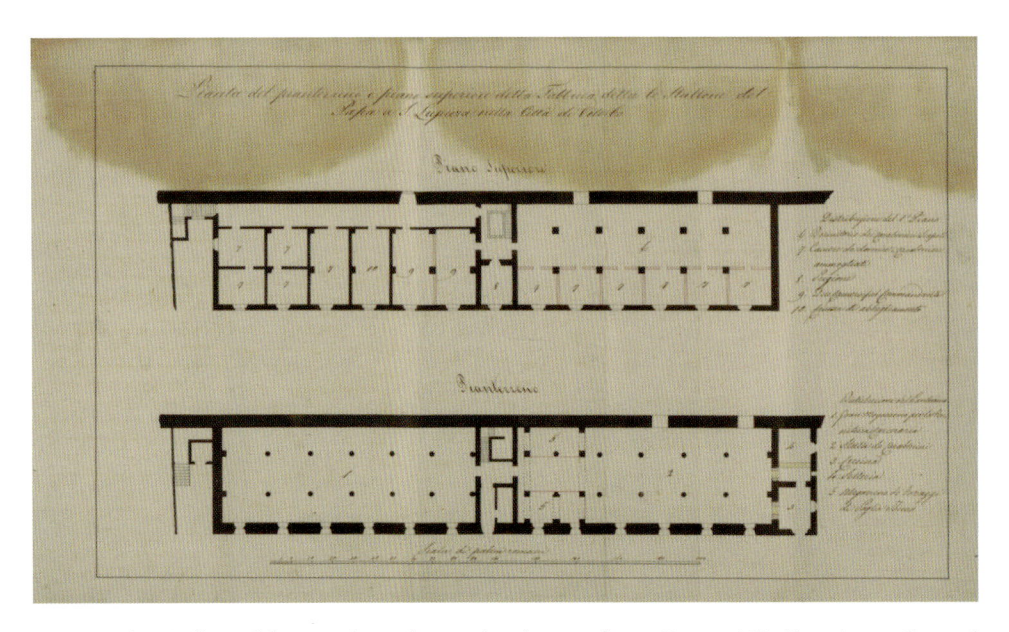

6.28. Viterbo: Stallone del Papa, plans of ground and upper floors. Rome, ASR, Tesorierato Generale, Amm. V. Lavori Camerali, b.64, Federici, drawing 1832. Courtesy of Minstero dei beni e le attività culturali –Archivio di Stato di Roma

6.29. Pienza, Palazzo Piccolomini stables, buttressed south wall

at Cafaggiolo, the windows on the north side are approximately one third smaller than those to the south – a design of which Corte would later approve.

Both treatises and court ordinances stressed the importance of keeping the stables well lit at all times so that the horses could be inspected regularly or fed. The *ordini* for the Duke of Urbino are particularly interesting for giving an insight to the night time duties of the stable boys,

> During the night the stables should always be lit for any situation that might happen, and so each of the servants should have a tallow candle for himself to manage the horses and to go to sleep and to get up in the night when necessary, taking diligent care not to put the flame in anything nor to go about with torches, nor into any dangerous areas without lanterns, for which the stables should not be lacking these or other implements.[121]

To keep the stables lit at night both Corte and Caracciolo suggested two large oil lanterns should be kept permanently lit. But Caraccciolo warned that the stable staff should take great care when carrying candles, which should be hung up far away from hay, straw or any other flammable materials, as 'only one spark causes great fires'. For this reason, he recommends that everything possible in the stable should be made of stone rather than wood.[122]

Of course, the stable complex consisted of more than the suitably designed accommodation for the horses. Although the central stabling area might be an overtly impressive part of the building, it was the other secondary areas, tack and harness rooms, blacksmiths' and saddlery workrooms, fodder storage, treatment rooms and accommodation for stable staff which contributed to the horses' welfare. Such 'back stage' areas also served to keep the stable clear of any visual distraction from the horses themselves as, according to Corte, anything kept in the central aisle impeded the movement of the horses or riders and was 'ugly to look at'.[123] Caracciolo

6.30 and 6.31. Medici stables at Poggio a Caiano: pillar and diagrams showing holes and iron stains, possibly used for attaching dividing rails and for hanging up saddles, bridles and other accoutrements

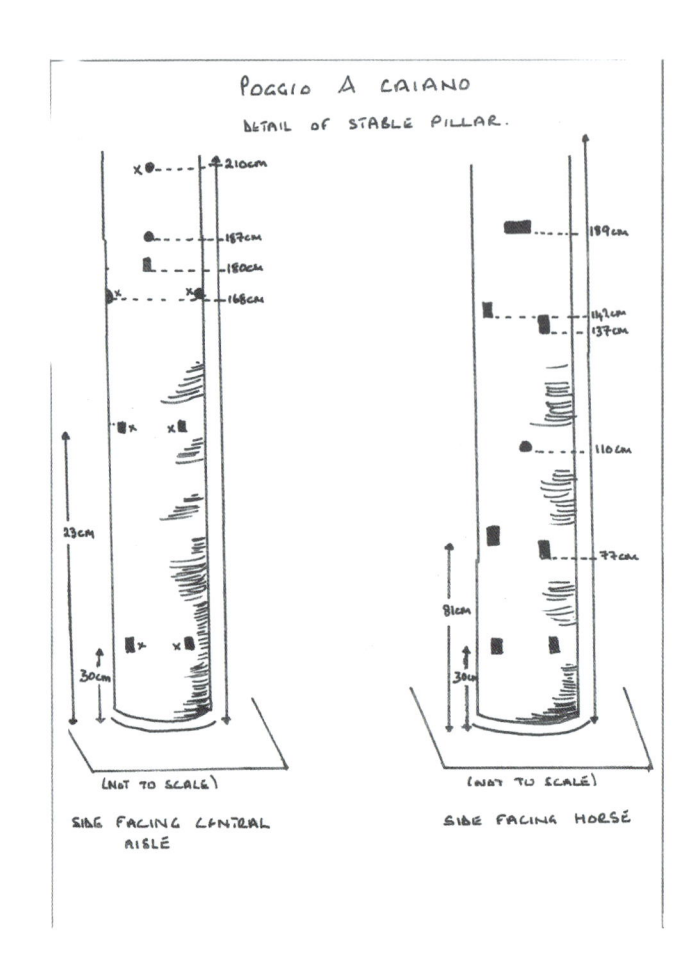

also recommended keeping tack away from the stalls because horses found bits of harness or tack annoying, trying to chew anything they could reach or eating pieces of cloth and leather.[124] However, such advice was not always followed, as Cesare Nubolonio's detailed description of the Vigevano stables explains, 'between one [column] and the next, there were as many small columns for placing the horses' tack'.[125] And certainly at Poggio a Caiano the many iron stains and fragments remaining in the columns indicate that these may well have been used both for dividing rails and for hanging up bridles, head collars or even saddles at the end of each stall, even if only on a temporary basis when the horse was being groomed before or after riding (6.30, 6.31).

Secure storage of cleaning implements and tack was also important: saddles and bridles required suitable supports, linen summer rugs – as protection against flies – and wool winter rugs required dry storage, while valuable decorative comparisons required locked *cassoni* in much the same way as human clothes would do. With hundreds of horses housed in some court stables, such items required considerable space, although no evidence remains of exactly where these storage rooms were located. The most logical explanation is given by Corte, who suggested that they should be at either end of the stable, each with its own fireplace, and that the furnishings should include 'racks for hanging bits, harnesses and other things' and 'trestles on which to put the saddles'.[126] These rooms, which were also used for the stable boys and grooms to eat their midday meal, must be kept 'clean and without any smell'.[127] In 1510, Paolo Cortese suggested that the saddles and harnesses for the cardinal's British horse or trotting mule should be stored separately from those of the other horses in the cardinal's palace stables. These, he advised, should be kept close to the vestibule, in a vaulted room used as an armoury so that 'time will be saved [and] arms ready to hand' if there is any danger.[128] Francesco di Giorgio describes the Urbino stables as having a room 'next to the Master of the Stable's room . . . in which [the staff] can practise [medicine], shoeing, decorate the saddles and other necessary things',[129] although it is more likely that shoeing and medical treatments took place in one room and saddlery repairs in another.

Many larger stables had covered areas or atria where horses could be mounted and saddled. At Urbino, the atrium was used for 'saddling and unsaddling and shoeing the horses [and included] a fountain with two drinking troughs',[130] while the large atrium at Poggio a Caiano served the same purpose with its drinking trough stretching halfway across the width of the stables (see 5.44). Some writers would describe the ground immediately outside the stable building where horses could be groomed, exercised or cooled down. Quoting Xenophon, Caracciolo writes that immediately outside the stable four or five cartloads of round stones should be scattered, which should then be broken up with a hammer so that they fit into the hand and don't move. By walking on these stones the soles of the horse's feet will become tough and ready for walking on stony roads.[131] But the Neapolitan horseman also suggested that the horses should have a covered strawed area, where they could 'jump about before they are given water' or, once unsaddled, the horse could 'leave his work behind and throw himself on the ground', becoming reinvigorated in much in the same way as a horse rolling in the field after hard work.[132] Like many ideas on the horse's well-being this reiterates earlier advice, in this case Vegetius, who had added that if the horse does not tumble and roll 'after his usual manner' this may well be a sign that it is ill.[133] It is quite likely such stables would have had this strawed area and that it would have been used regularly as, if not turned out in a field, horses would certainly not have been able to roll whilst tethered in their narrow stalls. Certainly, Caracciolo's idea complements Leonardo's suggestion of a pool outside the stable in which the horses could splash about after a journey.[134]

As for the storage of fodder and straw, several stables are described as having trap doors over the central aisle from which the straw and hay could be thrown down to the stables from a storage space on the upper level. Francesco di Giorgio mentions the 'beautiful vault where the straw and hay are held, with square hatches through which the fodder is thrown down'.[135] Archaeological evidence shows that there were two chutes from the top floor of Tibaldi's Rotonda, Pietrasanta's drawing showing that they were situated either side of the main entrance, marked by an 'E' (see 6.9).[136] For Leonardo, the priority was to keep the stable clean and neat. But unlike other stable designers, he not only suggested where to store the hay and straw, but devised a way of bringing it into the stable, which not only kept the stable tidy but which was labour-saving. His Manuscript B shows the storage space in the centre of the upper floor, with four side access aisles: two for the stable staff and two for supplying hay directly to the hayracks via funnel shaped chutes set into the cavity walls. His notes explain that the chutes 'should be well plastered and cleaned' so 'that the hay is not stopped on the way' to the hayracks. He had also devised a rope hoist, a *carro*, for taking hay and straw up through the large first-floor window directly into the storage corridor (see 6.20).[137] There is no evidence that either of these ingenious devices was put into practice in Renaissance Italy but, in late seventeenth-century England, a tube connecting a loft to a horse's manger was recorded at Richard Fermor's Tusmore stables in Oxfordshire.[138]

Stables were designed to impress, both through the use of decorative details and in the way horses were displayed in their stalls. With the horse becoming increasingly valued for its peace-time qualities, it was no longer just the number of horses which counted as a show of wealth and power but also the quality of their care and stabling. And so the interior of the stable was accorded considerable attention, with many Renaissance architects and equestrian experts prescribing significant details, some of which had been recommended centuries earlier, others ingenious innovations. Many aspects of a stable's interior benefited the horses' health, but carved capitals and decorative wall frescoes did not benefit the horses in any way; they were elements of display, acting as theatrical scenery in front of which valuable horses could be exhibited.

For maximum effect, stables also needed to be clean, tidy and well managed. Consequently, as the Renaissance progressed many sixteenth-century writers stressed the importance of a clean stable and efficient drainage, reflecting the increased importance attached to human health and urban cleanliness. This made new demands of the staff, many of whom were required to spend most of their life with the horses, dedicated to their care. It could be said that court horses were more privileged than the stable boys who cared for them and, in many ways, they were. But they were also restricted in their movement, being tied up and hobbled not for their benefit but primarily for man's convenience. Echoing Vegetius, the writings of both Leonardo da Vinci and the Neapolitan horseman, Pasqual Caracciolo, must have recognised the everyday restraint imposed on these court horses, offering them a respite after hard work; a 'playground' where they could jump about or roll and a pool in which they could splash and refresh themselves.

1 G. Worsley, 'The Design and Development', 1989, p. 104.
2 See Chapter 5 for letter dated 3 July 1515, re. expenses for the Pietole decoration. Mantua, ASMa, AG, b.2491, 166r.
3 Rubbiani, *Il castello di Giovanni II Bentivoglio* (1989), p. 35, *Tutta la scuderia appare all'interno ancora dipinta e compartita in rombi che incorniciano nitriti teste di cavalli*. The stable is now part of a medical laboratory and no trace of this decoration remains.
4 Vasari, *Vite* (1966), III, 'Piero della Francesca', p. 260.
5 Ugo Caleffini, *Cronica della Casa d'Este*, in A. Cappelli, ed., *Atti e memorie della Reale Deputazione di storia patria per le province modenesi e parmensi*, II (1864), pp. 267-312. See 22 January, 1487, . . . *et che havea insino ali colonelli ove se atachano le selle et breve in la stala tuta in volta per 20 cavali de marmoro*, cited in Tuohy, *Herculean Ferrara* (2002), p. 38, n. 50.
6 Alberti, *On the Art of Building* (1988), I, ch. 10, p. 25.
7 F. Bussi, *Istoria della città di Viterbo* (Rome, 1742), p. 305. Cited in F. T. F. Zeni Buchicchio, 'Quale intervento per lo Stallone del Papa a Viterbo?', *Biblioteca e Società* XVII, 1-2 (June, 1990), pp. 7-14, p. 9, n. 2.
8 Buchicchio, 'Quale intervento' (1990), pp. 9-11. Buchicchio suggests Bramante's involvement with these stables from two documents dated 1506 and 1508. One shows Bramante was involved with the Rocca during this period, the other that the columns are identical to those in the Rocca.
9 See Chapter 2 for a description of Agostino Chigi's banquet.
10 Milan, ASMi, Frammenti, b. 4, 325r-v, *havendo Ionetto da Mandello presente osteansore havuto caricho di condure ad Vigevano tutti quelli possoni de sarizo che sono necessarie pro uso de le nostro stalle là . . .* , cited in R. Schofield, 'Ludovico il Moro and Vigevano', *Arte Lombarda* 62 (1982), pp 93-140, p. 108.
11 Milan, ASMi, reg. ducale, 120, LX, 1489-90, 488r, 6 July, *le columne necessarie de preda alla fabrica delle stalle nostre principiate ad Milano et ad Vigevano*. Cited in R. Schofield, 'Ludovico il Moro and Vigevano', *Arte lombarda*, 62 (1982), pp. 93-140, p. 108 and n. 82.
12 L. Gremmo, 'La vicenda costruttiva', in Bombi *et al.* eds, *La biscia e l'aquila* (1988), pp. 145-79, pp. 161-2.
13 See hypothetical plan and cross section of La Data in M. Bruscia, ed., *La Data (Orto dell'abbondanza) di Francesco di Georgio Martini*, 1990, p.61.
14 Worsley, 'The Design and Development', 1989, p. 29.
15 Milan, Bib. Triv. MS 2162, 21v -22r and Paris, IF, MS 2173-manuscrit B, 38v-39r.
16 M. Kemp, *Leonardo da Vinci: the Marvellous Works of Nature and Man* (Oxford, 2006), 'Abbreviations and references', pp. xxviii-xxix.
17 L. Firpo, *Leonardo architetto e urbanista* (Turin, 1971), pp. 88-93.

18 C. Pedretti, *Leonardo architetto* (Milan, 1978), pp. 259-63.
19 Chapter 36, 'Della stalla & sue pertinentie' is in both editions of Corte's treatise but are on different pages: *Il cavallarizzo* (1562), I, 45v-47v; *Il cavalerizzo* (1572), I, 53r-55r.
20 See Chapter 1.
21 Paris, IF, MS. B, 39r. Leonardo proposes each stall is 1.75 metres wide and 3.50 metres long.
22 The *canna* varies between 2 and 2.90 metres.
23 Corte, 1562, I, ch. 36, 47r.
24 The two earlier stables at Vigevano are 56m and 50m long.
25 Lamberini, 'Il Tribolo ingegnere', in E. Pieri *et al.* eds, *Il Tribolo* (2001), p. 192, n. 60.
26 The stable's capacity for 200 horses has also been suggested by C. Conforti, 'Recupero delle scuderie medicee di Poggio a Caiano', *Casabella* LXV (June, 2001), pp. 16-17, p. 16.
27 See Chapter 2.
28 Two and a half *palme* is approximately 73 cm or 28½ inches.
29 Corte, 1562, I, ch. 36, 46v – 47r.
30 Ruffo, *Libro della mascalcia,* (2002), chs. II and III, pp. 18-9.
31 Corte, 1562, I, ch. 36, 46v.
32 Caracciolo, 1589, p. 572.
33 Ibid. pp. 572-3.
34 G. B. Ferraro (1560), II, p. 85 in P. A. Ferraro, *Cavallo frenato* (1602).
35 Corte, 1562, I, ch. 36, p. 47.
36 *Ordini*, ch. 29, pp. 43-4, *La stalle è da essere divisa da cavallo a cavallo cum stanghe o cum tavole.*
37 Rome, ASR, Camerale III, b. 518, 'Libro delle misure della fabbrica del palazzo del Ill.mo e R.mo Farnese a Caprarola', 11r, *Lo haver messo 50 stanghetti dj legno long luno palmi 8 che tramezano li cavalli et busciato le colonette, per ataccare ditte stanghetti insieme mote_____c._____87 5*
38 Taking the Florentine *braccia* as 58.3 cms.
39 Corte, 1562, I, ch. 36, 46v.
40 Worsley, *The British Stable* (2004), p. 185.
41 Vegetius, *Of the distempers* (1748), I, ch 56, p. 99.
42 Ruffo, *Libro della mascalcia* (2002), pp. 19-20.
43 Alberti, *On the Art of Building* (1988), p. 142.
44 *Ordini*, ch. 29, p. 44.
45 Paris, IF, MS B, 39r.
46 Sebastiano Serlio, 'On Architecture', VI, 'On habitations', 72v.-73r
47 Caracciolo, 1589, VII, pp. 571-2.
48 Corte, 1562, I, ch. 36, 46v.
49 Naples, ASNa, AF, Carte Farnesiane (CF), b. 1358.1. Letter signed by Cristoforo Balduccini, . . . *mangiatore e lo fatta bona provesione di calce et se ne fara de mano in mano ancio no manchi si attende ancora altre facevole necessarie . . .* Although the word *calce* means limestone, Florio has *calce vergine* as 'unflaked lime' and it seems likely this is a limewash for the mangers.
50 Vegetius, *Of the distempers* (1748), I, ch. 56, p. 99.
51 The Duke of Calabria was later Alfonso II of Aragon. The building work was carried out between 1488-93. It is not certain if there were stables prior to 1488 or whether this was a new construction. For an account of the construction work and the relevant archival documents see L. Gennari, *Struttura e manutenzione della cavallerizza regia di Marcianise (1488-1493)* (Salerno, 2006).
52 Naples, ASN, Dipendenze della sommaria, II, fasc. 36.1, 30r, 10 December 1491, *Cunto de la dispesa se fay a la cavallaricza de Marczanise de lo illustrissimo signor duca, ciò èy per intavolare le mangiatore davanti lo pecto de li cavalli de tavole per cento cavalli, ciò èy cento stancie, et a quatro chiovi per tavola per ordinacione de messer Lionardo Como et sonno de li introyto de li dinari ge so bisogno per dicta dispesa ut supra. In primis.* Cited in Gennari, *Struttura e manutenzione della cavallerizza* (2006), p. 49.
53 Rome, ASR, 'Libro delle misure . . . a Caprarola', CAM III, b. 518, 11r, *Le doi magnatore [sic] fatte nella stalla granda di Signor Giulio long: palmi 100 con sua limarelli sopra et messo dinanzi le sua archa reggie et piantanto li passoni numero 10 incollata et fattolj l'astrio insieme mote c._____10 [?]_____.*
54 Francesco di Giorgio Martini in ed. C. Maltese, *Trattati* (1967), II, pp. 339-40.
55 Scamozzi, *L'idea della architettura* (1615), Part 1, II, ch. XXII, 'De luoghi da munitioni e vittovaglie & alloggiamenti de' soldati e da guarnigioni e stalle publiche da cavalli', p. 178.
56 Alberti, *On the Art of Building* (1988), p. 142.
57 One Florentine *braccia* is approximately 58.36 cm or 23 inches.
58 Paris, IF, Bib., MS B, 39r.
59 *Ordini*, p. 42, *Li strami non voriano stare in rasteliera perchè la polvere cade nel naso a li cavalli et li imbolisse, ma nelle mangiotore cum les traverse de sopra.*
60 Ruffo, *Libro del mascalcia* (2002), pp. 19-20.
61 Probably Gioachino Camerario I (1500-74), who translated various Greek and Latin texts such as Galen and Xenophon or possibly his son, the humanist Gioachino Camerario II (1534-74).
62 Caracciolo, 1589, VII, p. 523.
63 Ibid. p. 572. See also Vegetius, *Of the distempers* (1748), I, ch. 56, p. 99.
64 Caracciolo, 1589, VII, p. 572.
65 Paris, IF, Bib., MS B, 39r and Sebastiano Serlio, *Tutte l'opere d'architettura et prospettiva*, VI 'On habitations' 72v-73r, 'The final details of the royal palace at number XXII'.
66 *On Horsemanship*, 1962, pp. 298-9.

67 Alberti, CV, p. 65. Videtta, p. 144.
68 D. Biow, *The Culture of Cleanliness in Renaissance Italy* (Ithaca and London, 2006), p. xi.
69 Alberti, *On the Art of Building* (1988), IV, ch. 7, 'On public works', p. 113.
70 Paris, IF, Bib., MS B, 38r-v.
71 Paris, IF, Bib., MS 2173, 37v, 'Design for a city with a system of canals and quays'.
72 Biow, *The Culture of Cleanliness* (2006), see p. 56, where Biow lists: Sperone Speroni, *On the Care of the Household* (1542), Paolo Caggio, *Economics* (1552), Giacomo Lanteris *On the Household* (1560), Francesco Tommasi *Regimen of the Father of the Family* (1580), Torquato Tasso, *The Father of the Family* (1580) and Niccolò Vito di Gozze, *Governing the Household* (1589).
73 Torquato Tasso, *Il Padre di famiglia* (Venice, 1583), pp. 106-9.
74 *On Horsemanship*, 1962, p. 315.
75 Columella, *On agriculture* (1968), II, Book VI, p. 203.
76 Palladius, *The fourteen books* (1807), I, ch. XXI, 'On stables and ox-stalls', p. 32.
77 Vegetius, *Of the distempers* (1748), I, ch. 56, p. 98.
78 See Paris, IF, Bib., MS. B, 39r.
79 *Ordini*, p. 44.
80 Alberti, *On the Art of Building* (1988), V, p. 143.
81 Corte, 1562, I, ch. 36, 46v.
82 Ibid. 46r-v.
83 Scamozzi, *L'idea della architettura* (1615), Part 1, III, ch. XVII, p. 301.
84 Blundeville, *The Fower Chiefyst Offices* (1565), p. 10. The book includes Blundeville's revised translation of Grisone's treatise, *Gli ordini di cavalcare*.
85 Ruffo, *Libro della mascalcia* (2002), V, p. 27.
86 B. Gerbier, *A Brief Discourse Concerning the Three Chief Principles of Magnificent Buildings* (London, 1662), p. 34.
87 Gerbier, *A Brief Discourse* (1662), p. 34.
88 Francesco di Giorgio Martini, *Trattati,* in ed. C. Maltese, (1967), II, pp. 339-41.
89 Paris, IF, Bib., MS. B, 39r.
90 Milan, ASMi, Bib. Triv., MS 2162, Codice Trivulziana, 21v.
91 The Milanese *braccia*, most likely used by Leonardo, is 0.59 metres, see R. Schofield, 'Ludovico il Moro and Vigevano', *Arte Lombarda* 62 (1982), p. 114.
92 Stale: to urinate.
93 Pedretti (1977), II, p. 37.
94 Scamozzi, *L'idea della architettura* (1615), Part 1, II, ch. XXII, p. 178.
95 Thomas de Grey, *The Compleat Horseman and Expert Farrier in Two Books* (London, 1639; fifth edition, 1684), I, p. 16, 'for in raising your flore so much, I do abstract from the ancient ill custom, by reason than a horse standeth higher before than he doth behind, his hinder legs will swell, and so he becometh lame; and besides, it giveth him a taint in the back and kidneys and to conclude, his long standing in this uneasie manner begetteth in the poor beast much pain and grief . . . '
96 François A. de Garsault, *Le Nouveau parfait maréchal ou la connoissance générale et universelle du cheval* (La Haye, 1741; fourth edition, Paris, 1770), 'De l'écuyer', ch 1, p. 92, *Chaque place . . . doit avoir une pente douce écoulement à urine, & pour que le devant du Cheval étant un peu plus haut que le derriere, il ne pese pas tant sur ses épaules, & ait plus de grace à la vue: chaque place doit être pavée . . .*
97 Corte, 1562, I, ch. 36, 46r.
98 Worsley explains that the benefits of the sloping floor were much debated in England during the seventeenth century and sloping floors were thought by some to put too much pressure on the horse's rear legs, causing them to swell. See *The British Stable* (2004), pp. 86-7.
99 Corte, 1562, I, ch. 36, 47r.
100 Ibid. 46v.
101 Corte, 1562, I, ch. 36, 47r, *Saria anco più utile assai per lo passagio de cavalli stracchi, sudati, bagnati, & ammalati al tempo del freddo, venti, & poggie.*
102 Caracciolo, 1589, VII, p. 575.
103 Alberti, CV, p. 73. Videtta, p. 148.
104 Alberti, *On the Art of Building* (1988), p. 143.
105 Ibid.
106 Mantua, ASMa AG b. 2441, 8 August 1492, *Maistro Lorenzo dice che la stalla di Gonzaga sie molto frigida a questi tempi perché l'è discoverta e che se li cavalli staranno lì el crede che se ne amalerà una gran parte.* Cited in Malacarne, *Il mito* (1995), p. 30.
107 Corte, 1562, I, ch. 36, 47r-v.
108 Piccolomini, *The Secret Memoirs* (1988), p. 277.
109 R. Kirkbride, *Architecture and Memory: the Renaissance Studioli of Federico da Montefeltro* (New York and Chichester, 2008), p. 157.
110 Excavations at Cafaggiolo, show that brick kilns may have been placed directly under the west end of the stables, although in November 2009, evidence of a furnace was found further away in the grounds of the *castello*. Visits to the site have not yet established whether horses were definitely stabled on the floor above these kilns. It may be that another part of the pottery production was on the ground floor level. In either case, heat would have penetrated into the adjacent stabling. The Fattorini's pottery was originally under the patronage of Lorenzo di Pierfrancesco de' Medici and functioned until the early seventeenth century.
111 Vitruvius, *De architectura*, 10 books, VI, ch. 9, trans. W. Newton, *The Architecture of M. Vitruvius Pollio*, 2 vols (London, 1791), II, p. 143. Newton refers to cattle here, although others such as F. Granger, *Vitruvius on architecture* (London and New

York,1934), specify horse stables.
112 Vegetius, *Of the distempers of horses* (1748), I, ch. 56, p. 100.
113 Francesco di Giorgio Martini in ed. C. Maltese, *Trattati* (1967), II, p. 339.
114 Thomas Blundeville recommended windows were glazed or latticed to prevent birds entering the stables, Blundeville, *The Fower Chiefyst Offices* (1565), p. 10.
115 Naples, ASN, Cavallaricza de Marczanise, Sommaria, Dipendenze, I, 36, fasc. 2, 39v, 20 July 1492 . . . *per facitura de tredice fenestre facte a la stalla per ordinacuie de messer Mactheo Crispano* and 40r, 25 July 1492, *vinty octo bracza de tela de càndano per comissione de messer Mactheo Crispano, presente Galiocto Caldrarone, per serrare tredice finestre alla stalla* . . . cited in Gennari, *Struttura e manutenzione della cavallerizza* (2006), Appendix II, p. 60. See also 40r, 27 July 1492, *per stippareli per chiavare dicte tele a le dicte finestre, che non intrassino le mosche, liberato grana octo et per centruni grana septe et per czagarelli intorno le dicte telle grana dudice et per certi meczi chyovi per le sbarelle* . . . , Gennari, p. 61.
116 Gandini, 'Viaggi, Cavalli, bardature e stalle degli Estensi'(1892), p. 85. Gandini gives no reference for these records.
117 Modena, ASMo., Camera Ducale (CD), Amministrazione Principi (AP), vol. 997, which covers the rebuilding, redecorating and stocking of the Palazzo in 1534-5. Cited in M. Hollingsworth, *The Cardinal's Hat* (London, 2005), p. 36.
118 The walls of the earliest Vigevano stable show evidence of Gothic windows, which have been subsequently filled in. The windows were probably altered to match those of the two later stables.
119 Corte, 1562, I, ch. 36, 47r–47v.
120 Scamozzi, *L'idea della architettura* (1615), Part 1, II, ch. XXII, p. 178.
121 *Ordini*, ch. 28, p. 43.
122 Caracciolo, 1589, p. 571.
123 Corte, 1562, I, ch. 36, 47r.
124 Caracciolo,1589, VII, p. 571.
125 C. Nobilonio, *Cronaca di Vigevano* (1584) ed. R. di Marchi (Pavia, 1988) pp. 62-3. Cited in Giordano, 'La polita stalla' (2009), p. 12 and p. 13, n. 14.
126 Corte, 1562, I, ch. 36, 47r.
127 Ibid. ch. 38, 49v.
128 Cortese, *De cardinalatu* (1510), II, ch. 2, 'De domo cardinalis', trans. in K. Weil-Garris and J. F. d'Amico, *The Renaissance Cardinal's ideal Palace: A chapter from Cortesi's De Cardinalatu* (Rome, 1986), p. 77.
129 Francesco di Giorgio Martini in ed. C. Maltese, *Trattati* (1967), II, p. 340.
130 Ibid. p. 339.
131 *On Horsemanship*, 1962, pp. 315-6 and Caracciolo, 1589, p. 574.
132 Caracciolo, 1589, VII, p. 574, 'Dee ancora star vicino alla stalla un luogo di pagliaccia coverto, dove i cavalli innanzi al bere si possano voltare . . . ' and 'et levatagli la sella, ò barda, si lasci bene a sua posta voltolare per terra: egli mirabilmente rinforzato sorgerà in piè si fresco, e voglioso di caminare . . . '
133 Vegetius, *On the distempers* (1748), I, ch. 56, p. 101.
134 Paris, IF, Bib., MS B, 38r.
135 Francesco di Giorgio Martini in ed. C. Maltese, *Trattati* (Palma, 1967), II, p. 339.
136 Carlo Federico Pietrasanta (1656-1729), 'Pianta della Scuderia nel Palazzo Archiepiscovile di Milano', Archivio Storico Diocesano di Milano.
137 Paris, IF, Bib, MS B, 39r, trans. E. MacCurdy, *The Notebooks of Leonardo da Vinci* 2 vols (London, 1954), II, p. 391.
138 Robert Plot, *The Natural History of Oxfordshire* (Oxford, 1677), p. 263. Cited in Worsley, *The British Stable* (2004), p. 43.

PART THREE

Caring for the Court Horse

Introduction

> It is the mark of a good horseman . . . to see that his groom, like himself, is instructed in the way in which he should treat the horse.
> Xenophon, fourth-century BC.[1]

If the Renaissance stable was to serve as a gallery in which to display valuable horses, it was important that both the building and its contents were kept in good condition. An unkempt stable or neglected and unfit horses not only suggested a lazy or badly-trained staff, it also reflected the ignorance of the owner. Many equestrian treatises concentrated on the care of the horses and, whether descriptive or prescriptive, it is these texts – their theories often based on earlier works – together with court ordinances, which allow an insight into the standards of care expected for court horses. The stable staff's responsibilities were wide ranging, involving horse breaking and training, careful administration of fodder and water, routine grooming and washing, elaborately decorating and plaiting the horses' manes and tails, as well cleaning the stable and maintaining the many pieces of tack and extravagant caparisons. Ordinances show that the court stable had its own *famiglia* and although, unlike the household *famiglia*, the stable staff was all male, it functioned in much the same way. As Gregory Lubkin has explained in his book *The Renaissance Court*, the whole court required 'an active and efficient logistical organisation' carried out under the auspices of three officials which, at the extensive Sforza court, consisted of the seneschals (*sescalchi*), responsible for lodgings, stewards (*spenditori*), in charge of the kitchens and wardrobe, and masters of stables (*maestri di stalla*); each of whom were responsible for, and supported by, a staff, which carried out most of the physical labour.[2]

The first chapter looks at the hierarchy and living conditions of the stable *famiglia* and the various responsibilities individuals were assigned. The second chapter discusses the methods used to maintain the horses' health both through cleanliness in the stable and care of the horses. It also considers the treatments available to the court *maniscalco* in his work as both a farrier and horse doctor.

1 *On Horsemanship*, 1962, p. 317.
2 G. Lubkin, *A Renaissance Court* (1994), p. 35.

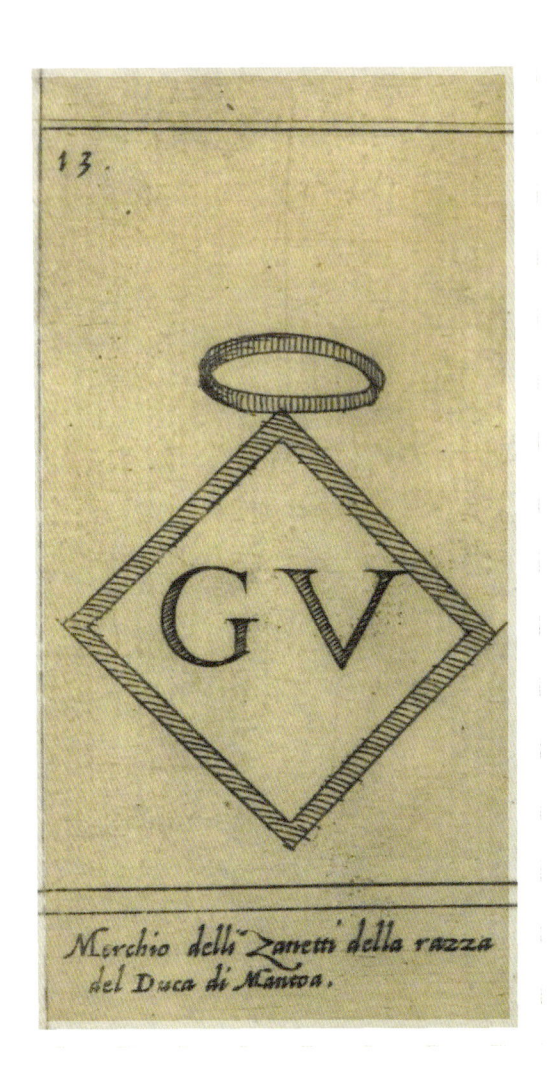

Marchio delli Zanetti della razza del Duca di Mantoa.

Brand for the *gineti* of the Duke of Mantua

Chapter 7

Faithful and loving: Stable Staff and their Duties

> Seeing you are forced to meddle with horses, don't you think that common
> sense requires you to see that you are not ignorant of the business?
> Xenophon, fourth-century BC[1]

Both the fitness and the presentation of the court horses were the responsibility of a hardworking and tightly regulated male staff who washed, groomed, fed, watered and exercised their charges, often sleeping in the stables at night to protect them from theft, fire and other hazards. As with any commodity, the horse's value was partly dependent on its quality (breeding and schooling) and partly on its presentation (appearance and performance) – both aspects of horse care dependent on a well-informed and conscientious staff. The importance attached to equestrian care is evident from the many chapters dedicated to it in works not necessarily written specifically for horsemen but also for court households. Certainly, members of stable staff were sometimes referred to in book titles, suggesting that these men were either literate or that particular chapters were read to them to encourage a high standard of conduct and work,[2] Corte's brief chapter on the responsibilities of the stable boys reading more like a sermon on behaviour than advice on equine care (see Appendix Two).[3] Unlike the wide readership of printed treatises, court ordinances were written for a more specific audience such as those for Federico da Montefeltro's household,[4] for the Sforza secretary, Cicco Simonetta[5] and those outlining the responsibilities of the governor of the royal Neapolitan stud farms in Calabria.[6] Whilst treatises and ordinances prescribe advice and give orders, it is court correspondence and stable records which show that much of this theory was put into practice.

Overall responsibility for court stabling belonged to the stable master, *maestro di stalla*. It was he who hired and fired the staff, gave them orders and paid the stable boys and head grooms. It was he who ordered fodder and bedding, provided the horse-trainers with their equipment and who called the farrier-surgeon, *il maniscalco*, if a horse was ill or required new shoes. Certain contemporaries, such as Priscianese, rated his role more highly than those who looked after other valuable court commodities.

> Truly in the stable, it is of no less importance to be an excellent master than to be a capable master of the chamber. [I am] conscious that a beautiful and well-kept stable would, in my judgement, be of more honour to the signore than a beautiful bedroom, even if it is hung with gold brocade. Because, with all the decoration in the world, in the end the bedroom is a dead thing and cannot go outside to accompany the master to show off its beauty. On the contrary, if you wish it to be seen, it is necessary to go to it. But a beautiful stable of well-tended horses . . . can go outside and accompany the master wherever he wishes [to go] and, being seen in public, delight everyone who sees it, giving the patron such honour that he himself will maintain it well, because of the benefit it provides.[7]

This admiration for eye-catching and well-tended horses, and the attention they could draw, recalls the classical values of Xenophon over one thousand years earlier,

> A prancing horse is a thing so graceful, terrible and astonishing that it rivets the gaze of all beholders, young and old alike. At all events, no one leaves him or is tired of gazing at him, so long as he shows off his brilliance.[8]

To produce these admirable prancing horses, the stable master required a large efficient *famiglia* under his jurisdiction. Sometimes supported by assistants, stable masters worked with riding masters (*cavallarizzi*) and farrier-surgeons (*maniscalchi*) who, as well as shoeing horses, were responsible for medication and surgery. Inside the stable, the grooms – both men and young boys[9] – carried out the physical work while outside the stable the horses were schooled by trainers and professional riders (*cavalcatori* and *equitatori*) or by specialist racehorse trainers (*barbareschi* or *barbarescatori*). With the magnificence of the rider dependent on both the performance and appearance of his horse, expensive accoutrements were worn and ribbons woven into elaborately plaited manes and tails, all of which required not only experienced grooms but also skilled tradesmen such as the saddler, stirrup maker, bridle maker and bit maker. Tailors and goldsmiths cut, sewed and decorated elaborate caparisons with gold and silver buckles, bells and other decorations. In addition, there was a much larger section of the community whose livelihood depended on the court horses and the culture surrounding them. Many were artisans and tradesmen such as armourers and spur makers, broom and rope makers, builders and carpenters, those who mined and smelted iron for the horses' shoes, who cured leather for the tack and harnessing and who traded in exotic spices, metals and dyes for the health and appearance of the horses.

Of particular importance for the day-to-day running of the stable were those who provided the fodder and bedding. Priscianese's mid sixteenth-century assessment of a stable's expenses gave the daily requirement of hay for each horse as twenty-five pounds[10] which, for forty horses, he priced at 360 *scudi* a year. Two hundred cartloads of straw were also required per year totalling 30 *scudi*;[11] some used for fodder, the rest serving as bedding or for filling staff mattresses.[12] The fodder varied according to the season: for the six winter months only barley (costing 131 *scudi*) was fed to the horses and in summer oats or spelt, giving each horse two measures per day,[13] which for the six summer months cost half as much as for the winter.[14] In addition, Priscianese added the shoeing costs which for forty horses was estimated at 50 *scudi*, medicines costing 10 *scudi* and a total of 40 *scudi* for saddlery, stirrups and bridles as well as for the stable implements. These calculations gave the annual expenses for the stable at 686 *scudi*, 50 *baiocchi* which, excluding any of the staff salaries, worked out at 17½ *scudi* per horse per year. This sum is put into perspective when compared to Priscianese's suggested annual salary for a stable boy, which was only 9 *scudi*.

The responsibilities of the stable staff were numerous and are listed in Garzoni's late sixteenth-century work detailing different professions, *La piazza universale di tutte le professioni del mondo*. They had

> to take care of the stable litter, the fodder in the mangers, the feeding troughs and the hayracks; to serve the stable master, manage the horses, put on the [horses'] head-collars, tie them up, give them their food and water, sieve the fodder, put on and take off their stable blankets, make up their bedding, tidy the stable, currycomb and comb them, knot the tails, saddle them for riding, fasten the girths, clean the tack, take [the horse] outside,

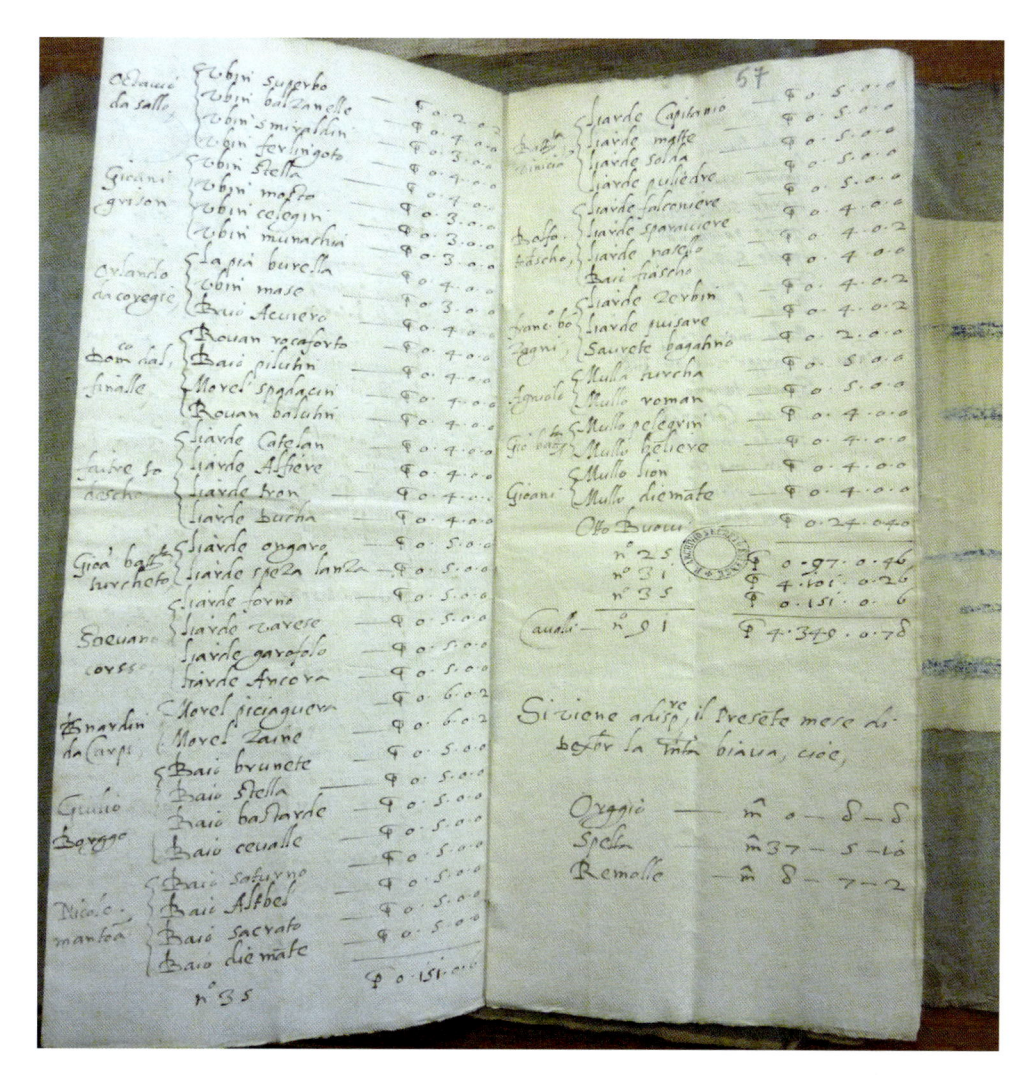

7.1. Este stable book, 1598, showing the horses' names and the grooms responsible for them. Modena, ASMo AE, Camera Ducale. Amm. Della Casa, Stalla, b.2, fasc.1. 'Elenchi di cavalli e cose relative 1480-1597, 'Ordinamento de tutti gli cavalli et altre bestie che a questo di primo dexembre si ritrovano nella ducale stalla, 56v-57r'. Courtesy of Ministero per i beni e le attività culturali – Archivio di Stato Modena, prot n. 955

hold the stirrup, then walk beside their master's stirrup; and supply any journey with saddle and bridle, rub down the [horses], wash and dry them, see if the saddle has harmed them, make sure they are shod and take them to the farrier.[15]

This list, together with other ordinances and treatises, suggests that the Renaissance stable was a bustling and busy place. In fact, a comparison can be made between Corte's advice on the responsibilities and living conditions of the staff and Alberti's prescribed standards for an ideal household a century earlier, where 'no-one is ever idle' and the house has an 'orderly routine'.[16] And while Alberti's housewife is ordered to 'check whether things are in their places, and how everyone is working',[17] Corte's stable master is held responsible for the security and storage of stable equipment as well as ensuring the staff fulfil their duties.[18]

It was, however, inevitable that the stable master's social standing, and the number of staff under him, varied according to the status of his patron and the size of the stable. Priscianese suggested that a city court stable with forty horses required one stable master with his own servant and ten grooms.[19] Writing about twenty years later, Corte suggested a slightly higher ratio of grooms to horses with sixteen stable boys and at least two head grooms (*baccallari*) in charge of forty-eight horses[20] – a ratio found in 1598 Este stable records which show each groom's name bracketed against the three or four horses in his care (7.1). If this ratio was practised at Vigevano or Urbino, the stable master would have overseen as many as 100 stable boys at the central court alone. In the larger courts rulers would regulate both their courtiers' stable staff and the number of horses they stabled. For example, in Milan Duke Galeazzo Maria gave Francesco ('Cicco') Simonetta[21] – a senior advisor and secretary to the Sforza for thirty years – the *ordini* for his household which identified the stable staff and described their daily responsibilities.[22] The orders were to be implemented at all times and wherever Simonetta and his household went. As would be expected, the horses were to be kept fit and well shod with their tack clean and in good order. They were also to be guarded day and night with a member of staff in the stable at all times. But the orders also stipulated that Simonetta's head groom, Zohanne Todesco, must never, under any circumstances, stable visiting horses, even for a single day, unless he has specific permission to do so; he must also inform on any visiting horses in the stable. If he broke these conditions or stabled horses for longer than the time allowed, the stabling costs would be deducted directly from his salary.[23] As noted earlier, 1,000 of the Sforza courtiers were entitled to stable their horses at their patron's expense[24] and the control over visiting horses may well have been because there was not the capacity to stable them. But it is also possible that either there was fear of visiting horses bringing viruses into the court stables or a concern for the overall security and safety of the court.

For patrons who had their own breeding programmes, the management and care of the court horses went far beyond the immediate confines of the principal court stable, extending to various outlying stud farms. At Governolo, the Gonzaga had created their own breed, Margonara, by cross breeding Italian horses with Barbary or Turkish breeds and at Roversella in the Sermide basin they kept their destrier mares. Meanwhile, the extensive Este stud farms went as far as the Garfagnana north of Lucca and, in the south of Italy, the Neapolitan rulers owned extensive stud farms in Calabria and Puglia – as did the Venetian Republic from 1495-1530.[25] In addition stable masters or trainers sometimes acted as agents for their courts, buying horses from abroad and then accompanying them to Italy by sea and land,[26] or escorting Italian-bred horses far afield as gifts for foreign princes and dignitaries. Whether these horses were exported or imported they were often part of extensive breeding programmes run by some of the great Renaissance rulers, such as the Este and Gonzaga in the north of Italy and the Neapolitan rulers in the south. Each stud farm had its own independent staff responsible for their herd's safety. This involved checking that good quality water and grass were available for mares and foals and ensuring that the horses came to no harm, particularly from theft or attack by predators such as wolves or wild dogs. Hunting would have been impractical near young horses, with records showing that, as an alternative at the Neapolitan Marcianise stables, wolves were lured into deep pits, *lupare*, which had been lined with oak and baited with pig meat.[27] For security, guards were employed to watch over the various herds. In the event of theft, a horse's brand mark could help identify the rightful owner or breeder, as was the case in 1529 when a letter to the Duke of Ferrara asked for his help in finding a lost Gonzaga horse, described first by her age, colour and white markings and then by the breed's mark of the sun on her right flank.[28] Tight security was also used to keep a breed pure. This was certainly the case in Spain, where Philip II gave orders for his guards to fire at any stray stallion or donkey attempting to reach his

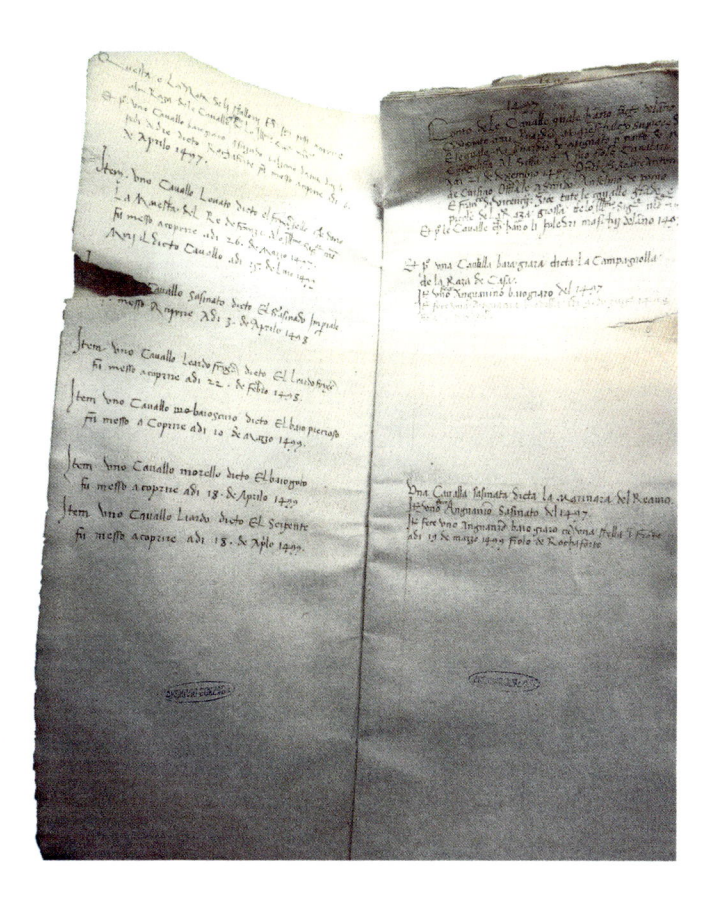

7.2. Gonzaga stud book, 1497-99. Entry showing the dates that stallions were put to stud. Mantua, ASMa, AG, b. 258, 'Vachetta in cui sono scritti li stallone e le cavalle dell'Illustrissimo Signor Marchese di Mantova'. Courtesy of Ministero per i beni e le attività culturali – Archivio di Stato di Mantova

valuable brood mares, pastured near the Guadalquivir river.[29] There is no reason to believe that the Spanish king or any other breeder would not have gone to the same lengths to protect their breeding stock in Italy.

To monitor breeding programmes stable employees kept detailed stud books, logging the stallion's name and the date a mare was covered, as well as the birth date and description of any subsequent foal – all details found in Gonzaga, Este and royal Neapolitan records. A parchment folder, dated 1497-9 and labelled 'Vachetta in cui sono scritti li stalloni e le cavalle dell'Illustrissimo Signor Marchese di Mantova,'[30] has been signed by Bernardino, the senior *mareschalco* on 21 December 1497.[31] The first page contains the names of stallions, with the phrase 'Fu messo a coprire' and the date they were put to stud, as seen written beneath the grey stallion, El Serpente (7.2). For the rest of the folder, half a page is allotted to each broodmare (*fattrice*), some of which were foaling in consecutive years.[32] Each entry gives the mare's name and distinguishing features, her foal's sex, date of birth, the name of the sire and, as in the following case, the date the mare died (7.3):

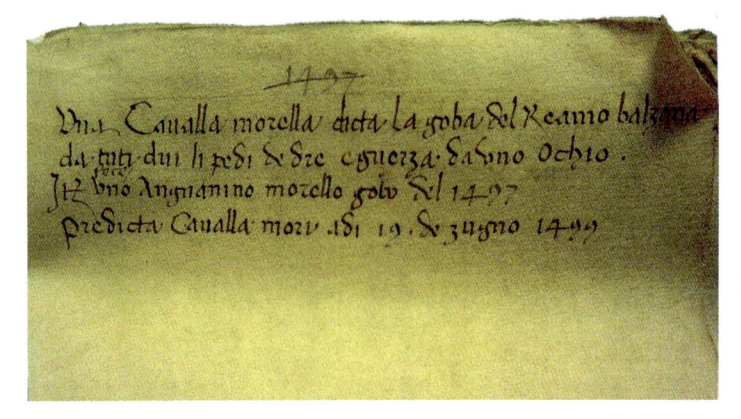

7.3. Gonzaga stud book, 1497-99. Entry for the mare La Goba, recording the birth of a colt foal in 1497 and the mare's death on 19 June, 1499. Mantua ASMa AG, b. 258. Courtesy of Minstero per i beni e le attività culturali – Archivio di Stato di Mantova

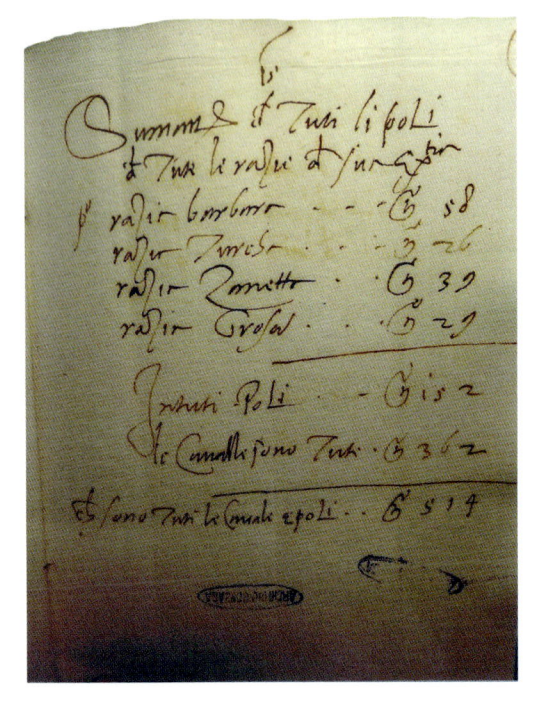

7.4. Gonzaga stud book 1540: total of all mares, foals and young horses. The breeds are listed as Barbary, Turkish, Zanetti and Grossa. Mantua, ASMa AG, b. 258. Courtesy of Ministero per i beni e le attività culturali – Archivio di Stato di Mantova

> A black mare, called La Goba, from the Kingdom,[33] with white socks on the two hind legs and blind in one eye, who produced a black colt foal Gobo in 1497. The said mare died on 19 June 1499.[34]

Forty-one years later a comprehensive list was made of all the broodmares (*cavalle fattore*) and foals owned by Duke Federico Gonzaga,[35] with breeds recorded separately, mares listed alphabetically and every one described in detail. The summary shows that in 1540, the year of the Duke's death, there were 222 broodmares and 91 colts and fillies still with their dams, which had been born between 1538 and 1540 and there were a further 49 offspring consigned to the stables (*consigli ala stalla*) presumably for breaking and training (7.4). These detailed records served two purposes: they helped breeders to develop specific qualities in their thoroughbreds and ensured that any horse could have its ancestry traced – a valuable asset when subsequent owners attached importance to owning a particular bloodline.

In addition to monitoring breeding programmes, the Gonzaga stud farm managers were also expected to show off their charges to visitors, either by parading the mares and foals or by displaying stallions in short entertainments, although it is difficult to ascertain whether they were pre-arranged or impromptu. Certainly, descriptions of the Cardinal of Aragon's visit to Marmirolo and of Isabella d'Este taking the Mantuan court to the Island of Te in 1515 show that these stables were used for equestrian entertainments.[36] Similarly in 1523 the stables at Pietole were visited by a group of Gonzaga officials: Geronimo Archario and 'M. Gaspare', a professional rider (*cavalcator*) 'M. Petronanione', the factor of Marmirolo and Bernardino da Bergamo. A letter from Archario, describing his visit to Marquis Federico, shows that Turkish, *gineta* and cavalry horses (*raza grosa*) were kept at the stables and that a total of 307 mares and foals were accommodated on the stud farm. The letter illustrates that crowds had gathered with the Gonzaga officials to watch these well-bred horses, as they were paraded in their elegant stable yard (see Appendix Three).[37]

Even though their responsibilities were so wide-ranging, it appears that most stable masters had no formal training or apprenticeship although, as Corte had written, some had learned their trade by progressing through the stable hierarchy. In his treatise he gives three examples: Giambattista da Cremona, who had spent eight years as Corte's stable boy before becoming a rider and then advancing to the rank of stable master; another stable boy, Cecco di Paliano, who had become a professional rider; and a 'much honoured' rider, known as Tomasso, who had started his court employment in the kitchens (see Appendix Two).[38] Inevitably, a stable master's situation varied considerably as, in some courts, the role was an honorary one. In 1535, the future Cardinal Ippolito d'Este, second son of Duke Alfonso II of Ferrara, chose five aristocratic courtiers to run his court one of whom, Ippolito Zuliolo, was chosen to be his stable master. This honorary appointment, overseeing twenty stable boys, a saddler, a *maniscalco* and four trainers,[39] was of equal status and pay as the master of the chamber, Scipio Assassino (41 *scudi* per year), although both earned considerably less than the head steward, Girolamo Guarniero (62 *scudi*).[40] Of course, Zuliolo may have had other privileges as compensation but, writing in the same decade, Priscianese, who had valued the stable master's role so highly, suggested an even wider gulf between the two salaries, recommending that a stable master should be paid 48 *scudi* and a steward 120 *scudi*.[41] At the much larger Sforza and Neapolitan courts the senior stable masters also had aristocratic backgrounds. Duke Galeazzo Maria would choose Count Giovanni Antonio Secco, known as 'Borella',[42] as his stable master, listed under 'li officiali dalla stalla' in 1471 and '76.[43] In fact both Borella's father, Count Antonio, and his father-in-law Franco Caimi, were Milanese courtiers.[44] In Naples, it had long been the tradition to appoint a member of the aristocracy to run the royal stables, the post known as *cavallericio* – Alfonso of Aragon (King of Naples, 1443-58) having set a precedent by appointing Paduano Pagano, a member of a leading Neapolitan family.[45] The tradition continued into the sixteenth century but in 1570 Philip II's Neapolitan stable master, the *caballerizo major*, had an additional administrative and judicial role. Not only could he hold tribunals in his house, he had civil and criminal jurisdiction over any officials under him such as riders, grooms and stonemasons. Similarly, the King's governor for the royal stud farm in Calabria was given exceptional power as, in addition to his normal stud-farm duties, he could jail, fine and punish 'at his discretion' or sentence anyone who caused damage to the 'breed's territory', having a jailer and three grenadiers at his disposal.[46]

The stable master was also expected to make detailed inventories with other members of household staff. Both the Urbino *ordini* and Priscianese's treatise required him to make an inventory of all the stabled animals and then, with the chief steward, to record all the bridles, saddles, harnesses as well as the stable implements.[47] In Urbino, this inventory was shown to the man in charge of weapons, before the stable master and *maniscalco* accounted for all locks and medicines.⁴⁸ Archives show that even recording the saddlery would have been a laborious and detailed task, with Aligueri's eighteen-page inventory listing at least ten different styles of saddle in use at the Ferrarese court in 1521, all of which needed to be kept in good repair.⁴⁹ Whether responsible for a relatively small or a large imperial stable, a patron's personal horses or his stud farm, the stable master required more than competent horsemanship; he also needed the skills of man-management, accountancy and diplomacy.

As for other members of staff, court orders and treatises also define the ideal character for a stable master. In Urbino the court *ordini* suggested he was to be a 'wise and diligent' man who 'feared and respected' his master. A century later Giovan Battista Ferraro who, like his son Pirro Antonio,⁵⁰ had been riding master at the royal Maddalena stables in Naples, advised that care should be taken to 'find a good man, [who was] god-fearing, conscientious and honourable'.⁵¹ But Corte would also demand total commitment, explaining that the stable master should be so in love with his stable that any external pleasure should be considered an 'enemy' to his work.⁵² As for administration, Ferraro wrote that the stable master should know 'not only how to order but at times to demonstrate to the stable boys', having a comprehensive understanding of the many trades concerning horses⁵³ which both Corte and Priscianese referred to as 'arts',⁵⁴ in particular those of the *maniscalco*, the saddler and the bridle maker. Corte wrote 'if not competent, at least he should not be totally ignorant' of them.⁵⁵ Priscianese also expected the stable master to be capable of shoeing the horse 'with his own hands [and to] know if it is well shod', to understand which breeds or colours of horses have hard or brittle feet and with which kind of shoe and quality of iron they should be shod.⁵⁶ And in understanding the veterinary side of the *maniscalco*'s work, the stable master was expected to be able diagnose illness and administer the necessary remedies.⁵⁷ He was also expected to have a considerable knowledge of saddles and bridles, knowing 'which [style] is best for this or that mount' and how to check every detail of its construction so it does not 'cause any harm to the horse in any area'.⁵⁸ Similarly, he should 'check that the harnesses and bridles such as the headpieces, reins, breastplates, cruppers,⁵⁹ straps and stirrup leathers are double, strong and of good leather' and that they are 'well sewn and expertly attached'.⁶⁰ Varied as they might seem, these specifications are extremely important as they are all concerned not only with the safety of the rider but also with the welfare of the horse.

Some writers felt the necessity to explain how a stable master should handle his staff with both Corte and Ferraro, men who were directly involved with leading stables, encouraging harmony rather than domination. Corte recommended the stable master should not only be 'quick-witted and trustworthy in management' but also 'attentive', 'feared and loved by the stable boys, because it is this quality, which . . . will equip him, without any doubt, for his position'.⁶¹ Ferraro also emphasised the importance of harmony in the stable, first warning that the stable master had 'great power not only in the lives and salaries of the stable staff' but also in every aspect of equine care,⁶² before comparing stable management with running a ship,

> At the break of day, [the stable master] should be found inside his riding school⁶³ giving orders, so that the mucking out starts and this should happen immediately at the first signal, without tumult or any contradiction . . . in the style of a galley, that is to say with care, but full of affection because it is through love, rather than fear, that he is obeyed.⁶⁴

Unlike these two professional horsemen, Priscianese's primary concern was that the stable master should recognise a good thoroughbred horse and be able to control its behaviour, rather than indulge in sympathetic staff management. His first specification is that the stable master should have the 'information and understanding of the features . . . that are needed for a beautiful horse . . . so that he can show his master [what is beautiful or ugly] in this or that horse'. When he is riding, the stable master should always be well dressed, sitting high and straight, with his legs stretched out so that, with 'the point of his foot in the stirrup', his toe should be 'level with the horse's ears',[65] a style of horsemanship that would soon become outdated as seen in Ferraro's treatise, where horsemen sit with their toes either in line with the knee or further back.[66] In addition, Priscianese suggested that the stable master should know how much force should be used to get the horse to respond to a rider's commands; whether or not it needs to be struck hard by the rider's heel, pricked by spurs, hit with a stick, or shouted at. He should also know whether the horse needs a soft or a vigorous hand[67] and understand the many different ways for controlling and riding it.[68] He should know which style of bridle, which bit and which thickness of curb-chain[69] is required and whether the horse's tongue should be tied down in order to make it more manageable – all factors which indicate that, in his opinion, the stable master's most important role was to contribute to his patron's appearance and public reputation.

It was, of course, the riding master (*cavallarizzo*) and professional riders (*cavalcatori*) who trained the horses to be responsive to riders' commands or prepared them for racing, and it was these men who were next to the stable master in the hierarchy of stable staff. The requirements and work of the *cavallarizzo*,[70] the profession that both Corte and his father had followed, are contained in three dialogues at the end of his treatise, whilst the sixty-one chapters of Book II give advice on training. It is not relevant here to consider Corte's many instructions on schooling horses but, in his first dialogue, it is notable that he compared the *cavallarizzo*'s craft to that of a painter or sculptor who carefully moulds his raw material into the perfect form

> As many painters do, who first adjust the colours and shapes in the composition, which they wish to create in their painting, and then create it; in the same way sculptors made marble, which they first polish, then trace it with charcoal lines almost painting it, [before] reducing it to the perfect shape, which they had already imagined; so it is correctly said that the shape and model, together with the finished result, is the first intention, and the last in execution; so, therefore, I have written this, hoping to create a good *cavallarizzo*.[71]

As for physical build and mental character of the riders, Corte explains that they should

> be good spirited and well built, attentive and loyal, vainglorious, without envy, of few words, not blameworthy or gambling but faithful and sincere.

He explains that when riders required anything for their work, they should 'tell the stable master who will give it to them' or, if he doesn't do so, they should inform the *cavallarizzo*. Characteristically, Corte was concerned with the staff's welfare, insisting that the stable master saw that the riders were well treated, not lacking for anything, 'neither food, drink nor salary'.[72] In return, each professional rider was responsible for training and exercising up to eight horses and was expected to ride them in displays of *maneggio* when required. For these displays certain jumps had been adapted from battle movements, in which the best cavalry horses had been admired for their ability to use kicks, bites and pounding hooves. Now performed in the confines of the court, these movements could be admired by men and women alike. However, this new court art was not for the war horse to perform; it was for the Spanish *gineta* whose physical strength and intelligence made it the ideal performance horse. A movement such as the *corbetta*,[73] where

7.5. The *capriola* in battle. Paolo Uccello, *The Battle of San Romano: Bernardino della Ciarda unhorsed*, c.1435. Florence, Uffizi Gallery. Peter Horree/Alamy stock photo

the horse stood on its hind legs to shield the rider's body from attack, was already known to Xenophon[74] and the most difficult jump, the *capriola*,[75] which required the horse to leap and simultaneously kick back its rear feet when parallel to the ground, was described by Massari in 1600 as necessary for both tournament and battle, as the horse could create a clearance around its rider if surrounded by the enemy.[76] Examples of the *capriola* can be seen in Piero della Francesca's frescos of the *Legend of the True Cross* for Arezzo's San Francesco (c.1452-c.1466)[77] and in Paolo Uccello's *Battle of San Romano: Bernardino della Ciarda unhorsed*, where a grey horse lies prone behind the chestnut, which is kicking out its hind legs (7.5). Uccello also depicts several other horses performing the *corbetta* in his composition.

For horses to be trained and to perform well it was essential that they and their riders had the correct equipment. In fact, the importance attached to saddles, stirrups and bridles led to them being celebrated among other important inventions in a series of early seventeenth-century frescoes at the Tesoro dei Granduchi in Florence (7.6, 7.7, 7.8). Together with inventions such as telescopes, clocks and the printing press, vignettes of saddles, stirrups and bridles show them hanging outside trade stalls with the appropriate tradesman helping a customer make a choice.[78] The emphasis on these pieces of equipment reflects their various benefits for both horse and rider. Firstly, they contributed to the rider's appearance, not only in helping him sit well on his horse and look competent but also by assisting in controlling the horse's movements and behaviour. More importantly, both saddle and stirrups helped keep rider and horse safe; the saddle protecting the horse's back and both it and the stirrups helping keep the rider secure. But whilst this equipment assisted in drawing attention to the rider's horsemanship, it also provided a means for him, or his court, to display his magnificence through the use of extravagant materials. This is evident from a 1597 inventory of Alfonso II d'Este's estate which lists: gilded and damascened brass stirrups and gilded bits, saddle cloths made of sable, lynx, wolf and silk, girths of black, white and crimson velvet, of green silk with silver thread and gold brocade amongst the hundreds of magnificent items of saddlery and caparisons for the Este horses.[79]

7.6. Assistants of Michelangelo Cinganelli, *Nova Reperta: the Invention of the Saddle.* Florence, Palazzo Pitti, Tesoro dei Granduchi

7.7. Assistants of Michelangelo Cinganelli, *Nova Reperta: the Invention of the Stirrup.* Florence, Palazzo Pitti, Tesoro dei Granduchi

7.8. Assistants of Michelangelo Cinganelli, *Nova Reperta: the Invention of the Bit.* Florence, Palazzo Pitti, Tesoro dei Granduchi. All images courtesy of the Ministero per i beni e le attività culturali, Gallerie degli Uffizi

7.9. Saddler and stirrup maker. Galle and Collaert engraving after Jan van der Straet (Stradanus), *Nova reperta: The Invention of Stirrups*, c.1590

It was, therefore, both for safety and aesthetic reasons that the saddler held a prominent role within the stable *famiglia*. Although the craft of the saddler was independent from that of the stirrup-maker (*staffiero*) and bit-maker (*morsaio*), tradesmen established their shops close to one another. This is shown in Galle and Collaert's engraving *The Invention of the Stirrup*, based on one of Giovanni Stradano's twenty-four late sixteenth-century drawings of new discoveries, which depicts the workrooms of saddler and stirrup-maker opposite one another in a narrow street (7.9).[80] It seems logical, therefore, that the larger court stables would have their own saddlery workshops where all trades could work together. Certainly, for the convenience of both saddler and stable master, Priscianese recommended that the saddler should have a workroom within the confines of the court stable, so that he could adjust or fit the saddles to individual horses.[81] From Francesco di Giorgio's description of the Urbino stables it is known that saddles were being 'decorated' in a room next to that of the stable master's, implying that other craftsmen were working there.[82]

Even the saddles were not solely the work of a saddler: carvers, gilders, painters and goldsmiths would have worked with him. These men would have made not only simple training saddles but elaborately decorated saddles with expensive fabrics or inlays which, together with ornate bridles, added to the magnificence of the horse and rider's display. Meticulous Este stable accounts show that, in addition to various coloured cloths,[83] as many as five different types of nail were used in the Este saddle workshop in 1554. Although some may have been studs for decoration, as many as 3,100 nails were used in January by the saddler Maestro Domenicho.[84]

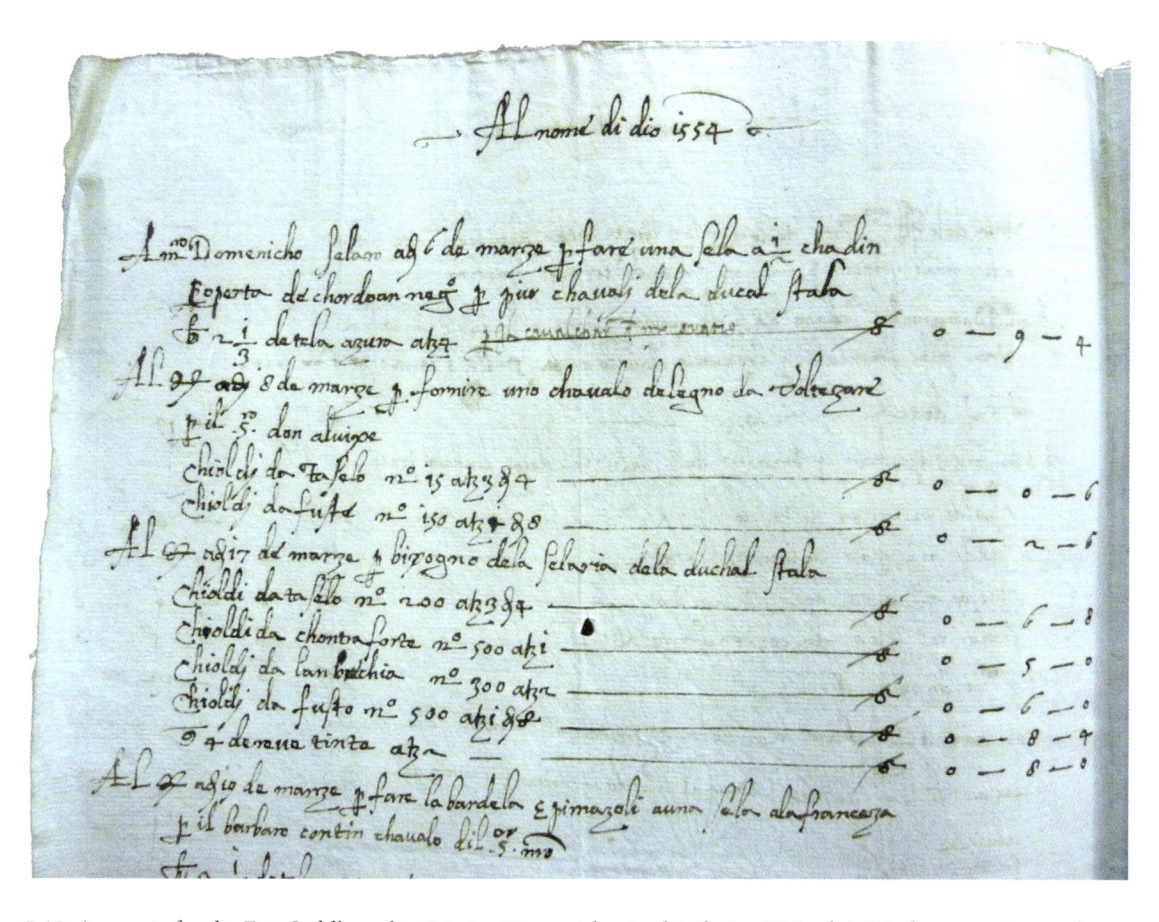

7.10. Accounts for the Este Saddle maker, Master Domenicho, Iv, detail. On 8 March 1554, the account records a wooden toy horse for five-year-old 'Don Aluigi' (Ercole II d'Este's youngest son, Luigi). Modena, ASMo, AE, b. 2, fasc. 3, Stalla: Note-spese-inventori, 1521-1713. Courtesy of Ministero per i beni e le attività culturali –Archivio di Stato di Modena, prot n. 955

As suggested, saddles were made for specific court horses – such as the blue saddle *a la Francesca* made in January 1554 for one of the Duke Ercole's horses, Pongarelo,[85] or, more unusually, the saddle made the following March for a wooden toy horse *da voltazare*[86] belonging to five-year-old Luigi, the Duke's youngest son (7.10).[87] It seems that the little boy's riding skills had improved by October that year, as accounts show that matching blue saddles *a la Francesca* were made for his grey pony, Gobo, and for Duke Ercole's horse, Alfonsino.[88]

While the quality of workmanship for the harnessing or tack might impress onlookers, this also drew attention to the rider indirectly by affecting the horse's performance. However, of all the tradesmen involved with the horse's tack it was the bit maker, the *morsaio*, whose craftsmanship produced the most important part of the horse's bridle; essential not only for training and control but also affecting the horse's performance and head carriage. Introducing the horse to the bit was an important part of its schooling and, if done incorrectly, could affect the horse's behaviour permanently. This mouthpiece was by no means a simple piece of equipment and the *morsaio*'s trade could well be compared to that of a goldsmith. As the sixteenth century progressed, a wider choice of bit became available. Although the simple snaffle bit, *filetto*, was used for training purposes, it was the more severe curb bit which evolved with styles described as Spanish, Polish, German and Turkish, sometimes with bizarre illustrations to identify them (7.11). In fact, by 1562 it was possible for a German spur maker to produce a four hundred-page book which consisted entirely of elaborate engravings and descriptions of 382 different bits.[89]

The many sections of the curb bit allowed for elaborate decoration not only of the visible

7.11. Pirro Antonio Ferraro, *Cavallo frenato* (Naples, 1602), IV. A Turkish bit

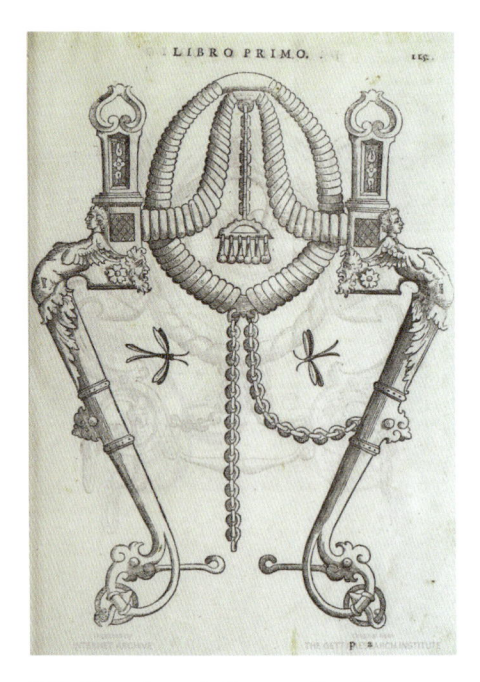

7.12. Pirro Antonio Ferraro, *Cavallo frenato* (Naples, 1602), I. A curb bit

elements such as the shanks, but also of the unseen sections inside the horse's mouth, which affected the severity and pain caused by the bit (7.12). For this reason, the rider's ignorance or malpractice could have disastrous effects on the horse's performance. Pirro Antonio Ferraro, who defined the bridle as 'the real rudder that guides this great machine', warns that without the 'true doctrine' of schooling the bridle alone counted for nothing. He adds,

> long will be the discourse if I wish to confine to memory the opinions of the ancient instructors, many of whom, practising this skill with few lessons and strong bridles, would like to punish their horses and also, without true and continuous discipline more often produce harm to [their] horses' mouths.[90]

Well-disciplined horses adorned with beautiful saddles, bridles and caparisons were what the public and a ruler's subjects expected to see. But this turnout took considerable work not only from trainers, riders and harness makers; inside the stable it was the stable boys who carried out most of the manual labour. A variety of names described these hard working young men – *garzoni*, *stallieri*, *fanti*, *putti* and *mozzi di stalla* – although these boys were of equal status, with only the *baccalari* immediately senior to them – a position that can be equated to a head groom.[91] Unfortunately, being at the lower end of the stable hierarchy little is known of these boys' origins but, as with other members of staff, they probably moved around from stable to stable, as happened following the collapse of the Bentivoglio regime in 1507 when three members of their Bolognese stables moved to Mantua.[92] But stable staff could also come from further afield. As already noted, a posthumous inventory included four black slaves working in a Neapolitan stable – two of whom had been given their freedom,[93] and names such as Giobattista Turcheto, Faitre Todesco and Borso Tedesco appear in stable records, suggesting these boys came from Turkey and Germany.[94] Lowly origins are suggested by Corte who described them as 'only hirelings',

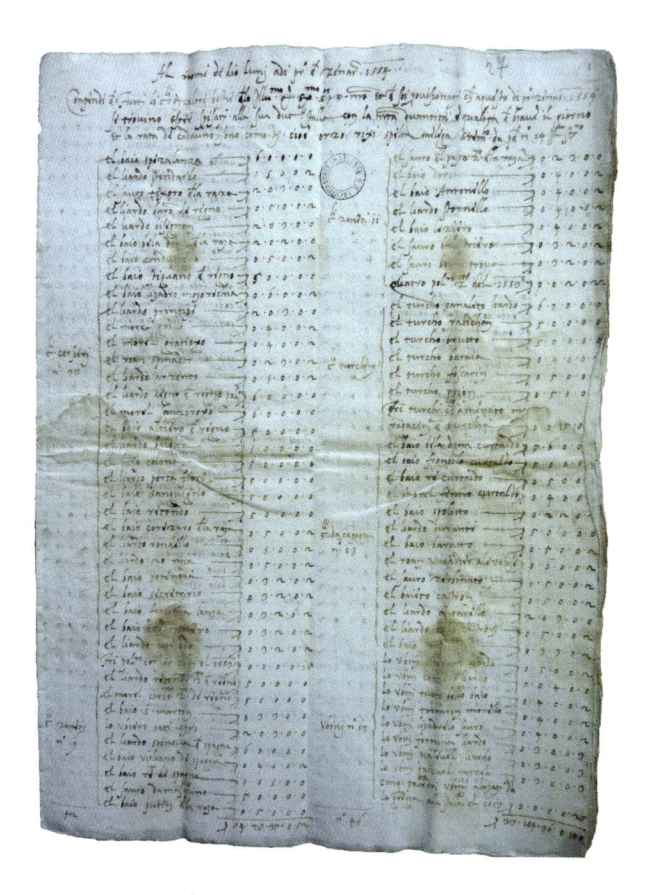

7.13. Este stable records, listing horses and their daily fodder, 1554. Modena, ASMo, AE, Amministrazione della casa: note-spese, b.1, 27r. Courtesy of Ministero per i beni e le attività culturali –Archivio di Stato di Modena, prot n. 955

who were 'naturally loutish' in their behaviour[95] but, wherever they came from, the standards set for them were high. Corte expects a stable boy to be faithful and loving, to work well, and not to 'have a wife and children . . . because he must not sleep outside the stables at night'. The concentration on their commitment to work differs significantly from Corte's requirements for jockeys who, he suggests, should be 'short, lean, vigorous, dexterous and courageous, having a good intellect and memory'.[96] This seems surprising as the stable boys' work was not only strenuous but also required intelligence and memory to administer the correct diet and to groom the horses correctly.

Administering the correct diet was not a simple matter. It was not only the quality of food that mattered, it was also important that each horse had the correct diet to achieve its potential. Not only were horses individually catered for, but there was an ongoing mixture of advice on feeding and no doubt stables varied in their feeding practices. Whilst Alberti and Leonardo, like Vegetius and Ruffo before them,[97] described the correct position of the food, Corte concentrated on how feeding should be conducted and Caracciolo focused on the ideal quality and types of fodder. Certainly, the correct diet depended on the horse's sex and breed as well as its expected workload, details that required the stable boys to administer carefully controlled amounts. The 1554 Este stable masters kept a precise record of each horse's fodder (7.13), with the daily amounts of barley, rice, spelt, lucerne and bran written beside each horse's name.[98] Later records bracketed the names of the boys beside their horses. Corte's chapter on the stallion recommends that, for at least two months before he is 'given to the mares', he should be fed 'the best barley to please and fatten him' and on the days when he is to cover the mares and for ten days afterwards, he should be given water mixed with *farraina* (a mixture of powdered cereal)

205

and salt (see Appendix Four).⁹⁹

In Corte's chapter devoted to the training of racehorses he again emphasises the importance of diet.¹⁰⁰ For the eight days before a race, the horse's care and feed are described in detail, indicating just how much work would go into this preparation by trainers and stable boys. Added to the horse's daily mash were two ounces of pine syrup and eight to ten eggs, the quantity of food to be doubled four to five days before racing. For these last few days, the horse was to be muzzled at night except during the twice-nightly check by the stable boy, who should then give him a quantity of rose-flavoured sugar or a bunch of Passerina grapes – presumably for high sugar content. On race morning, this feeding was followed by three slices of bread sprinkled with grated sugar and a fresh lettuce. Like the stallions, these horses were being prepared for specific events but, for every horse, it was important that diet was carefully controlled.

In addition to diet, Corte's advice on the racehorse's care while in training shows just how much might be expected of the stable staff. As for the special diet, preparation started eight days before the race with Corte advising that every day artemisia – a herb known to prevent bacteria – should be rubbed into the horse's back and any other place touched by the bridle or spurs. Then, for two to three days before the race, the horse's legs should be washed twice a day with a concoction of dried roses boiled with sage, rosemary, citrus leaves and camomile, adding half a glass of rose oil for the last three washes. Six days before the race, the horse was to be shod with extra heavy shoes before intensive training began. This started with a gallop of half the race distance, gradually increasing the distance and his speed until he exceeds the length of the race by 'the flight of an arrow' – about 400 metres. After each of these training sessions, the horse's legs were to be washed down with warm wine. On race day, lightweight shoes were once again fitted, his legs greased with red deer bone marrow and his head washed with sweet smelling wine mixed with rose oil and water in which herbs had been boiled. Before going to the start he was to be stroked, pummelled and wiped down, his nostrils and genitals wiped with wine, and a large cloth soaked in rose petal vinegar should be placed over his loins. Immediately before the race starts, Corte advises that the horse's legs, stomach and genitals should be coated with good quality oil. If this regime was carried out, it would have taken several boys to prepare the horse and, if rewarded with victory, there would be pride for all those involved. Certainly, Butteri's painting clearly shows the groom's admiration for his master's horse as he parades it through the streets (7.14). Believed to be Francesco de' Benci's horse, Il Seicento, it is thought that the *fleur de lys* on the elaborate saddle cloth may signify that this grey had won the *palio* of Florence.

Even if not specifically caring for stallions or racehorses, the stable boys had many other regular chores. They were expected to clean and tidy the stables, check the horses' feet and take them to the farrier if necessary. They also had to wash and groom the horses before and after their daily exercise to keep them looking their best. Writers describe grooming techniques at length and a brief analysis of the care prescribed for tired and sweating horses illustrates not only the contradictory advice given to them, but also the physical effort required of these court servants. Much of the equipment available to them is seen in the frontispiece of a work commemorating the stables of Don Juan of Austria, where combs, sponges and cloths for grooming, cleaning and drying the horse are depicted alongside the forks for moving and sifting bedding and various pieces of tack (7.15).¹⁰¹

Cleaning and grooming after exercise was a laborious job but almost all writers start their routine with the horse being washed, many contemporary and early writers describing the positive and negative qualities of different washing techniques, in either sea water or river

7.14. Giovanni Butteri, *The Return from the Palio*, 16th century. Dublin, National Gallery of Ireland

7.15. Cleaning and grooming equipment. Jan van der Straet (Stradanus), Equile. Ioannis Austriaci Caroli V. Imp. F., Antwerp 1578-80, title page. Courtesy Utah Museum of Fine Arts, Gift of E. Frank Sanguinetti

water.[102] Both Alberti and Corte preferred covering a sweating horse with a blanket and walking it at a leisurely pace to cool it down; Corte designating a specific area outside the stables for this gentle exercise[103] and Alberti, following Vegetius,[104] recommended that the horse be allowed to lie down and roll. Only after this should mud be removed with a scraper before the horse was coated with oil and his skin rubbed vigorously with handfuls of hemp to bring back condition but, Alberti warns, 'this friction must not be too frequent nor too hard on a tender skin'.[105] Many years before, Vegetius had suggested that the horse should be curried and rubbed down by the 'hands of many people' to teach the horse 'tameness and gentleness' and also to relax its skin.[106] With one groom appointed to as many as four horses, Vegetius' advice is unlikely to have been followed in the Renaissance. In fact, a rare scene of grooming in the background of Fra Angelico's and Filippo Lippi's mid fifteenth-century *Adoration of the Magi*, depicts each horse attended by only one groom – each man rubbing down or cleaning out the feet of his master's horse (7.16).

Once groomed, it is likely that the stable boys would have put blankets over the horses: linen in summer and wool in winter. In Ferrara, the Este horse blankets added to the spectacle of show in the stable as they were made of a red *scarlattino* fabric,[107] contrasting with the green ribbons woven into the horses' manes and their green leather head collars and ropes. Records show that, even taking a horse through the streets of Ferrara to be shod, this rug and head collar were exchanged for something more magnificent; the horse's blanket changed for one embroidered with the Este *impresa*[108] and the green head collar replaced by an elaborate green and red silk bridle.[109] Such extravagant displays of wealth could also be seen on racehorses. For example

7.16. Fra Angelico and Fra Filippo Lippi, *The Adoration of the Magi*, c.1440/60.
Washington, DC, National Gallery of Art, Samuel H. Kress Collection. Image courtesy of the Board of Trustees

in 1509, when Francesco Gonzaga's horses wore his green and crimson colours, their bi-colour velvet saddle cloths were decorated with tremblents made of the *Cresolo* impresa while small bells hung from their matching silk bridles which carried red and green feather plumes as head ornaments.[110] In addition to fitting and exchanging harnessing, the Gonzaga stable boys were also expected to dye the manes and tails of Turkish racehorses with valuable imported henna (see 3.13).[111] There is also evidence that horses were decorated with chequered patterns or other designs, often in the livery colours of their master, although no such evidence has been found for the Gonzaga stable.[112]

It was, no doubt, partly due to such decoration that Priscianese was prompted to describe horses as having more value to a patron than a 'bedroom hung with gold brocade',[113] or why Castiglione's Fregoso expected a courtier's horse to be 'beautifully caparisoned ... with appro-

7.17. Ippolito Andreasi, 1548-1608, Horse with richly decorated equipment

Both images: Sweden, Nationalmuseum, Åsa Lundén, public domain

7.18. Giulio Romano d.1546, Horse with a drum attached to the saddle

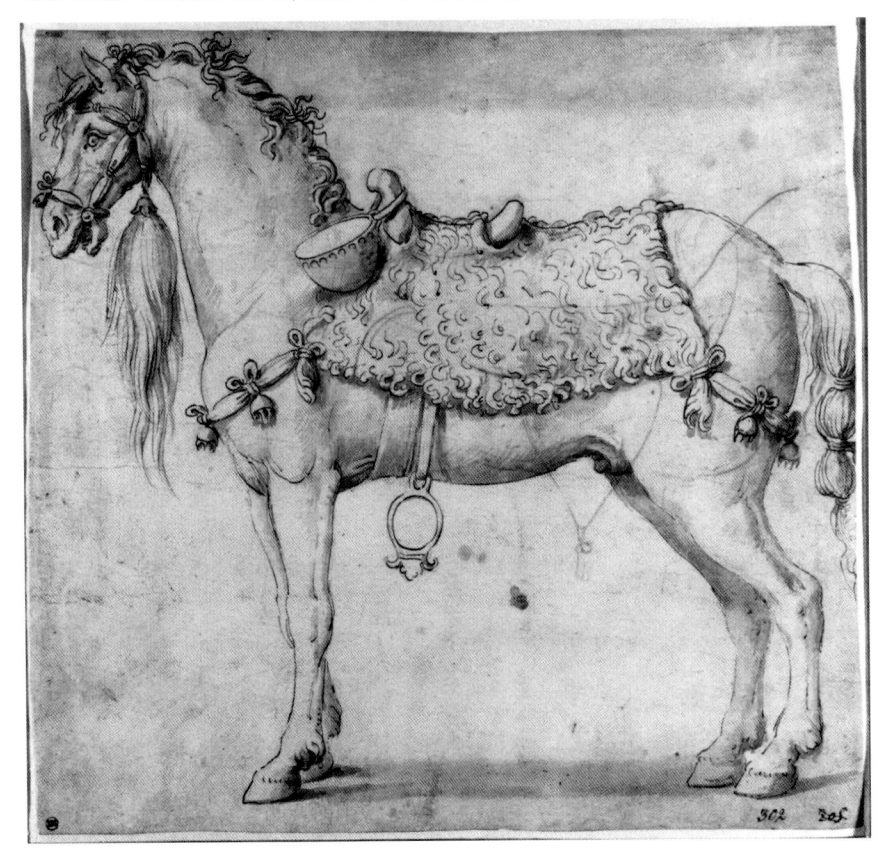

210

7.19. Decorative horse tails in Taddeo and Federico Zuccari's, *I fasti farnesiani: The Truce of Nice* c.1559. Villa Farnese, Caprarola, akg-images/De Agostini Picture Lib./G Dagli Orti

priate mottoes and ingenious devices to attract the eyes of onlookers in his direction'.[114] Many members of staff would have worked hard to create and maintain these elaborate harnesses, fancy dress costumes and caparisons, but it was the stable boys who fitted these intricate 'outfits' to the horses (7.17, 7.18). It was also their responsibility to decorate the horses' manes and tails – a skill described by Garzoni as 'knotting' (*aggroppare*)[115] – twisting, plaiting and interweaving the horses' hair with ribbons in designs not unlike Renaissance women's hairstyles of the period. This styling may well have been a conscious decision as Giovan Battista Ferraro had emphasised that, if well looked after, both mane and tail should resemble 'a lady's hair' of which 'long and blond [was] held to be the most beautiful'.[116] Ferraro goes into some detail on this decorative grooming explaining that the stable master must not only oversee the stable boys but also know how to create 'every sort of tail'.[117] First, he should monitor the tail's washing, which should be done in the morning so that it can be combed and fluffed out in the evening, the stable boy carefully separating the hairs by hand. The tail should then be shined with a cloth but not oiled in summer as this will make dust stick to it, nor in winter 'unless the occasion demands it'. He continues

> diligence should be used on the horse's [mane and tail], seeing that these two extremities are the most beautiful parts [of the horse]; I say this because this animal will become

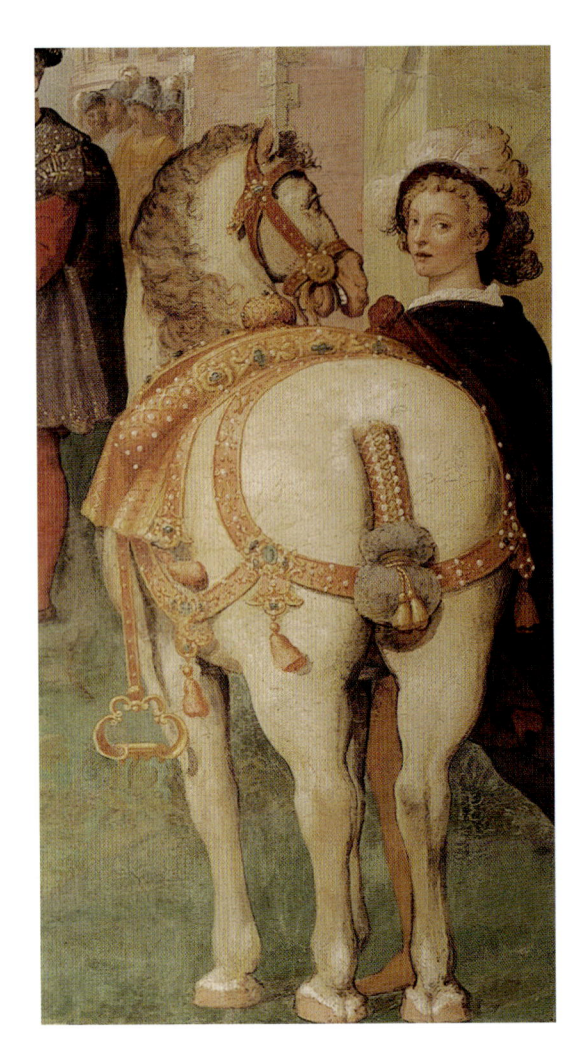

7.19a. Taddeo and Federico Zuccari, *I fasti farnesiani,* detail

graceful and beautiful when they are looked after well.[118]

Portrait medals, paintings and engravings (see 7.15) all contain images of elaborate mane and tail decorations; some very controlled such as in Zuccari's frescos, *I fasti farnesiani*, at Caprarola and others more free-flowing as seen in Lo Scheggia's cassone panel of *Trajan and the Widow* (7.19 *previous page,* 7.19a, 7.20). Much of this grooming and pampering might seem excessive, especially when preparing a racehorse for a *palio*, but it should be remembered that many of the writers were practitioners directly involved with horses, not simply theorists. There was, in the Renaissance, a clear belief that the more contact man had with the horse, the better the health of the horse. The elaborate grooming and washing techniques allowed for a close human-equine relationship to develop, with stable boys and trainers preparing the horses for their riders. If mishandled by the owner or stable boy, much of this preparation work was worthless and would need repeating, but mishandling was less likely if the advice given by theorists was followed correctly. Caracciolo, whose love for the horse is evident throughout his treatise, summarised the importance of the horse's trust in his handlers claiming that 'affection above all things will remove all those things which seem to upset these animals'.[119] He explains that while rubbing down soothes the horse, benefiting both its health and temperament, 'caressing'

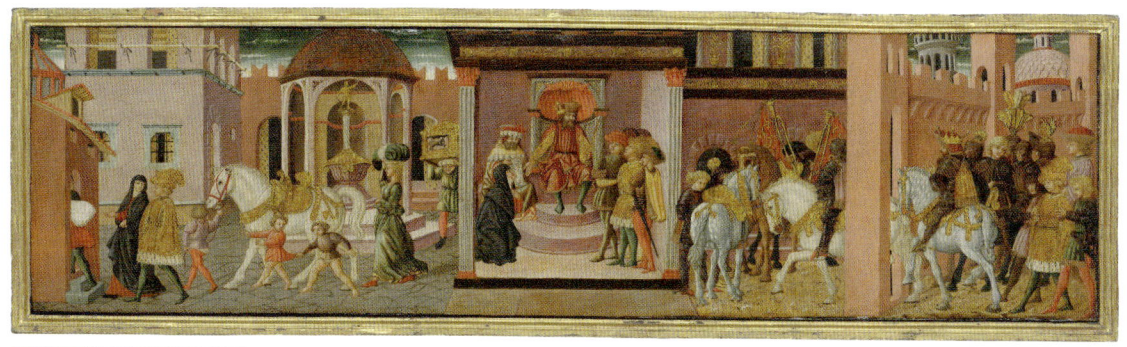

7.20. Decorative horse tails. Lo Scheggia, *Trajan and the Widow*, c.1450, cassone panel and detail. ©Christie's Images Limited

with the voice not only calms the horse down but also prevents him from being malicious.[120] This followed Xenophon's belief that 'a horse can be taught to be calm with a chirp of the lips' and 'roused with a cluck of the tongue'.[121] As Vegetius and, later, Caracciolo had rightly concluded, rubbing down was beneficial for both the health and for the grace of the horse.

In spite of, or perhaps because of the stable boys' wide-ranging duties both inside and outside the stable, it seems that gambling and theft occurred in stables. Both the Urbino *ordini* and later Corte had recommended stable boys should be kept away from gambling,[122] and Ferraro had warned that gambling at night provoked not only discord and blasphemy but, more importantly, made the boys 'tired and dazed, when it [was] necessary to look after the horses'.[123] To prevent the theft of fodder, Corte suggested the stable master should patrol the stable during feeding times to check that all the horses were eating properly. If they weren't, this could be because the horse was ill or a stable boy had coated its teeth with tallow or pig fat in order to steal its food.[124] Whether the stolen fodder was for the stable boy's consumption or for him to sell is not explained, but even Xenophon had suggested that 'it [was] a good plan to have the stall so contrived that it will be as difficult to steal the horse's fodder out of the manger as the master's victuals out of the larder'.[125] Nevertheless, records show that it was generally the responsibility of the employer to feed the stable boys as well as providing them with their bedding. In Urbino, for example, the stable boys were to be given two meals a day as well as bread and wine once or twice a day, which was to be eaten discreetly.[126] A century later Corte suggested that, whenever possible, the stable boys should eat together at midday in the harness rooms at the end of the stable, where they should eat quietly and quickly, eight per room whilst the *baccallari* kept watch over the horses.[127]

If fodder was stolen for gain, this may well reflect poor pay and living conditions, both of which must have varied from stable to stable. Certainly, the recommended pay varied in different parts of Italy. Mid sixteenth-century accounts for Ferrara, show that Ippolito d'Este's stable boys were paid 5 *scudi* a year, one seventh of the chief horse-trainer's salary of 34 *scudi*,[128] which was enough money for them to have bought them two capons a week or two small pigs a year.[129] Unlike other members of the Este stable staff, they did not eat in the palace and were only given one hundredth of a *scudo* a day for food, equivalent to the value of a pound's weight of poor quality beef or 800 grams of bread.[130] In 1540, Priscianese had advised that a stable boy in Rome should be paid almost double this amount, 9 *scudi* a year. But these costs are put into perspective when compared to Federico Gonzaga's annual income at the other end of the scale – 90 to 100,000 ducats – or even to Priscianese's suggested annual maintenance cost for a court horse – 17½ *scudi* – almost double the stable boy's annual salary, even though the maintenance cost would be higher if the staff's salaries were taken into account.[131] Corte, who was concerned with the effect of poor pay on performance, quoted the proverb 'According to how much you pay me, I will serve you' and continued

> therefore, treat those servants well who deserve it, and throw out the idlers, [that is to say] the presumptuous and ignorant ones. Because very often idleness is full of presumption and ignorance and this can be dangerous not only for the stable but for the whole court.[132]

Nevertheless, he believed that there was spiritual reward for the stable boys' hard work and it is easy to imagine a stable master reading out the following extract from Corte's *Cavallarizzo* as a source of encouragement for his staff,

> [Stable boys] must be prompt and ready for their work, quick and cheerful, of few words, not drunk or thieving but reverent and humble. And this will come to them when they consider that God has made them poor but strong so that they can earn themselves bread with their sweat, they remain dependent but believe that in another life they will be given incomparable wealth. And in this way they will content themselves with their vocation.[133]

Reward promised 'in another life' may well have seemed inadequate recompense for the exceptional amount of work expected of these hard-working servants. Corte had, of course, mentioned some who had managed to rise through the ranks to honourable positions but by the time he wrote his treatise, in 1562, he had worked in several large court stables and chose to name only two stable boys and one kitchen boy who had achieved promotion. It is, therefore, perhaps not unexpected that both gambling and theft of fodder by those who were not so gifted would remain problems for stable masters throughout this period.

A study of the staff's accommodation shows that all those working with the court horses had lodgings either inside or adjacent to the stabling. Unusually, Priscianese suggested that the stable master could also have a canopied bed in the stable, so that he can be woken in the morning with 'sweet and gentle sounds . . . a music of combs and stable songs, harmonised with the sound . . . beat and movement of hands', presumably as the stable boys groom and pummel their horses.[134] There is no recorded evidence of this sleeping arrangement being put into practice and, in this instance, Priscianese seems to be 'romanticising' about the working practices of stable life. Nevertheless, the Urbino *ordini* certainly stipulate that the stable master should be lodged close to the stables and that a junior stable master should be continuously in the stable, when his superior is not there.[135] Certainly, the stable boys were expected to be with their horses day and night, with Corte explaining that their straw mattresses should be placed along the length of the stable's central aisle so as 'to help the horses and scold them when necessary'. He preferred this arrangement to stables where boys slept on platforms or in separate rooms, where they cannot be 'seen by their superiors'.[136] If the boys did sleep in the aisle presumably their mattresses were placed on the raised part of the wide central aisle, as this was the only area that would have been clean and dry throughout the night. In any event, even if the stable master did not have a bed inside the stable itself, this important court position was a twenty-four-hour job, with Corte insisting that everything should be in order before he retired:

> [The stable master] must never go to sleep before checking that all the horses are well tethered, as they should be, that their bedding is good, that the stables are clear of any danger of fire, that each horse [stall] has a torch, that the horses' hooves are greased and that they are well shod; so that nothing can happen that is not foreseen, thought of or proven. For if anything indicates that the stable boys in their last hours are kneeling down, chattering and singing in the stable, he must make them go to rest quietly.[137]

The watchfulness of a conscientious stable master and his staff could not guarantee security for a stable in peaceful or troubled times as the following examples show. In April 1469 a letter to Sigismondo d'Este[138] informs him that during the night the Reggio stable had burnt down, killing forty-one horses belonging to him and his brother Ercole, thirty-two of which were 'of great value'. One stable boy had also died in the fire which, it is suggested, may have been caused deliberately.[139] In 1495, Giacomo Gallo records that during the sack of Naples horses had escaped from the burning royal *cavallarizzo*, causing King Ferdinand II himself, together with 400 Swiss guard and some courtiers, to catch the thirty-two horses and return them to the safety of the castle.[140] One of the worst stable disasters occurred during the wars with France when in November 1501, forty-five destriers, half of the Gonzaga's cavalry, died during the night. Although there was no apparent cause, it was believed they had been poisoned, possibly on the orders of the King of France. The Gonzaga's senior stable master, Roadino Evangelista,[141] was held responsible, compounding his supposed guilt by fleeing the same night – an action which resulted in Francesco Gonzaga offering the enormous sum of two thousand ducats if Roadino were to be found and proved guilty.[142]

Evidence shows that the stable staff were expected to work hard day and night to maintain the court horses in good condition. As such, the time and attention given to the horses at least matched – if not exceeded – that given to other valuable commodities. But this commodity was not like any other. It was vulnerable, temperamental and potentially dangerous although, at the same time, it provided unlimited opportunities for its owner to display wealth and magnificence. This was partly due to the horse's thoroughbred ancestry but also to its intelligence, which could be exploited for the benefit of its owner. Consequently, every part of the horse's life was nurtured – from its conception and birth, its training, harnessing and care in the stable and the more aesthetic elements of its grooming. Like some early texts, fifteenth- and sixteenth-century court ordinances and treatises explained at length the minutiae of the horse's daily routine, often prescribing the conditions of its stabling and its feeding in more detail than those given for the living conditions of the stable staff. For the stable boys many of these conditions could be compared to those of a monastic life: working in an all-male environment, forbidden to have a wife or children, having to live within the stable's 'community' and eating their meals in silence. Even the meticulous regularity suggested for the horses' feeding and grooming routines, is comparable to religious ritual. Above all, it is Corte's belief that God made the stable boys poor but strong so that, through hard work, they could earn incomparable wealth in another life – which shows just what was expected of these court servants.[143]

Certainly, it was the staff's support and care which allowed the horse to develop from a raw product into a valuable Renaissance commodity. But horses could only show off their qualities if they were healthy, willing and able to perform for their riders. It was, therefore, essential that their feet were suitably shod, their diet appropriate and for any sickness or injury, they were treated appropriately. For these aspects of the horses' welfare it was the *maniscalco*, the farrier-surgeon, who was responsible and it is this indispensable post which will be considered in the final chapter.

1 Xenophon, *Memorabilia and Oeconomicus* (1923), III, p. 387.
2 See Corte, *Il cavallarizzo* (1562) addressed to riding masters. Fiaschi's *Trattato* (first published 1556) on breaking in, schooling and shoeing horses, Ruini's *Anatomia* (1598) on equine sickness and remedies addressed to princes, horsemen, philosophers, doctors, riding masters and farrier-surgeons and Filippo Scaccho da Tagliacozzo's, *Trattato di mescalzia* (1603) addressed to princes, gentlemen, soldiers and farrier-surgeons.
3 Corte, 1562, I, ch. 37, 47v-48r, 'Del officio de' garzoni di stalla'.
4 *Ordini*. It is not known who wrote the 'Ordini et Officij', nor exactly when they were written. The existing 'Ordini' is a late fifteenth- or early sixteenth-century manuscript copy. See S. Eiche, ed., *Ordini et officij de casa de lo illustrissimo Signor Duca de Urbino* (Urbino, 1999), p. 16.
5 'Ordini per il governo della famiglia di Cicco Simonetta' c.1476, in C. Magenta ed., *I Visconti e gli Sforza* (1883), II, 'Galeazzo Maria Sforza', pp. 371-5.
6 Naples, BNN, MS XI.B.39, 84r and 86r-v. Cited in Hernando Sánchez 'La Gloria del cavallo' (1998), p. 302, nn. 69 and 70.
7 Priscianese, *Del governo* (1883), ch. XXVI, p. 52.
8 *On Horsemanship*, 1962, pp. 355 and 357.
9 This variation in names comes from the different texts consulted and although their responsibilities were similar, the men sometimes held a different status within the stable hierarchy.
10 Approximately half a rectangular bale of hay in the present day.
11 Priscianese, *Del governo* (1883), ch. XV, p. 20.
12 Priscianese does not specify the type of straw. Oat straw can be fed to horses although its quality as fodder is not as high as hay. It can also be used as bedding. Wheat straw is the most suitable for bedding. Barley straw should not be used at all. If eaten, barley husks can irritate or scratch the throat, causing a cough.
13 Priscianese refers to the 'Campo di Fiore measure' although the measure's quantity is not specified.
14 Priscianese, *Del governo* (1883), ch. XVI, p. 20.
15 Tommaso Garzoni, *La piazza universale di tutte le professioni del mondo*, 2 vols (Venice, 1589), eds. P. Cherchi and B. Collina (Turin, 1996), *Discorso* lv, 'De' cavallari, asinari, mulattieri overo somieri ò somegini, e stabulari e servitori ò famegli da stalla, e fabricatori di scove', p. 800.

16 L. B. Alberti, 'I libri della famiglia' *c*.1434 trans. and ed. R. Neu Watkins *The Family in Renaissance Florence*, 4 books (Columbia, SC, 1969), III, p. 218.
17 Alberti, *The Family* (1969), III, p. 222.
18 Corte, 1562, I, ch. 36, 'Della stalla, & sue pertinentie'; ch. 37, 'Dell'officio de' garzoni di stalla'; ch. 38, 'Del governo de' cavalli in istalla'; ch. 48, 'Dell'officio del maestro di stalla, de i cavalcatori, & baccalari'.
19 Priscianese, *Del governo* (1883), 'Proemio', pp. 4-6.
20 Corte, 1562, I, ch. 38, 48v.
21 Francesco ('Cicco') Simonetta (1410-80). After Galeazzo Maria's murder in 1476, Simonetta was put in charge of finding the murderers. In 1479 Simonetta and his brother, Giovanni were arrested and imprisoned in Pavia. Simonetta was beheaded in 1480.
22 Milan, ASMi, 'Ordini per il governo della famiglia di Cicco Simonetta' in C. Magenta (1883), II, pp. 371-5.
23 Ibid. II, p. 374, *Item ch'esso Zohanne non debba acceptare in stalla niuno cavallo de forestieri, nè tenerli più de uno dì senza licentia, et ogni sira debba notificare quilli cavalli forestieri che serano in casa, altramente retenerdoli più de uno dì senza licentia, serano metuti in conto ad lui sopra il suo salario.*
24 See Chapter 5.
25 The Venetian Republic had an extensive stud farm and equestrian school near Alberobello in Puglia. See G. Notarnicola, *La cavallerizza della Serenissima in Puglia* (Venice, 1933. Reprint, 2008).
26 The Gonzaga sent agents to various breeding centres in Europe, North Africa and Turkey.
27 Naples, ASNa, Sommaria, Dipendenze, I, 36, fasc. 2, 'Cunto et libro de le dispese se fando a la cavallaricza de lo illustrissimo signor duca in Marczanise, per me, notario Monaco scrivano de racione, in quella et primo per incasare paglia de fare mete de quisto anno VI indictione 1488, 17r-50v'. See 27r, '*a mastro Cola Meczone per una tavola de cerqua, per fare fare duye tanelle per parare a li lupe che amaczavano li cavalle a lo pascone de Carbonaro*' and 28r, '*per una porcastra grossa tare uno et meczo per quella dare a li lupare de lo signore re che facessiro lo carnagio a li lupe che venivano a li cavalle*'. Cited in Gennari, *Struttura e manutenzione della cavallerizza regia* (2006), Appendix II, pp. 47 and 48.
28 Mantua, ASMa, AG, b. 2932, l 298, 70r-v, Copialettera to the Duke of Ferrara, *Nella raza mia trovo che manca una cavalla poledra d'anni tre baya fazauda et balzana di dreto con il marchi del razo che'l sole sulla cossa dextre, et e della raza grosa*.
29 Madrid, Archivo del Palacio Real (APR), Sección Administración. Dehesas arrendada (Rented pastures), 'La Ribera, lg. 1.013, punto 8°, 5r-6v. Cited in Juan Carlos Altamirano, *Historia y origen del caballo Español: las caballerizas reales de Córdoba (1567-1800)* (Malaga, 1998), p. 112, n. 7.
30 Mantua, ASMa, AG, b. 258, 'Vachetta in cui sono scritti li stalloni e le cavalle dell' Illustrissimo Signor Marquise di Mantova'.
31 Bernardino handled the stallions and oversaw their mating. He is from Bergamo. See Nosari and Canova, *I cavalli Gonzaga* (2005), p. 87.
32 Mantua, ASMa, AG, b. 258, *Una cavalla learda pomellata dicta la faxana de la Raza de Casa fece una anguanina lovata con una stella in fronte balzana dal pie stancho de dre adi 16 marzo 1498. Fiola del frixozelo. Ill fece uno anguanino sasinato balzano dal pie drito de dietre con una stella in fronte adi primo de marzo 1499 fiolo del leardo frixone.*
33 The phrase 'del Reamo' suggests that the mare is from the royal Neapolitan breed.
34 Mantua, ASMa, AG, b.258, '1497, *Una cavalla morella dicta la goba del Reamo balzana da tuti dui li pedi de dre e guerza da uno ochio. Ilche fece uno anguanino morello gobo del 1497. Predicta cavalla mori adi 19 de zugno 1499*'.
35 Mantua, ASMa, AG, b. 258, 'D. IV no. 4 1540', 'Libro che contiene lo inventario o sia descrizione di tutti le cavalle da razze dei Signor Duca di Mantova ed' insieme poledri nati dal 1538 al soprascritto 1540'. The leather bound book is 16 x 22 x 1.5cms.
36 Descriptions of these two visits are found in Chapter 5.
37 Mantua, ASMa, AG, b. 2504, 455r, 19 October, 1523. The letter is printed in full in C. Cavriani, 'Le razze gonzaghesche dei cavalli nel mantovano e la loro influenza sul puro sangue inglese', *Quaderni storici mantovani*, VII (Mantua, 1974), pp. 25-6.
38 Corte, 1562, I, ch. 37, 47v.
39 Hollingsworth, *The Cardinal's Hat* (2005), p. 36.
40 Zuliolo and Assassino, earned 41 *scudi*, per annum and Guarniero, 62 *scudi*. See Hollingsworth, *The Cardinal's Hat* (2005), pp. 31-3, and a chart of courtiers' salaries', p. 33
41 Priscianese, *Del governo* (1883), ch. XVIII, pp. 21-2.
42 Secco's nickname, Borella, came from the area in Calabria, where his family originated.
43 On at least two occasions, Borella is listed with another stable master, Spagnolo. In February 1471, the men are included as part of the Duke Galeazzo Maria's entourage going to Florence. See ASMi, AS, 898, 9r, 'Lista de landata da fiorenza facta et ordinata a di 14 de februario de lanno 1471', and in 1476, they are included amongst courtiers entitled to have their stabling paid for by the Milanese court. See ASMi, AS, c. 932, 2v, '1476, Lista de li deputati acavalcar dreto ala corte del nostro Illustrissimo Principe et Exellentissimo Signore ali quali se ha adare alogiamento'. These lists are included in Lubkin, *A Renaissance Court* (1994), p. 268, Appendix 2 and p. 276, Appendix 4.
44 On Borella and his family, see Lubkin, *A Renaissance Court* (1994), p. 288, n. 41 and p. 297, n. 188.
45 On Alfonso of Aragon's stable masters and huntsmen see A. Ryder, *The Kingdom of Naples under Alfonso the Magnanimous* (Oxford, 1976), pp. 70-73.
46 Naples, BNN, MS XI.B.39, 84r and 86r-v, cited in Hernando Sánchez, 'La Gloria del cavallo' (1998), p. 285 and p. 302, nn. 69 and 70.
47 *Ordini* ch. 28, p. 41 and Priscianese, *Del governo* (1883), ch. XXVI, p. 58.
48 *Ordini*, ch. 28, p. 41.
49 Modena, ASMo, AE, Camera Ducale, Amm. della casa, Stalla, Note-spese-inventori, 1521-1713, b. 2, fasc. 3, 1521, Selleria, 'Inventario di le robe pertinente ali mano di M Signor g Aligueri quale sone intro note ō la quarta robe et la salari de lo Illustrsssimo Signor Nostro'. See Chapter 2.
50 Pirro Antonio was at the Royal Maddalena stables, in 1572. See Naples, ASN, Inv. N. 90-1. R. Cam. della sommaria, Patrimonio, Dipendenze 1 serie, b. 1.39, f. 4, where he is listed in a stable book as *Cavalluriero delli cavalli de sua maiasta. Notamente de tutti li cavalli che restono ne la regia cavalleriza de la Madalena . . .*

51 G.B. Ferraro (1560), II, p. 79, 'Obligo del mastro di stalla', in P.A. Ferraro, *Cavallo frenato* (1602).
52 Corte, 1562, I, ch. 48, 57r.
53 G.B. Ferraro (1560), II, p. 79 in P.A. Ferraro, *Cavallo frenato* (1602).
54 Corte, 1562, I, ch. 48, 57v, and Francesco Priscianese, *Del governo* (1543), ch. XXV, pp. 54-5.
55 Corte, 1562, I, ch. 48, 57v.
56 For a horse that is low at the heel, Priscianese suggests it should be fitted with a studded shoe which has been treated 'in the Turkish way' (*il ferro imbrunito alla turchesca (come dicono) si assetta meglio in su l' piedi*), see Priscianese, *Del governo* (1883), ch. XXVI, p. 54.
57 Priscianese, *Del governo* (1883), ch. XXVI, p. 54.
58 Ibid. pp. 54-5.
59 The breastplate is a wide leather strap that runs across the horse's chest, attached to the saddle at either side. It is to prevent the saddle slipping back towards the tail. The crupper is a strap that runs from the back of the saddle along the horse's spine to be looped round the tail. This strap prevents the saddle from slipping forward.
60 Priscianese, *Del governo* (1883), ch. XXVI, p. 55.
61 Corte, 1562, I, ch. 48, 57r.
62 G.B. Ferraro (1560), II, p. 79 in P.A. Ferraro, *Cavallo frenato* (1602).
63 *Cavallerizza*: riding school. In southern Italy, a *cavallerizza* was a riding complex with school and stables.
64 G.B. Ferraro (1560), II, p. 79 in P.A. Ferraro, *Cavallo frenato* (1602).
65 Priscianese, *Del governo* (1883), ch. XXVI, pp. 53-54.
66 Pirro Antonio Ferraro, *Il cavallo frenato*, Venice, 1602, Book III, p. 275.
67 A 'soft hand' would indicate that the horse's mouth is sensitive to the rider's instructions through the reins and the bit. A 'vigorous hand' would indicate that the horse's mouth was 'hard', that is to say, he rejects instructions given gently and, therefore, needs more force to respond positively.
68 Priscianese, *Del governo* (1883), ch. XXVI, p. 53.
69 The 'curb-chain' runs under the horse's chin, joining both sides of the bit together. The severity of the chain depends on its composition as well as on the rider's use of it. For example, a thick short chain could cut into the horse's lower jaw if used severely, whilst a lighter and longer chain would only put slight pressure on the jaw.
70 Book III of *Il cavallarizzo* consists of three dialogues between Corte and the 'Milanese gentleman', the Commendador Fra Prospero Ricco, whom Corte describes as the best *cavallarizzo*, see *Il cavallarizzo*, III, 111r. *Commendador* or *commendatore* is a grade of professional rider, between 'Rider' and the highest official.
71 Corte, 1562, 'Dialogue I', 113r.
72 Corte, 1562, I, ch. 48, 57v.
73 Corte, 1562, II, ch. 15, 70v.
74 *On Horsemanship*,1962, p. 355.
75 Corte, 1562, II, ch. 18, 73v.
76 Alessandro Massari, *Compendio dell'heroica arte di Cavalleria* (Venice, 1600), 37r, *Capriola è necessaria per cavallo da torneo, & anco da guerra, per il besogna, quando il Cavaliere fusse circondato da' nemici facendo far piazza*.
77 Arezzo, San Francesco, Piero della Francesca *The Legend of the True Cross: The Battle between Heraclius and Chosroes*, (*c*.1452-*c*.1466).
78 Assistants of Michelangelo Cinganelli, *Nova Reperta*, early seventeenth century, Loggetta dei Mestieri, Tesoro dei Granduchi, Palazzo Pitti, Florence.
79 P. Sella, ed., *Inventario di Alfonso II d'Este 1597* (Ferrara, 1931).
80 Theodore Galle and Johna Collaert engraving after after Jan van der Straet (Giovanni Stradano), *Nova Reperta*. Stradano's drawing *The Invention of Stirrups* is held in the Cooper Hewitt Museum, New York, inv. n. 1901-39-300.
81 Priscianese, *Del governo* (1543), ch. XXVI, p. 54.
82 Francesco di Giorgio Martini in ed. C. Maltese, *Trattati* (1967), II, p. 340.
83 Modena, ASMo, AE, b.2, fasc. 3, Stalla: Note-spese-inventori, 1521-1713', Accounts for Maestro Domenicho sellaro' 1554 *tela azura, chordoan negro*.
84 Modena, ASMo, AE, b.2, fasc.3, 'Stalla: Note-spese-inventori, 1521-1713'. The accounts for 'Maestro Domenicho sellaro' dated 2 January 1554, list *200 chioldi da tafolo, 300 chioldi da lanbrachia, 400 chioldi da fusto and 500 chiodi da contraforte*. On 27 January, he lists more of these types, totalling 1,700 nails. His entry for 5 March also lists *chioldi da mora*.
85 Ibid.
86 *Volteggiare*: to turn around. Whether this is a wooden horse on a small track or a wooden horse on wheels is not clear.
87 Modena, ASMo, AE, b. 2, fasc. 3, Stalla: note-spese-inventori, 1521-1713.1554, Maestro Domenicho, p. 2, 8 March 1554 *per fornire una chavalo da legno da voltazare per il 5 vo don Aluige/ Chioldi da tafolo 15/ Chioldi da fusta 150*.
88 Ibid. Maestro Domenicho, p. 4, 23 October 1554, *2 bardelle & primarzola & 2 selle francese*.
89 Hans Kreutzberger, *Eygentliche/Wolgerissene Contrafactur und Formen der Gebiss* (Augsburg, 1562). For bit books, see Pia F. Cuneo, 'Just a bit of control: the historical significance of sixteenth- and seventeenth-century German bit-books' in Raber and Tucker eds, *The Culture of the Horse* (2005), pp. 141-73.
90 P.A. Ferraro, *Cavallo frenato* (Naples, 1602), I, p. 16, *Et essendosi già per varie opinione conchiuso, che la briglia è il vero timone che guida questa tanta machina, perciò ingegnato mi sono, chiarirla, in modo che ciascuno la capisca . . .*
91 Corte, 1562, I, ch. 48.
92 The racehorse trainers, Giocomo Vallino, Falamischia da Bologna and Zandino, all moved to Mantua following the collapse of the Bentivoglio regime in 1506. See G. Nosari & G. Canova, *I cavalli Gonzaga della Raza de la Casa* (Reggiolo, 2005), p. 90.
93 The posthumous inventory of Count Onorato II Gaetani, who died on 24 April, 1491, includes 12 black (*nigro*) slaves of whom 4 were working in the stable. See Chapter 2, n.43.
94 Modena, ASMo, AE, Stalla, 'Elenchi di cavalli & cose relative 1480-1597', b. 2, fasc. 1, *1598, Ordinamento de tutti gli cavalli et altre bestie che a questo di primo dexembre si ritrovano nella ducale stalla*.

95 Corte,1562, I, ch. 48, 57v.
96 Corte, 1562, I, ch. 37, 47v. and Corte, 1562, II, ch. 52, 100v, 'Boys who are racing should be short, lean, vigorous, dexterous and courageous, having a good intellect and memory'.
97 See Chapter 6.
98 Modena, ASMo, AE, Amminstrazione della casa: note-spese, b.1, 27r. See also Amm. della casa, Stalla b. 2 fasc. 1, 'Elenchi di cavalli e cose relative 1480-1597, 56r-57v, 1598.
99 The recipe for *farraina* is described in Corte, 1562, I, ch. 41, 52r-53v, 'Come dev'essere la farraina & in che modo & tempo si dee dare'.
100 Corte, 1562, II, ch. 52, 98r-100v.
101 Jan van der Straet, *Equile Ioannis Austriaci Caroli V. Imp. F. in quo omnis generis equorum ex varijs orbis partibus insignis delectus ;ad vivum omnes delineati a J. Stradano, et à P. Galleo editi* (Antwerp, 1578-80). The engravings are by Adriaen Collaert, Hieronymous Wierix and Hendrik Goltzius. Van der Straet, also known as Stradanus and Giovanni Stradano (Bruges, 1523 – Florence, 1605).
102 Crescenzo, Ruffo, Xenophon, Camerario, Pirro Antonio Ferraro and Caracciolo all write on the positive and negative qualities of washing the horse.
103 Corte, 1562, I, ch. 36, 47v.
104 Vegetius, *Of the distempers* (1748), I, ch. 56, p. 101.
105 Alberti, CV, p. 79. Videtta, p. 154.
106 Vegetius, *Of the distempers* (1748), I, ch. 56, pp. 100-1.
107 Gandini, 'Viaggi, cavalli, bardature' (1892), p. 86.
108 Modena, ASMo, AE, 'Libro de le calzamenta de lo Illustrissimo Nostro Signore 1442, 56v, *et a di dicto (9 Nov) taia bra 3 de verde de 50 in uno mantello chon le arme de pano per meter suxo li chavali del Signore quando se mena atorno et a ferrare*'.
109 Modena, ASMo, AE, Cred et Deb. 1471, c. 53, 'E a di dicto per le apresso scripte robe a Biasio del bailo strazarollo per fornimenti di duo manteliti di citanino crimsino per chavali grossi del N.S. quando vano fora a la marescalcaria che se fieceno fare per la andata de S. Ex.a a Roma – videlicet – Onze ½ de seda vergina – Onz. 1 de revo – Onze 10 de seda da friso a divisa biancha rossa et verde lavorata in franze basse et in fiocchi 8 grossi a sol. 15 per onza,* cited in Gandini, 'Viaggi, cavalli, bardature' (1892), p. 87, n. 1.
110 Mantua, ASMa, AG, b. 2416, lib. 205, c. 58, Isabella d'Este to Berardo Ruta, 26 May, 1509, *Nota del le robe de li barbari e palii, li quali ha mandati messer Berardo Rutha a lo Illustrissimo Signor Marchese per mezo de messer Cabriel Farahone, videlicet: Primo, mantelletti tri da barbari de veluto cremesino e verde, temperatati de tremolanti cum la impresa del Crosolo . . . item brillie 3 da barbari de tesuti de seta verde e cremesina cum li sonaglii; item penachii sei verdi e rossi, cioé 3 celate e 3 per li testeri da li cavalli*, cited in Malacarne, *Il mito* (1995), p. 230.
111 See Chapter 3.
112 Dresden, Staatliche Kunstsammlungen, Kupferstich-Kabinett, Inv. Nr. Ca 213, 'Klebeband mit Tierarstellungen', shows a hennaed horse, with crescent and star.
113 Priscianese, *Del governo* (1543), ch. XXVI, p. 52.
114 Castiglione, *Cortigiano* (1528), II, ch. VIII, lines 32-5.
115 Garzoni, *La piazza universale* (1588), *Discorso* lv, see p. 497. Florio gives the translation for *aggroppare* as 'to knot'.
116 G.B. Ferraro (1560), II, p. 82 in P. Ferraro, *Cavallo frenato* (1602).
117 G. B. Ferraro (1560), II, p. 86 in P. A. Ferraro, *Cavallo frenato* (1602).
118 Ibid. pp.81, 82.
119 Caracciolo, 1589, VII, p. 589.
120 Ibid. pp. 589-90.
121 *On Horsemanship* (1962), p. 345.
122 *Ordini*, p. 43 and Corte, 1562, I, ch. 37, 47v.
123 G. B. Ferraro (1560), II, p. 85, in P. A. Ferraro, *Cavallo Frenato* (1602).
124 Corte, 1562, I, ch. 38, 49r. The problem of grooms stealing horse food is also mentioned by Ferraro. See G.B. Ferrraro (1566), II, p. 80 in P. A. Ferraro, *Cavallo frenato* (1602).
125 *On Horsemanship* (1962), pp. 313 & 315.
126 *Ordini*, p. 43.
127 Corte, 1562, I, ch. 38, 49v. G. B. Ferraro also recommended that the boys should eat at either end of the stable. See G.B. Ferraro (1560) II, p. 84 in P. A. Ferraro, *Cavallo frenato* (1602).
128 Hollingsworth, *The Cardinal's Hat* (2005), p. 38.
129 This comparison of values has been made by Hollingsworth, *The Cardinal's Hat* (2005), p. 36.
130 Hollingsworth, *The Cardinal's Hat* (2005), p. 36.
131 In the 1540s, Bernardo Navagero wrote, *Mantova ha d'entrata 90 in 100,000 ducati*. The Duke's expenses were said to be very heavy, because he 'spent a great deal on stables and buildings, and much in maintaining a great court, which amounted to 800 or more mouths to feed', see A. Segarizzi, *Relazioni degli ambasciatori veneti al senato*, 4 vols. (Bari, 1912), I, p. 52.
132 Corte, 1562, I, ch. 48, 57v.
133 Corte, 1562, I. ch. 37, 48r.
134 Priscianese, *Del governo* (1543), ch. XXVI, p. 56.
135 *Ordini*, p. 40.
136 Corte, 1562, I, ch. 37, 47v – 48r.
137 Ibid. ch. 48, 57r.
138 Sigismondo d'Este (1433-1509).
139 G. Pardi ed., 'Diario ferrarese dall'anno 1409 sino al 1502', *Raccolta degli storica italiani (RIS)*, New Series, 24:7 (Bologna, 1928-33), p. 60
140 Giacomo Gallo, *Diurnali di Giacomo Gallo e tre scritture pubbliche dell'anno 1495* (Naples, 1846), p. 9, for 19 February, 1495.

141 Roadino had been a professional rider for the Kingdom of Naples, and then an expert in selecting horses for Milan. He became responsible for Marquis Francesco's stables in 1495 and was highly influential in advising the Marquis on buying purebred horses to improve the Gonzaga breed ('Raza Gonzaga'). See Nosari and Canova, *I cavalli Gonzaga della Raza de la Casa* (2005), p. 99.

142 For more information on this incident see Nosari & Canova, *Il palio nel Rinascimento* (2003), p. 270 and *Il cavalli Gonzaga* (2005), p. 99. Nosari and Canova do not mention if Roadino was caught.

143 Corte, 1562, I, ch. 37, 48r.

Chapter 8

Il Maniscalco: Spells, Potions and Prayer

> We think it necessary to show by what methods the health of horses &c may be preserved . . . for it is better by diligence and care to preserve their health, than to administer remedies to them when they are sick.
> Vegetius, fifth century.[1]

Working alongside the stable master and his staff was the court *maniscalco*, who was responsible for helping maintain the horses' general health: caring for their feet and giving them appropriate treatments when necessary. His work was not confined to the court stables; he would also travel with the court and set up a temporary forge to fit horse shoes whenever it was necessary. In fact Priscianese advised that as the *maniscalco* 'would not know what was needed when travelling', he should take the 'well-provided forge' with him.[2] Neither was the *maniscalco*'s role confined to horses. Valuable exotic animals would also have been dependent on him for their health; a letter to Duke Cosimo I mentioning that one of the Medici tigers had been treated by a young maniscalco in 1550.[3] This chapter, however, concentrates on the *maniscalco*'s responsibilities for the court horses. It starts by explaining the various misconceptions attached to the profession. It then considers the precautions taken to maintain cleanliness and health in the stable, before looking at the different methods available to the *maniscalco* for curing horses of both sickness and behavioural problems.

Although during the Renaissance the words *maniscalco* and *marescalco* were interchangeable, over time the responsibilities associated with these two titles have evolved and it is worth explaining how this has occurred. In *La gloria del cavallo*, Caracciolo explained that the word *maniscalco* was actually a vulgarisation of *marescalco*, which was derived from *mara*, signifying 'horse'. He continues,

> Thence also *marescalco* is said, which when corrupted becomes *maniscalco* [and is] now used in the vulgar tongue; and which seems to be accepted by Rauisio,[4] who says that horse doctors are called *equinarij*, *mulomedici*, and *manucalci*; in Latin *veterinarij*; as *veterini* is said to be appropriate for all animals suitable for [pulling] coaches.[5]

And in 1908, Pietro Gargano explained that, over time, the word *marescalco* evolved into the French military title of *maréchal* or marshal,

> For the French, the word *maniscalco* would have the honour of becoming the origin of a more sought-after military title, that is to say *maréchal*, which corresponds to *equorum magister* in philology and to *marestalla* (and also *marexallus*) in Giordano Ruffo, a title that was obtained by Alberico Clemente, who from *comes stabuli*, or *conte della stalla*,

8.1. Florence, Orsanmichele, Tabernacle for the Guild of Farriers, Nano di Banco, *S. Eligius*, 1411-15, detail

became *constable* and then *maréchal,* beginning the series of Marshalls of France, and having the honour of following King Philip August in the Holy Land.[6]

This more recent meaning of 'marshall' has sometimes led to an historical misinterpretation of the responsibilities of the *maniscalco*. However, when, in 1480 Zanino Ottolengo signed himself *merescalchus*,[7] his letter suggested his knowledge of both the shoeing and the medical treatment of the Gonzaga's court horses and mules – evidence of his position as a farrier-surgeon. Therefore, during the Renaissance, no distinction should be made between *la veterinaria* and *la mascalcia*, despite Gargano separating these skills: *la veterinaria* as 'the art of conserving health in animals and restoring them to it, when they have lost it', and *la mascalcia* as a means of maintaining the 'natural state of the foot' and restoring 'a ruined or deformed foot to [its] conformation'.[8] Such a distinction is misleading for fifteenth- and sixteenth-century Italy, when the *maniscalco* was responsible for making potions and ointments and carrying out surgery and was knowledgeable in both the theory and practice of remedial shoeing.

The *maniscalco*'s responsibilities were not as diverse as they might first appear; the condition of a horse's feet equating to its usefulness in the same way as its general health would do. In order to keep the horses well shod, new or existing iron shoes needed fitting every four to six weeks, depending on the work the horse had done and how fast the hoof grew, with both manual skill and anatomical knowledge required by the farrier. Corte suggested that stable boys should check the horses' feet at least twice a day to make sure that they were clean and the shoes securely attached. In *Il cavallarizzo*, he warned of the dramatic consequences of losing a nail:

> A nail very often loses a shoe
> A shoe, the foot;
> The foot, a horse;
> One horse, two or three
> And this, the company,

8.2. Cesare Fiaschi, *Trattato dell'imbrigliare, maneggiare, e ferrare cavalli*, Bologna, 1556, Frontispiece to Book III

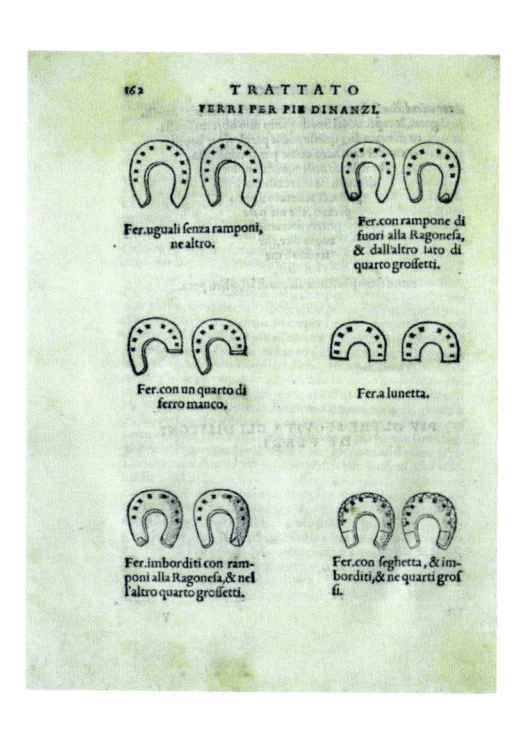

8.3. Cesare Fiaschi, *Trattato dell'imbrigliare, maneggiare, e ferrare cavalli*, Bologna, 1556, Book III. Diagrams of remedial horseshoes

> Which can also lose an army and so, from a nail that is missing from the shoe of a horse, one can see what disorder and inconvenience can arise.[9]

Nanni di Banco's early fifteenth-century relief sculpture of S. Eligius for the Florentine Guild of Farriers at Orsanmichele[10] and an illustration in Cesare Fiaschi's 1556 treatise show that the methods of shoeing a horse remained largely unchanged in the intervening years (8.1, 8.2). However, the fact that Fiaschi's treatise contains thirty-five chapters on shoeing horses, as well as three pages illustrating different shoes for specific purposes, indicates the amount of knowledge a *maniscalco* was expected to have on this part of his practice (8.3). As with other aspects of care, writers encouraged sympathetic handling when shoeing. In a chapter on how to shoe 'a horse that does not want to be shod', Fiaschi warns against cruel contemporary methods especially if a horse was normally gentle. For example, he dislikes *moraglie* – a version of the modern day 'twitch' – a cord tightened around the horse's upper lip.[11] And he disapproves of hitting the horse around the ears with a rope attached to a stick, which could affect the horse for the rest of its life, making it fierce and angry and always difficult to shoe. Instead, he suggests that the stable boy should scratch the horse's neck and head in order to calm him or, if that does not work, that a cloth should be put over the animal's head. If still distressed, a bandage should be wrapped around the animal's leg with a ring attached to a rope in order to hoist the weight off the foot to be shod.[12]

Most court stables had a resident *maniscalco* although some, such as the Gonzaga, had several working under a senior farrier-surgeon such as Ottolengo, whose manuscript is exceptionally useful for learning first hand his techniques for curing horses and other duties he was expected

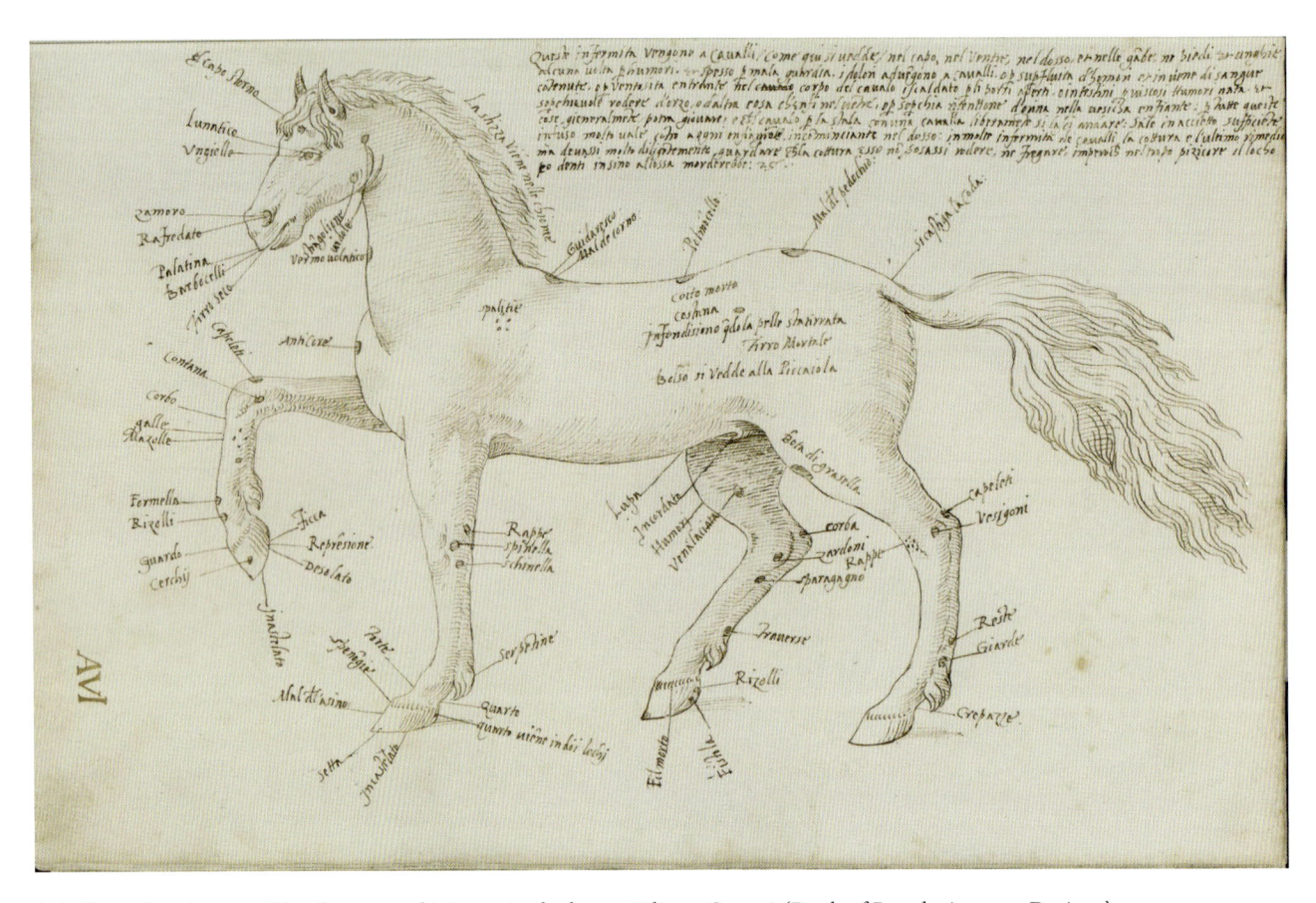

8.4. Chart showing possible ailments and injuries to the horse. Filippo Orsoni, 'Book of Parade Armour Designs' Italy, 1554. London, Victoria and Albert Museum

to perform. Unlike Ruffo's *Libro della mascalcia*, Ottolengo's manuscript was never printed and it is Ruffo's work, printed at the end of the fifteenth century, that is often referred to by later writers. In contrast to the stable master, the *maniscalco* would probably have learned his trade through both apprenticeship and practical experience. And assuming he was literate, he would have consulted contemporary or classical texts, such as the Greek *Hippiatrica*, composed by various authors and printed in Italian in 1543.[13] By the beginning of the seventeenth century there was a wide variety of books on equine care, medical treatments and shoeing, all of which were in print. In addition to the *Hippiatrica*, these included Ruffo's *Liber mareschalchie* (Rome, 1490), Grisone's *Gli ordini di cavalcare* (Naples, 1550), Fiaschi's *Trattato dell'imbrigliare, maneggiare & ferrare cavalli* (Bologna, 1556),[14] Giovan Battista Ferraro's *Delle razze, disciplina del cavalcare, et altre cose pertinenti ad essercitio cosi fatto* (Naples, 1560), Corte's *Il cavallarizzo* (Venice, 1562), Caracciolo's *La gloria del cavallo* (Venice, 1566), Marco de Pavari's *Escuirie de M. de Pavari* (Lyons, 1581), Carlo Ruini's *Anatomia* (Bologna, 1598), Ottaviano Siliceo's *Scuola de' cavalieri* (Orvieto, 1598) and Filippo Scaccho da Tagliacozzo's *Opera di mescalzia* (Rome, 1591). Even Isabella Cortese's treatise on household hints, which ran to twelve editions between 1562 and 1677, contained eight equine treatments: for distemper and colic, dressing a kick to the groin and an open wound, expelling worms, 'curing a bone tumour on the hock' and, curiously, how to make a black star on the forehead of a white horse.[15] Some of these books, such as Fiaschi's, used a chart to indicate the various ailments the horse could suffer. And although not a book on *mascalcia*, Filippo Orsoni also included a chart amongst the many elaborate designs for costumes and armour (8.4). At the top of his drawing Orsoni gives a guarded warning,

> These illnesses can affect horses, as shown here: on the head, on the body, on the back, on the legs, feet and hoof walls and include psychological problems. This often happens if they are not kept well.[16]

Methods of treatment varied and, as in human medicine, traditional medieval aspects of health and medicine such as physiognomy, astrology and magic, were practiced alongside newer theories of cleanliness and the isolation of sick animals. In the mid-fifteenth century, Alberti had advised gentle and sympathetic treatment in which there was minimal medical intervention,

> As to yourself, do not hasten to give medication, but so that the horse fights with his own strength, in waiting, against illness, supply him with everything which can help Nature. And if Nature has already well started her healing work, do not stir up the precipitation of her work. If she seems a little slow, do not search for an assault on the illness, as if by violence, with a strong medication, but bring her quietly to accomplish her work – this will restore health.[17]

This naturalistic form of healing, which apart from bloodletting was not invasive, very much followed Columella[18] whose first-century book on husbandry influenced some Renaissance writers by suggesting practical, naturalistic remedies. Judging by Ottolengo's many cures and treatments for sprains, bruises and broken bones, it seems that such advice was not widely followed.

As a form of preventative medicine, Alberti stressed the importance of cleanliness and suitable conditions in the stable, with the correct diet administered and an eye kept on the quantity of work the horse undertook. Or, as he summarised, 'supply[ing the horses] with what is necessary for them and ask[ing] them to do what they can reasonably accomplish';[19] values which would continue throughout the Renaissance. Cleanliness was considered important to the health both of man and horse; a belief in preventative medicine that was already evident in classical works. For example, to preserve the horse's health Vegetius recommended good drainage with raised hardwood flooring for the horse stalls and a trench leading to an underground pipe to drain any urine away. In addition, he emphasised that the manger should always be clean 'lest any filth be mixed with [the horses'] food', fodder must be clean of dust, drinking water should be clear flowing and the stable should be light and airy.[20]

During the Renaissance, cleanliness would be considered more than a method of preserving health. It became, as Biow has indicated, linked to culture, self-discipline and self-control, which, depending on the person in authority, provided the possibility to 'fashion and be fashioned'.[23] Biow's argument can easily be extended into the stable environment where horses, washed, rubbed down and groomed regularly by stable boys, would benefit from constant human contact – a form of 'fashioning' which not only enhanced their natural beauty but also affected their temperament. Equally important is that Renaissance theories of cleanliness in the stable meant that the health, life and usefulness of the horse was maintained, in the same way as a suitable environment helped preserve the beauty or usefulness of other valuable commodities. As already noted, in 1580 Tasso had suggested that cleanliness not only benefited health it also conferred 'nobility and dignity on things that [were] base and mean by nature'.[22] This theory can surely extend to the stable as, whilst benefitting the horse's appearance and temperament, cleanliness could also contribute to the horse's nobility.

Again, it was the stable boys whose hard work maintained the stable's clean and healthy environment. But while the results of their expert grooming were immediately evident to those admiring the court horses, their equally important but less obvious tasks of mucking out and washing the stable contributed to the horses' health. The late fifteenth-century *ordini* for the Duke of Urbino actually stipulated that every part of the stable, both inside and out, should be kept as clean as 'every part of the house'.[23] Each morning, the stable boys were expected to help one another clean out the stalls, using carts to take the manure outside.[24] Of course, the sloping stalls and drainage channels advocated by many Renaissance horsemen and architects, assisted the stable boys in washing down the stable floors, but keeping it 'as clean as a house' involved more than the removal of manure, washing surfaces and keeping out dust. For centuries, writers had been advising against allowing certain farm animals to be housed in the same vicinity as horses – pigs, chickens and sheep being considered particularly harmful. Even Vegetius had warned of the dangers to a horse of ingesting chicken dung, explaining that it caused the horse 'great torment' as if it was 'stung by venomous beasts' which resulted in 'inflation', 'tumbling' and a 'harsh cough'.[25] Certainly, writers such as Caracciolo continued this fear of chickens, warning that if the horse swallowed a chicken feather or droppings this could damage the stomach and bladder, as well as the throat.[26] He followed with a remedy as indigestible as the initial problem,

> The remedy for the [horse ingesting a] feather (according to Ruffo[27]) would be this; that the horse is [first] warmed around the navel . . . then put cold ox manure into the horse's mouth and draw blood from him, and afterwards put all the entrails of a chicken onto his throat and, not being cured in this way, carefully draw more blood.[28]

Other farm animals such as pigs and sheep should also be excluded from the stable, with Caracciolo suggesting that a horse ingesting pig manure might result in an outbreak of plague, because 'everything porcine was loathsome to all kinds of horses, whether it is the grunting, breath or smell'.[29] Then, at the end of *La gloria*, on two unnumbered pages, Caracciolo also excluded sheep from the stable, believing they caused horses to become blind.[30] Oddly, he sees the male goat as beneficial, explaining that the goat's smell makes the air healthy for horses and chases away certain maladies.[31]

Whilst it must have been relatively easy to exclude larger animals and chickens from the stables, fabric was placed over the stable windows to prevent insects from entering, and burning essences was suggested for expelling vermin and cleaning the air. Listing common flies, horse-flies, mosquitoes, worms, cockroaches and scorpions as 'direct enemies of horses through their noise, stench, breath and biting', Corte was emphatic that the stable should be kept clear of the dirt and rubbish which attracted them.[32] To get rid of rats, mice and snakes he suggested burning scented perfumes in the stable, both to expel the vermin and rejuvenate the horses.[33] Quoting from Virgil's *Georgics*, Corte suggests burning cedar wood and galbanum[34] and from Columella's *On Agriculture*, he recommends burning a woman's hair or a stag's antler – ideas that had originally been recommended for expelling snakes from sheepfolds and hen houses.[35] A more extreme suggestion is given in the 1573 version of Corte's treatise: that the smell of a roasted [she] cat will rid the stables of mice[36] – a remedy that must surely have alarmed the horses.

The exterior cleanliness of the stable was also the responsibility of the stable staff. In fifteenth-century Ferrara, the ducal *senescal* Francesco Ariosto recorded that neither edicts issued by the Duke's stable masters nor those of the head of the Duke's household, Baldassare da Montecchio, had prevented the Volta del Cavallo[37] outside Ercole d'Este's court stable from becoming a rubbish tip where disreputable people gathered. In 1471, Nicolò Calavrese, a stable boy annoyed by the amount of rubbish – and presumably concerned that it might affect the horses' health – had taken matters into his own hands and, hoping that it would protect the area from further vices, he attached a paper image of the Virgin Mary onto a column forming part of the archway's decoration. Subsequently, the image performed miracles, the first concerning a stable boy, Andrea da Modena, whose debilitating fever ceased whilst he was lying on a bench facing it.[38] Calavrese's remedy not only cleansed the immediate vicinity but quickly rendered it a centre for devotion, bringing a continuous flow of people to the stable's entrance. This resulted in an enclosure being built around the image, with candles lit and regular services performed, the ducal choir assisting at Mass on a Sunday. Three years later, in 1474, Duke Ercole arranged for the image to be placed in a specially built chapel[39] and by 1477 Francesco Ariosto,[40] known as 'Il Pellegrino', was able to record fifty-one miracles associated with this image, which he recorded for Pope Sixtus IV,[41] many of them involving stable staff or injuries to riders.[42]

As for the horse and the stable itself, cleanliness was paramount in every aspect of watering and feeding, with Caracciolo insisting that 'above all you should know that both the horse's feed and his drink is better when it is cleaner'.[43] Records show that stud farm staff were often concerned with maintaining the correct conditions for the horses' health, whether within the stables or in the pastures. There was, for example, concern over stables being too cold and damp and of contaminated drinking water in the fields of the Sermide basin.[44] And when in the summer the grass became scarce or the heat intolerable, it was the Gonzaga stable masters or riders who requested their master's permission to move large herds of horses from one part of the country to another, to find fresh grazing either at a different stud farm or further afield in the pastures of Monte Baldo towards the Tyrol. The fact that many letters are concerned with the lack of grass or with outbreaks of sickness would indicate that fields were sometimes overgrazed or that there was no way of isolating sick horses to prevent contagion.

Similarly, there was a fear of substandard fodder affecting the horses' health. Caracciolo's advice to 'invest enough on good care, take away everything dirty and diligently clean the manger', was only repeating well-established principles[45] but he stressed that the fodder should be pure, carefully chosen and well sieved 'so that the barley is not mouldy or rotten through age, or too fresh; and likewise the hay, straw or bundles of vetch'. None of these should be put in front of the horse unless it had been 'turned over by hand to inspect it, so that it does not trap dust or dirt';[46] an indication that either it was substandard or had been stored in unsuitable conditions. In fact, a century earlier, the Urbino *ordini* had specified that one stable servant should be solely responsible for sifting through the fodder outside the stable to get rid of any dust.[47] According to Caracciolo, the consequences of 'dust in hay, barley, oats or anything else amongst the fodder' were that horses developed coughs and dried out guts'.[48] Claiming that this could lead to incurable illness, he offered three remedies for horses that had eaten poor quality barley: a drink of dry figs cooked in sweet smelling wine; a concoction of old wine, honey, powdered incense and pepper mixed with the ground-up skin of a smoke-dried chicken; or, if both these remedies failed, he advised standing the horse in a cold river facing upstream which, he wrote, should encourage it to drink and thus cool any fever.[49]

It is no doubt partly to monitor the effects of fodder on the horse's health and performance that, at the large Este stable, precise records for fodder were kept throughout the year.[50] However, as well as monitoring fodder, further steps could be taken. In 1569 the anonymous author of the *Libro de marchi* included fourteen pages of equine recipes and cures, ending with 'a beautiful new way of conserving horses and of curing them of every great infirmity'.[51] He advised that the horse's diet should change according to the season and that certain simple treatments should be administered when necessary. In winter, the horses should be kept inside and fed hay, straw and fodder and allowed to drink tepid water twice a day. In spring, they should be bled from under the tongue, given bran and water as well as fresh grass. In summer they should eat straw and spelt as well as melon rind, bran and cool water and, in autumn, hay, barley and bran. For internal ailments the horse should be given a precipitator (*precepitato*)[52] with some bran, whilst scabs (*broze*) and wounds should be rubbed with a pure lead oxide (*litargirio crudo*) ointment, probably as an anti-inflammatory. By following these suggestions, the reader is told he will see 'miracles in the horse's body, such as have never been heard in the world'.

Despite preventative measures, horses did become sick and a wide range of illnesses with their symptoms and cures are described in Renaissance texts. Certainly, in some stables it was possible to isolate sick horses in a loosebox (*cassetta*) within the stable if, as Corte had suggested, they were ill but not contagious.[53] If contagious, the sick animals needed to be moved further away. But, whether isolated or not, texts and letters show that, as in human medicine, a variety of treatments was available to the *maniscalco* and it is evident that science and magic had not yet parted company. One of the most important factors in determining treatment was the horse's age because, as Caracciolo explained, 'as for man, some remedies are worthwhile when they are young and fevered, and others when they are old and cold'.[54] Once age was ascertained, either by the teeth or the number of wrinkles at the edge of the mouth,[55] there were several methods of treatment available to the *maniscalco*. In addition to regular seasonal bleeding, he could also bleed the horse for specific ailments with charts and diagrams indicating which vein, or veins, should be bled for particular illnesses. This was not as straightforward as it might seem as it was believed that certain areas of the body could not be bled or have surgery if the moon was in the corresponding sign of the Zodiac. Giovan Battista Ferraro advises that if the moon was in Aries or Taurus neither the head nor the neck could be cut or cauterised; if in Gemini or Cancer, the shoulders and ribs could not be touched; if in Leo or Virgo, the stomach, loins or back were excluded; if in Scorpio the croup;[56] if in Sagittarius, Capricorn, Aquarius or Pisces, the legs, feet and thighs. If the moon was in these signs, the *maniscalco* should consult either a current almanac or an astrologer (8.5). In addition to bloodletting, the *maniscalco* could administer liquid medication by pouring it into the horse's mouth through a horn – a method known as drenching. Enemas were administered, the chest tapped with a cannula, or the horse made to inhale with its head held over a brazier – all of which are crudely illustrated in several editions of Scaccho's *Opera di mescalzia* (8.6, 8.7). While Ottolengo's manuscript describes poultices and compresses for sprains and bruises, it seems that surgery was a significant part of the *maniscalco*'s work, as he describes methods for removing arrows and metal fragments, the wounds and nerves being sutured with silk. For these more serious procedures, there is no doubt that the horse would have to be immobilised. As early as the fourteenth century, Rusio had described ways of anaesthetising a horse through the use of oral drugs. In a chapter entitled 'How the *marescalco* can practise surgery on an angry horse',[57] Rusio gives three recipes, all of which include the seeds of the poisonous black henbane, already known by Dioscorides in the first century for procuring sleep and allaying pain.[58] Rusio's first recipe of three or four ounces of henbane seeds mixed into the horse's fodder, suggests that 'for the whole day [the horse] will be unconscious – even appearing dead – so that you can operate wherever you wish'. For the 'same effect', his second recipe,

8.5. Giovan Battista Ferraro, d. 1569, *Delle razze, disciplina del cavalcare, et altre cose pertinenti ad essercito cosi fatto*, Book III, included in the first part of Pirro Antonio Ferraro's *Cavallo frenato*, Naples, 1602. The effect of the Zodiac on equine treatments

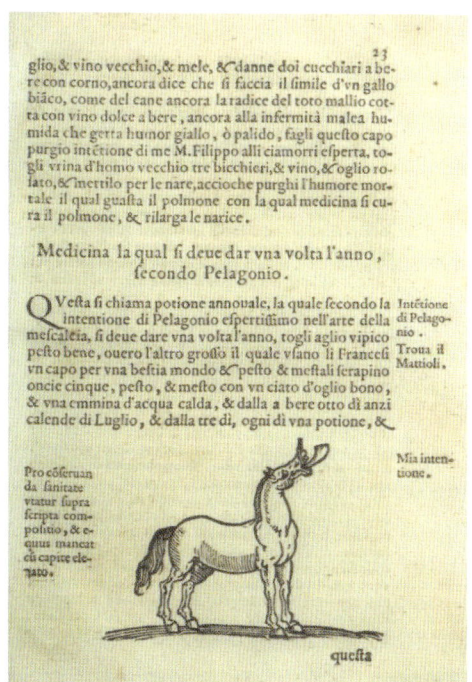

8.6. Filippo Scaccho, *Opera di mescalzia*, Rome, 1591 Book I. Drenching the horse

8.7. Filippo Scaccho, *Opera di mescalzia*, Rome, 1591 Book I. The horse inhaling

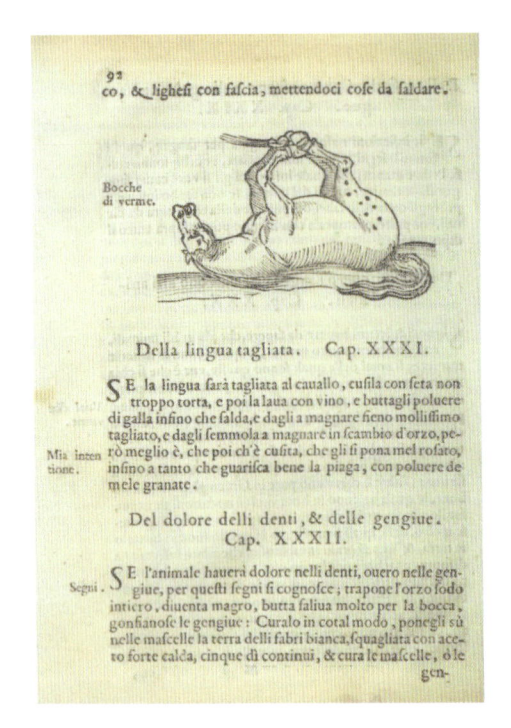

8.8. Filippo Scaccho, *Opera di mescalzia*, Rome, 1591, Book II. The dorsal position for surgery

consisting of mandrake[59] or opium, henbane, nutmeg and aloe wood[60] – cooked until dissolved in water – is given as a draught and the third recipe, consisting of myrrh, *persigia*, henbane, galangal[61] and cloves,[62] is mixed with wine and given as a drink to the horse. After surgery, Rusio suggests splashing cold water on the head and genitals so that the animal 'wake[s] up immediately'.

Anaesthetised or not, the horse needed to be immobilised in order to operate safely and it is likely that the technique illustrated in Scaccho's late sixteenth-century treatise would have been used. The image shows the dorsal position into which a horse was placed for surgery, with its four legs tied together and the animal lying on its back (8.8). The rope tying the legs would then be attached securely to a beam above the horse, preventing its body mass from crushing its internal organs. Once immobilised it was possible to operate. However, one operation, mentioned by several authors, required the horse to stand upright. This was 'firing' (*dare il fuoco alle gambe*), where hot irons were inserted into the horse's legs, either to strengthen the tendons or to prevent or cure lameness by deadening the nerves. As early as the fifth century Vegetius mentioned firing[63] and records show that the operation was performed on a Gonzaga horse, Pisanello, in 1492.[64] This was by no means without danger. Cito explained that, because of the horse's humours, if the horse was fired in cold damp conditions it would suffer for nine days and might have spasms, especially if fired close to the foot (an area he associated with a humid humour). It was, he added, better to fire a horse in hot weather.[65]

Many treatises included recipes for a wide variety of medicines and ointments although some authors such as Ottolengo also included a panacea to cure all ailments, a *medicina triacale*. The recipe shows that Ottolengo must have had access to expensive imported ingredients as it included myrrh and frankincense, in addition to more mundane apple skins, red acacia, burnt stag's horn and saxifrage, all of which should be made up and stored in a tin vase so that it can be given at any time at the onset of illness. When required the potion was diluted with tepid water and administered as a drench through a stag's horn, with the horse's head tied up high for an hour so that the medicine reached the whole body. If the horse had a fever, Ottolengo advised

8.9. Drenching a reluctant horse, Zanino de Ottolengo, 'Trattato' 15th century. Fondazione d'Arco, Inv.547, 17v-18r (With permission of the Fondazione d'Arco, Mantua)

the addition of rose oil, with the draught administered two or three times, not just once. He also added that it would be 'better to exchange the tepid water with the same quantity of white wine' and boasts that this medicine is of 'such virtue that it has been proven to cure every internal illness of the horse'.[66] A miniature in Ottolengo's manuscript (8.9) illustrates that not all horses were willing recipients of this treatment. It shows a reluctant grey horse backing away from the *maniscalco* and throwing up its head, while tethered to a tree outside a stable. Meanwhile, a stable boy is filling a horn held by the *maniscalco*, who is preparing to pour the potion down the horse's throat.[67] Unlike Ottolengo, Priscianese's nineteen short chapters on horse ailments form only a small part of his treatise but the ingredients he suggests for his remedies are more likely to be found in gardens and farms in Italy, rather than imported at great expense. They include eggs fried in oil, honey, animal blood, rosemary, chickpeas and broad beans as well as *fili greci* – possibly fenugreek stalks.[68]

Both Priscianese and Ottolengo suggested cures for diverse behavioural problems, such as the horse's reluctance to move forward, a fear of shadows and a horse that keeps its mouth wide open (a sign of resistance) – all of which would have been an embarrassment to the rider and damaging to his public image. As for Alberti, some cures are sympathetic to the horse, as when Priscianese suggests using a light bit carried low in the mouth for a resistant horse, dismissing a vice with a strong hard bit which, he says, will always cause the mouth to bleed and make the problem worse.[69] Whatever the case, many documents and treatises show that the *maniscalco*'s repertory for dealing with badly behaved or even wounded or sick horses included not only science and astrology but also magic and religion. Ottolengo's treatise included seven spells (*incanti*) and various treatments assisted by prayer, amongst which is his advice for stopping 'a wicked or disreputable' horse:

> Speak these words directly into his ear: 'In the name of the Father, Son and Holy Ghost: Caspar catches you; Melchior ties you up; Balthasar whips you'. Then release the horse and immediately he will calm down and be patient and he will stop.[70]

The inclusion of Christian prayer or appeals to biblical characters and saints was not unusual in human medicine, curing the patient through auto-suggestion or self-belief, but there is no logical explanation for why it might succeed with a horse or any other animal. Even so, a cure 'For any manner of evil horse', included in an English manuscript dating from *c.*1420, has several similarities to Ottolengo's advice,

> Say this charm in the right ear of the horse and set your foot on his right foot and make a cross on his head and say, 'In nomine patris. Amen. Our Lord God was born and hanged on the rood, so surely as this is truth be the horse whole. Amen'. Say this on his four quarters in front and behind and at the end of each limb and say a *Pater noster* and take five raw chicken eggs and cast them into his mouth.[71]

But Ottolengo's cure for worms – an illness causing a serious loss of weight and condition – was even closer to a magical incantation: after saying three Our Fathers and three Hail Marys, a young innocent boy should attach a leather label to the horse with the written words,

> Maga: Magabu: Magabulu: Sancto: Job: Magalut: Magabult: Malla: Macula: Sancto: Job

Following this, three masses should be said in honour of the Trinity and St Job – indicating the seriousness of the condition.[72] Contemporary illustrations of worm infestation show a significant inflammation of the horse's skin and this may well be why St Job, protector from the bubonic plague, is called on in this instance (8.10). Whilst Ottolengo's words are incomprehensible, his phrase mirrors a sixteenth-century English cure for ague in which the words diminish in length, rather than increase. The author suggested writing 'Arataly, Rataly, Ataly, taly, aly, ly' on a paper, which is then wrapped round the sick man's arm, before saying three *Pater noster*s to Saints Peter and Paul for nine days.[73] These examples show that both horse doctors and physicians appealed to God, Christ and the saints for protection, according horses equal status to human beings during outbreaks of the plague or other medical problems – a further indication that the health of horse and man were seen as equally important. Letters from the Este *maniscalco* Andrea show that the use of spells in curing horses was sometimes successful when all other treatments failed. A letter to Duke Alfonso II, dated 3 November 1545, informs the duke that seven brood mares at the Garfagnana stud farm to the north of Lucca had become ill after

8.10. Filippo Scaccho, *Opera di mescalzia*, Rome, 1591 Book I. Skin eruptions believed to be caused by worms or maggots and for which St Job was sometimes invoked

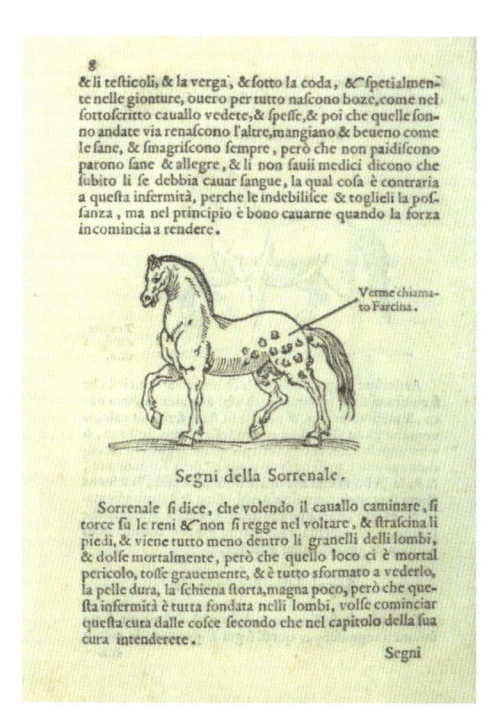

foaling. Having failed to heal them, Andrea and a certain Messer Oratio had found it necessary to seek the aid of a witch from the adjacent Lunigiana valley who, 'with spells around these ills, had created miracles' resulting in the horses being completely cured.[74]

Just as curious are the various recipes given for changing the colour of a horse's hair, sometimes for cosmetic reasons, such as Isabella Cortese's for creating a black star on a white horse[75] or Ottolengo's bizarre cure for making the hair grow back in its natural colour, presumably to hide a scar from a battle wound or surgery. Entitled 'Cura per fare venirli pili al cavallo, dove mancano', the reader is advised to,

> take a mole that has just surfaced from the ground and is without eyes, and take it alive and put it in a pot without water and cook until it becomes burnt and can be made into a powder. Take some oil and anoint the place that lacks hair, then add the powder . . . and the hair will grow.[76]

Ottolengo also offered recipes for turning black hair white, one based on sulphur smoke and another on sheeps' milk.[77] Unfortunately, there is no record showing that the recipes were used in the Gonzaga stables, although this seems quite likely given the later interest in dying horses' manes and tails. Whatever the case, these recipes have been listed by the leading Gonzaga *maniscalco*, indicating that it was he who was responsible for contributing not only to the health but also the appearance of the horses.

It was, therefore, both the conditions within the stable and the *maniscalco*'s treatments and potions that contributed to the horses' well-being. As court farrier, and in his role as both physician and surgeon to the horses, the *maniscalco* – together with the stable staff – was expected to maintain health in the stable. He required a sound knowledge of the horse's anatomy and of remedial shoeing; he had to be capable of making diagnoses and prescribing the correct treatments. Evidence shows that environmental cleanliness was advised and that, in the event of sickness, it was possible to isolate horses to prevent disease spreading. For treating the horses, the *maniscalco* was expected to understand the different properties of spices and herbs while having a considerable range of recipes to call on. Even so, letters and treatises show that the established medical practices of astrology, prayer and magic were also used when treating sickness, injury or even behavioural problems. The stable staff were expected to keep the stables, the horses and their food spotless – work which filled much of their day – and although the *maniscalco* might prescribe and carry out surgical procedures, many of the poultices, dressings and medicines would have been administered by the stable boys.

It could be said that both the care and treatment of these court horses was excessive. But in exchange for the luxury of a clean stable, daily pampering and expensive medicines, these privileged animals underwent methods of training and medical procedures that were sometimes far from sympathetic, suggesting that, in many instances, horses must have been less than willing servants. Willing or not, it is evident that many professional horsemen and owners felt a great affection for these animals; and seldom did an author write about a horse's bad characteristics unless to explain how they had resulted from ill-treatment or poor training. These thoroughbreds and the culture surrounding them had become important to many aspects of Renaissance court life. And, while they, and the men who owned, bred and looked after them, have long since disappeared remaining records and paintings, letters and verse are proof of the regard in which horses were held. Fortunately, some of the stables which housed them still exist – although it is rare to find evidence of the original fittings or elaborate decoration that once made them so spectacular. These magnificent buildings stand as memorials to an elegant equestrian culture that, from the Italian princely courts, swept through the rest of Europe. It is not too extreme to describe the great stables, such as at Vigevano and Poggio a Caiano with their statuesque classical columns, and at Caprarola with its soaring barrel vault, as equine cathedrals, monuments to past traditions and values. With this in mind, it is appropriate to conclude with Alberti's words, which reflect man's desire to find perfection in both the horse and in architecture:

> As for the Italians, their inborn thrift prompted them to be the first who made their buildings very like animals. Take the case of the horse: they realised that where the shape of each member looked suitable for a particular use, so the whole animal itself would work well in that use. Thus they found that grace of form could never be separated or divorced from suitability for use.[78]

1 Vegetius, *Of the distempers of horses* (1748), I, ch. 56, p. 98.
2 Prisciánese, *Del governo* (1883), p. 58.
3 Florence, ASF, Mediceo, 613, insert 6, 14r, cited in The Medici Archive Project, doc. 18081. March 10 1551, letter from Pier Francesco Riccio to Cosimo I de' Medici '*Ho trovato un giovine maniscalco ch'è entrato a medicar il tigre che sta male. Halli raso tucte due le gambe di dietro, cosi il groppone, così andrà seguendo se potrà guarirlo*'.
4 Rauisio – probably Lorenzo Rusio (Laurentius Rusius). See F. Smith, *The Early History* (1976), I, pp. 92-8.
5 Caracciolo, 1589, II, p. 71, '*Indi ancora Marescalco si disse, che corrottamente Maniscalco dice hora il vulgo*'.
6 P. Gargano, *Origini della mascalcia e suo sviluppo in Sicilia* (Palermo, 1908), p. 16. Cited in G. B. Palma, 'Per un trattato di mascalcia in dialetto siciliano del secolo XIV', *Archivio storico siciliano*, New Series, 45 (Palermo, 1924), pp. 209-19, pp. 208-9, n. 4.
7 See Ottolengo , 'Prefazione' and 'Proemio', pp. 7-12.
8 Gargano, *Origini della mascalcia* (1908), pp. 4 and 5. Cited in G. B. Palma, 'Per un trattato' (1924), p. 209, n. 1.
9 Corte, 1562, I, ch. 38, 49r. This is the phrasing that Corte uses. It is possibly the earliest known printed version of this saying, the origin of which is not known, although the saying was used in France and England in the seventeenth century. The clergyman Thomas Adams (*c.*1583-1652) in one of his sermons (collected 1629) said, 'The Frenchmen have a military proverb, 'The loss of a nail, the loss of an army''. See *The Oxford Dictionary of Nursery Rhymes*, eds, I. and P. Opie (Oxford, 1951), pp. 324-5, which discusses the nursery rhyme based on this saying.
10 Florence, Orsanmichele, Nanni di Banco, *S. Eligius* (1411-15).
11 According to Florio, the *moraglie* is 'a kind of pincher, or device to pinch a horse about the nose to tame him when he is shoeing or let blood'. This is a severe version of the modern-day 'twitch', in which a loop of cord at the end of a stick is twisted tightly around the top lip and 'quietens' or 'stills' the horse. It is now believed that the 'twitch' actually reduces the rate of the horse's heartbeat and makes it more docile.
12 Fiaschi, 1603*,* III, ch. 29, p. 132, '*Del cavallo che non si vuole lasciar ferrare*'.
13 *Opera della medicina de' cavalli composta da diversi antichi scrittori, et a commune utilità di greco in buona lingua volgare ridotta* (Venice, 1543). Two more editions were printed in 1548 and 1549.
14 Cesare Fiaschi, *Trattato dell'imbrigliare, maneggiare & ferrare cavalli* (Bologna, 1556). This is the first edition of Fiaschi's treatise.
15 Isabella Cortese, *I secreti della Signora Isabella Cortese. Ne quali si contengono cose minerali, medicali artefìciose & alchemiche. Et molte de l'arte profumatoria, appartenenti a ogni gran Signora* (Venice,1561), chs 73-80.
16 Filippo Orso (illustrator) in Filippo Orsoni "Book of Parade Armour Designs", Italy, 1554. London, Victoria and Albert Museum, National Art Library.
17 Alberti, CV, p. 97. Videtta, p. 176.
18 Columella, *On Agriculture* (1968), chs XXX – XXXV, pp. 201-13.
19 Alberti, CV, p. 89. Videtta, p. 166.
20 Vegetius, *Of the distempers* (1748), ch. LVI, 'Of the diligence to be used in preserving animals in a good state of health', pp. 98-100.
21 Douglas Biow, *The Culture of Cleanliness in Renaissance Italy* (Cornell, 2006), p. 63.
22 Tasso, 'Il padre di famiglia' (1583), Cesare Guasti, ed., *I dialoge di Torquato Tasso* 3 vols (Florence, 1858), I, p. 378.
23 *Ordini*, ch. 28, p. 43.
24 Ibid.
25 Vegetius, *Of the Distempers* (1748), III, ch. LXXXV, 'Of an animal that has eaten hen's-dung', p. 373.
26 Caracciolo, 1589, VII, p. 570.
27 There is no evidence that Giordano Ruffo suggested this treatment. This may be Annibale Ruffo who Caracciolo mentions as a famous rider. See Caracciolo, 1589, p. 141.
28 Caracciolo, 1589, VII, p. 570.
29 Ibid. pp. 569-70.
30 Caracciolo, 1589, penultimate page unnumbered, '*ma bisogna avertire che nelle stalle dove stanno cavalli, non vi fusse peccore, percioche dove stanno peccore & cavalli insieme, li cavalli diventano ciechi*'. This belief was already in a *Libro de marchi* printed in Venice, 1569.
31 Caracciolo,1589, VII, p. 570.
32 Corte, 1562, I, ch. 37, 48r.
33 Ibid. ch. 38, 49v.
34 *Galbona*: the resin formed from milky juice that flows when the root of *ferula galbaniflua* (galbanum or giant fennel) is cut. There are two kinds - from the Levant and from Persia. It has a pungent smell and is used for relieving air passages and, externally against inflammatory swelling. See M. Grieve, *A Modern Herbal*, 2 vols (New York, 1971), I, 340-1.
35 Corte, 1562, I. ch. 38, 49v: '*Disce & odoratum stabulis accendere cedrum/ Galbaneoq[ue]; agitare graves nidore chelydros*' which Corte translates as '*Impara accender nelle stalle cedro: Et galbano che suol fugar serpenti*'. Taken from Virgil, *Georgics* III, 414. Columella also quotes Virgil, but the remedy is for sheepfolds. Columella, *On Agriculture* 5-9 (1968), VII, p. 261 and VIII, pp. 351-3.
36 Corte, 1573, I, ch. 38, 57v: '*Potrete disfacciare i sorici dalle stalle con l'odore di gatta arostita*'. This is not included in Corte's earlier version of *Il cavallarizzo* (1562).
37 The Volta del Cavallo was named for the equestrian statue of Niccolò III d'Este, which was erected nearby in 1451.
38 F. Ariosto, Modena, Bib. Est., LAT. 309, Alpha W.4.4. 1 November 1477, 56r. '*Origine e sito del novo saccello dedicato ad honore e per reventia de la gloriosissima vergene Madre de Jesu Cristo Salvadore nostro intro el magno e magnifico palazo Ducale de ferrara cum elso cermoniale culto e cū la translatione de la so admirabile ymagine e cum molti miraculi et etiamdio cuz la ducale instavatione de esso sacello de scripti e ilitulati per Francesco Ariosto peregrino furisconsulto alla Beatissima Sititade del sūmo pontifice Hieronimo sixto quarto savonense*'. The manuscript – known as *Il Peregrino* – is written first in Latin and then Italian, starting the Italian section at 56r with the above title.

39 For a brief history of the miraculous image and the chapel's description see Tuohy, *Herculean Ferrara* (1996), pp. 54, n. 5 and 92-5.
40 Francesco Ariosto (Ferrara 1415-1484) studied under Guarino da Verona and was uncle to Ludovico Ariosto (1474-1537).
41 Modena, Bib. Est., LAT. 309 Alpha W.4.4, Nov. 1 1477.
42 The first nine miracles include three stable boys: Miracle 1, Andrea da Modena (56r-v), Miracle 7, Francesco Francio (64r), Miracle 9, Sigismondo Tosco (64r); one stable master, Miracle 5, Tadeo Mazone (63r) and one rider, Miracle 3, 'Il Magnifico cavaliere Messer Niccolo di Contrary' (56v).
43 Caracciolo, 1589, VII, p. 524.
44 See Chapter 4.
45 See Vegetius, *Of the distempers* (1748), I. ch. 56, p. 99.
46 Caracciolo, 1589, VII, pp. 524-5.
47 *Ordini*, ch. 28, p. 42: '. . . et uno famiglio che non atendesse ad altro che a vagliare la biada, ma fuore de la stalla perchè la polvere noce multo li cavalli'.
48 Caracciolo, 1589, VII, 524-5.
49 Ibid. p. 525.
50 See Chapter 7.
51 *Libro de marchi* (1569), p. 15.
52 *Precipitato*: Florio translates this as 'a corrosive powder used by surgeons to eat away dead flesh', although, in this instance, it seems unlikely that the horse would be given this with its food.
53 Corte, 1562, I, ch. 36, 46v.
54 Caracciolo, 1589, III, p. 177.
55 The horse's teeth become more protruding as it ages. According to Alberti the wrinkles on the mouth also increased with age. See Alberti, CV, pp. 25, 27, 29. Videtta, pp. 104, 106, 108.
56 The croup is the area on the back between the top of the loins and the root of the tail.
57 Rusio, *La mascalcìa* (1867), I, p. 383, ch. CLIX, 'In che modu in delu cavallu furiusu lu maresclcu poza operare la cirlugia'.
58 Hyoscyamus – 'Black henbane' or 'stinking nightshade'. Found in central and southern Europe.
59 Mandrake was used as an anaesthetic in Pliny's day – the patient being given the root to chew before an operation. It grows in Southern Europe and the Levant.
60 *Anabola*, Greek for the wood of the Aloes, probably Socotrine Aloes, which is a dark reddish-brown and is almost entirely soluble in alcohol.
61 Galangal – from the Arabic Khalanjan, possibly a perversion of a Chinese word meaning 'mild ginger'. Used as both a stimulant and as a carminative (ie. stops flatulance).
62 *Garofali*. The *garofalo* is the dried flower bud of the clove tree, *caryophyllus aromatica*. The flower is also known as the 'gillyflower' (Florio). The clove is sometimes used as a painkiller, to calm flatulence or to expel worms.
63 Vegetius, *Of the distempers* (1748), I, ch. XXVIII, 'Of the manner of giving the fire and cautery'.
64 Mantua, ASMa, AG b. 2441, 9 October 1492, letter signed Lorenzo *marescalco*, 'Lo ho snervato e dato il foco al Pisanello', cited in Cavriani, *Le razze Gonzaghesche* (1974), p. 13.
65 See Giovanni Antonio Cito, *Del conoscere le infirmità che avvengono al cavllo et al bue, co' remedij à ciaschedun di esse* 3 Books (Venice, 1589), II, p. 49, 'Il fuoco à quali infirmità si dia'. Cito's 3 books were often included as an appendix to Caracciolo's *La gloria*, printed in Venice the same year.
66 Ottolengo, p. 96.
67 Mantua, Fondazione d'Arco, Inv. 547, Ottolengo, title page, 17v. The miniaturist and the scribe are unknown.
68 *Fieno Greco* (Greek Hay) was the name for fenugreek. *Fili greci* may be the stalks of the fenugreek.
69 Priscianese, *Del governo* (1883), p. 61.
70 Ottolengo, p. 94.
71 London, British Library, MS Sloane 3285 (c. 1420), 'Medicine for all diseases of horses' cited in Smith, *The Early History* (1976), I, p. 109.
72 Ottolengo, p. 95.
73 K. Thomas, *Religion and the Decline of Magic: Studies in popular Belief in Sixteenth and Seventeenth Century England* (London, 1971), pp. 180-1.
74 Modena, ASMo, AE, Amm. della Casa, b. 2, fasc. 2 , 'Stalla: carteggi diversi per cavalli e cose relative, 1502-1789, Letter dated 3 November 1545, '. . . e stato neccessario fine a mandare in Lunisiana a torre una stregha che con incanti intorno a tali mali fa miraculi & si ni è visto experientie de maniera che da scette or otto in fuori tutte le altre son guarite libere'.
75 Cortese, *I secreti* (1561), ch. 73. The other six remedies are for distemper, for dealing with bruises, cuts and kicks as well as treatments to cure worms and colic, chs 74–79.
76 Ottolengo, p. 91.
77 Ibid. p. 92.
78 Alberti, *On the Art of Building* (1988), VI, ch. 3, p. 158.

A Summary of the Stables
in alphabetical order of their location

Not all the stables listed here are mentioned in *Privileged Horses*. Some of them are only known from documents and, even for those which still remain, the amount of detail varies considerably for each site.

Where the size of the stable is known but the quantity of horses housed in it is not recorded in contemporary documents, Leonardo da Vinci's recommendation for a stall's correct measurements has been used to work out the stable's approximate capacity. Taking the Florentine *braccia* as 58.36 cms the width of the stall should, therefore, be 1.75 metres (3 *braccia*) and the length 3.50 metres (6 *braccia*). However, Leonardo's proposed width allows the horse little room to manoeuvre and it would need to be tethered at all times to prevent it trying to turn around. In the 1560s, the Royal Spanish stables in Madrid allowed 2.80 metres width per horse stall and it is quite possible that the Spanish stables, built during the same period in the south of Italy, also allowed this width. It is for this reason that two of Philip II's stables from the Spanish mainland are included in this summary, justified by the fact that Naples, Sardinia, Sicily and Milan were under direct Spanish rule from 1559.

Where possible, a brief bibliography for each stable, including archival material and lesser known publications, has been included although this is by no means comprehensive. The stables are listed in alphabetical order of their locations or the town closest to them. The two royal Spanish stables, Córdoba and Madrid, are included at the end of the summary.

Italy

Alberobello
See **Venetian Republic**

Bentivoglio
(formerly Ponte Poledrano), 1460s
Patron: Giovanni II Bentivoglio
Architect: Pagno di Lapo Portigiani[1]
Dimensions: Length 70m, width 10.5m
Capacity: 50-60 horses
Water supply: well water
Design features:
The stable forms part of a walled and moated castle complex. It runs east -west. There are large arched entrances at both ends with a smaller south-facing entrance towards the castle. Rectangular windows on stable level and arched windows on upper level. Hayloft, granary and possibly accommodation are on first floor. Basilica style with three aisles, the central aisle being slightly wider and the flooring of stone. The cross-vaulted ceiling is supported by columns in the form of a Greek cross. The exterior was once painted to match the castle – a white background with lozenges containing the Bentivoglio *imprese* of joined and divided canes. The interior is said to have had paintings of neighing horses in *trompe l'oeil* lozenge-shaped frames.

The castle complex belongs to the Ramazzini Institute and is not open to the public.
Bibliography:
Alfonso Rubbiani, *Il castello di Giovanni II Bentivoglio a Ponte Poledrano* (Bologna, 1914, reprint Bentivoglio, 1989)

Bologna
Messer Annibale's stables
Castello Bentivoglio, 1480s

Patron: Giovanni II Bentivoglio
Architect: Pagno di Lapo Portigiani
Capacity: about 48 horses
Design features:
Basilica style stable with a vaulted ceiling. The castle was razed to the ground in 1507.
Image:
MODENA, GALLERIE ESTENSI, Bib. Estense Universitaria, MS a.J.8.1, Cherubino Ghirardacci, *Historia di Bologna*, 17th century, Part III, 1393-1509, 445r. Plan of Giovanni II Bentivolgio's palace.
Bibliography:
ARMANDO ANTONELLI & MARCO POLI, *Il Palazzo dei Bentivoglio nelle fonti del tempo* (Venice, 2006)
C. ADY, *The Bentivoglio of Bologna: a Study in Despotism* (London, 1937)
GEORGIA CLARKE, 'Magnificence and the city: Giovanni II Bentivoglio and architecture in fifteenth-century Bologna', *Renaissance Studies* 13:4 (December, 1999), pp. 397-411
ALBANO SORBELLI, *I Bentivoglio, signori di Bologna* (Bologna, 1987)
WILLIAM E. WALLACE, 'The Bentivoglio Palace; Lost and Reconstructed', *Sixteenth century Journal* X:3 (1979), pp. 97-114

Bologna
Bentivoglio garrison stables
Second half of 15th century
Patron: Giovanni II Bentivoglio
Dimensions: Length, *c.*100m, width *c.*12m
Capacity: about 110 horses
Water supply: Three rivers flow under Bologna and it is likely water was drawn from these.
Design features:
 Two storey brick stables, with the principal entrance under a portico. The exterior walls were once painted with equestrian scenes. The interior is a basilica design with three aisles. Twenty-two octagonal brick columns, with pietra serena stone capitals and pedestals, support a cross-vaulted ceiling, the vaults terminating on stone corbels on the outer walls. Large tall windows are set *c.*3m from ground level.
 The stables are now used as a student bar and recreation area for the University of Bologna. The octagonal pillars are now covered with a thick layer of plaster and are painted.

Bibliography:
As for 'Messr. Annibale's stable' above.

Cafaggiolo
Mid 15th century
Patron: Cosimo de' Medici (Il Vecchio)
Architect: Michelozzo
Dimensions: Length 90m, width *c.*10m
Capacity: Probably 60 horses
Water supply: Tributary of the Sieve running parallel to stables
Design features:
The stables run east-west and have two levels. There is a large arched entrance door at the east end and two rectangular doors leading into central hallways on the south side. The west end has a large chamber, spanning three bays, under which is a vaulted brick chamber. The remainder of the building is divided into bays by stone arches with *pietra serena* details, each bay holding three or four horses on each side. For this section of the stable, the cross-vaulted ceiling terminates in *pietra serena* corbels on the outer walls. The east end has a high wooden ceiling (*c.*5.85m high). Each of the stable bays has a window set high up with sloping sills, the windows on the south side being considerably larger than those on the north. Horses stood on cobbled floors, which sloped down gently to a central aisle, paved with grey stone slabs and with narrow (25cm) gutters on either side.
 The upper floor at the west end is served by an internal stone stairway leading to several large rooms, which are linked by narrow arches. The upper floor at the east end is reached via a stone staircase leading

directly from an external door in the south façade. This area has a series of small rooms leading off a narrow corridor and has one large space at the east end, possibly for fodder storage.

Together with the Villa, the much-altered stables now form part of a luxury resort.

Caprarola
Lo Stallone
c.1580-1585
Patron: Cardinal Alessandro Farnese
Architect: Giacomo Barozzi da Vignola (d.1573). Work overseen by Giovanni Antonio Garzoni da Viggiù
Dimensions (internal): Length 100m, width 15m. External height 20m to cornice
Capacity: 120 horses
Water supply: Probably piped from several miles away, as for the Palazzo's fountains and gardens. There is a well-head to the north of the stable.
Design features:
The stables run east to west, the principal east-facing entrance is heavily rusticated, with alternating *tufo* and *peperino* stone. The first-floor west end entrance is reached via a wide ramp running beside the north side of the stables and leading into a large hall. There is also an entrance half way along the south-facing wall. The impressive stable area is barrel vaulted and would have had heelposts dividing the horse stalls. Large high windows, with sloping sills, allow light onto both sides of the stable. The east end has herring-bone brick flooring with stone drainage channels running down each side. The upper three floors, which are served by several staircases, were used for staff accommodation and storage.

Most of the building was occupied by a catering and hospitality school, while the main part of the ground floor stabling was being restored in 2011.
Bibliography:
Naples, ASN, CF, b.1358.1 includes various letters on the earlier Caprarola stables
Rome, ASR, Camerale III, 518, 'Libro delle misure della fabbrica del Palazzo del Ill.mo e R.mo Farnese a Caprarola', 17th *misura*, from 20 June 1581 to 5 February 1583
Enzo Bentivoglio, 'Le scuderie di Palazzo Farnese a Caprarola; I 'remedi' proposi da Giovanni Battista Contini e Sebastiano Cipriani dopo il terremoto del 1703 (dai MSS 34 K13 e 34 K14 della Biblioteca Corsiniani di Roma)', *Quaderni del Dipartimento Patrimonio Architettonico e Urbanistico*, Anno XIV 27.28 (1981), pp. 181-90
L.W. Partridge, 'Vignola and the Villa Farnese at Caprarola, Part 1', *Art Bulletin* LII (1970), pp. 81-7
Luciano Passini, *Caprarola – il paese e la sua storia* (Rome, 2002; reprint 2008)
C. Robertson, *'Il Gran Cardinale', Alessandro Farnese, Patron of the Arts* (New Haven, MA & London, 1992)

Ferrara
Belfiore hunting lodge and park
1491
Patron: Duke Ercole I d'Este
Carpenter: Girolamo Zuchola paid to make stable
Dimensions: Length 21.80m, width 10.90m

Ferrara
Belriguardo, near Voghiera
c.1453
Patron: Niccolò III d'Este and Duke Ercole I d'Este
Architects: Biagio Rossetti and Pietro Benvenuti
Capacity: possibly 500 horses[2]

Ferrara
Palazzo San Francesco
1485-7
Patron: Duke Ercole d'Este. Built for a ducal favourite Giulio Tassoni
Capacity: 20 horses

Design features:
The stable had marble columns supporting a vaulted ceiling.
   The palazzo is now part of the University of Ferrara.
Bibliography:
Ugo Caleffini, *Cronica della ill.ma et ex.ma Casa d'Este*, in ed. A Cappelli, *Atti e memorie della Reale Deputazione di storia patria per le province modenesi e parmensi*, II (1864), pp. 267-312 gives some details of the stables

Ferrara
Reggio
Mid 15th century
Patron: Borso d'Este
A fire, which killed 49 horses, is recorded there in 1469.

Bibliography for all Este stables
J. Bentini, ed., *Gli Este a Ferrara; una corte nel Rinascimento* (Milan, 2004)
G. Bertoni and E. Vicini, *Il Castello di Ferrara ai tempi di Niccolò III* (Bologna, 1907)
L.A.Gandini, 'Viaggi, cavalli, bardature e stalle degli Estensi nel Quattrocento', *Atti e memorie della regia deputazione di storia, patria per le provincie di Romagna*, 3:10 (Bologna, 1892), pp. 41-94

Florence
San Marco
1515-6
Patron: The Medici family. Built for the visit of Giovanni de' Medici (Pope Leo X)
Architect: Probably Baccio Bigio (Bartolomeo Lippi)
Dimensions: Length *c.* 64m (110 *braccia*), width 23m (40 *braccia*)
Capacity: 128 horses[3]
Design features:
Built opposite the Medici San Marco library, the stable runs south-east to north-west and is a double width basilica (as at Poggio a Caiano) with 4 lines of horses. Each line is divided into 16 bays, each holding 2 horses. Cross vaulting was supported by 'beautiful columns'.[4] It is known that on a wall facing a covered area, under which horses could be exercised in bad weather, there were equestrian paintings of various stances and movements by Alessandro Allori (1535-1607).[5] These stables are said to have inspired those at Poggio a Caiano.
   The site is now occupied by the Museo de Storia Naturale (Geologia e Paleontologia), which is built to similar dimensions. The paved entrance archway to the Via La Pira is probably original.
Image:
Milan, Biblioteca Ambrosiana, Leonardo da Vinci, Codice Atlantico, 96v shows a sketch of the floorplan
Bibliography:
Carlo Pedretti, *Leonardo Architetto* (Milan, 1978) pp. 258-261
Carlo Pedretti, *A Chronology of Leonardo da Vinci's architectural Studies after 1515* (Geneva, 1962)

Florence
The Uffizi stables
1560s
Patron: Cosimo de' Medici, Duke of Florence
Architect: Giorgio Vasari
Dimensions: Following the ground plan of the Uffizi. The west wing is 90m long
Capacity: *c.*120 horses and 50 mules (17th-century figures)
Design features:
The vaulted subterranean U-shaped stables follow the ground plan of the Uffizi Galleries. In addition to stabling, this underground space had workrooms – including a *maniscalco*'s workshop, staff apartments

and areas for isolating sick horses. Eighteenth-century drawings by Giuseppe Ruggieri show that, at this period, the west wing had an entrance via a long stepped ramp descending from the Via delle Carrozze (off the Via Lambertesca), while the east wing had two entrances, one from the Piazza di Guidici (which still exists), the other from the Piazza del Grano. The shortest wing, running parallel with the Lungarno terrace, was served by another ramped entrance leading up from the river Arno. The west wing stables were partially lit by ox-eye windows placed in the floor of the loggia above them

Vasari had always planned to use this sub-terranean space as stables and in 1560 had written to Duke Cosimo with his proposed plans of 'beautiful stables that had their entrance along the river and one could also enter directly from the houses' but the Duke had reservations, his secretary writing 'As to the stables you have designed, these do not please the Duke'. Even so, the basement area was used for stabling and workshops. The Duke's objection was well-founded when, in November 1589, the river flooded the stables and several of the court horses drowned. But despite the Arno's tendency to flood, certain sections of the stables continued to be used into the late 18th century.

The stables are not open to the public although the stepped ramps from the Via delle Carrozze and from the Arno serve as entrances for the Società Canottieri Firenze – a rowing club.

Bibliography:

DANIELA MIGNANI, 'Le scuderie granducali nei sotterranei del fabbricato degli Uffizi' in eds C. di Benedetto & S. Padovani, *Governare l'Arte*, Oct. 2008 (Prato), pp.228-234, from which the information above is taken. The article includes several plans of the Uffizi stables.

Mantua
Island of Te
1502
Patron: Marquis Francesco II Gonzaga
Dimensions: Length *c*.54m, width 10.70m, height to apex of roof 10.30m. Side walls height 8.40m
Capacity: The dimensions allow for two lines of 30 horses
Design features:
The stables ran east to west. Evidence of painting on both interior and exterior of the stable, consisting of friezes with arabesques and the exterior walls painted with rustication. The exterior of the west facing façade had Francesco Gonzaga's initials and the date 1502. Both east and west façades were crenellated and have various Gonzaga devices painted on them. There is evidence of a pitched roof.

The building was almost entirely destroyed when Giulio Romano built the north wing of the Palazzo Te for Duke Federico II Gonzaga in 1524-34. A few sections of the frieze can be seen in the north-facing alcove and in the Sala d'Ovidio. Other sections remain in the roof space.

Bibliography

UGO BAZZOTTI, '"Un luogo e certe stalle" sull'isola del Te prima di Giulio Romano', *Civiltà Mantovana*, 3:122 (2006), pp. 141-61

A. BELLUZZI, *Palazzo Te a Mantova* (Modena, 1998), esp. pp. 23-44

A. BELLUZZI and W. CAPEZZALI, 'Le scuderie dei Gonzaga sul Te', *Civiltà Mantovana*, 1.42 (1973), pp. 378-94

L. FIENI, 'Palazzo Te a Mantova: indagine stratigrafica del sottotetti. Preesistenze e trasformazioni al progetto di Giulio Romano', *Archeologia dell'architettura*, VIII (2003), pp. 209-19

Mantua
Island of Te
c.1525
Patron: Federico II Gonzaga
Architect: Giulio Romano
The stables are situated south west of the Palazzo Te and border the gardens. Much altered. No decoration remains although in 1958 Hartt suggested that there had been elaborate stucco decoration on the stable's façades, for which Giulio Romano's drawings still exist.

Bibliography:

FREDERICK HARTT *Giulio Romano* (New Haven, 1958). See especially pp. 88-9 and figures 149-51

Mantua
Gonzaga stud farm
1458-90
Capacity: 125 horses on the farm
Water supply: Stables situated on a tributary of the Po
Design features:
The stables are known to have had a portico, under which horses were led out to be shown.
Bibliography:
CLIFFORD M. BROWN, ANNA MARIA LORENZONI, '"Concludo che non vidi mai la più bella casa in Italia": The frescoed decorations in Francesco II Gonzaga's suburban villa in the Mantuan countryside at Gonzaga (1491-1496)', *Renaissance Quarterly*, 49:2 (1996), pp. 268-302

Mantua
Pietole stud farm
c.1509-14
Patron: Francesco II Gonzaga
Design features:
Like the Te stables, this building also had friezes painted on the interior and exterior walls with painted *trompe l'oeil* rustication covering exterior walls.
Bibliography:
MANTUA, ASMA, AG, b. 2491, c. 166 for letter giving evidence of painted decoration dated 3 July 1515.

Mantua
Margonara stud farm
Governolo
Patrons: the Gonzaga
Water supply: Mincio river
The Gonzaga's barbary horses and brood mares were stabled here. Only the horses bred here were referred to as the 'Margonara' breed.

Mantua
Marmirolo stud farm
First half of 15th century with later additions
Patron: Marquis Gianfrancesco Gonzaga, developed by Duke Federico II Gonzaga
Architect: Alterations by Giulio Romano in the 1520s

Mantua
Roversella stud farm
Sermide basin
Patron: the Gonzaga
Water supply: wells
The *cavalle grosse* (destrier mares) were kept here.

Milan
'La Rotonda'
1580s
Patron: Archbishop Carlo Borromeo.
Architect: Pellegrino Tibaldi (Pellegrino Pellegrini)
Dimensions: Decagonal building. Each wall 4.40m wide. Total height of two main floors (ground to roof) 12.40m. Width of *pronaos* 8.46m
Capacity: 18 riding horses and 18 mules
Water supply: A well accessed through a window at each stable leve
Design features:
On three floors, the decagonal stable housed mules in a semi-basement, horses on the main level and a

hay store at the top, from which hay could be supplied to the stables via two chutes. The mule stable is reached from the Via del Ore by a wide ramp. The principal access to the horses' stable, which faces the Archbishop's Palace, is through a *pronaos* entrance with Doric columns supporting a pediment. A small circular tower on the north-west side, which contains a narrow spiral staircase, connects the horses' stable to the upper level, while a wider external staircase leads down from the main entrance to the entrance of the mule stable. Every floor has a window in the centre of each wall (with the exception of the *pronaos*), those at semi-basement level being slightly smaller. Similarly, each level has an ambulatory, divided from the central decagon by ten pillars, which support a cupola; the cupola becoming more acute on the upper levels. The semi-basement and the central level have Doric capitals, whilst the top floor hay store has Ionic capitals. The spaces between the pillars were subdivided by heelposts. Urine and waste water from both stables is taken down narrow gulleys to a central drain, leading through a hollow pillar to a cistern under the building.

The building now houses the Fondazione Culturale Ambrosianeum.

Images:

CARLO FEDERICO PIETRASANTA (1656-1729) Detailed cross section and floor plans in Archivio Strorico Diocesano di Milano, Milan

Bibliography:

ALBERTO FALCK, ed., *I cinquant'anni dell' Ambrosianeum 1948-1998* for Fondazione Ambrosianeum (Franco Angeli, Milan 1998), pp. 77-96

RICHARD HASLAM, 'Pellegrino de' Pellegrini, Carlo Borromeo and the public architecture of the Counter Reformation' in 'Pellegrino Tibaldi: nuove proposte di studio: Atti del convegno internazionale Porlezza-Valsolda, 19-21 settembre, 1987', *Arte Lombarda,* New Series 3-4 (1990), pp. 17-30

ANGELO PAREDI, *La Rotonda del Pellegrini* (Milan, 1950)

M. ROSSI AND A. ROVETTA, eds, 'Pellegrini Tibaldi pittore e architetto dell'età borromaica: atti delle giornate di studio 8-9 novembre 1996', *Studia Borromaica: saggi e documenti di storia religiosa e civile della prima età moderna*, 11 (Milan, 1997)

PELLEGRINI TIBALDI, *L'architettura*, ed. G. Panizza (Milan, 1990

Milan
Near the Porta Vercellina
1490s
Patron: Galeazzo Sanseverino
Architect: Leonardo da Vinci
Design features:
According to Vasari, Bramantino had painted frescoes of life size horses on the stable's interior walls.[6]

Milan
c.1498
Patron: Mariolo de' Guiscardi
Architect: Leonardo da Vinci

Naples
The Caserta *cavallerizza* and stables
Falciano
1490s
Patron: Ferdinand I Aragon, subsequently given to his personal doctor, Giovanni di Leone Galluccio, Bishop of Caserta

Bibliography:

L. GIORGI, 'Le residenze dei vescovi di Caserta dalla fine del 1400 e gli interventi barocchi nella cattedrale di S. Michele Arcangelo di Casertavecchia', *Rivista di Terra di Lavoro, Bolletino dell'Archivio di Stato di Caserta*, 3:1 (April 2008), the Cavallerizza is only mentioned briefly.

Naples
Maddalena stables
1570s renovation
Patron: Originally Aragonese. Renovated on orders of King Philip II of Spain in 1570s
Capacity: A stable book for 1572 lists 112 horses although Jacques de Villamont mentions 95 stabled there in 1595.[7]
Water supply: Probably wells as the stables were close to the swampy estuary of the Sebeto river

Naples
The royal Marcianise *cavallerizza* and stables
Rebuilt *c.*1488-93
Patron: Alfonso of Aragon, Duke of Calabria (Later Alfonso II of Naples)
Architect: Master builder Pietro Loniardo
Capacity: Stalls for 100 horses
Water supply: wells with specialist workmen to keep them clean. In 1488 a new well was constructed 1.59 x 2.10m and 15m deep.[8]
Design features:
The stable is said to have matched the 'Masseria Cavallerizza' in its plan,[9] which was built by Alfonso I. It was a walled complex consisting of several buildings for horses and for staff. Two large doors lead from the stables onto the courtyard. The stables were built of brick and wood, divided into stalls with enough space for horses to remain untethered. There were 13 windows, which had hemp covers for insect screens. Stone flooring and wide central aisle. Staff accommodation was on the first floor but the stable master had a separate house within the complex. Oil lamps and tallow candles were used for night lighting. Straw and hay were stored in a separate building.
Bibliography:
NAPLES, ASN, Sommaria, Dipendenze, I, 36, fasc. 1, cc. 1r-16v and 2, cc. 17r-50v
LUCIA GENNARI, *Struttura e manutenzione della cavallerizza regia di Marcianise (1488-1493)* (Salerno, 2006).
 Gennari includes a transcription of all the Neapolitan archival material relevant to the Marcianise stables.

Naples
S. Giovanni a Carbonara
1480
Patron: Alfonso of Aragon, Duke of Calabria
These stables were built close to the city walls at Carbonara. Entries dated 1489 mention that Alfonso went to visit his new stables 4 times in November and December that year.[10]

Pavia
Castello Visconteo
14th century
Patron: Galeazzo Il Visconti but later also used by Galeazzo Maria Sforza from 1469
Dimensions: Length *c.*100m, width *c.*10m, height 5.35m
Capacity: about 100 horses
Design features: A semi-basement stable, spanned by a single barrel vault. The rectangular space is divided by pointed Gothic arches into 9 bays, each of which would probably have held five or six horses on each side. Continuous stone feeding troughs run along the outer walls.
 The main part of the stable can now be hired for entertaining or conferences.

Pienza
*c.*1460
Patron: Pope Pius II (Enea Silvio Piccolomini)
Architect: Bernardo Rossellino
Capacity: 100 horses
Water supply: a complicated network of cisterns and wells, with a large drinking trough or cistern inside the stables

Design features:
South-facing stables, including workshops and a wide passageway leading to kitchens and storage areas. The stables are subterranean on the north side, with only small windows on south, east and west walls. Buttresses on the south façade are interspersed by one large and two smaller doors. The cross-vaulted brick ceiling is supported by circular *arenaria* and brick columns, with carved stone Tuscan Doric capitals. There is a void between the stable vaulting and the palace's hanging garden above. This vacuum served to keep the stables dry and to store hay and straw.

One corner of the stable is a gift shop. The remainder is unsafe and is not accessible.

Bibliography:
G. GIORGIANNI, ed., *Pio II, la città, le arti: la rifondazione umanistica dell'architettura e del paesaggio* (Siena, 2006)
C.R. MACK, *Pienza: the Creation of a Renaissance City* (Ithaca and London, 1987)
JAN PIEPER, *Pienza, il progetto di una visione umanistica del mondo* (Felbach, 2004)

Poggio a Caiano
c.1540- c.1560[11]
Patron: Cosimo de' Medici, Duke of Florence
Architect: Niccolò di Rafaello di Niccolò (Pericoli) il Tribolo[12]
Dimensions: Length 108m, width 31m, height 15.6m (to apex of roof)
Capacity: 200 horses
Water supply: Fresh spring water and River Ombrone
Design features:
The stable is said to have been inspired by the Florentine San Marco stables built and probably designed by Baccio Bigio. The building runs north to south and is connected to the Villa's garden by a bridge at first floor level and also by an underground passage leading to the north end. It is a double-basilica plan, having a total of six parallel aisles, allowing for four lines of horses. The principal façade at the south end has a large central rectangular door with a *pietra serena* rusticated surround, and a small door at each side. The central door leads to a large atrium which is supported by hexagonal columns and contains a large drinking trough. The north façade has two large arched doors with brick surrounds, each leading to the central aisle of one of the stables. Inside the cross-vaulting is supported by four lines of *pietra serena* Tuscan Doric columns, (two lines for each basilica plan) and by *pietra serena* corbels on the out walls. Each stable has 26 bays – each 3.60m wide. The two central aisles are 4.20m wide and the four side aisles are 3.10m wide. Both ends of the building have large cruciform windows lighting the first-floor central corridor, which runs the full length of the building and is 6.30m wide and 9.30m high. Above this corridor a wooden framework supports a terracotta tiled roof. On both sides of this corridor are 13 doors with *pietra serena* surrounds, leading to the 26 individual apartments, each with a floor area of c.7.40 x 7m, an external window and a fireplace. Every apartment had a small wooden attic space above it.

The building now houses the municipal library, two conference rooms and the Museo Soffici. The first floor also contains an art gallery.

Bibliography:
C. CONFORTI, 'Recupero della scuderia medicea di Poggio a Caiano', *La Casabella* 690, LXV (Milan, 2001), pp. 10-15
F. GURRIERI & D. LAMBERINI, *Le scuderie della Villa Medicea di Poggio a Caiano* (Bologna, 1980)
F. GURRIERI & D. LAMBERINI, 'Le Scuderie Medicee di Poggio a Caiano, una potenziale strutture museale', *La Toscana e l'Arte*, 2:4-5 (1982), pp. xxviii-xxxi
E. PIERI & L. ZANGHERI, eds, *Niccolò detto il Tribolo tra arte, architettura e paesaggio* (Signa, 2001)
FRANCO PURINI, 'Ricostruire modificando le scuderie medicee di Poggio a Caiano', *Costruire in Laterizio*, XIII:77 (Sept/Oct 2000), pp. 22-7
FRANCO PURINI, 'Recupero delle scuderie medicee (Restoration of the Medicean Stables) Poggio a Caiano, 2000', *La Casabella* 690, LXV (Milan, 2001), pp. 16-17
PROVINCIA DI PRATO, COMUNE DI POGGIO A CAIANO, Ufficio Tecnico Comunale, *Analisi di prefattibilità per il project financing: Recupero delle Scuderie della Villa Medicea di Poggio a Caiano*, 3° Lotto (April, 2007)

Rome
Chigi stables
Via della Lungara, Trastevere
c.1512
Patron: Agostino Chigi
Architect: Raphael
Dimensions: Length 41m, width 12m, height of stable interior 9m
Capacity: 48 horses at ground floor level (*c.*100 if semi basement area was also used)
Water supply: wells and the Tiber
Design features:
The stables, situated at the end of the Villa's gardens, run north-south. The building had 4 levels: a semi-basement with half windows (possibly used for stabling), the main stable at a slightly raised ground floor, the first floor *foresteria* for guests, and an attic level for staff. The principal entrance into the stables had partially recessed Tuscan pillars and Chigi's name above it. The exterior was lavishly decorated with carved *peperino* mouldings, Doric columns on ground floor and Corinthian columns between balconied windows on the first floor. It is also possible that, like the Villa, frescoes may have decorated the flat wall surfaces. The stable's layout followed the basilica plan of three aisles, in this case divided into three sections by two arches supported by stone columns with Doric capitals. The brick barrel vaulting terminated on pilasters on the stable's outer walls. Drawings show that two sections of the stable had heelposts for dividing the horses while the third section was open and was probably for grooming. The stalls had sloping flooring.

Chigi's villa was bought by the Farnese family in 1577 and is now known as the Villa Farnesina. The stable quickly fell into ruin due to poor construction and weak foundations and was pulled down at the beginning of the 19th century, leaving only the lower section of 2 exterior walls on the Via Lungara.

Images:
BERLIN, KÜNSTBIBLIOTEK, Anon. French, Elevation of the stable façade and entrance door and other details, 16th century
FLORENCE, UFFIZI, Gabinetto di disegni e stampe, 1474, Esp. v. Raphael, 'Progetto per le stalle Chigi'
NEW YORK, THE METROPOLITAN MUSEUM OF ART, Inv.49.92.44v, Anon Franco-Flemish, Villa Farnesina Stable plan and cross section (drawing) 16th century and Inv 49.92.50r, Anon Franco-Flemish, Villa Farnesina, elevations (drawing), 16th century
ROME, ISTITUTO CENTRALE PER LA GRAFICA, Cherubino Alberti, 'Membri di la stalla di agustino Ghisi in trastevere di preta di baldasari opera architetura'

Bibliography:
D. COFFIN, *The Villa in the Life of Renaissance Rome* (Princeton, NJ, 1979)
C. L. FROMMEL, ed., *La Villa Farnesina a Roma* (Modena, 2003)
C. L. FROMMEL, *et al.* eds, *Raffaello Architetto* (Milan, 1984)

Rome
Vatican (plans only)
1505-7
Patron: Pope Julius II (Giuliano della Rovere)
Architect: Bramante
Capacity: Probably 20 horses
Water supply: possibly the Tiber and wells
Design features:
Proposed stable runs east to west, situated to the north of the Sala del Conclave. Basilica plan with three aisles of equal width, defined by two lines of 11 columns, each with a corresponding pilaster on the outer wall. Each aisle has a doorway at the east end. Frommel suggests that the stable also served to support the upper level, which would have contained a library.[13] A drawing in the Uffizi Gabinetto di disegni e stampe shows Bramante's plan for redeveloping part of the Vatican complex for Pope Julius II. According to Shearman, in 1506 the existing ceremonial staircase connecting the portico of the old basilica, via the old Scala Regia to the Sala Regia, was demolished and replaced by a *cordonata*, a ramp staircase, negotiable by horses, known as the Via Giulia Nova.[14]

In 2009 Henry Dietrich Fernández suggested to the author that Bramante may have planned to have horses on both the lower and upper levels. However, despite the *cordonata* being suitable for horses, the plan shows no internal access to this staircase from the stable, nor is there any external staircase drawn, making this theory unlikely.

Image:

Florence, Uffizi, Gabinetto di disegni e stampe, n. 287. A, Workshop of Bramante, *c*.1507, drawn by Antonio da Sangallo the Younger, 'Progetto per il rinnovamento del Palazzo Vaticano'

Bibliography:

Henry Dietrich Fernández, 'The Papal court at Rome, *c*.1450-1700' in ed. J. Adamson, *The Princely Courts of Europe: Ritual, Politics and Culture under the Ancien Régime, 1500-1750* (London, 1999), pp. 141-63

C.L. Frommel et al., *Raffaello Architetto* (Milan, 1984), p. 361

John Shearman, 'The apartments of Julius II and Leo X' in G. Cornini *et al* eds, *Raphael: In the Apartments of Julius II and Leo X* (Milan, 1993), pp. 15-36

Rome
La Magliana hunting stables
c.1513-21 – unfinished
Patron: Pope Julius II
Architect: Bramante. After Bramante's death, the work was carried out by his assistant, Giuliano Leno, and Giovan Francesco da Sangallo (nephew of Giuliano da Sangallo)
Dimensions: Length 69m, width 20m
Capacity: Approximately 160 horses
Design features:
The stable has an interior wall running along the centre of the building for two-thirds of its length and allowing for a total of 4 lines of horses. This leaves a third of the building as an open space on the aspect opening towards Rome. Large external buttresses support the outer walls.
The Castello della Magliana was started by Pope Sixtus IV della Rovere in the 1480s but the stables remained incomplete during Julius II's reign.
　In the twentieth century, the stable building became a hospital for the Knights of Malta.
Image:

Eugenio Lendesio, *Casale della Magliana fuori di Port Portese alle 7 miglia*. Lithograph by Weiller, 1835 Rome

Trebbio
Mid 15th century
Patron: Pierfrancesco de' Medici
Water supply: well or spring water
Design features:
Brick vaulted space with single span. Separate storage areas for fodder and straw.
　The privately owned Castello del Trebbio has a vineyard and restaurant and is available for hire.

Urbino
La Data
c.1480
Patron: Federico da Montefeltro, Duke of Urbino
Architect: Francesco di Giorgio Martini.
Dimensions: Stabling area: Length 127m (360 *piedi*),[15] width 9.89m (28 *piedi*), height 12.70m (36 *piedi*)
Capacity: Said by Francesco di Giorgio Martini to hold 300 horses, although this is unlikely
Water supply: A spring serving 2 large drinking troughs
Design features:
Three-storey building made of brick: a cellar (3.85m high) lit by small windows; a single barrel-vaulted space, the vaulting resting on half-pilasters and a hayloft with square trap doors for distributing fodder. The space allowed for two lines of horses, divided by a central aisle 3.90m wide. Large windows, on the west-facing wall only, were set 2.60m from the original floor, and were 1.60m wide and 4.20m high. Sloping floors were of volcanic tophus rock. Water could flow through the continuous covered mangers

and be released at various points to clean the stables.

The stable was already in ruins by 1587.[16] However, various sections have been redeveloped.

Images:
Federico Barocci, *Crucifixion*, 1604, Museo Nacional del Prado Madrid, in which the stables are shown in the left background

G. Cialdieri, *The Assumption*, 1630, Museo Albani, Urbino in which the stables are in the background.

Gaspar van Wittel (Gaspare Vanvitelli) (1653-1736), A preparatory drawing of Urbino from the West (Morgan Library, New York). The completed painting is in a private collection

Bibliography:
Bernardino Baldi, "Descrittione del Palazzo ducale d'Urbino", ed. A. Siekiera, *Studi e ricerche*, 87 (Alessandria, Italy, 2010)

G. Ermini, *Ordini et officij alla corte del serenissimo Signor duca d'Urbino dal codice manoscritto della Biblioteca Vaticana N. 1248* (Urbino, 1932), chs XXVII-XXX and XXVII-XXXVIII

Marta Bruscia, ed. *La Data (Orto dell'abbondanza) di Francesco di Giorgio Martini; Atti della giornata di studio, Urbino, 27 settembre 1986* (Urbino, 1990)

Francesco di Giorgio Martini, *Trattati di architettura ingegneria e arte militare*, ed. C. Maltese, 2 vols (Milan, 1967), II, 'Architettura civile e militare; dai codici senesi S. IV. 4 e Magliabechiano II. I. 141, pp. 339-40

Venetian Republic
Alberobello in Puglia
The Masseria cavallerizza and stud farm
1495-1530

Patron: Built by Alfonso I of Aragon in the mid-fifteenth century. Owned by Venetian Republic 1495-1530

Capacity: Not known, although in 1500 the stud farm had 20 stallions and 250 mares, presumably many of the mares would also have had foals

Water supply: the complex was served by cisterns and drinking troughs. The Canale di Pilo was served by several rivers which were prone to flooding

Design features:
This was the most important stud farm for Venetian military horses. Said to match the Marcianise stables in plan,[17] the Cavallerizza was much like a medieval fortress, with a surrounding wall and a look-out tower on the roof with spy holes and arrow slits. It included storage rooms, stables, a chapel and a two-storey building for the staff, with 15 rooms in the living area, which is barrel vaulted with pointed arches. Some buildings have conical roofs, typical of the *trulli* in Puglia. The wide flat plain, the Canale di Pilo, stretching out below the Cavallerizza, once had a figure-of-eight training ground for schooling horses. The area is well known for the black Murgese horse, taking its name from Murge in Apulia and developed from imported Barbs and Arabians cross bred with Andalusian horses.

The Canale di Pilo is now an important arable farming area. The buildings of the Cavallerizza were offered for sale for redevelopment in 2019.

Bibliography:
Giuseppe Notarnicola, *La Cavallerizza della Serenissima in Puglia* (Venice, 1933; Reprint Alberobello, 2008)
Franco Porsia, *I cavalli del Re* (Brindisi, 1986)

Vigevano
1471-1490s

Patrons: Galeazzo Maria Sforza and Ludovico 'Il Moro' Sforza

Architect: First two stables (1470s) attributed to Maffeo da Como. Third stable (1490) was built at the time both Bramante and Leonardo were working for Ludovico Sforza

Dimensions: Stable 1 (1471) length 50m, width 7m
Stable 2 (1471) length 56m, width 8m
Stable 3 (1490) length 91m, width 10m

Capacity: The three stables were said to hold a total of 300 horses although more likely to be 220

Design features:
The external walls of all three stables are painted to match the other courtyard walls, including the falconry

and the fortress. The *trompe l'oeil* design was a hexagonal geometric diamante pattern, interrupted by fluted Corinthian columns and a frieze of garlands, cornucopia and Sforza emblems at first floor level. Some of this decoration can still be seen. Each basilica style stable as 3 aisles of equal width. Cross vaulted ceilings are supported by rows of *serizzo* columns with Corinthian capitals, some showing evidence of the Sforza emblem. The vaulting terminates on *serizzo* corbels on the outer walls. The horse stalls are paved in stone and slope down to convex central aisles, which have drainage channels running down either side. There are windows on both sides of the stables. A grooming area is behind the first stable and behind the second stable is the blacksmith's workshop. The first floor[18] had accommodation for staff, or militia, and has a wooden coffered ceiling.

Stable 1 is now the Museo Archeologico Nazionale della Lomellina. Stable 2 is used for temporary exhibitions. Stable 3, although with no original flooring or fittings, is open to the public. The blacksmith's workshop is a visitor centre and ticket office. Over Stable 2 is the Museo della Calzatura and over Stable 3, the Pinacoteca Civica di Vigevano.

Bibliography:

G. BOMBI, M. LAVERONE, P. LUCCA EDS, *La biscia e l'aquila; il castello di Vigevano: una lettura storico-artistica* (Vigevano, 1988)

L. GIORDANO, '"La polita stalla": Leonardo, i trattatisti e le scuderie rinascimentali', *Viglevanum: Miscellanea di studi storici e artistici*, XIX (April, 2009), pp. 6-15

C.J. MOFFAT, 'Urbanism and Political Discourse: Ludovico Sforza's architectural plans and emblematic imagery at Vigevano' (University of California, Los Angeles, PhD thesis 1992)

R. SCHOFIELD, 'Ludovico il Moro and Vigevano', *Arte Lombarda*, 62 (1982), pp. 93-140

Viterbo
Stallone del Papa
1506-10
Patron: Pope Julius II (Giuliano delle Rovere)[19]
Architect: Bramante[20]
Dimensions (internal): Length *c*.63m, width *c*.11m
Capacity: Accounts say 100 horses or more
Design features:
The interior is divided into three aisles, defined by two lines of 12 large *peperino* Doric-Tuscan columns. The central aisle is wider than the two side aisles, under cross vaulted ceiling. Each side aisle vault rests on a corbel on the outer wall. The original principal entrance faced the Rocca; there was another entrance halfway down the side opening onto the piazza. There were no windows on the side against the Rocca's wall, and 12 high windows (one for every bay) on the side facing the Piazza Sallupara on ground level and 11 smaller windows at first floor level. The hayloft and accommodation above the stables were accessed via an external staircase.

Due partly to having been a prison and also to having been bombed in World War II the building is now a ruin although there are plans to restore it.

Bibliography:

ENZO BENTIVOGLIO & SIMONETTA VALTIERI, *Le Scuderie del Papa a Viterbo* (Rome, 2010 reprint as Digital Print, Città di Castello, 2012)

F. BUSSI, *Istoria della città di Viterbo* (Rome, 1742)

A.M. CORBO, 'La Rocca di Viterbo al tempo di Pio II', *Biblioteca e Società*, V:2 (April, 1980), pp. 11-15

FABIANO T. FAGLIARI ZENI BUCHICCHIO, 'Quale intervento per lo Stallone del Papa a Viterbo', *Biblioteca e Società*, XVII:1-2 (June, 1990), pp. 7-14

Spain

Córdoba
Las Caballerizas Reales
1568-1578
Patron: King Philip II of Spain
Architect: Diego López de Haro in charge. Master mason was Juan Coronado
Dimensions: Length 101m, width 15.5m, height 16m
Capacity: 104 horses
Water supply: a water tower from which water was piped. There was a drinking trough on the exterior wall of the stables, accessible from the courtyard. Later, a large drinking trough was added at one end of the central aisle.
Design features:
The complex consisted of some separate staff accommodation, stables, blacksmith's shop, storage and a riding school, all surrounded by a perimeter wall in which there were 12 doors. The stable runs north to south. At one end, the principal entrance door opened onto the street, with an iron balcony over it. This door had a spy hole and a large bolt for security. One façade faced the street, the other opened onto a large yard, on the opposite side of which was the riding school with a portico running along the side. The upper level of the stable had accommodation for the stable staff, including the accountant and the paymaster.

The stable building has 57 brick vaults supported by sturdy marble columns with Doric capitals and pedestals. The cross vaulting is supported by rounded arches, which are bordered in brick and terminate in marble corbels on the outer walls. Between each pair of pillars, two horses could be stabled. The floors were paved; those of the stalls with rectangular cobblestones, the central aisle with large pebbles. The doors and the interior arches were once painted blue. The stall partitions and the tabletop covers for the mangers ('pesereras de tablas') are made of pinewood, bound with iron bands at regular intervals. Windows were on the upper and lower floors. The 12 external windows (ie those facing the city street) had iron grills attached to the outside wall with rosette nails. For lighting at night, there were 12 tin-plate lamps fitted with glass, which were attached to the ceiling. To replace oil and wicks, the lamps were lowered and raised by pulleys. The building was given a certificate of completion in 1578.

The stables are open to the public.

Bibliography:
MADRID, ARCHIVO DEL PALACIO REAL (APR), Sección Administración, 'Instrucciones de la Caballeriza de Córdoba', 'Dehesas arrendada' and 'Instrucciones al Gobernador de la raza'
SIMANCAS (VALLADOLID), Archivo General de Simancas (AGS), 'Sitios reales', 'Sec. de Estato', 'Contaduría'
JUAN CAROLOS ALTAMIRANO, *Historia y origen del caballo Español: las caballerizas reales de Córdoba (1567-1800)* (Malaga, 1998)

Madrid
Royal stables and Armoury in the Alcázar
1553
Patron: King Philip II of Spain
Architects: Luis de Vega for the stabling and exterior; Juan Bautista de Toledo for the armoury.
Dimensions: Length 78.5m, width 10ms. Each horse stall was 2.80m wide
Capacity: 50 horses
Design features:
The exterior had step gabled ends in the Franco-Flemish/Burgundian style adopted by Philip II and dormer windows. On the principal north-facing façade there were 19 large rectangular windows with grilles, each placed between a pair of pillars. This façade also had an arched doorway. De Vega was to have put similar windows on the first-floor level but de Toledo changed them to balconies with grilles. The lower level was constructed of stone and the upper level of brick. The basilica style stable was divided into three aisles – the central aisle being wider. The roof was supported by 34 stout stone columns, with Doric capitals and pedestals. There were 36 grey granite ('piedra berroqueño') mangers – each probably

serving two horses. Each horse stall was 2.80m wide. The vaulted first floor armoury, designed by de Toledo, had the Tuscan order and had glazed ceramic tiles on the floor. The room was used to display six, life-size wooden horses, adorned with the most valuable caparisons in the armoury and coloured feather plumes, which were surrounded by Philip's war trophies, some placed in a tall cupboard running down one side of the building. The armoury walls had large mirrors, which multiplied the number of horses and their visual impact. These stables probably influenced the King's renovation of the Neapolitan Maddalena stables. A letter dated August 1559 shows that Juan de Toledo had been called to Spain from Naples by the King, to complete the stables which had begun six years earlier.

The building was pulled down in 1894 to make way for the crypt of the Almudena Cathedral.

Bibliography:

J.M. BARBEITO, *El Alcázar de Madrid* (Madrid, 1992), see Ch. 3, 'La Armería Real'

J. RIVERA, 'Las caballeriza reales y la armeria. Dirección de Juan Bautista de Toledo' in *Juan Bautista de Toledo y Felipe II: la implantación del clasicismo en España* (Valladolid, 1984), pp. 231-43

1 Pagno trained in the workshops of Donatello and Michelozzo.

2 Giovanni Sabadino degli Arienti (d. 1510) in Book V, 54v of his *De triumphis religionis*, Vat. Rossiano 176, suggested the stables could hold up to *c.*500 horses, '*Lì sono s[t]abuli per cavalli circa cinquecento, dele cuì li è de poste ducento cinquanta cavalli, che sia superbo vedere.*' See W. Gundersheimer, *Art and Life at the Court of Ercole I d'Este: the 'De triumphis religionis' of Sabadino degli Arienti* (Geneva, 1972), p. The Medici 65-6.

3 Leonardo da Vinci explained that there were 32 bays and the stable could hold 256 horses, although he has actually drawn 16 bays. See Pedretti, *Leonardo Architetto* (Milan, 1978) p. 261.

4 De Villamont, *Les voyages du Seigneur de Villamont, Chevalier de l'ordre de Hierusalem, Gentilhomme du pays de Bretaigne, divisez en trois livres* (Paris, 1595), I, ch. VII, 20r, '*Quant aux escuries du Duc elles sont toutes coultees & basties sur belles coulonnes, où que i' y fus y avoit quatrevingts treize pieces de chevaux, la plue-parts desquels estoient dressez*'.

5 See M. Francesco Bocchi and M. Giovanni Cinelli, *Le Belleze della città di Firenze* (1677 version), pp. 16-17, '. . . *in faccia d'un Corridore, che vi è coperta per poter far gl'esercizi in tempo di pioggia sono dipinti al naturale sei cavalli di mano d'Alessandro Allori, i quali son oltre modo vaghi, mostrando ogn'uno di loro diversa attitudine, e varia movenza.*'

6 Vasari, *Vite* (1966), III, 'Piero della Francesca', p. 260.

7 Jacques de Villamont, *Les Voyages du Seigneur de Villamont, Chevalier de l'ordre de Hierusalem, Gentilhomme du pays de Bretaigne. Divisez en trois livres* (Paris, 1595), II, ch. XXIIII (sic), 57v.

8 L. Gennari, *Struttura e manutenzione della cavallerizza regia di Marcianises (1488-1493)* (Salerno, 2006), p. 21.

9 Ibid. p. 15.

10 Gaetano Filangieri, ed., *Documenti per la storia, le arti e le industrie delle province napoletane* 6 vols (1883, reprint Naples, 2002), I, p. 275, entry dated 4 November 1489, '*satis bona hora surrexit et audita missa cavalco et ando a vedere si cavalli novamente venuti da marcenese a la nova stalla ad carbonara*'. Alfonso visits the stables again on 8 November and on 8 and 10 December.

11 In a letter dated 14 November 1562 Duke Cosimo asks Raffaello della Vacchia to expedite work on the rooms above the stables at Poggio. Florence, ASF, AMe. 216. Doc. 1187. fol. 143, letter from Cosimo de' Medici to della Vacchia, '*Sollecitate che si finischino le stanze sopra le stalle*'.

12 Formerly attributed to Baccio Bigio (Bartolomeo Lippi) a generation earlier (1516-21) and thought to have been altered by Il Tribolo (1548). See Lamberini's argument that Il Tribolo was responsible for the design: see Lamberini, 'Il Tribolo ingegnere e i lavori al Poggio a Caiano', *Niccolò, detto il Tribolo* (2001), pp. 173-85. The stables were completed after Il Tribolo's death in 1550.

13 C.L. Frommel *et al.* eds, *Raffaello Architetto* (Milan, 1984), p. 361.

14 J. Shearman, 'The apartments of Julius II and Leo X' in R. Caravaggi, ed, *Raphael: In the Apartments of Julius II and Leo X* (Milan, 1993), p. 35, n. 32.

15 One metre = 2.83 *piedi*. Calculation inferred in Bruscia's *La Data* (Urbino, 1990), p. 60 where Francesco di Giorgio's 36 '*piedi urbinati*' are said to equal 12.70m.

16 B. Baldi, "Descrittione del Palazzo ducale d'Urbino", ch. IV, 'Del fondamento del Palazzo' in ed. A. Siekiera, *Studi e ricerche*, 87 (Alessandria, Italy, 2010), for Baldi's description dated 10 June 1587.

17 L. Gennari, *Struttura e manutenzione della cavallerizza regia di Marcianise (1488-1493)* (Salerno, 2006), p. 15.

18 The first and third stable's upper floors were not seen by the author.

19 Buccicchio makes a credible argument for Julius II building the stables at this date. In 1742, Feliciano Bussi had incorrectly identified the *stemma* over the portal as belonging to Pope Sixtus IV and suggested that the stables were built for him *c.*1481. See F. Bussi, *Istoria della città di Viterbo* (Rome, 1742), p. 305.

20 See article by Bucchicchio who explains that two documents link Bramante to the Rocca in Viterbo between 1506 and 1508.

Appendices

One

'Codice dei palii gonzagheschi' 6r-v, *c*.1499-1518
Private Collection

Poem in praise of Francesco II Gonzaga's racehorse, Dainosauro

Non Dayno o Pardo o fuggitiva fera
né sagitta da chorda a furia spinta
né fulgure dal ciel per l'aria tinta
passò sì presto mai mattina ò sera

Né Febo cho destrier de la sua spera
la cui velocità gia mai fu vinta
né vento che ogni forza ha sempre extinta
mostrò furia nel mondo mai sì fiera

Come correndo fece il legier Sauro
passando in mezzo la città del fiore
per vincer del Baptista il premio dauro

Gloria del mio Francesco eterno honore
per cui Gonzaga dal mar Indo al Mauro
phama harà sempre del suo gran valore

Ponendoti le piume e l'ali adosso
tu hai fatto di te tal pruova Sauro
che sempre sen dirà dal Indo al Mauro
e l'uno e l'altro ciel ne sia percosso

Tu non fosti dal segno così presto mosso
che teco ti portasti il premio dauro
che tu sii vera floria e ver restauro
del Duca mantuan dir non tel posso

Tu fusti honor di tutti li altri armenti
nel correre, e nel corso senza guida
vincesti senza dubio tutti i venti

La virtù del Signor ch'in te si fida
s'è sparsa con rumor fra tante genti
che Turcho, Turcho, tutta Italia chrida.

Two

Claudio Corte, *Il cavallarizzo* (Venice, 1562), I, 47v-48r

Chapter 37
The responsibilities of the stable boys

The responsibility of the stable boy is principally to be faithful, loving and to work well; he must not amuse himself in gambling nor in anything base. He must not have a wife or children. This is because he must not sleep away from the stables at night. For which I would like the boys to have the comfort of sleeping with straw mattresses, sheets [and] blankets along the length of the main aisle; so that they can quickly and more easily help the horses [or] scold them when it is necessary. And, I do not praise those riding establishments that have raised platforms on which the lads can sleep, [as when they are] on these platforms and in bedrooms [the lads] can also cause many dangerous and dirty problems, without being seen by their superiors. The said stable boys must always clean very well underneath the horses and keep the whole stable spotless. Because it is through this that health and happiness will come to them as well as to the horses, in addition to honour; [whereas] the contrary would cause danger from one part to the other: because dirt and garbage corrupts the air, and rotten air is the worst and most annoying thing you can have. Besides, when one keeps the stable clean, it will not give rise to those small dirty animals, which are born from putrefaction and corruption of the air, and from filth and stench, such as flies, horseflies, mosquitoes, worms, cockroaches, scorpions and also mice, which are direct enemies of the horse through [their] noise, stench, breath and bites. Having in such an environment, a way of pleasing so vile, useless and dangerous an animal, [which is also an] irritation and the would-be enemy of such a worthy, generous and extremely useful animal. The stable boys must give bedding to the horses, being very careful that it is not dusty, nor anything else noxious in it; the same with the fodder. They must be prompt and ready in their work, quick and cheerful, of few words, not drunk or thieving but reverent and humble. And this will come to them when they consider that God has made them poor but of good strength, so that by earning themselves bread with their sweat, they remain subjects, but nevertheless to believe that, in another life, He will give them incomparable wealth. And in this way they will be content with their vocation. Expecting also that with good service they will be called upon to do more honourable and better-paid work. Because it was not many years ago that a stable boy was called from the stable of Captain Mario Muti to become the much honoured rider, Mister Cecco di Paliano, and before this the *cavaliero* Tomasso, so famous and excellent in the art of riding, was taken from the kitchens, and why should I not continue, Giambattista da Cremona, family name Capelletto, who was my stable boy for eight years, during which [time], seeing that he was very loving towards the horses and how well he rode in the *bardella*,[1] and in the management of a single Barbary horse in the last year, I promoted him from that management to rider in the saddle and to [then] become Master of the Stable with a salary suitable for his status; and now he can live respectably.

---

1 *Bardella*: a light-weight saddle pad.

Three

A letter from
Geronimo Archario to Marquis Federico II Gonzaga,
19 October 1523,
concerning the stud farm at Pietole.
Mantua, ASMa, AG, b. 2504, c. 455[2]

My illustrious and most excellent Lord and most valued patron,

Today, in the company of Messer Gaspar and Messer Petroantoni, *cavalcator* at the Marmirolo stud farm and of Bernardino da Bergamo, we went to Pietole to see the entire stud of mares and foals, which is one of the most beautiful things, not only in Italy but in the world and, because he has separated the foals of one and a half years from those of *cavalcator* Suso, we made all these yearlings come out of the stable one by one. And first there were eight very beautiful Turks of one and a half years old, four beautiful *gineti* of the same age and forteen little heavy horse foals,[3] which seemed much like coursers and are extremely beautiful and a bay mule of the same age. The above Turkish, *gineta* and heavy horse foals were consigned to the trainer Rizo and were in total twenty-seven, including the mule. Then similarly we made the two and a half year olds come out one by one with *cavalcator* Suso, first 10 Turks, then twelve *gineti* and thirteen heavy horses, which one must agree are beautiful in every way, and totalled thirty-five and were consigned to Messer Petroantoni for training, to whom I gave everything necessary for the said yearlings. I then left four one and a half year old Barbaries at Soave, which are very beautiful and, after handing over the yearlings, made all the mares pass by way of the Pietole courtyard. First, the thirty-one Barbary mares with seven colt foals and four filly foals from this year, then sixty-six Turks with twelve colt foals and five fillies, also from this year and finally the heavy horse mares passed through, which seemed like coursers and were one hundred and three in number, with twenty colt foals and fourteen filly foals from this year. And all the said horses and foals total three hundred and seven in number, and they are fat and look well and of such beauty as has ever been seen. And the horseman Scaramella has been to see the mares, Messer Lodovico Ottolino already under factor and a great crowd of men marvelled at the beauty of these mares and foals saying that, during the time of happy memory of the late Illustrious Lord,[4] there were never such well-built horses as there are now. Messer Gaspar, *cavalcator*, swears to me that, out of the eight hundred foals in the King of Naples' breed, only ten are as beautiful as these and I trust in God that on your Excellency's happy return, they will please you even more than this, as they are more beautiful than I have written, as it seemed to me to give a detailed opinion of them to Your Excellency for your satisfaction. I kiss your hand and in good grace, I commend myself to you.

    Mantua, 19 October, 1523
    Di S. ill Suo Hiero. Archario

---

2 The letter is printed in full in Carlo Cavriani, *Le razze Gonzaghesche dei cavalli nel mantovano e la loro influenza sul puro sangue inglese* (Mantua, 1974), pp. 25-6.
3 Heavy horse ('*razza grossa*') is a breed used as war-horses.
4 Federico's father, Francesco II Gonzaga had died in 1519.

Four

Claudio Corte
Il cavallarizzo (Venice, 1562), I, 52r-53v

Chapter 41
How *farraina* should be made and in what way and at what time one should give it.

Farraina should be [made] as it used to be in ancient times by some really wise men and as the name sounds, it is a mixture of many kinds of fodder, that is to say of yeast, barley, oats and rye, to be used for feeding horses, because this will cleanse them marvellously and refresh them considerably. Such is the strength of *farraina* that you must give it to the horse for ten days continuously, not giving anything other than this; from the eleventh day until the fourteenth day, one should begin to give barley together with this mixture, increasing it little by little until you reach his former ration. And when he is at this point, you must give him the *farraina* for another ten days continuously, together with his correct ration of barley; and throughout this time you must exercise the horse but not tire him [but if he is] sweating, you should grease him all over with tepid oil. If it is cold you must make a fire in the stable; this is as Varro wishes it to be.[5] But Apsyrtus and other Greeks preferred that *farraina* is [made] either of yeast, or of pure barley,[6] which would be better if it comes from and is sown close to the sea; because it purges the stomach more easily and gets rid of the sad humours. Not being able to have this, you must use that which you have. Also they would like you to give [the horse] barley in the manner above and then to give him grass without any pause, so long as he does not have too much. And that from the fifth day that he has begun to eat his *farraina*, he should be taken to water, where you wash him all over, and make him swim and dry him well with cloths and other things, and then pummel him by hand, going against the hair, and rub him well with rose oil and wine, that should be tepid for the whole body from the head down, outdoors. And after this you should pummel him again, this time [going] with the grain of the hair. But they, themselves, say it is necessary that whilst we give *farraina* to the horse, we should bleed him, by cutting the chest vein and we should also cut the palate.[7] They would prefer that we should give him salt on a table, next to where he eats the grass, so that he can take it when it suits him;[8] and this is so that there is no putrefaction in his mouth, caused by moisture in the grass. They also say that he should be kept inside and that it is better if he is purged before being put out to grass. This is how the Greeks speak of it: Apsyrtus, Hierocles and Theomnestus, who, it seems to me, talk very confusingly about it, even if there are some good ideas. But I would like to suggest a distinct and clear rule: that when you want to put your horse to *farraina*, before you do so, for one day and one night you pasture him on dirt[9] and I advise you that this is particularly important with horses of great value. And, afterwards, blow this well-pulverised recipe, written below, into his nostrils with a small pipe and then keep him tied up with his head high for half an hour.
The ingredients are:
    Roots of saffron, ½ ounce

---

5 This feeding plan and the fire are exactly as recommended by Varro, *On Agriculture*, ed. J Henderson (Cambridge, MA and London, 2006), pp. 389, 391.
6 *Orzo schietto* can mean wild barley.
7 The word *ferriamo* is used here. Reading to the end of the cure where there is talk of the horse swallowing blood, I believe this may mean slicing into the palate with an iron implement.
8 This is to give the horse the necessary minerals.
9 Corte uses the term 'in terra'.

    Pepper when possible, 1 *carlino*[10]
    Pennyroyal mint, ½ ounce
    Oregano, ½ ounce,
    Leaves of costmary,[11]
    Roots of wild cucumber, over 1 *giulio* of each if possible.

And all of the above must be well ground up and put through a sieve, mixing the snuff together so that you can put it up the horse's nostrils. Then detach the horse's head from the high post where he is tied and re-pasture him in a field, where there is clover and other good grass, so that all the damp humours that have accumulated in the winter, and the humidity in the head, will be distilled and purged through the nostrils, because the head is near the ground. And you must pasture him for three continuous days, but not during the night: because at the twenty-fourth hour he must be brought back to the covered stable, and there have the same grass from the field, but eating it from the floor in the same way. Horses managed in this way purge themselves more effectively and will get rid of many ills. Truly, when you cannot do this or do not have the means to pasture him in a field as we have said, you can make him eat the grass from the floor continuously for three days and nights in the stable. In which, for four other days, you should give him *farraina* of yeast or barley, after which you should bleed him from the common vein in the neck; then mix the blood with vinegar, rose oil and some white of egg and anoint the whole of the horse's body, tethering him to the floor whilst the ointment remains and then dries. Then putting him in the stable again, give him his *farraina* of yeast or barley for ten or eleven days continuously, during which time you must not groom him nor do anything else to the body nor to the legs but wipe down the head, which is not greased or oiled, with cloths. You must keep the area beneath him clean for the whole time that he eats the *farraina* and the grass; and if the stable is cold you should light a fire inside. On the eleventh day, you should take him to water, washing and drying him well, with large linen cloths; do this on calm days when there is no wind. And not having access to flowing water, a pool or the sea, which for this treatment is perfect, wash him with well water that is tepid and pure. Then put him back in the stable, and give him grass during this time, as you think is appropriate, which if clover would be best; you cannot give the horse a better grass than this. You must keep him covered, either with wool or linen as is necessary. And he must be groomed very carefully once every other day, [and] wiped down with cloths every day. I praise salt being put down beside the horse, but I praise more that in the morning and the evening you should give him bran[12] mixed with salt, from which he will become sanguine for the rest of the time that he eats grass. And it does not please me to give him barley, because having weak stomachs through the coarse dampness and frigidity of the grass, unfortunately they may not be able to digest it; and also because of the little exercise they have. For which exercise I would like every morning to be like this, or if not every morning, at least every other morning, they should be walked for one hour, and it pleases me if they start sweating, so they are rubbed with oil and tepid wine. And that they are pummelled by many hands first against the hair, oiling it, and then with the hair, but only the head must be wiped and dried. It does not please me to bleed from the vein in the chest at this time; unless it is necessary, don't do it; but I very much praise cutting the palette when the moon is waning, and you must make the horse swallow this blood because it has miraculous results, killing worms and other grubs which live in the horse's body and trouble him. During this time, you must often wash the horse's mouth with vinegar and salt, in order to descale his teeth, and make him eat with a good appetite. And make sure that the *farraina* does not become too strong. And that is enough.

---

10 This is Neapolitan currency. The *carlino* is a small silver coin used in Naples and Sicily, first struck in the 13th century and named after Charles of Anjou

11 Costmary is also known as 'alecost' and 'balsam herb' and is a close relative of the Tansy. Green's *Universal Herbal* (1532) states that a strong infusion of the leaves is 'good in disorders of the stomach and the head'. It originates in the Orient. See M. Grieve, *A Modern Herbal*, 2 vols (Mineola, NY, 1971), I, p. 226.

12 Corte uses the word *semola*.

Currency, Weights and Measurements

Different currencies existed in the different states and republics, making a true comparison of value difficult. For example, in the mid-fifteenth century, one Papal ducat (*ducato*) was worth the same as one Florentine florin (*fiorino*) and as 5 Sienese lira (*lire*).[1] It is, therefore, easier to ascertain the buying power of any Renaissance currency. With steady employment, a skilled worker in mid fifteenth-century Rome might earn 60 ducats a year, with a third of his income going on food, shelter, clothes. The following comparisons might help the reader appreciate the value attached to the horse in early sixteenth-century Mantua.

Comparative values using the Mantuan ducat in 1517[2]
1 ducat = 4 lire and 13 soldi or 930 imperial lire
'Una biolca da terra' (3,138 sq. metres) = 30 ducats
One ox = 300 lire
1 pair maroc leather shoes = 1 lire
1 lb of cheese = 4 *soldi*
A Gonzaga horse sold for 160 ducats in 1517.
In 1502 Francesco II Gonzaga offered a 2,000 ducats reward to find the supervisor of his stables, who was accused of poisoning 45 horses.[3]

In the Papal States and some other individual states, the currency was the *scudo*.
1 *scudo* = 100 *baiocchi* (singular: *baiocco*)
1 *baiocco* = 5 *quattrini*
In addition
1 *grosso* = 5 *baiocchi*
1 *doppia* = 3 *scudi*
1 *carlino* = 7½ *baiocchi*
1 *giulio* or *paoli* = 10 *baiocchi*
1 *testone* = 30 *baiocchi*

Weights and Measurements
These also differed considerably throughout the peninsular during the period 1450-1600, both by location and according to the commodity. An architect might use measurements from his home town or from the state or city in which he was working. Where it is possible, measurements have been explained in a footnote.

Weights[4]
In most of Italy including Sardinia and Sicily:
1 *livre* (pound) = 12 *onces* (although the ounce varied throughout Italy between 26.4 and 30.7 grams)
1 *once* (ounce) = 8 *ottavi* or *drachme*
In other parts of Europe 1 *livre* = 16 ounces

---

1 Valuation taken from Charles R. Mack, *Pienza:the Creation of a Renaissance City* (Ithaca and London, 1987), p. 180.
2 Taken from Nosari and Canova, *I cavalli Gonzaga* (2005), p. 308.
3 Nosari and Canova, *Il palio nel Rinascimento* (2003), p. 270.
4 Weights and measurements taken from H. Doursther, *Dictionaire universel des poids et mesures anciens et modernes, contenant des tables des monnaies de tous les pays* (Amsterdam, 1965).

Measurements

Linear measurements: *palmo*, *braccia* and *canna* are all used for stable measurements.

Palmo = varied between 24.3 and 29.2cms

Braccia = literally 'arm' but actually the distance between a man's fingers and his elbow. The measurment varied between $c.47$ and $c.58$cms.

Braccia (Florentine architecture) = $c.58.36$cms
Braccia (Mantua) = $c.46.7$cms
Canna (Florentine, commerce) = 4 *bracci* = 8 *palmi* = 2.30m
Canna (Florentine, architecture) = 5 *bracci* = 10 *palmi* = 2.90m
Canna (Naples) = 8 *palmi* = 2.10m
Canna (Pisa, Tuscany) = 5 *bracci* =10 *palmi* = 2.90m
Canna (Rome, commerce) = 8 *palmi* = 2m
Canna (Rome, architecture) = 10 *palmi* = 2.23m

Area measurement

Biolca = 3,138 square metres or 0.775 of an acre.

Notes to the Reader

Jean-Yves Boriaud's French translation of Alberti's *De equo animante*, *Le Cheval Vivant* (Paris, 1999), has been used by the author. References to *De equo animante* include both a reference to Boriaud's translation and to the Latin text in Antonio Videtta's *Il cavallo vivo* (Naples, 1991), the latter marked 'Videtta'. The translations of Leonardo da Vinci's manuscript notes are taken from two sources: E. MacCurdy, *The Notebooks of Leonardo da Vinci*, 2 vols (London, 1954) and C. Pedretti, ed., *The Literary Works of Leonardo da Vinci: Compiled and edited from the original Manuscripts by Jean Paul Richter*, 2 vols (Oxford, 1977). Unless otherwise stated, all other translations are the author's and, in some instances, the English has been modernised.

Abbreviations

Archival Material

AE	Archivio Estense
AF	Archivio Farnese
AG	Archivio Gonzaga
AMe	Archivio Mediceo
AS	Archivio Sforzesco
ASF	Archivio di Stato, Florence
ASR	Archivio di Stato, Rome
ASMa	Archivio di Stato, Mantua
ASMi	Archivio di Stato, Milan
ASMo	Archivio di Stato, Modena
ASN	Archivio di Stato, Naples
Bib. Amb.	Biblioteca Ambrosiana
Bib. Est.	Biblioteca Estense, Modena
BNN	Biblioteca Nazionale di Napoli, Naples
Bib. Triv.	Biblioteca Trivulziana, Milan
IF	Institut de France

Primary Sources

Alberti, CV
Leon Battista Alberti, *De equo animante* (c.1445), trans. into French and ed. J-Y Boriaud, *Le Cheval Vivant* (Paris, 1999)
Caracciolo, 1589
Pasqual Caracciolo, *La gloria del cavallo* (Venice, 1589)
Corte, 1562
Claudio Corte, *Il cavallarizzo* (Venice, 1562)
Corte, 1573
Claudio Corte, *Il cavalerizzo* (Lyons, 1573)

Fiaschi, 1603
Cesare Fiaschi, *Trattato dell'imbrigliare, atteggiare e ferrare cavalli* (Venice, 1603)

Ottolengo
'Treatise' ascribed to Zanino de Ottolengo, transcribed and collated by Gilberto Carra and Carlo Golinelli as *Sulle infermità dei cavalli. Dal codice di Zanino de Ottolengo (secolo XV)* (Mantua 1991)

Ruini, 1618
Carlo Ruini, *Anatomia del cavallo, infirmità et suoi remedii* (Venice, 1618)

***On Horsemanship*, 1962**
Xenophon, *On the Art of Horsemanship*, in E.C. Marchant, trans. *Scripta minora* (London and Cambridge, MA, 1962), pp. 295-363

Ordini
Ordini et offitij alla corte del serenissimo duca d'Urbino: dal manoscritto della Biblioteca Vaticana (Urb.Lat. 1248), ed. G. Ermini (Urbino, 1932)

A Glossary of equestrian terms and terminology

A

Anguanino/a
Yearling: a one-year-old horse or a horse in its second year.

Allevatore
Horse breeder: a man in charge of breeding and rearing horses.

Aloepatico
Aloes: imported via Alexandria and from the Greek island Socotra. Used as an intestinal purgative.

Anabola see also *Xiloaloes* (Greek)
The wood from aloes. It was probably the Cabaline or Horse Aloes that Rusio used in his horse anaesthetic. This is a powerful purgative and had been used by the ancient Greeks (e.g. Dioscorides and Pliny, but not mentioned by Hippocrates or Theophrastus). It came into Europe via the Red Sea and Alexandria but also came from the Greek island of Socotra. It is still used for veterinary purposes in the UK.

Anticore
Angina: known in humans as 'Ludwig's angina'. An inflammation in the chest close to the heart.

Appanare/appannare
To wipe down a horse with cloths.

Appannatoio
A cloth for wiping down horses, usually made of wool or silk or a blindfold (Battaglia 'a cloth for putting over/covering the eyes of a nervous horse when harnessing him').

Aratia
Stud farm; from old French *haraz* giving rise to *arazzo*, *razzo* and *razza*. See Porsia, *I cavalli* (1986), p. 23.

Arcendo or *Arzeglio*
Adjective describing a horse with a white rear right foot. According to Caracciolo this horse will be a disaster in battle. *La gloria* (1589), IV, p. 298.

Archenna
Henna: a reddish brown dye used for colouring the Gonzaga grey horses' tails. Imported from the Levant or Turkey.

Arena
Sand mixed with lime to make mortar and plaster. Used in building construction.

Armellino
Florio describes this colour horse as 'apricot coloured'. It may also be named after the ermine (*ermellino*), ie pale cream with black mane and tail.

Armento
A herd of horses or cattle.

Artemisia
Artemesia: herb used in poultices for aching muscles and rubbed into a racehorse's back with sandarac (*sandaraca*) in preparation for a race. Corte (1573), II, ch. 52, 117v.

Arzeglio see *Arcendo*

Asse
Planks of wood or straight wooden boards, used for construction and for some horse stalls.

Assongia
Pig fat/lard: rubbed into horse's hooves to prevent cracking and used in medicine.

Attafanato/a
'Flea-bitten': when the horse's white hair is flecked with black, causing a flea-bitten effect.

Avelignese w
A breed from La Venaria Reale, Savoy.

Avena
Oats: more commonly *vena*.

B

Baccallario/baccallaro
Head lad: Corte explains that this is a senior groom in charge of the stable boys. Corte, 1562, I, ch. 38, 48v. (Derived from the medieval Latin *baccalarius*, meaning yeoman farmer).

Bacchetta
Stick or cane for schooling the horse.

Baglio/baio/bayo
Bay: usually a pale golden brown coloured horse with black legs, mane and tail. However, some Renaissance writers indicate that *baio* is a single colour with no black.

Balzano/a
Signifying white markings, especially on the horse's legs.

Balzano calzato
When the white on the horse's leg reaches its knees.

Barbaro/barbero
Barb: the Barbary horse from north Africa. The word would evolve in some stables to signify any racehorse.

Barbaresco/barbarescatore
A groom entrusted to care for and train racehorses.

Barbozzo
The horse's lower lip and lower jaw.

Barbozzale/barbazzale
Curb chain: the chain that fits onto the bit and runs from cheek to cheek behind the horse's underlip in the chin groove. It is 'controlled' by the lower of the rider's two reins. When the lower rein is pulled, the chain presses into the jawbone behind the underlip, forcing the horse to lower its head.

Bardatura
The horse's tack or harness.

Bardella/bardellone
An extremely soft saddle, having no wooden frame and made of deeply padded leather. Used for breaking in young horses and for schooling (La Crusca).

Bastardo
A cross-bred horse where the dam and sire are of different breeds.

Bertino
Dark iron grey coloured horse.

Biada
Fodder: Any kind of dried food.

Biolca
An area of land equal to 3,138 square metres or 0.775 acres. The area corresponds to the amount that could be ploughed in a day by a peasant, *bifolco*, with two oxen.

Biverone/beverone
A bran mash. Fodder made from soaking and cooking bran or other cereals. Served warm and often given as a tonic or for medicinal reasons.

Bocca di lupo
Ground level window, which lets light into a cellar or vault via a shaft.

Bolso/bolsaggine
Adjective describing a broken-winded horse, making it useless. See also *polezivo*. See Porsia, *I cavalli* (1986), Appendix B p. 135.

Braccia
Linear measurement equal to the distance between a man's fingertips and his elbow. Usually equal to 46 – 58cms.

Branca orsina
'Bear's claw' or common hogweed, cow-parsnip, used in an anti-inflammatory poultice.

Brenda/ brenna
Bran: made from cereal husks, this coarse food is used to bulk out other fodder. (*Brenna* also means a worn-out horse).

Briglia
Bridle: part of the harness attached the horse's head, which includes the bit, headpieces, brow band, noseband and reins. Sometimes, *briglia* can refer to the bit itself.

Broccare
To decorate with metal studs. Also meaning 'to spur' or 'to prick with the spurs'.

C

Caczola/cazzuola
A small round footbath used for soaking a horse's foot.

Caditoia
Manhole/trapdoor.

Calzane
'Socks': describing the lower part of the horse's legs as white.

Calzato/i
Adj. describing a horse with one or more white 'socks' (*calzane*), which only reach a short distance above the foot.

Càndano (Spanish?)
[*Canapa*]: a fibre made from the leaves of *Cannabis sativa* (hemp) used for sacking and ropes and for fabric fly screens for stable windows. See Gennari, *Struttura* (2006), pp. 20 and 60 citing ASN, Sommaria, Dipendenze, I, 36, fasc. 2, 40r.

Cunnu
Canes: the game of canes, where mounted combattants used canes in place of swords, as training for war.

Canoncello
A type of bit.

Canone
A whip made of cane.

Capestro
Halter: a rope or leather headpiece for tethering the horse.

Capezone
Cavesson: a kind of head collar used on young horses to break them in. It has a padded noseband with rings attached for schooling reins.

Capezza/capecza/cavessa
Halter.

Capo gacto/capo gatto/capostorno
Staggers: a sickness where the horse stumbles and falls down, usually a problem of the brain but sometimes caused by indigestion.

Capostotica
'Vapours': Florio describes this as caused by blood boiling in the body.

Capriola
Capriole: The most difficult *maneggio* movement in the 'Airs above ground', which takes much strength and courage on the horse's part. The horse jumps off the ground and, when his body is horizontal to the ground, he simultaneously kicks out his two back legs parallel to the ground, before landing all four feet on the ground at the same time. The move was used in battle in defence to create space, when surrounded by the enemy. According to Corte, the *capriola* is named after the goat's jump ('saltar del caprio'), hence the movement's name. Corte, 1562, II, 73v, ch.18.

Carnagio/carnaggio
Bait of meat. For example, the large pig used as bait in a wolf trap at the Marcianise stud farm. Naples, ASNa, Sommaria, Dipendenze, I, 36, Fasc. 2, 28r. See Gennari, *Struttura* (2006), p. 48.

Carrettoni
Waggoners.

Caryophyllon/Garyophyllon
Clove: the dried flower bud of the clove tree *Caryophyllus aromatica*. Sometimes used as a painkiller.

Castagno
Bright golden chestnut coloured horse.

Cavalcatore
A professional rider, who helped train and show the court horses.

Cavallarizzo/cavallerizzo
Riding master or 'professor of horsemanship' (Florio).

Cavallerizza
Riding school, which often included a stable complex, food storage and staff accommodation.

Cavallina
Filly: A young female horse.

Cavallo a pardo
A horse used for carrying a leopard on its rump for hunting.

Cavallo a petto
Florio explains that this is a strong, brave horse of value.

Cavallo a vettura
Carriage horse.

Cavallo castrato
Guelding, a guelded/castrated stallion.

Cavallo da soma
A packhorse.

Cavallo di legno
Child's wooden 'hobby horse'.

Cavallo di mezza sella
A horse that is partially trained.

Cavallo di tutta sella
A fully trained horse.

Cavallo fatto
A 'made horse': a mature, trained horse.

Cavallo frenato
A horse that is broken in, or schooled.

Cavallo gradaro
Carthorses for pulling heavy loads.

Cavallo grosso
Large horse, suitable for war or for transport. See also *Destriero*

Cavallo pezzato
Painted horse, Pinto or piebald horse, i.e. of more than one colour.

Cavalli purpurei
'Purple' horses: the best quality or royal horses.

Cavallo saltatore
A jumping horse: probably used for jumping displays or competitions.

Cavezza/capezza
Headcollar made of leather or rope, for tying up or leading the horse.

Cedro
1. A large citrus fruit, like a lemon.
2. Cedar: a large conifer tree.

Cegnia/cinghia/cingnyali
The girth or other straps made of leather, canvas or other strong fabrics. The girth is a wide strap running underneath the horse's ribcage, from one side of the saddle to the other, thus keeping the saddle in place.

Cerqua/Quercia
The wood from the oak tree.

Chiappe
The horse's rump.

Chinea/schinetto
Hackney: from French *haquenée* or English 'hackney' meaning 'a horse of ambling gait' and, therefore, suitable for riding or as a packhorse. The Chinea was also a white horse which the Kings of Naples presented to the Pope each year, until the end of the eighteenth century.

Ciambetta
A *maneggio* movement where the horses rises on its hindquarters with the forelegs elevated and leading with one foreleg, navigates round a tight circle, crossing one leg over another. No longer performed, but Tobey suggests it is the forerunner of the canter pirouette, where the horse pivots its body in a circle. E. Tobey, 'The Legacy of Federico Grisone', *The Horse as Cultural Icon* (2012), p. 152. Mentioned with other *maneggio* movements by Caracciolo, *La gloria* (1589), V.

Chyuppo/Pioppo
Wood from the poplar tree, used for separating the stalls in the stables of the Marcianise cavallerizza. See Naples, ASN, Sommaria, Dipendenze, I, 36, fasc. 2, 30v.

Ciffetto/ciuffo
Forelock: the section of mane falling forward between a horse's ears, over its face.

Cillaro
The name of the Duke of Calabria's horse. The same name as for Castor's horse in mythology. Castor was considered the great trainer of horses and protector of riders.

Cimurro/ciamorro
Equine 'flu' or distemper: a serious cold in the head with the nose running and which can be fatal (also *cziamorio/ czamurro*).

Cincorente
A rake with five teeth made of iron or wood to remove straw or manure from stalls.

Cocomero salvatica
Ecballium elaterium, 'Exploding cucumber'/'Asinine watermelon' or *asinino* –used in equine medicine as a purgative.

Consolida maggiore
Comfrey: *Synphytum officinale* used as an astringent.

Coppa
A measuring cup with the capacity of about 1.09 litres.

Corba
Bursitis: the inflammation around a joint.

Cordonata
A ramped stairway, which is easily negotiated by horses.

Corona
Coronal band: the area where the hoof meets the skin of the horse's leg.

Correre vuoti/a scosso
To race without a jockey.

Correre pieni/a pelo
To race bareback/ without a saddle.

Corsiero
A light warhorse also used for jousting and tournaments.

Cortaldo/curtaldo
A stocky, solid horse like the English cob, originally bred in Suffolk. Called *cortaud* in France (literally 'bob-tail') since Middle Ages. Often the tail is 'docked' (shortened) and the mane is cut, sometimes the ears are also clipped. Suitable for war, hunting and transport.

Corvetta
Courbette/corbette: one of the *maneggio* movements known as 'Airs above ground'. In the courbette the horse lifts his front legs off the ground as if rearing up and jumps forward on his back legs. This movement was used in battle, with the horse's body shielding the rider from the enemy. See Corte, *Il cavallarizzo* (1562), II, 70v, ch. 15 and Caracciolo, *La gloria* (1589) p. 427.

Coscia/cosce
The horse's thigh/thighs.

Cozzone/coczone
Middleman or horse-breaker. From *scozzonare* meaning to break in and train animals to the saddle or carriage work.

Credenza
A fault in the horse's movement, in which it finds it harder to turn on one side than the other.

Crepacze traverse/crepaccio traverso
A crack at the back of the horse's foot.

Crinaro
The crest of the horse's neck.

Crine
Horsehair.

Criniera
The mane.

Crippioni
Feeding troughs.

Cristiero
A clyster or enema.

Crivo, crivello
A sieve or riddle for filtering dry food or medicines.

Croupade
A *maneggio* movement where the horse jumps high tucking his hind legs under his stomach.

Ciuffo
Horse's forelock (see also *ciffetto*).

Czagarelli/zaganelli
Ribbons or tapes used to tie the canvas cloth onto stable windows, to keep flies and other insects out.

D

Destriero
A heavily built powerful warhorse, usually led by a groom on the right side, hence the name. Sometimes referred to as *Cavallo grosso*.

A digiuno
On an empty stomach.

Disarcionare (-ato)
To unseat a rider (unseated).

Domare
To break in or train a horse to be ridden.

E

Efippio
The caparison on which the rider sits.

Empiastro/impiastro
Poultice: used either as an anti-inflammatory or to soothe pain.

Equitatore
Horse trainer.

F

Fabricatori di scove/scope
Broom and brush makers.

Falbo/falvo
Light bay/dark yellow coloured horse with black skin and black legs, mane and tail.

Falso quarto/quartifalsi
False quarter: an inflammation of the coronet at the top of the horse's hoof, which affects the horn of the hoof and causes lameness. Rare and difficult to cure.

Famiglio di stalla
Groom or stable boy.

Fantino
Small boy or jockey in the *palio*.

Farraina
A mixture of fodder, such as yeast, barley, oats and rye, used as part of a purging and refreshing process for the horse. It is used together with washing, bleeding and massaging and, depending on the quality of the horse, the inhaling of snuff. The horse was usually given the purging treatment for several days. See Corte's recipe and instructions in Appendix 4. See also Caracciolo, *La gloria* (1589), VII, p. 541.

Fattrice
Broodmare.

Fegare/fregare
To rub down the horse with cloths.

Fenu gregu/fieno greco
Fenugreek

Ferraro
Artisan who works with iron, making nails, pins, rings and buckles for harnessing.

Ferro
The horse's iron shoe. Usually heated and moulded by the farrier (*maniscalco*) to fit the individual horse, the shoe could also serve a remedial purpose for a damaged foot. It is attached to the 'dead' part of the hoof wall by five or more iron nails, depending on the weight of shoe and workload of the horse.

Fesso
Adj. literally 'cracked' but, when describing the horse's mouth, it means 'wrinkled'.

Fettone
The 'frog': the soft raised triangular section on the sole of the horse's foot.

Fiammate vaccine
Cooked cow dung, which was made into a compress and put into the horse's foot to harden it and inhibit disease. Corte, *Cavalerizzo* (1573), II, ch. 52, 116r. where he suggests that ox dung is best, when preparing a race horse. Dried cow dung can also be used as an antiseptic dressing.

Fianco, fancho
Flank: the area between the horse's ribs and loins, extending down to the stomach.

Fienile
Hay barn, or hayloft.

Fieno
Hay.

Filetto
Snaffle: a simple and gentle style of horse bit.

Filonio
An antidote against poison, taking the name of its discoverer, the first-century doctor, Filone of Tarso.

Finimenti
The tack or harness.

Fornimenti da cavallo
The horse trappings, sometimes made of expensive fabrics such as gold brocade and adorned with tassels, bells or fringes. Cut and sewn by the court tailor, the saddler would have had the responsibility of assembling it.

Fraina
Pastures.

Freno
The bit: the mouthpiece attached to the reins, through which the horse is controlled by the rider.

Frisone
The Friesian breed of horse. Usually all black, but occasionally brown, they are strong and elegant with long flowing manes and tails.

Froge
The nostrils.

Fronte
The horse's forehead, i.e. below the crest of the head between the eyes.

Frontale
Browband: part of bridle, which passes in front of the horse's ears across the brow.

Fumento
A vaporising medication that is inhaled by the horse to cure chills and colds.

Fuoco/foco, 'dare il fuoco alle gambe'
To fire a horse's legs: red hot irons are inserted into the horse's leg either to strengthen the tendons, or to prevent lameness by blocking the nerves (*snervare*). In a mild form it could also mean blistering.

G

Galanga
Galangal: from the Arabic *Khalanjan*, a perversion of Chinese meaning mild ginger. The Arabs used this as a stimulant to make horses fiery. From China and Java.

Galbano
Galbanum the gum from *ferula galbaniflua*. Used as a stimulant, antispasmodic, for relieving air passages and in dressings for inflammation. From the Levant and Persia.

Galoppo gagliardo
Lit. Galliard gallop/lively gallop: a *maneggio* movement when the horse kicks out regularly between a specific number of galloping paces.

Galle
Galls: sores caused by the friction and chafing of the harness or tack.

Galluppo
A mounted servant, usually of low status.

Gandioni
Glanders: a highly dangerous and contagious disease, causing a thick nasal discharge, ulcers in the nostrils and swollen glands in the neck.

Garofano
The pink, from the carnation family used in equine medication.

Garrese
The withers: raised part of spine at the base of the neck. The saddle sits immediately behind the withers. It is from the ground to the highest point of the withers that the horse's height is measured. See also *guidalescho*.

Garretto
The hock – the joint in the back leg. It contains 6 bones and its formation can indicate the quality and durability of a horse.

Garofalo
A clove or 'gillyflowre' (Florio): the dried flower bud of the clove tree, *caryophyllus aromatica*. Sometimes used as a painkiller.

Garze
A disease in the horse's mouth.

Gaza
Adj. *Gazza* = magpie: *la coda gaza* may indicate a tail with black and white hair.

Gazzo
'Wall-eyed': a pale china-coloured eye. It is not a sign of blindness.

Giavazzo
Adj. describing the shiny black coat of a horse.

Gineta/zanetta/jinetta
Jennet: the Spanish breed of horse used for light armour but especially valued for its skills in *maneggio*. The word *gineta* comes from the zanete tribe of the Mahgreb lancers, light horsemen. In England the word also referred to the mounted Spanish men-at-arms after the *gineta* style of riding with shortened stirrups.

Alla gineta
This riding style and its saddle were brought to the Iberian peninsular by the Arabs of north Africa. The horseman's weight is totally supported by the saddle and not by the stirrups.

Girello/zirello
Girth: the leather or fabric belt securing the saddle to the horse.

Giumenta/iumenta/ jumenta
Mare: mature female horse.

Giumente molari
Lit. 'mule-mares': mares used for cross-breeding with donkey stallions to produce mule foals.

Giumento
Riding horse.

Giusquiamo see *Iusquiamu*

Glomo
Bulb: the fleshy part at the heel of the horse's foot.

Goza/gozzo
A swelling of the thyroid gland.

Gramegna/gramigna
Wild natural pasture, named for the wild dog-tooth violet (*gramigna*) growing there.

Groppa
The croup: the part of the horse's back between the top of the loins and the top of the tail.

Gucta/gutta
Laminitis: also known as equine gout or founder. Often the result

of too much rich clover or grain, which causes fluid to build up in the soft tissue of the foot and results in lameness.

Guaragno
A vulgar Milanese word for a stallion. From 'cavallo guadagno' signifying a stallion that will make money for its owner by serving other owner's mares (*guadagno* = an economic profit). F. Cherubino, *Vocabulario milanese-italiano* 2 vols (1839), I, p. 262.

Guernimenti
Harness.

Guidalescho
The withers: the ridge of bone at the top of the shoulders behind where the neck meets the back. It is from the top of the withers to the ground that the horse's height is measured. See also *garrese*.

Guizzare degli orecchi
To twitch the ears. An indication that a horse is attentive and listening.

H

Herbetta
Short, new sprouting grass.

I

Imboccatura
The bit or mouthpiece of a bridle.

Impastoiare
To hobble or fetter the feet of an animal, tying either the two front, two back or two side feet loosely together so the animal is restricted in its movement.

Impennarsi
To rear up so that the horse is standing on its hind legs.

Inchiavature
Infection in the horse's foot, caused by incorrect placing of the horse shoe nails.

Infrenare
To break in and school a horse to the bit (*freno*).

Incrocio
A cross bred horse, i.e. a mixture of breeds.

Insogna/sogna
Lard used for rubbing into galls/sores caused by harnessing or girths. Also used as a base for poultices and ointments.

Iusquiamu
Hyoscymus/black henbane or 'stinking nightshade': a poisonous plant used in Rusio's horse anaesthetic. In the 1st century, Dioscorides used henbane to procure sleep and allay pain.

L

Lasagne
Cito mentions this as *pasta* to feed horses.

Leardo/liardo
Grey horse or, according to Florio, *liardo* is grey flecked with red making a roan colour and, in England, the work 'liard' was used for a roan horse.

Leardo argento
White horse, the coat flecked with silver.

Leardo moschato
White flecked with black – known as 'flea-bitten grey'.

Leardo pomellato/pomato/rotato
Dapple grey horse.

Levada
One of the more difficult *maneggio* movements, known as 'Airs above the Ground'. In the *levada*, the horse lifts his front legs off the ground, lowering his hind quarters so that he stands at a 30° angle to the ground. He holds the position for as long as possible.

Limarelli
Wooden planks covering the manger, making a 'table-top' cover.

Linusa
Linseed, used as a mild laxative and for its soothing effects.

Liscia
Buck-lye (Florio).

Lisoia
Probably *lisolo*: creosote, a dark syrupy liquid containing creosol – distilled wood tar - which was used as an antiseptic.

Lovato/a
Adjective indicating that a horse has hairy feet (Nosari & Canova).

Lupara/Lupaia
A wolf trap for which a deep hole is dug into the ground, lined with wood and covered with a net. It is then baited with meat or a live animal to attract the wolves. In the Neapolitan kingdom, the Marcianise stud farm used a fat sow ('una porcastra grossa') as bait.[1] Naples, ASNa, Sommaria, Dipendenze, I, 36, fasc. 2, 28r. See Gennari, *Struttura* (2006), p. 48.

Lupini
A type of pulse called 'lupines' or 'fig-beans'. Highly nutritious for horses, anti-worms and good externally in an ointment for ulcers.

M

Maestro di stalla
The stable manager or stable master responsible for the day-to-day running of the stables and the stable staff.

Man della briglia
The 'near fore' or front left leg. Named for the hand in which the rider held the bridle.

Man della staffa
The 'near fore' or front left leg, named for the stirrup by which the rider mounts the horse.

Man lancia
The 'off fore' or front right leg, named for the side the lance was carried.

Mandragora
Mandrake: used in making an anaesthetic for horses. Already used in Pliny's day, where human patients were given a root to chew before an operation. It grows in the Levant and southern Europe.

Mandria
Herd of horses or cattle.

Maneggiare
To handle, train and show off a horse's paces and movements in *maneggio*.

Maneggio di volta d'anche
Maneggio movements used over jumps for the purpose of combat. See Caracciolo, *La gloria* (1589), summary of Book V.

Mangiatoia/mangiatore/magnatora
Manger: a feeding trough usually fitted to the wall of the stable. Made of stone or wood and sometimes having a hinged wooden tabletop.

Maniscalco/marescalco
Farrier-surgeon responsible for the health and shoeing of the horses.

Mano
A horse's foreleg (*Piè/Piede* is a rear leg).

Marchiare
To brand or mark with hot irons.

Marchi/merchi/mierchi
Brand marks, which signified the breeder or owner of a horse and could also indicate the horse's breed or quality within a breed.

Marescalco
The hammer used by the *maniscalco/ marescalco* to drive nails into the horse shoes.

Margonara
The Gonzaga horse breed, bred at Governolo.

Maristalla/marestalla
The origin of the word *stalla*/stable, according to Caracciolo.

Mascalcia
The trade of the *maniscalco/marescalco*.

Mascarizo
Leather cured with allum to make it more supple (from the Milanese *mascaria*). Used for belts and straps.

Masseria
A fortified farm in southern Italy – sometimes a stud farm as for the Venetian Republic near Alberobello, Puglia.

Mellone
The rowls on a horse's bit.

Menare
To thresh: to extract the corn after harvesting by beating it.

Menare cani
Whippers-in: the professional huntsmen who control the hounds when hunting, by voice, horn and whip (Lit. to whip dogs).

Meta
Stook: a cone shaped structure made of wooden poles, used for drying grass or harvested sheaves of corn, which are placed against it so that water runs off.

Mezzo sangue
Half-blood horse, ie. half thoroughbred.

Moraglie/muraglia
A 'Twitch': a pinching device or loop of cord at the end of a stick, which is used for twisting round the upper lip of fidgety or vicious horses, to quieten them when handled.

Morsaio
Bit maker.

Morso
A bit: the metal or wooden mouthpiece of the horse's bridle.

Mosarola see *Museruola*

Mozzo/mozzo/muczo di stalla
Stable boy.

Mulattiere/molictere/molicterio
A man in charge of the mules.

Mumia
Pulverised mummy (a mummified body), which was used in healing ointment. See Giovan Battista Ferraro, *Delle razze* (1560), p. 97.

Murghese/Murgese
A breed of black horse taking its name from Murge, Apulia. It was developed from Barbs and Arabian cross bred with Andalusians.

Muraglia
The hoof wall: the exterior hard surface of the hoof.

Museruola/musarola
Muzzle or noseband.

Muzone
The horse's snout/muzzle – the end of the nose.

N

Nare/nasche/narice
Nostrils.

Nastri
Dividers between the horse stalls (Lit. cartilage which separates the nostrils).

Nerviti
Sinews or nerves.

Nodello
Fetlock: the joint protruding above the hoof, connecting the cannon bone to the pastern.

Non domato
An unbroken horse, ie. not schooled.

Nubini/e
Nubian horses bred by the Este at Belfiore. In 1504 Nubia became part of Egypt.

O

Olivirare
To rub oil into the harnessing in order to soften the leather.

Orzo
Barley: a major part of the horses' diet.

P

Paglia
Straw: the stalks of any cereal, used not only for bedding but as fodder. Also used for filling mattresses for the stable staff.

Palafreno
Palfrey: a horse suitable for travelling as it has an easy relaxed walk.

Paleta/paletta
Cantle: the highest part of the back of the saddle.

Pastoia/pastorale
Pastern bone: part of the leg between the hoof and the fetlock.

Pennacchio/piumaggio
Plume of feathers sometimes worn on the horse's head, either for decoration or for identification in a race.

Peperino/peperigno
A green/brown volcanic rock, formed of small grains of sand. It has minute pepper-like black spots, from the cinders, giving it its name. A typical *peperino* is found in the Alban Hills near Rome. Unlike another volcanic rock, *tufo*, *peperino* can be cut and polished to create decorative effects. It was widely used in small blocks. Used at Caprarola and at the Chigi stables in Rome.

Pesate
Pesade: One of the *maneggio* movements known as 'Airs above the Ground'. In the pesade the horse lifts his front legs up and lowers his hindquarters. It is much like the *levada*, but the horse lifts his fore legs higher off the ground. See Corte, *Il cavallarizzo* (1562), II, ch. 15, 70v.

Pezzato/piezzato
Piebald or 'painted horse' in which the coat is of more than one colour.

Piaffe
Piaffe: a *maneggio* movement when the horse arches his back and raises his diagonally opposed feet at an even space, as though he is trotting on the spot.

Piccolo pastorale
The small pastern: the area between the hoof and the fetlock.

Pictima/pittima
Poultice: used for reducing swelling or for helping wounds heal, depending on the formula.

Piede/piè
Horse's back leg (*mano/man* – foreleg).

Piè della staffa
The horse's 'near-hind' or rear left leg. Named for the left hand stirrup by which the rider mounts the horse.

Piè stancho/stanco
Horse's left hind foot.

Pila di abbeveramento
Drinking trough.

Pili
Hair as in *capelli*.

Platone
Young foal ('puledro giovane di primo pelo', Battaglia).

Poledro/pollistro/puledretto and Poledra/pollistra/puledretta
Colt: Young male horse and Filly: young maiden mare.

Polezivo/polsivo/pulcino
Adj. describing a horse that is broken-winded: a quality making it unfit and useless. Also *bolso/bolsaggine*. See Porsia, *I cavalli* (1986), Appendix B, p. 135.

Pomellato
Adj. describing the dappled effect of the horse's coat.

Portanta
A pregnant mare.

Purosangue
Purebred, thoroughbred: a horse whose sire and dam are from the same breed.

Q

Quartierino
The skirt of a saddle: the loose flap of leather in front of the seat and under the rider's legs, beneath which the girths are fixed.

R

Raddoppare
Lit. to redouble: a trick or double turn in *maneggio*.

Ragazzo/ragazzino
A jockey, a boy of 12-15 years old.

Rapicano
White rump or tail on the horse.

Rastrelliera
Hayrack: made of wood, the rack was placed above the manger.

Recalcitrare
To buck: the horse jumps so that its hind quarters are higher than the fore, usually trying to throw the rider off its back.

Redini/redeni/retene
The reins: made of leather or silk, the reins connect the rider's hands to the bit, thus giving his commands to the horse.

Remula/remola
Bran, usually made from the outer layer of wheat grain. Although not nutritious it bulks out other food and stops the horse bolting his food. A bran mash serves as a gentle laxative or to encourage a sick or exhausted horse to eat.

Repolone
From the Spanish *repelón* or short gallop. A *maneggio* movement now called the *passade* from its French translation. After a short gallop, the horse is taught to stop abruptly and then turn quickly on its hind quarters, to face the opposite direction. Used in battle when turning to face the enemy. Caracciolo, *La gloria* (1589), V, pp. 430-1.

Rezentino
Silver colour of a horse's coat. Malacarne, *Il mito* (1995), p. 61.

Rimessa/e
Outhouse/s.

Roano/rouano
Roan horse: the coat is a solid colour, such as chestnut or black flecked evenly with the same amount of white. Originally from Spanish *rojo*.

Rogna
Mange or scabies: a contagious skin disease caused by insects attracted by dirt, which burrow under the horse's skin.

Ronzino/roncino
A large service horse suitable for transport.

Rozzo
A nag or ruined horse.

Roxada de grana
Red dye of dried cochineal beetle, giving a carmine colour.

S

Salimastro/salmastro
Adj. describing salty or brackish water.

Sandaraca
Sandarac: a gum resin from a small cypress-like tree (*tetraclinis articulata*), native to north-west Africa, particularly the Atlas

Mountains. Used with *artimesia* for rubbing into a racehorse's back in preparation for a race. See Corte, *Il cavalerizzo* (1573), II, ch. 52, 117v. Used also as a varnish for paintings and as an incense for burning.

Sasinato/saginato
Roan horse: the coat is of white and chestnut hair, usually with black legs mane and tail.

Sasinato rosso
Roan, but chestnut hair predominant.

Sassonato
A horse from Saxony, usually a warhorse.

Sauro
Sorrel coloured horse, a pale bright chestnut, mane and tail the same colour.

Scalcheria
Blacksmith's shop, also a forge or 'smithy'.

Scalfato/scarfato
Adj. describing a horse as heated or excitable.

Scamonea
Scammony or 'Syrian bindweed': used as a purgative. Known to Greek and Arab physicians. Probably from Smyrna or Aleppo, although can be grown on any very dry soil.

Scarafaggio/Scarafoni/scarasoni
Scarabfly or hornet (Florio).

Schinancia/cincancia
Cough caused by a swelling in the throat that can lead to suffocation.

Scrova
Broom for cleaning the stable

Scrinato
Adj. 'Hog-maned': meaning without a mane because it has been cut.

Scrufole/scrufola
Swollen lymphatic neck glands.

Scuderia
A stable or the collection of horses within it.

Scugliare/scuoiare
To flay or skin an animal. Skins were sometimes sent to owners as proof of a horse's death, showing that they had not been sold or stolen.

Secchio
Bucket.

Segala
Rye. Used as fodder.

Sego
See *sevo*

Sella
Saddle: made of leather and often elaborately decorated with precious metals, or stud work and sometimes covered in expensive fabrics. Many different saddle styles are recorded in the Renaissance.

Sellaio/sellaro
Saddler. Saddlers often had their own businesses making and repairing harness, saddles and bridles. However, the large court stables employed their own in-house saddler. Most saddles were made for, and fitted to, individual horses.

Selvadeghi
Foals, the same as *poledri*.

Semi di lino
Linseed: used for many purposes after it is softened by soaking in water for 24 hours. Used as laxative, also works on the kidneys. Linseed meal can be used in poultices. Linseed 'tea' (mixed and cooked in water) benefits sick horses.

Serbatoio
Water cistern.

Setola
A sand crack: fissure in the hoof wall.

Sevo/sivo/sego
Tallow: animal fat used for candles and soap.

Sfioratore
Spillway. Part of a drainage system.

Snervare
Lit. 'de-nerve': to block the nerves in a horse's feet or legs. See *Fuoco*.

Soda/la carne soda
Firm flesh (of a horse) from *sodo*: tough, strong, stiff.

Sopracapo
The headpiece of a bridle.

Sorcino
Adj. lead coloured horse with black mane and tail. From *sorcio*: mouse.

Spaga/spaghe
A kind of resin or pitch from Asia (Florio).

Spalle
Shoulders.

Spavano
Spavin/bone spavin: an enlargement of the inner and lower part of the hock. It can be caused by hard work or concussion, which results in inflammation and lameness.

Spelda
Spelt: a kind of wheat used in fodder.

Spicanardi
Spikenard: good for wounds. Taken for bruising, pains and ruptures. The juice can be used to cure itching and the smell was said to repel and kill insects. Also known as 'Great Fleabane'. Grows on chalky soil and limestone.

Spiritale/i
The 'vital' or breathings parts, or pertaining to them. From the Latin *spiritalis* (Florio).

Sponghe
Sponges: used for cleaning the horses and wiping them down.

Sprone/i
Spurs: Made of different, sometimes, precious metals, there are several different designs. They are used to urge the horse forward by touching the horse's flank with pricking. Incorrect and harsh use can puncture the horse's skin and cause it to bleed and leave scarring.

Stabbie
Manure.

Staccato/steccato
A hurdle or fence, either to be jumped by horses or as a barrier separating livestock.

Stacca/stacche
Fillies: young maiden mares.

Staffa/Staffa da giostra
Stirrup/Stirrup for jousting.

Staffiere/stafero
Stirrup footman, whose primary duty is to help his master mount and dismount as well as walk alongside the horse as he rode. Sometimes a privileged appointment.

Staffile
Stirrup leather: a leather strap, which attaches the stirrup to the saddle. Sometimes made of silk. Also a thin whip.

Stallatico
Manure. Also the name of a tax.

Stallaggio
The livery or stabling charge.

Stallare
To stable a horse but it also means to stale or urinate.

Stallone
Stallion: a male horse. The name *stallone* is sometimes given to a stable as in the Stallone del Papa in Viterbo or the Farnese stables at Caprarola.

Stancho
The left hand/near side of the horse. For example, *piè stancho* is the left foot.

Stanche/stancie
The stall in which the horse is contained in the stable. *Stalla* and *stavolo* can also mean stall.

Stanghetto/i
Wooden bars often used to separate the stalls in a stable.

Stavolo
A horse's stall in the stable.

Stinco
The cannon bone: the large bone which lies between the knee and the fetlock in the foreleg and between the hock and the fetlock in the rear leg.

Stipia
Stubble or chaff: finely chopped hay or straw given as bulk in fodder (Florio).

Stornello/storno
A black horse with flecks of white in the coat.

Storta
A sprain.

Strame
Straw: the dried stalks of a cereal crop such as wheat, barley or oats. *Strame* can also mean the horse's 'bedding'.

Stramente
Straw put into pallets or mattresses.

Stranguglioni
'Strangles': a highly infectious equine disease, which can be fatal, due to a swelling in the throat, which prevents ingestion.

Streggia
Curry comb: usually metal, the currycomb has several parallel rows of shallow teeth for grooming the horse. Useful for removing surface dirt and mud.

Streggiare
To groom with a curry comb.

Streglie
Combs.

Strenghette
Part of the bit.

Strigliare
To comb the horse.

Strofinare
To rub the horse with bunches of hay or straw.

Stuchye/stocco
Stook: a conical shape made of wooden poles over which hay or straw is put to dry in the open air.

Stroppicciare
To scour or scrub.

Sumacco
Sumach: a black dye.

Supraposta/sovraposta
Overreach: the hind foot over-extends striking the back of the fore-leg or front foot and causing injury.

Supracigni/sopracinghia
An extra girth, which goes over the saddle in order to fasten the horse's caparison and stop it slipping to one side. The saddle girth would be underneath the caparison.

T

Tafani
Horseflies.

Talpa/topa
Mole: the animal is used in several 'cosmetic' recipes for changing the colour of the horse's hair.

Tavola/ Tavolato
A wooden plank: used as a division between horses in the stable and hung from either chains or leather straps at either end of each stall.

Terra a terra
A *maneggio* movement, a short intense gallop, with the 'croup in' but which is 2 time and not 4 time like the gallop.

Terriaca/tirriaca/tirriaco
A treacle used against poison. Also a grape from which a wine is made, which cures venomous snake bites (Florio).

Testiera
Browband: part of the bridle which passes across the horse's brow, in front of the ears.

Tirella/e
Traces: part of a harness, which connects the horse's collar to the cart or carriage it is pulling and is attached to the wooden shafts.

Tirelle di corda
Rope traces.

Tiro
A drench or draught: any liquid equine medicine, usually administered through an animal horn.

Torbido
Adj. cloudy or muddy as in *acqua torbida* – cloudy water.

Trabocchetto
Trap door or hatch.

Trastravato
A horse with white markings on diagonally opposed legs. According to Caracciolo, 1589, IV, pp. 297-8, this indicated that the horse had tangled up his legs whilst in his dam's womb and was, therefore, liable to stumble or fall.

Travato
A horse with two white legs on the same side. According to Caracciolo, 1589, IV, p. 297, this was a bad sign, especially if on the right side.

Trementina/tirmintina
Turpentine used in medical recipes.

Trinacri
Adj. describing horses from Sicily. From *Trinacria* – the earlier name for Sicily, as used by Dante in *The Divine Comedy*.

Tufo/tofo/tuffo
Tufo: a grey/yellow porous rock of volcanic origin and usually cut into large blocks. Used at Caprarola.

Turco/turcho
Turkish breed of horse, partly from Arabian stock, used for light cavalry and racing.

U

Ubino/i
Hobby. Small Irish and English bred horses, known for their speed over short distances. Henry VIII gave these horses to the Gonzaga. The hobby is the ancestor of the Irish Connemara horse.

Ungaro
Adj. describing a Hungarian horse.

Untare/ungere
To annoint: to rub oil or ointment into the hoof, legs or body of the horse.

V

Verga
Rod, stick or whip.

Villano
A country horse used for service. See Cavriani, *Le razze* (1974), p. 16.

Viuoli/vivuli/vivuoli
A swelling of the glands which are between the neck and the head, preventing the horse from swallowing or eating. Probably tetanus. See Lorenzo Rusio, *La mascalcia*, ch. LXII.

Volte a botte
Barrel vaulting.

Volto/voltoio
The mobile part of the bit.

X

Xiloaloes see anabola
The Greek for *anabola* the wood of aloes.

Z

Zemina
A type of damascened work, using gold wire. Used on swords, stirrups and armour.

Zipadura/e
A long sewing stitch that goes through two or more layers of fabric or leather.

Zirello/girello
Girth: the belt securing the saddle to the horse

Zoccolo
The horse's hoof.

Zoppicare
To limp.

Bibliography

Manuscripts

Florence, ASF, AMe, 216, doc. 1187

Madrid, Archivio del Palacio Real, Sección Administración, "Instrucciones de la Caballeriza de Córdoba", "Dehesas arrendada" and "Instrucciónes al Gobernador de la raza"

Madrid, Bib. Nacional, MS 2790, Zapata de Chaves, "Miscellánea, ó varia historia"

Mantua, ASMa, AG, b. 2491

Milan, ASMi, Biblioteca Trivulziana, MS 2162, Leonardo da Vinci, Codex 2162

Modena, Bib. Est., LAT. 309, Alpha W.4.4, Francesco Ariosto, 1 November 1477, 'Origine e sito del novo saccello dedicando ad honore e per reverentia de la gloriosissima vergene Madre de Jesu Cristo Salvadore nostro intro el magno e magnifico palazo Ducale de ferrara… etc'

Naples, ASN, Carte Farnesiane, b. 1358.1

Naples, ASN, Sommaria, Dipendenze

Paris, Bibliothèque Nationale de France, MS Portuguese 5, 99-128, Dom Duarte, "Livro da ensinança de bem cavalgar toda sela", *c*.1438

Paris, Bibliothèque National de France, MS It. 1711, Giuiano Maio, "La opera de maiesta composta da Iuniano Maio, cavaliero nepolitano", Naples, 1492

Paris, Institut de France, MS B, Leonardo da Vinci

Rome, ASR, Camerale III, 518, 'Libro delle misure della fabbrica del Palazzo del Illustrissimo e Reverendissimo Farnese a Caprarola', 17th *misura*

Simancas (Valladolid), Archivio General de Simancas, 'Sitios reales', 'Sección de Estato', 'Contaduria'

Vatican City, Biblioteca Apostolica Vaticana, MS Chigi, a.I.1, "Chigiae familiae commentarii"

Zanino de Ottolengo, "Trattato", transcribed by G. Carra and C. Golinelli, *Sulle le infirmità dei cavalli: dal codice di Zanino de Ottolengo (sec. XV)* (Mantua, 1991)

Primary Printed Sources

Aelian (Claudius Aelianus), *c*.170-*c*.235, *De natura animalium*, trans. A. F, Schofield, *Aelian on the Characteristics of Animals*, 3 vols (Cambridge, MA and London, 1958-9)

Leon Battista Alberti, *De equo animante* (*c*.1445), trans. and ed. J-Y. Boriaud as *Le Cheval Vivant* (Paris, 1999), trans. to English by the author

_____, *De equo animante* (*c*. 1445), trans. and ed. Antonio Videtta as *Il cavallo vivo* (Naples, 1991)

_____ *I libri della famiglia* (1440s), trans. R. N. Watkins as *The Family in Renaissance Florence* (Columbia, SC, 1969)

_____ *De re aedificatoria*, trans. J. Rykwert, N. Leach and R. Tavernor as *On the Art of Building in Ten Books* (Cambridge, MA and London, 1988)

Albertus Magnus, *On Animals. A Medieval summa zoologica*, trans. K. F. Kitchell and I. M. Resnick (Baltimore, 1999)

Aristotle, *Nichomachean Ethics* 10 books (350 BC), trans. D. Ross, notes by L. Brown (Oxford, 2009)

Antonio di Pietro Averlino, *Libro architettonico*, 25 vols, *c*.1464. See Filarete

Athenaeus of Naucratis, *The Deipnosophists* (3rd century), trans. C. B. Gulick, 7 vols (London and New York, 1933)

Bernardino Baldi, 'Descrizione del Palazzo ducale d'Urbino di Bernardino Baldi da Urbino Abbate di Guastalla' (1586-7) in *Descrittione del Palazzo ducale d'Urbino*, ed. A Siekiera, *Studi e ricerche*, 87 (Alessandria, Italy, 2010)

Thomas Bedingfield, *The Art of riding, conteining diverse necessarie instructions, demonstrations, helps and corrections apperteining to horssemanship, not heretofore expressed by anie other Author: Written at large in the Italian toong, by Maister Claudio Corte, a man most excellent in this Art* (London, 1584)

The Bible, King James' edition

Thomas Blundeville, *The Arte of Ryding and Breakinge Greate Horses* (London, 1560)

_____, *The fower chiefyst offices belonging to horsemanshippe* (London, 1565)

Francesco Bocchi and Giovanni Cinelli, *Le bellezze della città di Firenze dove a pieno di pittura, di scultura, di sacri templi, di palazzi, i più notabili artifizj, e più preziosi si contengono* (Florence, 1677)

Ugo Caleffini, 'Cronica della ill.ma et ex.ma Casa d'Este', in ed., A. Cappelli, *Atti e memorie della Reale Deputazione di storia patria per le province modenesi e parmensi*, II (1864), pp. 267-312

_____, 'Croniche di Ferrara 1471-1494', in *Deputazione provinciale ferrarese di storia patria* (2006)

Calendar of State Papers Relating to English Affairs in the Archives of Venice, Volume 2:1509-19, ed. Rawdon Brown (1867), 'Venice, June, 1514'

Pasqual Caracciolo, *La gloria del cavallo. Opera del l'illustre signor Pasqual Caracciolo. Divisa in dieci libri. Ne' quali si descrivono gli ordini appartenenti alla Cavalleria, & a far un eccellente Cavaliero, insieme con tutti i particolari, che son necessari nell'allevare, custodire, maneggiare, e curar Cavalli sì in pace e viaggio, come in Guerra, & alla Campagna; accommodandovi essempi tratti dall' Historie Antiche, & Moderne* (Venice, 1589)

Baldassare Castiglione, *Il libro del cortegiano* (1528), ed. V. Cian (Florence, 1947)

William Cavendish, *A New Method and Extraordinary Invention to Dress Horses, and Work Them According to Nature: Which was never found Out, But by the Thrice Noble, High and Puissant Prince, William Cavendish, Duke of Newcastle* (London, 1667)

Charles IX of France, *La Chasse Royale* (1625)

Giovanni Antonio Cito, *Del conoscere le infirmità che avvengono al cavallo et al bue, co' rimedij à ciascheduna di esse di Gio. Antonio Cito napolitano, libri tre, aggiunti alla gloria del cavallo* (Venice, 1589)

Gaspare Codibò, *Diario bolognese dal 1471 al 1504, con note e cronotassi dei priori e cappellani di Santa Maria Maddalena in Bologna*, ed. A. Macchiavelli (Bologna, 1915)

Lucius Junius Moderatus Columella (Columella), *On Agriculture*, Books 1-4, trans. H. B. Ashe (Cambridge, MA and London, 1941-55)
_____, *On Agriculture*, Books 5 – 9, trans. E. S. Forster and E. H. Hefner (Cambridge, MA, 1968)

Philippe de Commynes, *Mémoires de Philippe de Commynes*, 2 vols, ed. B. E. Mandrot (Paris, 1903)

Bernardino Corio (1459-1519?), *Storia di Milano*, ed. A. M. Guerra, 2 vols (Turin, 1978)

Claudio Corte, *Il cavallarizzo di M. Claudio Corte di Pavia. Nel quale si tratta della natura de' cavalli, del modo di domarli, e frenarli, e di tutto quello, che a' cavalli, e a' buon cavallarizzo s'appartiene* (Venice, 1562)

_____, *Il cavalerizzo di Messer Claudio Corte di Pavia. Nel quale si tratta della natura de' cavalli del modo di domargli, & frenargli e di tutto quello che à cavalli, & à buon cavalerizzo s'appartiene* (Lyons, 1573)

Isabella Cortese, *I secreti della Signora Isabella Cortese. Ne quali si contengono cose minerali, medicali, arteficiose, & alchemiche. Et molte de 'arte profumatoria, appartenenti a ogni gran Signora* (Venice, 1561)

Paolo Cortese, *De cardinalatu, libri tres* (Rome, 1510)

Dom Duarte, *The Royal Book of Horsemanship, Jousting and Knightly Combat. A translation into english of Dom Duarte's 1438 Treatise 'Livro da ensinança de bem cavalgar toda sela' (The art of riding on every saddle)*, trans. A. F. Preto, (Highland Village, TX, 2005)

Desiderius Erasmus, *The Education of a Christian Prince* (1516), trans. N. M. Cheshire and M. J. Heath (Cambridge, 2002)

Erasmus of Valvasone, *La caccia poema di Erasmo di Valvasone* (Milan, 1808)

G. Ermini ed., *Ordini et officij alla corte del serenissimo signor Duca di Urbino dal codici manoscritto della Biblioteca Vaticana N. 1248* (Regia Accademia "Raffaello", Urbino, 1932)

Giovan Battista Ferraro, *Delle razze, disciplina del cavalcare, et altre cose pertinenti ad essercito cosi fatto* (Naples, 1560), printed as the first part of P. A. Ferraro, *Cavallo frenato* (Naples, 1602)

Pirro Antonio Ferraro, *Cavallo frenato di Pirro Antonio Ferraro Napolitano, Cavallerizzo della Maestà Cattolica di Filippo Il Re di Spagna N.S. nella real cavallerizzo di Napoli. Diviso in quattro libri. Con discorsi notabili, sopra briglie, antiche,& moderne nel Primo; nel Secondo molte altre da lui inventate; nel Terzo un Dialogo trà Autore, & Illustriss. Sig. Don Diego di Cordova, Cavallarizzo Maggior di Sua Maestà; Con un Discorse particulare sopra alcune Briglie Ginette. Et el quarto un'altro Dialogo tra l'Autore, e l'Illustriss. Sig. marchese di Sant'eramo, Luocotenente del Cavallerizzo maggiore in questo Regno, & alcuni disegni di Briglie, Polache e Turchesche. Et à questi quattro libri suoi, precede l'opera di Gio. Battista Ferraro suo padre, Divisa in altri Quattro Libri, ridotta dall'Autore in quella forma, & intelligenza, che da lui si desiderava à tempo si stampò, dove si tratta il modo di conservar le razze, disciplinar cavalli, & il modo di curargli; vi sono anco aggiunte le figure delle loro anotomie & un numero d'infiniti Cavalli fatti, & ammaestrati sotto la sua disciplina con l'obligo del mastro di stalla* (Naples, 1602)

Cesare Fiaschi, *Trattato dell'imbrigliare, maneggiare, et ferrare cavalli, diviso in tre parti, con alcuni discorsi sopra la natura di Cavalli, con disegni di Briglie, Maneggi, & di Cavalieri a cavallo, & de ferri d'esso* (Bologna, 1556)

Cesare Fiaschi, *Trattato dell'imbrigliare, atteggiare, & ferrare cavalli di Cesare Fiaschi, nobile ferrarese, diviso in tre libri: ne' quali sono tutte le figure à proposito dell'briglie, de gli atteggiamenti, e de' ferri* (Venice, 1603)

Filarete, Antonio di Pietro Averlino, *Libro architettonico* (c.1464) trans. John R. Spencer, *Filarete's Treatise on Architecture*, 2 vols (New Haven and London, 1965)

J. Florio, *Queen Anna's New World of Words, or Dictionarie of the Italian and English tongues, collected, and newly much augmented by Iohn Florio, reader of the Italian unto the Soveraigne Maistie of Anna crowned Queen of England, Scotland, France and Ireland &c, And one of the Gentlemen of her Royall Privie Chamber, whereunto are added certain necessarie rules and short observations for the Italian tongue* (London, 1611)

François A. de Garsault, *Le nouveau parfait maréchal ou la connoissance général et universelle du cheval, divisé en sept traités* (La Haye, 1741; fourth edition, Paris, 1770)

Tommaso Garzoni da Bagnacavallo, *La piazza universale di tutte le professioni del mondo*, 2 vols (Venice, 1589), eds P. Cherchi and B. Collina (Turin, 1996)

Baldthazar Gerbier, *A Brief Discourse Concerning the Three Chief Principles of Magnificent Buildings* (London, 1662)

Cherubino Ghirardacci, *Historia di Bologna*, ed A. Sorbelli, part III, vol. I (Bologna, 1933)

Thomas de Grey, *The Compleat Horseman and Expert Farrier in Two Books* (London, 1639; fifth edition, 1684)

Federico Grisone, *Gli ordini di cavalcare et modi di conoscere le natura de' cavalli* (Venice, 1551)

François Robichon de la Guérinière, *L'École de Cavalerie* (Paris, 1733)

Stefano Infessura, *Diario della città di Roma*, ed. O. Tommasini (Rome, 1890)

Giovanni Filippo Ingrassia, *Quod veterinaria medicina formaliter una eademque cum nobiliore hominis medicina sit. Materiae duntaxat nobilitate differense* (Venice, 1564)

Johannes de Ketham, *Fasciculo de medecina* (Venice, 1494)

The Koran, trans. N. J. Dawood (London, 2006)

Hans Kreutsberger, *Eygentliche/Wolgerissene Contrafactur und Formen de Gebiss* (Augsburg, 1562)

Letters and Papers, Foreign and Domestic, Henry VIII, Volume 3:1519-1523, ed. J. S. Brewer (1867), 'Henry VIII: April 1519'

Francesco Liberati, *La perfettione del cavallo, libri tre di Francesco Liberati romano* (Rome, 1639)

Libro de marchi de cavalli con li nomi di tutti li principi & privati signori (Venice, 1569 and 1588)

Karel van Mander, *Den gronde der edel vry schilder-const* (Haarlem, 1604)

Francesco di Giorgio Martini, *Trattati di architettura, ingegneria e arte militare* ed. C. Maltese, 2 vols (Milan, 1967)

Alessandro Massario Malatesta, *Compendio dell'heroica arte di cavalleria del Sig. Alessandro Massari Tiburtino. Precetti Quattro* (Venice, 1600)

Michel de Montaigne, *The Complete Works: essays, travel journals, letters*, trans. D. M. Frame (London, 2003)

Nicholas Morgan, *The perfection of horse-manship drawne from nature: arte and practise* (London, 1609)

Gaspare Nadi, *Diario Bolognese di G. Nadi*, eds C. Ricci, A. Bacchi della Lega (Bologna, 1886; reprint 1981)

C. Nobilonio, *Cronaca di Vigevano*, 1584, ed. R. di Marchi (Pavia, 1988)

Opera della medicina de' cavalli composta da diversi antichi scrittori, et a commne utilità di greco in buona lingua volgare ridotta (Venice, 1543)

Ordini et offitij alla corte del serenissimo duca d'Urbino: dal codice manoscritto della Biblioteca Vaticana, N. 1248, ed. G. Ermini (Urbino, 1932)

Filippo Orsoni, "Book parade armour designs" (Italy, 1554)

Zanino de Ottolengo, "Trattato", eds G. Carra and C. Golinelli, *Sulle infermità dei cavalli: dal codice di Zanino de Ottolengo (sec. XV)* (Mantua, 1991)

Rutilius Taurus Aemilianus Palladius (Palladius), *The fourteen books of Palladius Rutilius Taurus Æmilianus, On Agriculture* trans. T. Owen (London, 1807)

Cesare Paoli, L. Rubini and P. Stromboli, eds, *Della venuta in Firenze di Galeazzo Maria Sforza, Duca di Milano, con la moglie Bona di Savoia nel 1471: lettere di due senesi alla Signoria di Siena* (Florence, 1878)

Marco de Pavari, *Escuirie de M. de Pavari venetien* (Lyons, 1581), eds P. Aquint, M. Gennaro (La Venaria Reale, 2008)

Pellegrino Pellegrini see Pellegrino Tibaldi

Aeneus Sylvius Piccolomini, *The Commentaries of Pius II*, Books I-IX, trans. F.A. Gragg (Northampton, MA, 1936-7)

G.B. Pio, *Annotamenta* (Bologna, 1505)

Pliny, *Natural History* VIII-XI, trans. H Rackham (Cambridge, MA and London, 1997)

Plutarch, *Moralia*, 15 vols. Vol. 12, trans. H. Cherniss and W.C. Helmbold (London and Cambridge, MA, 1957)

Antoine de Pluvinel, *L'instruction du Roy en l'exercise de monter à cheval, par messire Antoine de Pluvinel, son Sous-Gouverneur, Conseiller en son Conseil d'Estat, Chambellar ordinaire & son Escuyer principal* (Paris, 1625)

_____, *Maneige royal où l'on peut remarquer le défaut et la perfection du chevalier en tous les exercises de cet art, digne des princes, fait pratiqué en l'instruction du Roy par Antoine Pluvinel* (Paris, 1623)

Giovanni Pontano, *De splendore* (Naples, 1498)

Giambattista della Porta, *De humana physiognomia* (Sorrento, 1586) trans. as *Giovan. Battista della Porta: della fisonomia dell'uomo* (Vico Equense, 1599), ed. M. Cicognani (Parma, 1988)

Francesco Priscianese, *Del governo della corte d'un signore in Roma* (c.1540), ed. L. Bartalucci (Città di Castello, 1883)

Filippo Rinuccini, *Ricordi storici di Filippo di Cino Rinuccini dal 1282 al 1460, colla continuazione di Alamannno e Neri, suoi figli, fina al 1506, seguiti da altri monumenti inediti di storia patria estratti dai codici originali e preceduti dalla storia genealogica della loro famiglia e della descrizione della Capella Gentilizia in S. Croce,* ed. G. Aiazzi (Florence, 1840)

Giordano Ruffo, "Liber mareschalchie equorum" (c.1282), trans. into Italian as *Libro della mascalcia,* ed. P. Crupi (Soveria Mannelli, Calabria, 2002)

Lorenzo Rusio, ed. L. Barbieri, *La mascalcia di Lorenzo Rusio volgarizzamento del secolo XIV. Messo per la prima volta in luce da Pietro Delprato aggiuntovi il testo Latino* (Bologna, 1867)

Carlo Ruini, *Anatomia del cavallo, infirmità et suoi remedij. Opera nuova, degna di qualsivoglia principe, & cavaliere, & molto necessaria à filosofi, medici, cavallerizzi, & marescalchi. Del signor Carlo Ruini, senator bolognese* (Venice, 1618)

Marin Sanudo il Giovane, *De origine situ et magistratibus urbis Venetae, ovvero, La Città di Venetia (1493-1530),* ed. Angelo Caracciolo Aricò (Milan, 1980) pp. 21-2

Filippo Scaccho da Tagliacozzo, *Opera di mescalzia* (Rome, 1591) reprinted as *Trattato di mescalzia di M. Filippo Scacco da Tagliacozzo. Diviso in quattro libri: Ne' quali si contengono tutte le infermità de' cavalli così interiori come esteriori, & li segni da conoscerle, & le cure con potioni, e untioni & sanguigne per esso cavalli* etc. (Padua, 1628)

Vincenzo Scamozzi, *L'idea della architettura universale* (Venice, 1615)

Sebastiano Serlio, *Tutte l'opere d'architettura et prospettiva*, 7 books (1537-75)

Ottaviano Siliceo, *Scuola de' cavalieri di Ottaviano Siliceo, gentilhuomo troiano, nella quale principalmente si discorre delle maniere, & qualità de' cavalli, in che modo si debbono disciplinare, & conservare, & anco di migliorar le razze* (Orvieto, 1598)

J.R. Spencer, trans. and ed., *Filarete's Treatise on Architecture*, 2 vols (New Haven and London, 1965)

Jan van der Straet (Stradanus), *Equile Ioannis Austriaci Caroli V. imp. F. in quo omnis generis equorum ex varijs orbis partibus insignis delectus; ad vivum omnes delineati a J. Stradano, et a P. Galleo editi* (Antwerp, c.1578-80)

Suetonius, *The Twelve Caesars,* trans. Robert Graves (London, 2007)

Torquato Tasso, *Il padre di famiglia* (Venice, 1583)

Pellegrino Tibaldi (Pellegrino Pellegrini), "L'architettura" in G. Panizza ed., *L'architettura/ Pellegrino Pellegrini: edizione critica a cura di Giorgio Panizza; introduzione e note di Adele Buratti Mazzotta* (Milan, 1990)

Varro, *On Agriculture,* trans. W.D. Hooper and H.B. Ash (Cambridge, MA and London, 2006)

Giorgio Vasari, eds. R. Bettarini, P Barocchi, *Vite de' più eccellenti pittori, scultore e architettori nelle redazione del 1550 e 1568*, 11 vols (Florence, 1966)

Cesare Vecellio, *De gli habiti antichi, et moderni di diverse parti del mondo, libri due* (Venice, 1590)

Vegetius (Publius Vegetius Renatus), trans. Anon., *Vegetis Renatus of the distempers of horses, and of the art of curing them: as also of the diseases of oxen, and the remedies proper for them; and of the best method to preserve them in health* (London 1748)

Andreas Vesalius, *De fabrica corporis humani* (Basle, 1543)

De Villamont, *Les voyages du Seigneur de Villamont, Chevalier de l'ordre de Hierusalem, Gentilhomme du pays de Bretaigne, divisez en trois livres* (Paris, 1595)

Various authors, *Sermoni funebri de vari authori nella morte de diversi animali* (Venice, 1548)

Virgil, *Georgics III, Eclogues, Georgics, Aeneid I-VI*, trans. H.R. Fairclough (Cambridge MA & London, 1999)

Vitruvius Pollio, *De architectura* trans. W. Newton, The *Architecture of M. Vitruvius Pollio*, 2 vols (London, 1791)

Xenophon, *On the Art of Horsemanship* in *Scripta Minora*, trans. E.C. Marchant (London and Cambridge, MA, 1962), pp. 295-363

Xenophon, *Memorabilia and Oeconomicus*, trans. E.C. Marchant (London and New York, 1923)

Secondary Sources

J. Adamson, ed., *The Princely Courts of Europe: Ritual, Politics and Culture under the Ancien Régime, 1500-1750* (London, 1999)

C. Ady, *The Bentivoglio of Bologna: a Study in Despotism* (London, 1973)

Richard Almond, *Medieval Hunting* (Stroud, 2003)

Juan Carlos Altamirano, *Historia y origen del caballo Español: las caballerizas reales de Córdoba (1567-1800)* (Malaga, 1998)

A. Antonelli and M. Poli, *Il Palazzo dei Bentivoglio nelle fonti del tempo* (Venice, 2006)

Arjun Appadurai, *The Social Life of Things: Commodities in cultural Perspective* (Cambridge, 1992)

M. G. Arcamone, 'Il mondo animale nell'onomastica dell'alto Medioevo', *L'uomo di fronte al mondo animale nell'alto Medioeva: 7-13 aprile 1983*, 2 vols (Spoleto, 1985)

T. Astarita, *The Continuity of Feudal Power: the Caracciolo di Brienza in Spanish Naples* (Cambridge, 1992)

J.M. Barbeito, *El Alcázar de Madrid* (Madrid, 1992)

M.A. Barone, S. Gennari, C. Giovannini, 'Rilievi e indagine storica sulla Data', in M. Bruscia, ed., *La Data (orto dell'abbondanza) di Francesco di Giorgio Martini: atti del convegno, Urbino, 26 settembre 1986* (Urbino, 1990), pp. 21-44

Ugo Bazzotti '"Un luogo e certe stalle" sull'isola del Te prima di Giulio Romano', *Civiltà Mantovana* 3:122 (2006), pp. 144-61

A. Belluzzi, *Palazzo Te a Mantova* (Modena, 1998)

A. Belluzzi and W. Capezzali, 'Le scuderie dei Gonaga sul Te', *Civiltà Mantovana*, 1.42 (1973), pp. 378-94

J. Bentini, ed., *Gli Este a Ferrara; una corte nel Rinascimento* (Milan, 2004)

Enzo Bentivoglio, 'Le scuderie di Palazzo Farnese a Caprarola. I 'remedi' proposti da Giovanni Battista Contini e Sebastiano Cipriani dopo il terremoto del 1703 (dai MSS 34 K13 e 34 K14 della Biblioteca Corsiniana di Roma)', *Quaderni del Dipartimento Patrimonio Architettonico e Urbanistico* (Anno XIV), 27-28, pp. 181-90

G. Bertoni and E. Vicini, *Il Castello di Ferrara ai tempi di Niccolò III* (Bologna, 1907)

Umberto Bindi, *Pienza: i luoghi dell'acqua. Dalle fonti dela Pieve di Corsignano alla Bonifica della Val d'Orcia* (Montepulciano (Si), 2002)

Douglas Biow, *The Culture of Cleanliness in Renaissance Italy* (Cornell, 2006)

G. Bombi, M. Laveroni, P. Lucca eds, *La biscia e l'aquila: il Castello di Vigevano: una lettera storico-artistica* (Vigevano, 1988)

Jean-Yves Boriaud, *Le Cheval Vivant* (Paris, 1999), trans. and ed. L.B. Alberti's *De equo animante* (c.1445)

Franco Borsi, *Leon Battista Alberti: the Complete Works* (Oxford, 1977)

G. Bottari and S. Ticozzi eds, *Raccolta di lettere sulla pittura, scultura ed architettura*, 8 vols (Milan, 1822)

E. Brehaut, *An Encyclopedist of the Dark Ages: Isidore of Seville*, 2 vols (New York, 1912)

D. Brewster, *The Edinburgh Encyclopædia conducted by D. Brewster*, 18 vols (Edinburgh, 1830)

B.P.J. Broos, 'Rembrandt's portrait of a Pole and his horse', *Simiolus: Netherlands Quarterly for the History of Art*, VII:4 (1974), pp. 192-218

A. Brown, *Bartolomeo Scala, 1430-1497, Chancellor of Florence: the Humanist as Bureaucrat* (Princeton, 1979)

_____, 'Pierfrancesco de' Medici, 1430-1476: a radical alternative to elder Medicean supremacy', *Journal of the Warburg and Courtauld Institutes*, 42 (1979), pp. 81-103

Clifford M. Brown and Anna Maria Lorenzoni, '"Concludo che non vidi mai la più bella casa in Italia": the frescoed decorations in Francesco II Gonzaga's suburban villa in the Mantuan countryside at Gonzaga (1491-1496)', *Renaissance Quarterly*, 49:2 (1996), pp. 268-302

Marta Bruscia ed., *La Data (orto dell'abbondanza) di Francesco di Giorgio Martini: atti del convegno, Urbino, 26 settembre 1986* (Urbino, 1990)

F.T.F. Zeni Buchicchio, 'Quale intervento per lo Stallone del Papa a Viterbo?', *Biblioteca e Società* XVII, 1-2 (June, 1990), pp. 7-14

F. Bussi, *Istoria della città di Viterbo* (Rome, 1742)

A. Cappelli, ed., *Atti e memorie della Reale Deputazione di storia patria per le province modenesi e parmensi*, II (1864)

Carlo Cavriani *Le razze gonzaghesche dei cavalli nel mantovano e la loro influenza sul puro sangue inglese* (Mantua, 1974)

E. Celani, 'La venuta di Borso d'Este in Roma', *Archivio della società romana di storia patria* (1890)

David Chambers, 'The economic predicament of Renaissance cardinals', *Studies in Medieval and Renaissance History*, 3 (1966), pp. 287-313

David Chambers and Jane Martineau, eds, *The Splendours of the Gonzaga* (Milan, 1981)

Georgia Clarke, 'Magnificence and the city: Giovanni II Bentivoglio and architecture in fifteenth-century Bologna', *Renaissance Studies* 13:4 (1999), pp. 397-411

D. Coffin, *The Villa in the Life of Renaissance Rome* (Princeton, NJ, 1979)

A. Collins, *Letters and Memorials of State in the Reigns of Queen Mary, Queen Elizabeth, King James, King Charles the first, part of the reign of King Charles the second, and Oliver's usurpation*, 2 vols (London, 1746)

Comune di Poggio a Caiano, *Analisi di prefattibilità per il project financing: Recupero delle Scuderie della Villa Medicea di Poggio a Caiano*, 3°(Comune di Poggio a Caiano, April 2007), <http://allegati.comune.poggio-a-caiano.it/dl/ 20070428131531013>

C. Conforti, 'Recupero delle scuderie medicee di Poggio a Caiano', *La casabella* LXV:690 (2001), pp. 10-15

Guido Cornini *et al.* eds, *Raphael: In the Apartments of Julius II and Leo X* (Milan, 1993)

Anna Maria Corbo, 'La Rocco di Viterbo al tempo di Pio II', in *Biblioteca e Società*, V:2 (April, 1980), pp. 11-16

Pia F. Cuneo, 'Just a bit of control: the historical significance of sixeenth- and seventeenth-century German bit-books' in K. Raber and T.J. Tucker eds, *The Culture of the Horse: Status, Discipline and Control in the early modern World* (New York and Basingstoke, 2005), pp. 141-73

Francesca della Ventura and Daniele Ferrara '"Fe dipignere del vivo i più perfetti e più graditi cavalli" Enrico Pandone e il ciclo affrescato nel Castello di Venafro', *Dal cavallo alle scuderie: Visioni iconografiche e architettoniche* (Rome, 2014), pp. 65-80.

Pierre Desrey, 'Relation du voyage du Royal Charles VIII pour la conqueste du Royaume de Naples par Pierre Desrey de Troyes', *Archives curieuses de l'histoire de France depuis Louis XI jusqu'à Louis XVIII*, Series I (Paris, 1834)

H. Doursther, *Dictionnaire universel des poids et mesures anciens et modernes, contenant des tables des monnaies de tous les pays* (Amsterdam, 1965)

Sarah Duncan, 'The Italian Renaissance Court Stable' (Queen Mary, University of London, PhD thesis, 2013)

Peter Edwards, *Horse and Man in early Modern England* (London and New York, 2007)

Peter Edwards, Karl A. E. Enenkel, Elspeth Graham, eds, *The Horse as Cultural Icon: the Real and the Symbolic Horse in the Early Modern World* (Leiden and Boston, 2012)

S. Eiche, *Ordini et officij de casa de lo illustrissimo Signor Duca de Urbino* (Urbino, 1999)

A. Fabronius, *Laurentii Medicis Magnifici vita*, 2 vols (Pisa, 1784)

Noel Fallows, *Jousting in Medieval and Renaissance Iberia* (Woodbridge, Suffolk, 2012)

Henry Dietrich Fernández, 'The Papal court at Rome, c.1450-1700' in J. Adamson ed., *The Princely Courts of Europe: Ritual, Politics and Culture under the Ancien Régime, 1500-1750* (London, 1999), pp. 141-63

Laura Fieni, 'Palazzo Te a Mantova: indagine stratigrafica dei sottotetti. Preesistenze e trasformazione al progetto di Giulio Romano', *Archeologia dell'architettura*, VIII (2003), pp. 209-19

Gaetano Filangieri, ed., *Documenti per la storia, le arti e le industrie dells province napoletane*, 6 vols (1883; reprint Naples, 2002)

P. Findlen, 'Jokes of nature and jokes of knowledge', *Renaissance Quarterly*, 43:2 (1990), pp. 292-331

F.P. Fiori and M. Tafuri, *Francesco di Giorgio architetto* (Milan, 1993)

L. Firpo, *Leonardo architetto e urbanista* (Turin, 1971)

L. Fontebuoni, P. Refice, 'Verifiche documentarie', in ed. M. Bruscia, *La Data (orto dell'abbondanza) di Francesco di Giorgio Martini: Atti del convegno, Urbino, 26 settembre 1986* (Urbino, 1990), pp. 83-9

Antonio Frizzi, *Memorie per la storia di Ferrara*, 6 vols (Ferrara, 1791-1809)

C.L. Frommel ed., *La Villa Farnesina a Roma* (Modena, 2003)

C.L. Frommel, S. Ray, M. Tafuri eds, *Raffaello Architetto* (Milan, 1984)

J. and L. P. Froissard eds., *The Horseman's International Book of Reference* (London, 1980)

Giacomo Gallo, *Diurnali di Giacomo Gallo e tre scritture pubbliche dell'anno 1495* (Naples, 1846)

L.A. Gandini, 'Viaggi, cavalli, bardature e stalle degli Estense nel quattrocento', *Atti e memorie della regia deputazione di storia, patria per le provincie di Romagna*, 3:10 (Bologna, 1892), vol. 10, pp. 41-94

P. Gargano, *Origini della mascalcia e suo sviluppo in Sicilia* (Palermo, 1908)

L. Gennari, *Struttura e manutenzione della cavallerizza regia di Marcianise (1488-1493)* (Salerno, 2006)

L. Giordano, '"La polita stalla": Leonardo, i trattatisti e le scuderie rinascimentali', *Viglevanum: Miscellanea di studi storici e artistici*, XIX (April, 2009), pp. 6-15

G. Giorgianni, ed., *Pio II, la città, le arti: la rifondazione umanistica dell'architettura e del paesaggio* (Siena, 2006)

L. Giorgio, 'Le residenze dei vescovi di Caserta dalla fine del 1400 e gli interventi barocchi nella cattedrale di S. Michele Arcangelo di Casertavecchia', *Rivista di Terra di Lavoro, Bolletino dell'Archivio di Stato di Caserta*, 3:1 (April, 2008)

D. Godefroy, *L'Histoire de Charles VIII* (Paris, 1684)

G. Gozzi, 'Il territorio mantovano: studio di geologia', *Civiltà Mantovana*, 1:37 (1973), pp. 69-118

Lucia Gremmo, 'La vicenda costruttiva', *La biscia e l'aquila* (Vigevano, 1988), pp. 145-79

M. Grieve, *A Modern Herbal*, 2 vols (Mineola, NY, 1971)

Cesare Guasti, ed., *I dialogui di Torquato Tasso*, 3 vols (Florence, 1858)

W. Gundersheimer, *Art and Life at the Court of Ercole I d'Este: the 'De triumphis religionis' of Giovanni Sabadino degli Arienti* (Geneva, 1972)

F. Gurrieri and D. Lamberini, *Le scuderie della Villa Medicea di Poggio a Caiano* (Bologna, 1980)

_____ 'Le scuderie medicee di Poggio a Caiano, una potenziale strutture museale', *La Toscana e l'Arte*, 2:4-5 (1982), pp. xxviii-xxxii

V. Hart and P. Hicks trans., *Sebastiano Serlio on Architecture* (New Haven and London, 2001)
Frederick Hartt, *Giulio Romano* (New Haven, 1958)

Richard Haslam, 'Pellegrino de' Pellegrini, Carlo Borromeo and the public architecture of the Counter Reformation' in 'Pellegrino Tibaldi: nuove proposte di studio: atti del convegno internazionale Porlezza-Valsoda; 19-21 settembre 1987', *Arte Lombarda*, New Series 3-4 (1990), pp. 17-30

Mary Hollingsworth, *The Cardinal's Hat* (London, 2005)

W. Hooper, 'The Tudor sumptuary laws', *The English Historical Review* (1915), XXX, pp. 433-49

J.P. Hore, *The History of Newmarket and the Annals of the Turf*, 3 vols (London, 1886)

P. Howard, 'Preaching magnificence in Renaissance Florence', *Renaissance Quarterly*, 61:2 (2008), pp. 327-69

J. Huizinga, *Homo Ludens: a Study of the Play-Element in Culture* (Boston, 1955)

Ann Hyland, *The Medieval Warhorse: from Byzantium to the Crusades* (Stroud, 1994)

_____, *The Warhorse, 1250-1600* (Stroud, 1998)

_____, *The Horse in the Middle Ages* (Stroud, 1999)

C. James, 'Marriage by correspondence: politics and domesticity in the letters of Isabella d'Este and Francesco Gonzaga', *Renaissance Quarterly* 65 (2012), pp. 321-52

Lisa Jardine and Jerry Brotton, *Global Interests: Renaissance Art between East and West* (London, 2000)

Pita Kelekna, *The Horse in Human History* (Cambridge, 2009)

Martin Kemp, *Leonardo da Vinci: the Marvellous Works of Nature and Man* (Oxford, 2006)

R. Kirkbride, *Architecture and Memory: the Renaissance Studioli of Federico da Montefeltro* (New York and Chichester, 2008)

Jeremy Kruse, 'Hunting and magnificence at the court of Leo X', *Renaissance Studies* 7:3 (1993), pp. 243-57

Elizabeth LeGuin, 'Man and horse in harmony', in K. Raber and T. J. Tucker, eds, *The Culture of the Horse: Status, Discipline and Identity in the Early Modern World* (New York and Basingstoke, 2005), pp. 175-196

Daniela Lamberini, 'Il Tribolo ingegnere e i lavori al Poggio a Caiano', *Niccolò, detto il Tribolo tra arte, architettura e paessaggio,* eds E. Pieri and L. Zangheri (Signa, 2001), pp. 173-93

Donna Landray and Philip Mansel eds, papers from 'Horses and Courts: The Reins of Power', *The Court Historian: The International Journal of Court Studies*, 24:3 (December 2019)

G. Lubkin, *A Renaissance Court: Milan under Galeazzo Maria Sforza* (Berkeley, Los Angeles and London, 1994)

A. Luzio, 'Isabella d'Este e il sacco di Roma', *Archivio storico lombardo*, Ser. 4, 10 (1908), pp. 5-107

Charles R. Mack, *Pienza: the Creation of a Renaissance City* (Ithaca and London, 1987)

E. MacCurdy, *The Notebooks of Leonardo da Vinci*, 2 vols (London, 1954)

C. Magenta, ed., *I Visconti e gli Sforza nel Castello di Pavia e loro attinenze con la Certosa e la storia cittadine*, 2 vols (Milan, 1883)

Giancarlo Malacarne, *Il mito dei cavalli gonzagheschi: alle origini del purosangue* (Verona, 1995)

C. Maltese, ed., *Trattati di architettura ingegneria e arte militare*, 2 vols (Milan, 1967)

E. C. Marchant, trans. Xenophon, *Scripta Minora* (London and Cambridge, MA, 1962)

L. Martines, *Power and Imagination: City-states in Renaissance Italy* (New York, 1979)

D. Mazzini and S. Martini, *Villa Medici a Fiesole: Leon Battista Alberti e il prototipo di villa rinascimentale* (Florence, 2004)

A. McCabe, *A Byzantine Encyclopaedia of Horse Medicine: the Sources,*

Compilation and Transmission of the 'Hippiatrica' (Oxford, 2007)

E. MacCurdy, trans., *The Notebooks of Leonardo da Vinci* 2 vols (London, 1954)

H. Miedema, *Karel van Mander: Den grondt der edel vry schilder-const* (Utrecht, 1973)

Daniela Mignani, 'Le scuderie granducali nei sotterranei del fabbricato degli Uffizi', in eds C. Benedetto & S. Padovani, *Governare l'Arte*, Oct. 2008 (Prato), pp. 228-234

C.J. Moffat, 'Urbanism and political discourse: Ludovico Sforza's architectural plans and emblematic imagery at Vigevano' (University of California, Los Angeles, Ph. D. Thesis, 1992)

André Monteilhet, 'A history of academic equitation', in J. and L.P. Froissard eds, *The Horseman's International Book of Reference* (London, 1980), pp. 97-116

G. Nosari and G. Canova, *I cavalli Gonzaga della Raza de la Casa* (Reggiolo, Reggio Emilia, 2005)

_____, *Il palio del Rinascimento: i cavalli di razza di Gonzaga nell'età di Francesco Gonzaga, 1484-1519* (Reggiolo, Reggio Emilia, 2003)

G. Notarnicola, *La Cavallerizza della Serenissima in Puglia* (Venice, 1933; reprint Alberobello, 2008)

I. and P. Opie eds, *The Oxford Dictionary of Nursery Rhymes* (Oxford, 1951)

G.B. Palma, 'Per un trattato di mascalcia in dialetto siciliano del secolo XIV', *Archivio storico siciliano*, New series, 45 (1924)

Giuseppe Pardi, ed., 'Diario Ferrarese dall'anno 1409 sino al 1502', *Raccolta degli storici italiani (RIS)*, New series, 24:7 (Bologna, 1928-33)

A. Paredi, *La Rotonda del Pellegrini* (Milan, 1950)

L.W. Partridge, 'Vignola and the Villa Farnese at Caprarola, Part I', *Art Bulletin*, LII (1970), pp. 81-7

Luciano Passini, *Caprarola – il paese e la sua storia* (Rome, 2002; reprint, 2008)

C. Pedretti, *A Chronology of Leonardo da Vinci's architectural Studies after 1515* (Geneva, 1962)

_____, *Leonardo Architetto*: (Milan, 1978)

_____, *Leonardo da Vinci and the Royal Palace at Romorantin* (Cambridge, MA, 1972)

_____, *The Literary Works of Leonardo da Vinci: Compiled and edited from the original Manuscripts by Jean Paul Richter*, 2 vols (Oxford, 1977)

Jan Pieper, *Pienza, il progetto di una visione umanistica del mondo* (Felbach, 2004)

E. Pieri and L. Zangheri, eds, *Niccolò detto il Tribolo, tra arte, architettura e paesaggio* (Signa, Florence, 2001)
Robert Plot, *The Natural History of Oxfordshire* (Oxford, 1677)

S. Pollastri and C. Ramadori, eds, *Inventorium honorati gaetani: l'inventario dei beni di Onorato II d'Aragona 1491-1493* (Rome, 2006)

Franco Porsia, *I cavalli del re* (Brindisi, 1986)

A.F. and L. Preto, *The Royal Book of Jousting, Horsemanship and Knightly Combat: a translation into English of King Dom Duarte's 1438 treatise 'Livro da ensinança de bem cavalgar toda sela' (The art of riding on every saddle)* (Highland Village, TX, 2005)

Provincia di Prato, Comune di Poggio a Caiano, Ufficio Tecnico Comunale, *Analisi di prefattibilità per il project financing: Recupero delle Scuderie della Villa Medicea di Poggio a Caianop*, 3° Lotto (April, 2007)

F. Purini, 'Ricostruire modificando le Scuderie Medicee di Poggio a Caiano', *Costruire in Laterizio*, XIII:77 (September/October, 2000), pp. 22-7

_____, 'Recupero delle Scuderie Medicee (Restoration of the Medicean Stables) Poggio a Caiano, 2000', *La casabella*, LXV:690 (2001), pp. 16-17

K. Raber and T.J. Tucker, eds, *The Culture of the Horse: Status, Discipline and Identity in the Early Modern World* (New York and Basingstoke, 2005)

I.A. Richter, *The Notebooks of Leonardo da Vinci* (Oxford and New York, 1980)

J. Rivera, *Juan Bautista de Toledo y Felipe II: la implantación del clasicismo en España* (Valladolid, 1984)

Clare Robertson, *'Il Gran Cardinale', Alessandro Farnese, Patron of the Arts* (New Haven, MA and London, 1992)

Daniel Roche, 'Equestrian culture in France from the sixteenth to the nineteenth century', *Past and Present*, 199:1 (2008), pp. 113-45

_____, 'Le Livre d'équitation du XVIe au XVIIIe siècle: esquisse d'une réflexion', in F. Barbier, A. Parent-Charon, F. Dupuigrenet-Desroussilles, C. Jolly, D. Varry, eds, *Le Livre et l'Historien: Études offertes en l'honneur du Professeur Henri-Jean Martin* (Geneva, 1997), pp. 187-96

Dennis Romano, 'The gondola as a marker of station in Venetian society', *Renaissance Studies*, 8:4 (1994), pp. 359-74

J. Ross, *The Lives of the Early Medici as told in their Correspondence*, (London, 1910)

M. Rossi and A. Rovetta, eds, 'Pellegrini Tibaldi pittore e architetto dell'età borromaica: atti delle giornate di studio 8-9 novembre 1996', *Studia Borromaica: saggi e documenti di storia religiosa e civile della prima età moderna*, 11 (Milan, 1997)

A. Rubbiani, *Il castello di Giovanni II Bentivoglio a Ponte Poledrano* (Bologna, 1914; reprint Bentivoglio, 1989)

A. Ryder, *The Kingdom of Naples under Alfonso the Magnanimous* (Oxford, 1976)

D. Salazar, ed., 'Racconti di storia napoletana', *Archivio storico per le provincie napoletane* 34:1 (1909), pp. 78-117

J. Schiesari, *Beasts and Beauties: Animals, Gender and Domestication in the Italian Renaissance* (Toronto, Buffalo and London, 2010)

A.F. Schofield, *On the Characteristics of Animals*, 3 vols (Cambridge, MA and London, 1958). A translation of Aelian's *De natura animalium*

R. Schofield, 'Ludovico il Moro and Vigevano', *Arte Lombarda*, 62 (1982), pp. 93-140

Leopoldo Sebastiani, *Descrizzione e relazione istorica del nobilissimo, e real palazzo di Caprarola* (Rome, 1741)

P. Sella, ed., *Inventario di Alfonso II d'Este 1597* (Ferrara, 1931)

John Shearman, 'Raphael as architect', *Journal of the Royal Society of Arts*, CXVI (1968), pp. 388-409

_____, *Raphael in Early Modern Sources (1483-1602)*, 2 vols (New Haven and London, 2003)

_____, 'The apartments of Julius II and Leo X' in R. Caravaggi ed., *Raphael: In the Apartments of Julius II and Leo X* (Milan, 1993), pp. 15-36

Anna Siekiera, ed., *Descrittione del Palazzo ducale d'Urbino, Studi e ricerche*, 87 (Alessandria, Italy, 2010)

A. Segarizzi, *Relazioni degli ambasciatori veneti al senato*, 4 vols (Bari,

1912-16)

Frederick Smith, *The Early History of Veterinary Literature and its British Development*, 4 vols (London, 1919; reprint 1976)

A. Sorbelli, *I Bentivoglio, signori di Bologna* (Bologna, 1987)

F. Strazzullo, *Architetti e ingegneri napoletani dal 500' al 700'* (Naples, 1969)

K. Thomas, *Religion and the Decline of Magic: Studies in popular Belief in Sixteenth- and Seventeenth-century England* (London, 1971)

P.E. Thomson, *Contemporary Chronicles of the Hundred Years War* (London, 1966)

Elizabeth M. Tobey, 'The palio horse in Renaissance and early modern Italy', in K. Raber and T.J. Tucker eds, *The Culture of the Horse: Status, Discipline and Identity in the Early Modern World* (New York and Basingstoke, 2005), pp. 63-90

_____, 'The palio in Renaissance art, thought and culture', Diss. University of Maryland (2005)

S. Tramontana, *Il Regno di Sicilia: uomo e natura dall'XI al XIII secolo* (Turin, 1999)

T. Tuohy, *Herculean Ferrara. Ercole d'Este (1471-1505) and the Invention of a Ducal Capital* (Cambridge, 2002)

E. Verheyen, *Federico Gonzaga and the Palazzo del Te in Mantua: Images of Love and Politics* (Baltimore and London, 1977)

Antonio Videtta, *Il cavallo vivo* (Naples, 1991), trans. and ed. L.B. Alberti's *De equo animante* (*c.*1445)

W.E. Wallace, 'The Bentivoglio Palace; Lost and Reconstructed', *Sixteenth Century Journal*, X:3 (1979), pp. 97-114

K. Weil-Garris and J. F. d'Amico, *The Renaissance Cardinal's ideal Palace: a chapter from Cortesi's 'De Cardinalatu'* (Rome, 1986)

Evelyn Welch, 'Public magnificence and private display: Giovanni Pontano's "De splendore" (1498) and the domestic arts', *Journal of Design History*, 15:4 (2002), pp. 211-21

Giles Worsley, *The British Stable* (New Haven and London, 2004)

_____, 'The design and development of the stable and riding house in Great Britain from the thirteenth century to 1914', Ph.D. thesis, Courtauld Institute of Art, 1989.

Index

Adamantius 66
Adoration of the Magi, The (unknown artist) 25
Aelian 67, 84n26, 85n27, 86n76
agriculture, treatises/printed texts on 93–4, 127
Alberobello, Puglia: La Cavallerizza 103, 120, 127, *127*, 136, 248
Alberti, Cherubino 57
Alberti, Leon Battista 13–14, 100, 234; *De equo animante* 12, 13, 14, 28–9, 67, 161–2, 177–8; *De re aedificatoria* 95, 177–8; *Della famiglia* 67; on man/horse relationship 67, 94; on medical treatments 225, 232; on the 'perfect' horse 28–9, 32; on stable architecture 127, 137, 153–4, 161–2, 174–5; on stabling conditions 95, 102, 169, 171–2, 173, 177–8, 193, 205, 208
Albertus Magnus 65
Alexander the Great 77
Alexander, Robert 36–7
Alfonso I, King of Naples (Alfonso V, King of Aragon) 20, 197, 248
Alfonso of Aragon, Duke of Calabria (later Alfonso II of Aragon) 50, 185n51, 244, 248
Allori, Alessandro 143
anaesthetics 228–30
anatomy 29–32, 63, 70–5, *73*, 84
Andreasi, Ippolito 24, *24*, 210
Angelico, Fra and Fra Filippo Lippi, *The Adoration of the Magi* 208, *209*
Apsyrtus 14, 34, 71
Arabian horses *120*, 171, *171*
architecture *see* stable architecture
Ariosto, Francesco ('Il Pellegrino') 227
Aristotle 41, 42, 58, 63, 66, 94; *Nichomachean Ethics* 42–3, 65
Assassino, Scipio 197
Astorcone, memorial to 77
astrology/astrological charts 12, 16, 70, 71, 83, 225, 228, 232, 234
Athens, ancient 77

Babieca, memorial to 77
banquets 45, 58, 90
Barbary horses 23, 34, 102, 194; and racing abilities 26–7, 50, 82, 120
Barocci, Federico, *Crucifixion* 124, *124*
Baroncelli, Niccolò 14, 38n18, 86n91
Bedingfield, Thomas, *The Art of Riding* 15
Belfiore hunting lodge, Ferrara 239
Belriguardo, Ferrara 239
Benci, Francesco de' 206, *207*
Bentivoglio (place): castle 96, 97, 144; stables (*see* Bentivoglio castle stables, Bentivoglio)
Bentivoglio castle stables, Bentivoglio 96, *96*, 113, 144, 237; accessibility 93; wall decoration 10, *142*, 143, 153
Bentivoglio family 26, 48, 143, 204, 238–9; horses belonging to 48, 87n103; stables belonging to (*see* Bentivoglio castle stables, Bentivoglio; *see under* Bologna); *see also under individual names*
Bentivoglio, Giovanni II 48, 87n103, 101, 125, 143, 237, 238; stables belonging to (*see* Bentivoglio castle stables, Bentivoglio; *and under* Bologna)
Benvenuti, Pietro 239
Bertolaccio 82
Bigio, Baccio (Bartolomeo Lippi) 114n33, 134, 148n8, 161, 240
bit makers 192, 202, *202*, 203–4
bits 202, *202* 203–4, *204*, 232
blacksmiths' workshops *52*, 53, 109, 121, 178, 181
bleeding/bloodletting 70, 72, 225, 228
Blundeville, Thomas 13, 86n86, 175, 179
Bologna 48, *154*; Bentivoglio palace and stables 96, 97, 101–2, 125, 128, 143, 144, *144*, 154, 237–8
Bologna, Falamischia da 218n92
Bona of Savoy 51, 53, 120–1

books *see* treatises/printed texts
Borella (Giovanni Antonio Secco) 197, 217n43
Borromeo, Carlo 131, 242; stables belonging to (*see* La Rotonda)
Borromeo, Federico (Cardinal) 133–4
Bramante 10; La Magliana stables, Rome 247; Vatican (unbuilt) 17n4, 118, *119*, 246; Vigevano stables 248; Stallone del Papa, Viterbo 154, 249
Bramantino 153
brand marks 22, 23–6, *24*, *25*, *27*, *52*, 79, *116*, *152*, *190*, 194
bridle makers 121, 192, 198, 203; *see also* bit makers
bridles 46, 198, *199*, 200, 204, 209; storage of 182, *182*
Brogio, Giovanni 157
Bucephalus, tomb of 77
Buonsignori 134, *135*
Burgos: Monastery of San Pedro de Cardena 77
Butteri, Giovanni, *The Return from the Palio* 206, *207*

Caesar, Julius 77
Cafaggiolo, stables at 16, 100, *104*, 112, *128*, 238–9; building materials used 154–7; interior and ground plan 128, *128*, 154–7, *155*; and temperature regulation 113, 147, 178–9, *178*; water supply/drainage 104–7, *105*, 135; windows 113, 179–81
Calabrian horse breeds 26
Calavrese, Nicolò 227
Caleffini, Ugo 153
capitals, carved 43, *57*, 144, 153
Caprarola: stables ('old') 118, *119*, 167, 169, 171 (*see also* Lo Stallone, Caprarola); Villa Farnese 110, *111*, 211, *212*, 212
capriola 11, 17n11, 36, *37*, 200, *200*; *see also* maneggio
Caracciolo, Pasqual 15–16, 127, 228; on horse care 31, 32–4, 163–7, 172, 177, 181–2, 184, 205, 226, 227; *La gloria del cavallo* 12, 13, 15–16, 42, 65, 76, 77, 221, 224, 226; on man/horse relationship 64–5, 94, 212–13; on stable design/management 94, 169, 177, 183, 227
Carbonara, Naples: S. Giovanni stables 244
Cardiani horses 76
carro 183
carrousel 49–50
Casale, Giovan Vincenzo 131
Caserta *cavallerizza* and stables, Falciano 243
Castello, Erasminio da 157
Castello Visconteo, Pavia *122*; falconry 54, *55*; stables 94, 98, 122, *122*, 123, 160, 169, 244
Castiglione, Baldassare 41, 42, 45, 49, 50, 59n1, 60n33, 61n58, 61n60, 61n64, 67, 70, 85n34, 211, 219n114
cavallericio 197
cavalry horses 9, 26, 37, 38n8, 41, 124–5, 171, *197*
cavezza di Moro 34
ceilings, vaulted 10, 153–4, *154*, 160, *160*, 178; barrel 100, 127, *129*, 137, 147, 157, 160–1, *161*, 163, 167, 234; cross 54, 137, 154, *155*, 157, *157*; single 98–9, *98*
character (of horse) 27, 32–5, 35, 59, 68–9, 83–4; humanisation of 63–5, 66–7, 83–4; *see also* humours, the; intelligence
Charles IX, King of France 14; *La Chasse Royale* 42
Charles VIII, King of France 34, 44, 53, 77
Chigi, Agostino 55, *56*; stables belonging to (*see* Chigi stables, Trastevere)
Chigi, Fabio 56, 134
Chigi stables, Trastevere 16, 17n4, 55, *56*, 58, 102, 246; accommodation within 56–8, 118, 134; entrance/façade 53, 56, 138, 144–5, *145*, 148; interior/decorative details 10, 56–8, *57*, 90, 138, 157; layout/architectural plan of *57*, 134–5, *156*, 157, 163, 177
Cicero 41
cleanliness: and equestrian treatises 173, 184, 225–7; Renaissance theories of 16, 173, 184, 225–7, 233–4; and stables 64, 102, 103, 169–71, 173, 175, 177, 184, 225–6, 233–4
coats, horses' 32–4, 89, 179

Codibò, Gaspare 87n103
'Codice dei palii gonzagheschi' 82–3, 253 *see also* Lucca, Silvestro da
Colleoni, Bartolomeo, equestrian statue of 31, 78, *79*, 86n91
colour 28, 31–5
Columella 10, 14, 28, 31, 102; *On Agriculture* 94, 225, 226
columns 136, 144, 153–8, *154*, 162–3; Corinthian 54, *55*, *57*, 58, 157, *157*; Doric 56, 58, *58*, 131, 154, *155*, 157, 159, 163; Ionic 159–60; painted (*trompe l'oeil*) 54, *55*; Tuscan 56, 58, *58*, 131, 145, 154; *see also* capitals, carved
commodities, horses as 9, 16, 21, 23, 24, 26, 35, 36–7, 172
Como, Maffeo da 53, 96, 248
Compagnia de' Magi 51
corbetta 11, 17n10, 199–200
Córdoba: Las Caballerizas Reales 250
corsieri 26
Corte, Claudio 14–15, 199; Centaur theory 63–4; on horses' behaviour 64, 67–8, 74–5, 76–7, 83; on horses' care/training 15, 49, 205–6, 208, 222, 224; on horses' coats 32, 33, 34; *Il cavallarizzo* 12, 13, 14, 15, 32, 47, 49, 69–70, 94, 199, 214, 222–3, 224, 254, 256–7; on man/horse relationship 69, 79; on stable staffing/management 15, 47, 191, 193–4, 197, 198, 199, 204–5, 214–15, 222–3, 254; on stabling locations/layouts 92, 94, 112, 127, 128, 147, 162, 163, 167–8, 169, 177, 178, 181
Cortese, Isabella 224, 233
Cortese, Paolo 53, 182–3
costumes/dressing 41, 44–5, *45*, 47–8, 49, 51
coursers 26, 37, 38n8
Crac des Chevaliers, Syria: Knights Hospitallers' castle 98–9, *98*
Cremona, Giambattista da 47, 197
Cristoforo, Antonio di 14, 38n18, 86n91
Croatian horses 48
crupper 39n33, 198, 218n59
curb bits 203–4, *204*

Desrey, Pierre 53
Diaz de Vivar, Rodrigo ('El Cid'): horse of 77
diet (horses') 205–6, *205*, 213–14, 225, 227–8, 256–7; *see also* fodder
disease *see* illness
dogs *see* hounds, hunting
Domenicho, Maestro 202, *203*
Donato da Milano 120
drenching 228, *229*, 231, *231*
dressage, high school 11, 35–6; *see also* maneggio
Duarte, Dom, King of Portugal, *Livro da ensinança e bem cavalgar toda sela* 42, 70
Dunster Castle stables, Somerset *166*, 167

El Cid *see* Diaz de Vivar, Rodrigo
Eleanora of Aragon, Duchess of Ferrara 120
equestrianism 35–6, 69–70; *see also* horsemanship
Erasmus 69
Erasmus of Valvasone 29
d'Este, Alfonso, Duke of Ferrara 26
d'Este, Alfonso II, Duke of Ferrara 200, 232–3
d'Este, Beatrice, Duchess of Milan 44
d'Este, Borso 44, 50, 240
d'Este, Ercole I, Duke of Ferrara 44, 48, 50, 215, 239
d'Este, Ercole II, Duke of Ferrara 203
d'Este family 14; horses belonging to 24, *25*, 26, 48–9, 120, *202*, 203; stable accounts of *193*, 194, 202–3, *203*, 205, *205*, 227–8; stables of 42, 208–9, 214 (*see also* Belfiore hunting lodge; Belriguardo; Palazzo San Francesco, Ferrara; Reggio); stud farms belonging to 194, 232–3; *see also under individual names*
d'Este, Ippolito 197, 214

d'Este, Isabella 120, 197
d'Este, Luigi 203, *203*
d'Este, Niccolò III 239; equestrian statue of 14, 28, 86n91, 235n37
d'Este, Sigismondo 54, 215
eulogies 81–2
Eumelus 71
exhibitions (of horses) 41, 43, 59, 89; *see also* parades
'exotic' horse breeds 23, 26–8, 34–5, 36, 37, 49; *see also under individual entries*

façades, decorative: classical influence on 56, *57* (*see also* columns); painted 54, 58, 137–43, *140*, 148; rustication 136, 143, 145, 146–7, 148; *see also* frescoes; friezes
Falciano: Caserta *cavallerizza* and stables, Naples 243
falcons/falconry 26, 43, 45, 49, *52*, 54, 55
Farnese, Alessandro (Cardinal; grandson of Alessandro Farnese, Pope Paul III) 14, 107, 115n44, 115n45, 161, 167, 239
Farnese, Alessandro (later Pope Paul III) 115n44
farriers *see* maniscalco
Fattorini's pottery 179, 186n110
feast days/feasts 23, 51, 76, 82
feet, horses' 29, 206, 222–3; *see also* shoes/shoeing
Fera, Ruberto 12
Ferdinand I, King of Naples 43–4, 53
Ferdinand II, King of Naples 149n24, 215
Ferrara 35–6; Belfiore hunting lodge 239; Palazzo Diamante 54, *55*; Palazzo San Francesco stables 153, 179, 227, 239–40; Reggio stables 215, 240; riding academy 35; *palio/palia* 87n111
Ferraro, Giovan Battista, *Delle Razze* 76, 167, 198, 211–12, 224, 228, *229*
Ferraro, Pirro Antonio, *Il cavallo frenato* 68, *68*, 76, 204, *204*
Fiaschi, Cesare 13, 29, 35, 36, 76; *Trattato dell'imbrigliare, atteggiare & ferrare cavalla* 36, *37*, 223, *223*, 224
Fiesole, Medici villa at 100
Filarete, *Libro architettonico* 102
fire 147–8, 181, 215
firing (medical) 230
flooding 93, 100, 104, 135; *see also* drainage systems
flooring/floors 172–7, *176*; hump-baked (*gobbo*) 177; sloping *170*, 173, 174, 175–7, 226
Florence 41, 51; birds'-eye map of 134, *135*; Palazzo Medici Riccordi 44, *45*, 51; Palazzo Pitti 100, 200, *201*; palio 206, *207*; San Marco stables 10, 134, *135*, 143, 148n8, 161, 240; sumptuary laws (1420/1471) 41, 42, 51; Uffizi stables 100, 240–1
fodder 227–8; storage of 124, 128, 134, 136, 181, 183; and theft of 213–14, 215
Fontainbleau 136, 161
Francesco di Giorgio Martini 10, 127, 145, *145*, 247; architectural treatise 99, 123–4, 127, 169, 171, 175, 179, 202; stables designed by (*see* La Data, Urbino)
François I, King of France 26, 136, 161
frescoes 43, 136; exterior 10, 58, 89–90, 137, 138, 139–43, *140*, *141*, 148; interiors 10, 80–1, *81*, 138, 139, 143, 153, 184; *see also* trompe l'oeil
Friesian horses 35
friezes 139–41, *140*, *142*, 143
Frizzi, Antonio 26

Gaetani, Count Onorato II 47, 60n43
gambling 213, 215
Gandini 179
Garfagnana stud farm 194, 232–3
Garsault, François de, *Le Nouveau parfait marechal* 177
Garzoni, Giovanni Antonio 110, 115n45, 151n87, 239
Garzoni, Tommaso, *La piazza universal* 192–3, 211

281

Gerbier, Balthazar 175, 177
German horses 35
gifts, horses as 26–8, 36, 43
gineta 11, 23, 26, 30, 37, 38n2, 117, 197, 199–200
gondolas (Venetian) 46–7
Gonzaga (place): palazzina at 80, 178
Gonzaga family: brand marks of 24, *24*, 79; horse-breeding programmes 23, 26, 36, 194–6, *195*, *196*, 220n141; horses belonging to *24*, 38n3, 49, 79, 80, *81*, 82–3, 120, 124–5, 196, 209, 215, 230, 253 (*see also* Morel Favorito); stables belonging to 10, 34, 27, 115n54, 118, 143, 150n71, 178, 194 (*see also under* Palazzo Te, Mantua); stud farms belonging to 83, 103, *103*, 117–18, 141–3, 196–7, 242, 255; *see also under individual names*
Gonzaga, Federico I 12
Gonzaga, Federico II, First Duke of Mantua 38n3, 26, 82, 118, 196, 214, 241; favourite horses 24, *24*, 34, *35*, 79–80, *81*; Island of Te stables (*see under* Palazzo Te, Mantua)
Gonzaga, Francesco II 26, 27, 36, 38n3, 117–18, 120, 209, 215, 241; favourite horses 82–3, 253; stables/stud farms belonging to 80 (*see* Gonzaga (place); Marmirolo; *see also under* Palazzo Te, Mantua)
Gonzaga, Ludovico 12, 38n3, 51, 87n112, 124–5
Gonzaga, Sigismondo (Cardinal) 117–18
Governolo stud 27, 194
Gozzoli, Benozzo, *The Procession of the Magi* 44, *45*, 51
Greece, classical 11, 12–13, 14, 77, 94
Gregory XIII, Pope 45, 118
Grey, Thomas de 177
Grisone, Federico 11, 35, 36, 76; *Gli ordini* (1550) 11, 13, 15, 18n41, 18n42, 67, 86n69, 86n70, 186n84, 224
grooming/grooming techniques 206–13, *207*, *208*; tails/manes 80, *81*, 209–11, *210*, *211*, *212*, *213*
grooms 15, 46, 47, 192, *193*, 194
Guarniero, Girolamo 197
Guiscardi, Mariolo de' 30–1; Milan stables of 162, 243

Hampton Court 136
hanging bales *166*, 167
harnesses 192, 197; decorative 209–11; storage of 178, 181–2
Haro, Diego López de 250
haute école see maneggio
hay: for bedding 192; as fodder 141, 169, 173, 192, 227; storage of 10, 122, 124, 128, *129*, 134, 136, 141, *170*, 183; *see also* mangers
hayracks 10, 161, 171–2, *171*
heelposts *132*, 158, 160, 162, 163, 167, *168*
henna dying 80, *81*, 209
Henri IV, King of France 36
Henry VIII, King of England 26, 36, 50, 136
Hierocles 71
Hippiatrica 11, 71, 224
Hippocrates 14, 71
hobbies (*ubini*) 26
hobbling 163–7, 184
hoofs 29, 222; *see also* shoes/shoeing
horse-breeders 24–7, 38n6, 194; *see also under individual names*
horse breeding 28, 29, 93, 194–6, *195*, *196*; and 'exotic' horse breeds 28, 34–5; and importing horses 26, 34–5, 49, 194
horse trappings 26, 44–5, 47–8, 55, 59
horsemanship 9–13, 21, 34–7, 42, 49, 70
horseracing 23, 26–7, 50, 87n111, 206, *207*; *see also* racehorses
horses: anatomical studies of 30–2, *30*, *31*, 63, 70–4, *74*, 84; and beauty 28–31, 35, 44, 77, 83, 175, 225; breeds, desirability of certain 23–6, 27–8, 34–5; care/welfare of 10, 12, 13, 35–7, 46, 47, 48 (*see also* grooming/grooming techniques; medical treatments); colour of 28, 31–5; commemorations of 21, 77–83; displaying (*see* status, displays of); and economic value (*see* commodities, horses as); health of 16, 28, 29, 32, 70–1, 83, 89, 113, 153, 172, 177, 183, 212–13 (*see also* illness); and idealism (*see* 'perfect' horse, the); proportions of 13, 28–31, *30*, *31*, *32*, 37; provenance of 9, 23–6, 27; and psychology 13, 21, 35, 64, 75, 83 (*see also* character); selling 24, *25*, 34–5, 49 (*see also* horse breeding); *see also* man/horse relationships; training
hounds, hunting 43, 45, 50
humours, the 32–4, 64, 71, 230
hunting 10, 29, 41, 80, 93; animals/birds used for 43, 44, 45, *45*, 50; as spectacle 43–4, 46, 49, 50–1, 53, 58

Iberian peninsula 26; *see also* Spanish horses
idealism: and horses' proportions 13, 28–31, *30*, *31*, 37; and stable architecture 112, 161–2, *164*, 172, 174, 179; and staffing 193, 198; *see also* 'perfect' horse, the
'Il Libro di ricordi' 101–2
Il Tribolo (Niccolò Pericoli) 107, 114n33, 118, 126, 134, 148n8, 245
ill-treatment 64, 68–9, 75–6
illness 16, 32, 64, 74–5, 103–4, 198, 228; prevention of 64, 74, 225, 227–8; *see also* medical treatments
Ingrassia, Giovanni Filippo 70
intelligence 63, 67, 69, 70, 75–6, 199, 216
inventories 42, 47, 197–8, 200, 204
Isidore of Seville 65
Italian horsemanship 34–7
Italian horses, desirability of 26, 34–5, 36–7

Jacques, Duke of Nemours 14
João I, Dom, King of Portugal, *Livro da Montario* 42
jousting 42, 49, 51, 69, 73, 76
Juan of Austria, Don 206
Julius II, Pope 118, 124, 149n20; stables belonging to (*see* Stallone del Papa, Viterbo; La Magliana stables, Rome; Vatican stables (Julius II), Rome (unbuilt))

Ketham, Johannes de, *Fasciculo de medicina* 71, *71*
'knotting' (tails) 211

L'Incoronata stables, Naples 131
La Broue, Salomon de, *Le cavalerice françois* 36
La Cavallerizza, Alberobello 103, 120, 127, *127*, 136, 248
La Data, Urbino 16, 96, 123, *124*, *125*, 149n31, 214, 247; access to 99, 123; capacity of 89; floors 175; mangers 169, 171; stable design/layout 12, 123–4, 135, 160, 179, 183; storage and work rooms 183, 202
La Magliana, Rome 16, 51, 158, *158*, 247
La Rotonda, Milan: 90, 131–4, *132*, *133*, 143, 158–60, *159*, 242–3
Las Caballerizas Reales, Córdoba 250
Latham, Liévin van, *Les Miracles de Notre Dame* 121–2, *121*
legs, horses' 29, 30, *30*, *31*, 71, 72; caring for 89, 102, 163–7; markings on 32–3, 34
Lemercier, Jacques, *Palazzo di Caprarola* 118, *119*
Leno, Giuliano 158, 247
Leo X, Pope (Giovanni de' Medici) 26, 48, 90, 100, 157, 240; and hunting 10, 51–3, 58 (*see also* La Magliana, Rome)
Leonardo da Vinci: hayrack/manger designs 10, 162, 169–71, *170*, 172, 183, 205; horse drawings 29, 30–1, *30*, *31*, 78–9; stable architecture designs 110, 137–8, *137*, 161–2, *164*, *165*, *166*, 243, 248; stable drainage system designs 10, *170*, 173; stable interior designs 10, 162, 167, 174, 175–6
leopards 44, *45*, 50, 69
levada 11, 17n9
Liberati, Francesco 86n97
Libro de marchi... 27, 228

Libro di San Marco 24, 26
Lippi, Bartolomeo *see* Bigio, Baccio
Lippi, Fra Filippo *see under* Angelico, Fra
Lo Scheggia, *Trajan and the Widow* 212, *213*
Lo Stallone, Caprarola 16, 90, 118, 128, *129*, *147*, 239; barrel vaulting, use of 160–1, *161*, 234; building materials used for 136, 146–7; floors 175, *176*, 177; location/aspect 110–11, *111*, 113; water supply/drainage systems 111, *111*, *176*
Loniardo, Pietro 244
loosebox (*cassetta*) 167–8, 228
Louis XIII, King of France 36
Lucca, Silvestro da, 'Codice dei palii gonzagheschi' 82–3, 87n108, 253

Maddalena stables, Naples 38n7, 131, 198, 217n50, 244
Madrid: Alcàzar royal stables 250–1
magic 12, 224, 228, 232–3, 234
magnificence, displays of 9, 10, 21, 41, 42–9; and hunting 43–4, 50–1, 53, 58; and riding equipment 49, 55, 200, 202–4, *204*, 208–11, *210*; and stable architecture 9, 10, 12, 16, 41, 43, 48, 53–5, 59, 90, 93, 183–4; *see also* parades; status, displays of; sumptuary laws
Maio, Giuniano 43–4, 53
man/horse relationships 28, 64–5, 67, 69, 79, 94, 212–13, 225
Mandello, Giovanni da 157
Mandello, Ioanetto da 157
maneggio 8, 11, 17n11, 36, 37, 41, 49, 76, 143, 199–200
mangers 10, 90, 102, 121, 134, 162, 168–72, *170*, *171*, 183
maniscalco 121, 189, 198, 221–2; medical responsibilities 12, 16, 71, 191, 222–4, 228–32, 233; shoeing horses 191, 222–4; *see also* blacksmiths' workshops
Mantegna, Andrea 139
Mantovani, Rinaldo 79
Mantua 35–6, 120–1; Gonzaga stud farms 83, 103, *103*, 117–18, 141–3, 196–7, 242; *palio/palii* 87n111; Palazzo Te (*see* Palazzo Te, Mantua)
Mantuan horses 26
Marchi, Francesco de, *Architettura militare* 126
Marcianise *cavallerizza* and stables, Naples 104, 171, 179, 194, 244
marescalco 15, 221–2, 228; *see also maniscalco*
Margonara stud farm, Mantua 103, *103*, 242
Marmirolo stud farm, Mantua 80, 117, 197, 242
Massari 200
Master of Mazarine *120*, 121, *171*
medical treatments 12, 16, 64, 71, 72, 74, 198, 225, 228–34; and astrology 12, 16, 70, 71, 225, 228, 234; and cleanliness 225–7; and magic 12, 224, 225, 228, 232–3, 234; and religion 227, 232, 234; *see also* humours, the; medicines/ointments; surgery; *and under* treatises/printed texts
Medici, Cosimo de', Duke of Florence 51, 221, 240, 245; stables belonging to (*see* Uffizi stables, Florence; *and under* Poggio a Caiano, stables at)
Medici, Cosimo de' (Il Vecchio) 238; private chapel, Palazzo Medici Riccordi 44, *45*, 51; stables belonging to (*see* Cafaggiolo, stables at)
Medici family 51, 120, 240; horses belonging to 82; stables belonging to (*see* Cafaggiolo, stables at; Poggio a Caiano, stables at; Uffizi stables Florence; San Marco stables, Florence; Trebbio); *see also under individual names*
Medici, Giovanni de' *see* Leo X, Pope
Medici, Lorenzo de' 82, 126, 127; and sumptuary laws 42, 51, 82
Medici, Pierfrancesco de' 82, 247
Medici, Piero de' 48
medicines/ointments 230–1, 232, 233
Mediolano, Francisco de 178
memorials 77–83, 253
memory 64, 67, 76–7; *see also* intelligence

Michelozzo 100, 104, 151n83, 238
Milan: Archbishop's palace 131, 134; Galeazzo Sanseverino stables 162, 243; La Rotonda 90, 131–4, *132*, *133*, 158–60, *159*, 242–3; Mariolo de' Guiscardi stables 162, 243
Mirandola stud farm, Mantua 103, *103*
Modena, Andrea da 227
Montaigne, Michel de 45, 111
Montecchio, Baldassare da 227
Montefeltro, Federico da, Duke of Urbino 123, 191, 247; *ordini* 162, 169, 172, 174, 181, 197–8, 215, 226, 227; stables belonging to (*see* La Data, Urbino; *and under* Palazzo Ducale, Urbino)
Morel Favorito 34, *35*, 79, *80*
music 36, *37*, 49–50, 76, 77
mythology 63–4

Nadi, Gaspare 48
Nanni di Banco *222*, 223
Naples 11, 15, 35–6, 177; Caserta *cavallerizza* and stables, Falciano 243; L'Incoronata stables 131; Maddalena stables 38n7, 131, 198, 217n50, 244; Marcianise *cavallerizza* and stables 104, 171, 179, 194, 244; riding academies 11, 35; S. Giovanni a Carbonara stables 244; sumptuary laws (1533) 47
Navagero, Bernardo 219n131
Neapolitan horses 26
Nonio, Lodovico 103

Ombrone river 107, 134, 146
Orcia river 107, 110
Orsoni, Filippo: 'Book of Parade Armour Designs' 224–5, *224*
Ottolengo, Zanino de 12, 71, 222, 223–4, 228, *231*; recipes for medicines/ointments 230–1, 232, 233

Padovano, Lauro 82
Pagano, Paduano 197
pageants 21, 41, 47
Pagni, Benedetto 79
Pagno di Lapo Portigiani 114n19, 151n83, 237, 238
paintings *see* façades, decorative; frescoes; *trompe l'oeil*
Palazzo Ducale, Urbino: subterranean stables 96–8, *98*, 99, *99*, 107, 110, 123, 178
Palazzo Medici Riccordi, Florence 44, *45*, 51
Palazzo Piccolomini stables, Pienza 90, *100*, 107, 244: access to 99–100, *100*; blacksmiths' workshops 178; building materials used 136, *136*; interior 123, 154, *154*; water supply/drainage systems 107–10, *108*, *109*; windows 179, *181*
Palazzo Pitti, Florence 100, 200, *201*
Palazzo San Francesco, Ferrara: stables 153, 179, 227, 239–40
Palazzo Te, Mantua 138–41, *139*, 197; Sala dei cavalli 24, *24*, 34, *35*, 79–80, *81*, 139; stables (Federico II Gonzaga, c.1525) 80, 95, 113, 137, 138, *138*, 139, *139*, 158, 241; stables (Francesco II Gonzaga, 1502) 80, 138–41, *140*, *141*, 158, 241
Paliano, Cecco di 197
palii 14, 23, 27, 50, 69, 82, 87n111, 120, 206, *207*, 212
Palladius 94, 112
Pandone, Count Enrico 80–1
parades 37, 59; military 43, 45–6, 47, 48; private 41, 117; public 21, 41, 44–6, 47, 49, 197, 206
Paris: riding academies 36
Paul III, Pope *see* Farnese, Alessandro
Paul V, Pope 107
Pavari, Marco de, *Escuirie* 35, 64, 75, 224
Pavia: Castello Visconteo stables 94, 98, 122, *122*, 123, 160, 169, 244; Sforza court at 14, 80
Pelagonius 14, 71
Pellegrini *see* Tibaldi, Pellegrino
'perfect' horse, the 28–35, *30*, *31*, 37

performances/displays 11, 23, 25, 41, 50–3, 123; *see also* gineta
Pericoli, Niccolò *see* Il Tribolo
Persian horses 34
Peruzzi 56
Philip II, King of Spain 194–5, 197, 244, 250
physiognomy 65–7, 70–1; *see also* anatomy
Piccolomini, Aeneus Silvius *see* Pius II, Pope
Pickering, Sir William 15
Pienza: Palazzo Piccolomini, Pienza 99, *107*, *110*; stables (*see* Palazzo Piccolomini stables, Pienza)
Piero della Francesca 200
Pierozzi, Fra Antoninus (later St Antoninus) 41
Piètole stud farm, Mantua 103, *103*, 138, 143, 148, 153, 197, 255
pietra serena 145, 146, 154, 158
Pietrasanta, Carlo Federico, drawings of La Rotonda *132*, *133*, 158, *159*, 183
Pignatelli, Giovanni Battista 36
Pius II, Pope (Aeneus Silvius Piccolomini) 107, 110, 244; *Commentaries* 109; *see also* Palazzo Piccolomini, Pienza
Pius IV, Pope 15
Pliny 10, 14, 64, 77
Plutarch 63–4; *The Morals* 94
Pluvinel, Antoine de 36
poetry 79, 81–3, 253
Poggio a Caiano 16, 100–101; Villa Medici 126–7, *126*; stables (*see* Poggio a Caiano, stables at)
Poggio a Caiano, stables at *106*, 118, *130*, *135*, *147*, 183, 245; access to 100–101, *101*, 143–4; accommodation at 128–31, *130*, 162; building materials used for 136, *136*, 145, 154; capacity 53, 126–7, *126*, 163; drainage system 173, *174*, 176–7; location/aspect 93, 113, 134, *135*; rails 167, 192, *182*; stable layout/ground plan 134, 145–6, *146*, 154, *155*, 162, 163; water supply *106*, 107, 146, *146*; windows 146, 179
Polo, Marco, *Livre des merveilles* 120, *171*
Pontano, Giovanni 53; *De splendore* 42, 43, 46
Ponte Poledrano *see* Bentivoglio (place)
Porta, Antonio della 157
Porta, Giambattista della, *De humana physiognomonia* 65–7, *66*
porticos *132*, 143, 144, *144*
posts/poles and rails 163, *166*, 167
pottery kilns 178, 179, 186n110
Priscianese 209; on horse ailments and remedies 231–2; on stable expenses/salaries 192, 197, 214; on staff roles/responsibilities 191, 193–4, 198–9, 202, 215, 221
processions 43–6, 47, 48, 51, 59
provenance (of horses) 9, 23–6, 27–8
Puglian horses 26, 149n23

quintain 69, 85n46

racehorse trainers 192, 206, 218n93
racehorses 23, 26–7, 82, 206, *207*, 209–13
Raphael: *A marble horse on the Quirinal Hill* 31, *33*; stable designs 10, 17n4 (*see also* Chigi stables, Trastevere; Vatican stables (Julius II), Rome (unbuilt))
Ratto, Giovanni 36
Recordati, Aurelio 118, 144
Reggio stables, Ferrara 215, 240
religion 227, 232, 234
riders (professional) 192
riding 41, 42, 70, 199; *see also* hunting
riding academies 11, 35, 36, 76
riding equipment *see* tack
riding masters (*cavallarizzo/cavallarizzi*) 15, 36, 68, 192, 199
Rinaldino di Francia 86n89
Roadino Evangelista 215, 220n141

Romano, Giulio 82, 95, 139, *210*, 241, 242; Palazzo Te frescoes 35, 79–81, *81*, 138, *138*
Rome, ancient 77, 137
Rome: Chigi stables (*see* Chigi stables, Trastevere); panoramic map of 55, *56*; papal stables (Vatican) 94, 96 (*see also* Vatican stables (Julius II), Rome (unbuilt)); Via della Lungara 56, *58*, 102; Villa Farnesina 55, *56*
Rossellino, Bernardo 99, 107, 123, 244
Rossetti, Biagio *55*, 239
Roversella stud farm, Mantua 103, *103*, 194, 242
royalty 26, 36, 43, 44–5, 46, 50–1, 59, 197; *see also under individual rulers' names*
Ruffo, Annibale 235n27
Ruffo, Giordano 10, 14, 17n3, 163, 169, 172, 175; 'Liber mareschalchie' 13, 224
Ruini, Carlo, *Anatomia del cavallo* 31, 71, 72–5, *73*, *74*, 77, 224
Rusio, Lorenzo 10, 17n3, 228–30; *Hippiatria sive marescalia* 13

saddlers 181, 192, 198, 200–3, *202*
saddlery workshops 42, 181, 183, 202, *202*
saddles 42, 59n14, 60n38, 192, 198, *201*; decorated/extravagant 9, 46, 200, 202–3, 204, 208, 209, *210*; inventories of 42, 197–8, 200; storage of 182–3, *182*; *see also* tack
safety 163–7, 194
San Biagio stables 118, 115n54, 150n71
S. Giovanni a Carbonara stables, Naples 244
San Marco stables, Florence 10, 134, *135*, 143, 148n8, 161, 240
San Sebastiano stables 34, 115n54, 150n71, 143
Sangallo, Antonio da, the Younger 119, 115n44
Sangallo, Giovan Francesco da 158, 247
Sangallo, Giuliano da 126, 158, 247
Sanseverino, Galeazzo 30, 162; Milan stables 162, 243
Sanudo, Marin, *De origine* 46
Savelli, Paolo 78, *78*, 86n89
Savonarola 42, 51
Scaccho da Tagliacozzo, Filippo, *Opera di mescalzia* 71–2, *72*, 224, 228, *229*, 230, *230*, 233
Scala, Bartolomeo, 'Poem in praise of Pierfrancesco's horse' 82
Scamozzi, Vincenzo 90, 127, 135–6, 137, 171, 175, 177, 179; *L'idea della architettura* 95, 107, 112
Scaticia, Giovanni Antonio 36
Sebastiani, Leopoldo 118
Secco, Giovanni Antonio *see* Borella
serizzo 54, 157, 158
Serlio, Sebastiano 127, 141, 167, *168*, 169, 172, 177
Sermide basin 104, 113, 227
Sermoni funebri de vari authori… (funeral sermons) 81–2
Sestola, Girolamo 26
Sforza family: horses belonging to 30, 48; stables belonging to (*see under* Castello Visconteo, Pavia; Vigevano stables); *see also under individual names*
Sforza, Francesco, equestrian statue of 30, 78, 162
Sforza, Galeazzo Maria, Duke of Milan 44, 47, 50, 51, 53, 122, 248; falconry 54, 55; stables belonging to (*see under* Castello Visconteo, Pavia; *and under* Vigevano stables); staff employed by 80, 194, 197
Sforza, Ludovico 'Il Moro' 48, 53, 248; stables belonging to (*see under* Vigevano stables)
shoes/shoeing 13, 29, 53, 183, 192, 196, 206, 221, 222–4, *222*, *223*
Sibarites/Sibarite horses 76, 86n76
Sicilian horse breeds 30
Sidney, Sir Philip 15
Siliceo, Ottaviano 35; *Scuola de' cavalieri* 224
Simon of Athens 12–13, 28, 29, 32, 39n27, 64, 68–9, 75, 77
Simonetta, Francesco, 'Cicco' 125, 191, 194
Sixtus IV, Pope 227

slaves 47, 60n43, 90, 204, 218n93, 204
smithies *see* blacksmiths' workshops
Spagnola 80, 217n43
Spanish horses 34, 35; *see also* gineta
spectacle 43–4, 46–9, 53, 124, 208–9; *see also* hunting; tournaments
stable architecture 10, 90; aspect 111–13; building materials used 137–8, 154, 157–8; classical influence on 10–11, 43, 56, 94, 112, 113, 117, 127, 131, 138, 148; doorways/entrances 112, 136, 143–8, *145*, *147*; exteriors 127, 137–48; and idealism 112, 161–2, *164*; interiors 56–8, 127–9, 153, 161–2, 184; Medieval *120*, 121–2, *121*, *171*; ornamentation 43, 54, 56, 59, 89–90, 136–44, 148 (*see also* façades, decorative; frescoes); and status 9, 41, 53–55, 59, 89–90, 123–4, 143; windows 112, 113, 136, 179–81, 226; *see also* ceilings, vaulted; flooring/floors; stable ground plans/layouts; *and under* treatises/printed texts
stable boys 191, 194, 204–5, 206, 209, 211, 213–16, 226, 254
stable ground plans/layouts 56–8, 123, 127–36; basilica form 54, 56, 90, 122, 127–8, 131, 134, 148, 154, 179; 'cloister' 136, 148
stable masters 15, 191, 193–4, 197–9, 213–15
stable staff: accommodation 10, 53, 56–8, 121, 128–31, 134, 181, 215; organisation of 189, 191, 193–4, 198–9; pay/salaries of 192, 197, 214, 215; responsibilities of 9, 15, 41, 46, 184, 191, 192–3, 194, 215–16, 254; use of slaves 47, 60n43, 204, 218n93, 204; *see also* grooms; *maniscalco*; riding masters; stable boys; stable masters
stables: accommodation within 56–8, 118, 121, 127, 128–31, 134, 162, 181; architecture (*see* stable architecture); and cleanliness 64, 102, 103, 169–71, 173, 175, 177, 184, 225–6, 233–4; drainage systems 10, 104–7, *105*, 158–60, *170*, 173–4, 176–7, *176*, 225, 226; and horses' health 89, 94, 102, 113, 153, 172, 177, 183, 184; lighting 179–81; locations of, factors influencing 93–6, 102–3, 117; running costs 10, 50–1, 192, 197, 214, 215; and security 194–5; staffing of (*see* stable staff); as reflection of status 9, 41, 46, 48, 89–90, 117–20, 123–4, 125–7, 137, 153, 183–4; storage rooms 109, 121, 123, 128, 131, 136, 181–3; subterranean 94, 96–101, *98*, *99*, 122–4, *122*; temperature regulation 112, 113, 147, 177–9; visitors to 50–1, 125–7, 194, 196–7; water supply systems 10, 93, 102–11, *105*, *108*, *109*, 145, 227; owned by women 120–1; workrooms/smithies 52, 53, 109, 121, 178, 181, 202
Stallone del Papa, Viterbo 154, 179, *180*, 249
statues 18n46, 30, 31, 77–9
status, displays of 46–7; and horses/horse breeds 9, 11, 16, 26–7, 41, 46, 47, 51, 58–9, 83, 89, 117–18; and horsemanship 9–10, 11; and hunting 50–1, 58; and monuments 77–8; and parades 41, 45–6, 48, 59; and stable design/decoration 9, 89–90, 117–20, 123, 125–6, 137, 153, 183–4
Stella, Michele Martino 14
stirrup makers 200, 202, *202*
stirrups 200, *201*, 202
stornello 34
straw: for bedding 192; as floor covering 173, 174, 175; as fodder 169, 173, 192, 216n12, 227, 228; storage of 124, 128, 134, 136, 183
stucco work 43, 137, 138, 148
Stucco, Cristoforo 157
stud books 79–80, *80*, 195–6, *195*, *196*
Suetonius 66, 77
sumptuary laws 41, 42, 46, 47, 51
surgery 228, *230*, 234; *see also maniscalco*
Syrian horses 34

tack 47, 49, 55, 60n38, 189, 192, 194, 200, 203; decorated 208–9; storage of 46, 55, 121, 158, 181–2; *see also* bridles; saddles
tails: decorative 80, *81*, 209–11, *210*, *211*, *212*, 213; dying 80, *81*, 209, 233

Tasso, Torquato 173, 225–6
Te, Island of *see* Palazzo Te, Mantua
Téllez-Girón, Pedro, 1st Duke of Osuna 131
tethering (in stables) 163–7
theft 194, 213–14, 215
Theomnestus 71
Tibaldi, Pellegrino (Pellegrini) 90, 117, 131–4, 159, 179, 242
Todesco, Zohanne 194
Tomasso 197
tournaments 47, 69, 73, 200; *see also* jousting
trainers 192, 194, 199; *see also* racehorse trainers
training 10, 27, 35, 36, 67–9, 75–6, 143, 199, 203–4; and ill-treatment 64, 68–9, 75–6; and music 36, *37*, 76, 77, 86n76; and obedience 67, 68, 69, 73, 75–6, 84; and psychology 64, 75, 83; and punishment 68, 69
transport, methods of 46–7
treatises/printed texts: agricultural 93–94, 127; architectural 90, 101–2, 111–13, 123–4, 127, 141, 173, 184; equestrian 10, 12–16, 63, 70–1, 84, 94, 189, 216; medical 63, 70–3, 90, 224–5, 228–34; *see also under individual authors' names*
Trebbio: Medici stables at 160, *160*, 247
trompe l'oeil 54, 80, 138, 141, 148, 153
Trottus, Alphonso 36
Turkish horses 23, 26, 34, 80, *81*, 86n97, 117, 194, 197, 209

Uccello, Paolo, *The Battle of San Romano* 200, *200*
Uffizi stables, Florence 100, 240–1
Urbino: La Data (*see* La Data, Urbino); Palazzo Ducale stables 96–8, *98*, 99, *99*, 107, 110, 123; San Bernardino 145, *145*
Utens, Giusto: *Il Castello di Cafaggiolo* 104, *104*; *Il Trebbio* 160; *Poggio a Caiano* 106, 107, 134, *135*

Vallino, Giocomo 218n92
Van Mander, Karel 29
Varro 10, 14, 28, 32
Vasari, Giorgio 39n37, 95, 100, 138, 153, 240
Vasi, Giuseppe: panoramic map of Rome 55, *56*; *Prospetto di Caprarola* 110
Vatican stables (Julius II), Rome (unbuilt) 17n4, 118, *119*, 134, 246
Vecellio, Cesare 46–7
Vega, Luis de 250
Vegetius 14; on horse care/grooming 168, 169, 174, 208, 213; on horse health/illness 169, 179, 183, 221, 225, 226, 230; *Of the distempers of horses* 13; on stable design/management 225
Vellano da Padova 18n46, 78, *79*, 86n91
Venafro: Count Enrico Pandone's castle 80–1
Venetian Republic: stables/stud farms 103, 120, 149n24, 194, 217n25, 248; *see also* La Cavallerizza, Alberobello
Venice 80; public monuments 78, *78*, *79*; sumptuary laws (1562) 46, 47; *see also* Venetian Republic
Verrocchio, Andrea del 18n46, 31, *32*, 39n37, 78, *79*, 86n91
Vesalius, Andreas, *De humani corporis fabrica* 71, 73, 74, 75
veterinary medicine 63, 64, 70–5, 90, 232; *see also* medical treatments; surgery
Vigevano stables 10, 16, 113, 138, 148, 169, 179, 182, 248–9; Galeazzo Maria Sforza (1470s) 52, 53, 54, 95–6, *95*, 157, 163, *176*, 177; Ludovico 'Il Moro' Sforza (1494) 53, 54–5, *54*, *55*, 89–90, *95*, 96, 128–31, 136, 157–8, *157*, 162
Vigevano: Castello Visconteo Sforzesco 52, 53, 93, 95–6, *95*; *see also* Vigevano stables
Vignola, Giacomo Barozzi da 115n44, 118, 146, 151n87, 161, 239
Virgil 14; *Georgics* 28–9, 32, 226
Virgiliana stud farm, Mantua 103, *103*
Visconti, Bernabò: equestrian memorial to 78
Visconti, Gian Galeazzo 244
Visconti, Galeazzo II 98, 122, 123, 244

285

Viterbo 111; Stallone del Papa stables 16, 154, 179, *180*, 249
Vitruvius 179; *De architectura* 94
Vopiscus, Flavius 137

war horses 23, 77, 80, *81*; *see also* cavalry horses
warfare, training for 50, 76–7, 85n47, 199–200, *200*
wealth, displays of 9, 11, 41–6, 58; and stable architecture/location 90, 93, 123–4, 127, 137; and stable interiors 153, 157–8, 183–4; *see also* status, displays of; sumptuary laws
Wittel, Gaspar van, *La Data stables* 125
worms, treatments for 232, *233*

Xenophon 12, 14, 28, 69, 77, 93, 94; on care of horses 172–3, 189, 191, 192; *The Cavalry Commander* 12; on horse training 64, 67, 68–9, 75, 189, 200, 213; *On Horsemanship* 11, 12–13, 94, 95; on hunting 50; on stable design/management 89, 173–4, 175, 214

Zandino 218n92
Zapata de Chaves, Luis 34
zodiac signs/charts 33, 64, 71–2, *71*, *72*, 228, *229*
Zuccari, Taddeo and Federico, *I fasti farnesiani* 211, 212, *212*
Zuccaro, Federico 134
Zuchola, Girolamo 239
Zuliolo, Ippolito 197

The Author

SARAH GILCHRIST DUNCAN has a BA from the Open University (2003) and an MA in Renaissance Studies from Birkbeck College, London (2005). Her PhD from Queen Mary, University of London, 'The Italian Renaissance Court Stable' was completed in 2013.

Brought up in the English countryside, she was given her first pony at the age of five and has had an interest in horses ever since. She continues her research into the stabling and welfare of Italian Renaissance horses. She now lives in London.